LAW ENFORCEMENT

LAW ENFORCEMENT

AN INTRODUCTION TO POLICE IN SOCIETY

BRUCE L. BERG

Indiana University of Pennsylvania

ALLYN AND BACON
Boston   London   Toronto   Sydney   Tokyo   Singapore

Series Editor: Karen Hanson
Series Editorial Assistant: Laura Lynch
Production Coordinator: Holly Crawford
Editorial-Production Service: N. Caron Nelson/The Bookmakers,
    Incorporated
Cover Administrator: Linda K. Dickinson
Cover Designer: Suzanne Harbison
Manufacturing Buyer: Louise Richardson

Copyright © 1992 by Allyn and Bacon
A Division of Simon & Schuster, Inc.
160 Gould Street
Needham Heights, MA 02194

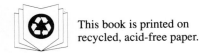

This book is printed on
recycled, acid-free paper.

Library of Congress Cataloging-in-Publication Data

Berg, Bruce Lawrence
    Law enforcement: an introduction to police in society / Bruce L.
Berg.
        p.   cm.
    Includes bibliographical references and index.
    ISBN 0-205-12257-4
    1. Law enforcement—United States.   2. Police—United States.
I. Title.
HV8138.B46   1991
363.2'3'0973—dc20   91-21018
                                                            CIP

Printed in the United States of America

10 9 8 7 6 5 4 3 2 1   96 95 94 93 92 91

CONTENTS

CHAPTER 6   **POLICE OPERATIONS: INVESTIGATIONS, JUVENILES, AND SPECIAL UNITS   82**

CHAPTER 7   **CONSTITUTIONAL REGULATIONS AND POLICING: LIFE, LIBERTY, AND THE PURSUIT OF CRIMINALS   100**

PREFACE

Law enforcement is perhaps the most diverse, intriguing, and changing social institution of modern society. Because of society's complexities, police officers must struggle with what many would describe as overwhelming problems and obstacles. In the face of the growing problems confronting police officers, research on policing has evolved into a more sophisticated, theoretical, and empirically grounded activity. This, in turn, has greatly improved the level of knowledge available to the police, police policymakers, and students of law enforcement. Customary and traditional police practices of the 1960s and 1970s have begun to fall by the wayside. Stereotypes of police officers are being pushed aside as police agencies increase their educational and training requirements and expectations.

To keep up with changes in society, police academies across the nation have shifted from mere skill training to police education. Communications and decision-making skills are reinforced with instruction in sociology, communications, psychology, and the law. Similarly, *Law Enforcement: An Introduction to Police in Society* moves beyond the usual limits of basic texts on police by introducing students to the theories that underlie police functions and the roles played by police in society. As a consequence, students are shown a number of critical issues not ordinarily examined in introductory books on policing and law enforcement.

Law Enforcement: An Introduction to Police in Society covers the usual basics of law enforcement but includes an examination of relevant sociological and criminological theory. The book is intended as a theoretically grounded textbook on the social implications of police, police functions, and police practice.

Police officers are the gatekeepers and standard-bearers of the American ideal of freedom. They must deal on a daily basis both with rule violators and law breakers. It is important to understand that not all persons who break rules are criminal. To this end, Chapter One attempts to familiarize the reader with the basic concepts of crime, deviance, and the law.

Policing has a rich and deep-rooted history, which began with customs and informal mechanisms of social control and evolved into today's more structured institutions of law enforcement and justice. Chapters Two and Three examine a socio-historical overview of policing. Much of this overview focuses on the effects on policing from changes in society. This review of policing's history is intended to place police activity in the context of its past and its future, as well as in the larger context of a necessary social control mechanism in our society.

As law enforcement has grown more structured and diverse, police agencies have emerged at different political levels. The basic structures of law enforcement agencies in the United States are outlined in Chapter Four.

Chapter Five examines a number of elemental patrol styles common in police agencies at a local level. As the chapter more fully describes, "patrol operations" are the backbone of municipal police agencies. Even one-officer police departments devote the majority of their time to pursuing patrol activities. This chapter also examines one of the fastest-growing areas rediscovered by law enforcement today, community policing strategies. As Chapters One and Two suggest, community policing has long been part of the Anglo-Saxon tradition of law enforcement. Yet, in recent years, this police–citizen cooperation has been touted as a new and highly effective policing strategy. In fact, recent empirical research has demonstrated the enormous benefits of improved police–community interactions. Several of these studies are highlighted in Chapter Five.

Chapter Six investigates the infrastructure of the typical municipal police agency. This includes discussion about such well-known police units as vice, narcotics, and undercover detectives. The chapter also considers internal affairs, the juvenile detail, and the role of the dispatchers—units frequently neglected in textbooks on police.

The criminal justice system in the United States operates under the criminal laws of our country and various state statutes and local ordinances. Police are expected to enforce these "laws of the land." However, before we can fully understand the role of the police officer as law enforcer, we must understand how, why, and under what circumstances police are entitled to enforce these laws. As previously mentioned, police officers are the gatekeepers of the American ideal of freedom. Officers are granted a considerable amount of official authority to preserve freedom. The question arises, however, whether a police officer is entitled to do *anything* the officer believes is justifiable to maintain the peace. Chapter Seven details the latitude and limitations that police officers have under the Constitution of the United States.

When an officer does make the decision to arrest a suspect, it is the first in a series of decisions that will be made throughout the criminal justice system. It is the first step in one of the more interesting relationships between police officers and other facets of the criminal justice system. An outsider might expect that police officers and the courts have strong working relations. Yet, police officers frequently blame their frustrations and job dissatisfaction on a failure of the courts to operate effectively. The cliché of "revolving-door justice" reflects the belief by many police officers that they arrest criminals only to have the courts set them free. Ironically, many court officials, judges, and district attorneys blame police officers for failing to make strong legal cases against criminals who must be released. Chapter Eight examines the roles of police officers and the justice system and considers a number of instances in which police officers must interact with the courts and correctional institutions. Chapter Eight also provides the student who knows little about the criminal court process with an opportunity to see how this element of the criminal justice system operates.

Chapter Nine offers a unique element for a textbook on policing: a chapter devoted to women and minorities in law enforcement. This chapter briefly sketches the history of women and other minorities in police work. This chapter also considers the impact hirings of women and minorities has had on police practice in general.

A number of people have argued that there is no substitute for experience in learning to become a police officer. Others argue that history demonstrates that many of the problems in policing stem from officers having had little or poor training before beginning their police careers. Chapter Ten will discuss how recruits receive much of their basic training in classrooms. This training will certainly not replace the lessons recruits learn once they begin working in the field. However, academy training provides recruits with important basic competence to perform any activity a police department may undertake. Chapter Ten will consider both the activities and directions of the modern police academy and the "culture of policing" new recruits enter at the academy.

To maintain both their own personal freedom and that of every other citizen, police officers are granted the discretion to arrest a suspect, issue a warning or citation, or do nothing at all. When this discretion is limited to such activities as writing a citation or calling a disruptive juvenile's parents about the child's behavior, many of us care little about the officer's decision. Yet, police officers also are granted the discretion to determine whether a given situation requires the use of physical force or even deadly force. Chapter Eleven examines the discretion of police officers, including the various elements that typically determine their decisions about use of force and deadly force.

One long-standing question among criminologists and others who study police is, "What exactly constitutes police corruption?" Chapter Twelve delves into this question by considering several possible definitions for police corruption. Chapter Twelve also attempts to suggest a distinction between what one might call police deviance and police corruption. In addition to these general definitions, Chapter Twelve considers some of the underlying theoretical explanations for why police officers sometimes become corrupt.

Modern police officers reside in the same society as everyone else. They are subject to the same stresses and strains of an increasingly endangered and polluted environment, an uncertain world political and economic structure, and the problems of living in a fast-paced, highly technological world. But police officers are additionally burdened with a number of serious health hazards because of their chosen occupation. It has always been difficult to determine the short-term and long-term effects of working in any hazardous occupation. Chapter Thirteen discusses a number of activities commonly regarded as police stressors. In addition, Chapter Thirteen examines a new stressor facing police officers, working with people who have AIDS. This examination includes discussion of legal implications arising from AIDS issues. Additionally, this chapter takes a slightly futuristic look at how the community might respond if police officers began to contract AIDS.

Chapter Fourteen takes both a pragmatic and a theoretical look at the attempt by police officers in the United States to become professionals. In order to look at this phenomenon, Chapter Fourteen considers the role played by police unions and a related innovation known as police agency accreditation.

Television has made forensic science a household phrase. In truth, technology *has* risen to quite a sophisticated level. It is not, however, the end-all in police investigations that television might have us believe. In fact, many of the technologies are too costly for the average municipal police agency. Chapter Fifteen details a number of activities associated with forensic investigations. Some are practical and likely to be used by a large number of police agencies. Others are used only in special cases or by large departments. This chapter also examines what has become the *business* of forensic experts—both the legitimate and useful, and the charlatans.

The final chapter considers several elements relevant to the future of policing. This includes discussion of the long-standing argument of education versus training in police work. This final chapter also considers the current movement toward securing private venders to provide what has been a public service.

Every chapter of *Law Enforcement: An Introduction to Police in Society* begins with a brief outline to orient the student reader to the chapter's content. At the conclusion of each chapter are several questions for class discussion or personal reflective thinking. Because this book includes a number of specialized terms and phrases, a glossary is included.

Law Enforcement: An Introduction to Police in Society is designed to achieve a number of goals for introductory courses on police and policing. First, it offers basic information on the history and practice of law enforcement and enforcement officers. In theme and perspective, this book provides a sociological and criminological approach to understanding police officers and how they operate in our society. Second, it attempts to present and debunk many of the myths, negative stereotypes, and folkways that pervade thinking about American police officers. Third, it has been written in a style intended to interest a wide range of students in learning about police and policing. This style of writing draws material from both the professional and popular media, as well as from academic and theoretical sources, and makes frequent use of examples to make abstract concepts more understandable. Finally, *Law Enforcement: An Introduction to Police in Society* presents many facets of the police in the context of the changing social and political forces that have shaped modern policing.

CHAPTER 1

SOCIAL CONTROL AND SOCIAL ORDER

*Policing is more than the high-speed car chases and bang-bang, shoot-
'em-ups that one sees so frequently on television shows. Police in the
United States embody the ideal and valued ways of behaving shared by
most Americans. These valued ways of behaving, started as tribal
customs, have changed in modern times into more formal rules and laws.
Adherence to these socially shared ways of behaving ensures preservation
of peoples' rights to safety and of their personal property. In fact, these
ways of behaving represent what most of us have come to see as the
American way of life. Yet, not every American is willing to follow these
ways of behavior all the time. Sometimes, society frowns but is not
sufficiently disturbed to take formal action. At other times, when the
deviations in behavior are sufficiently severe, the police may act to
restore a kind of social equilibrium.*

*The first chapter in this textbook describes rules, norms, and laws.
The purpose is to show both the need for having such behavioral
guidelines and a means of enforcing them. This chapter also will draw a
distinction between simple acts of deviance and criminal acts of law
violation. A major purpose of this chapter is to distinguish between
deviance and law violations. Making this distinction moves us toward an
understanding of the relationship between crime and the law. The
discussion of deviance and criminal acts also provides a background for
various perspectives on criminology and law enforcement.*

INTRODUCTION: POLICE OFFICERS, CRIME, AND THE LAW

The phrase **law enforcement officer** typically conveys the notion of one who enforces the laws. In fact, the primary purpose for the existence of law enforcement officers is to enforce the law. In the mind's eye of the average citizen, a law enforcement officer is a uniformed municipal police officer. Although this is essentially an accurate association, law enforcement officers are not limited to the level of the municipality. In this book, law enforcement officers are presented in a broader context. As several of the chapters will detail, law enforcement encompasses a wide variety of functions and may exist at different levels and branches of government.

In any context, the uniformed police officer is much more than an enforcer of laws. The uniformed police officer represents a personification of American social order. The officer is the front-line representative of the U.S. government at the local community level. To be colloquial, the police officer is "The Man."

For some, the police officer is the symbolic banner of the criminal justice system. For many others, the police *are* the criminal justice system. It is a uniformed officer who must often make the split-second decision to draw a service revolver and shoot a fleeing felon or simply to pursue the criminal on foot. It is the patrol officer who, upon seeing a suspicious person lurking in shadows late at night, must decide whether further investigation is warranted. It is the line officer who, upon discovering a store's open door after closing time, must enter the darkened building and perhaps face an armed intruder.

It is also frequently the uniformed line officer who must free the three-year-old boy whose mother has frantically, but unsuccessfully, tried to extricate him from the locked bathroom, or who must rescue the fabled kitten up a tree. Sometimes, the police officer must locate the appropriate social service agency when an aged community member

A trophy board of police uniform patches representing police agencies across the nation

phones the precinct to report that the utility company has turned off the gas.

The uniformed police officer carries a heavy burden, a friend to some, an enemy to others, and a social worker to many. In addition, members of society expect police officers to enforce criminal laws, maintain traffic laws, be knowledgeable on various regulatory laws, building and health codes, and maintain the peace throughout the community. How police officers accomplish all of these functions unfolds in the remainder of this book.

Before considering the various functions of police officers, it is important to understand several basic ideas, theories, and concepts. Let us begin with an examination of the need for social order and control in society.

HUMAN NATURE AND SOCIAL CONTROL

Humans are social beings. From the earliest cave dwellers to modern apartment dwellers, people seek the support and company of other people. Throughout history a tension has existed among humans between their need and dependence upon one another and their feelings of personal and group safety. A similar social tension exists between an individual's personal sense of freedom (liberty) and society's need for social order and control. This social tension represents a balance between total freedom leading to anarchy on one hand and total control leading to tyranny on the other hand (Critchley 1972). The police, as the social institution charged with representing the interests of the community, hold these elements of total freedom versus total control in balance.

Words such as order, control, constraint, and conformity tend to conjure images of bland robotic persons moving around under the governance of some Orwellian Big Brother. Yet, the essence of social cohesion and solidarity, which are much less affected words than "control," "constraint," and "conformity," is a consensual sharing of certain ways of doing things. In short, it is an agreement upon some set of rules. Unadministered, uncontrolled free activity ceases at once from being liberty and instead becomes anarchy.

Thus, without social controls, people could recklessly drive their cars, assault and steal from one another, or even kill. In this instance, unbridled activity ceases being freedom and becomes chaos. Free societies depend upon a balance between a person's ability to act independently and without fear of official reprisal and a person's responsibility not to infringe upon others' abilities to act independently as well.

In today's fast-paced, complex, and technologically advanced society, one witnesses many systems of social rules. There are rules of dress for certain occupations, rules of conduct in and out of the classroom, rules for different games, rules for the safe operation of motorized vehicles, rules of etiquette, rules for certain religious rituals, and the list goes on. Interestingly, each system of rules varies both in its degree of formal articulation and, when violated, its censure by society. Social scientists describe **norms** as the elemental units in social rules.

Briefly defined, norms are guidelines for conduct or basic social expectations for behavior. Knowledge of certain norms, therefore, provides one with the specifics of how one should behave in various social situations, especially social settings. Norms are sufficiently elastic to allow for some limited range of adherence and even violation.

For example, in the United States when one enters an elevator, the usual expectation is that one will turn around and face the door. If, however, one were to enter and remain standing facing the rear of the elevator car, one would violate a social norm (an elevator ritual). Although this norm violation might receive some puzzled or even pained expressions from other passengers, very little formal sanctioning is likely to occur. If, on the other hand, this same elevator-norm violator were to enter the elevator car, stand facing the rear, and curse or spit at another elevator rider, some greater sanctioning might result. In the first case, the norms were stretched, but not to the limit. In the second case, the elevator rider moved beyond the limits of social tolerance.

Most people in society follow norms more or less like the elevator rider. The adherence to social norms is not rigid, unyielding, or unchangeable. Norms adjust and adapt to such other fluid social contours in society as religious values, technology, societal needs, and the law. Violating norms beyond the social limits of a given society is called **deviance.** The process of responding to norm violation, enforcing rules and sanctions, and returning the group to a state of norm conformity is called **social control.** In later chapters, these terms are more fully examined.

Social controls are ever-present and powerful limitations on certain socially undesirable behaviors. Usually, social control manifests itself as a highly informal, frequently unwritten and unspoken, system of rules and norms. Yet, people in society operate in their daily lives both by adhering to various rules and norms and by assuming that others will share in and follow these norms.

For instance, when one goes shopping in a supermarket and is ready to pay a cashier, one queues-up behind the last person waiting to be checked out on a given line. Similarly, each person on the line expects that other shoppers will queue-up according to this general understanding of queuing rituals. If, however, someone pushes into the line ahead of those already waiting, that person is violating queuing norms. There are no statutes in any state's penal code on cutting into a supermarket check-out line. In spite of this, angry patrons may impose serious sanctions on the norm violator who cuts in ahead of them. In this particular situation, the invoking of what are essentially informal social controls (angry words, nasty looks, grimaces, and insults, etc.) are intended to reestablish social order, the queuing ritual. Unfortunately,

maintenance of social order of society in general cannot always be as neatly or effectively accomplished through **informal social controls** and sanctions.

To afford protection that preserves liberty in society, certain norms and rules have been established formally. These formal rules create required guidelines for behavior, rather than merely expected ones. In order to assure adherence to these required rules or **laws,** society has developed various formal sanctions that can be invoked whenever someone violates these laws. These formal laws, in contrast to informal norms, seek to assure safety and security for members of society, as well as to provide guidelines for ownership of personal property.

Laws, then, are a kind of back-up system that clarify and strengthen the importance of certain norms already supported by society. Unlike social norms, however, laws are politically legitimated rather than culturally or socially accepted. So, a person who violates a law in society enters a system that possesses the political backing of the entire society. It is on the basis of this political support that various institutions of society are empowered to apprehend, detain, adjudicate, and remand the law violator either out of or back into society.

The maintenance of liberty in our society requires that members be constrained from unbridled behavior. Although most members of society do follow appropriate norms of social behavior, many others do not. As a result, laws and politically backed methods for administering and enforcing them are necessary. Laws, then, are a formalized system of rules. In turn, laws are intended to complement and buttress the informal system of socially appropriate behavior represented by social norms.

The U.S. Constitution guarantees under law one's freedom to choose a particular life-style, manner of speech, religious preference, level of education, and occupation. Thus, one's freedom depends on provisions under law. Law, as described above, is a formal mechanism of social control. If members of society feel the need for greater constraint, they may enact more stringent or numerous laws. Conversely, if members of society believe that existing laws have outlived their usefulness or have not effected the kind of control anticipated, these laws may be repealed.

Deviance versus Crime

Deviant behavior refers to a very wide range of social activity. If one could witness the vast range of social conduct as a continuum, as illustrated in Figure 1.1, it would be possible to see that annoying, bizarre, eccentric, gross, bad, and good behaviors all can exceed the acceptable range of social tolerance.

As Figure 1.1 shows, within the range of acceptable behavior are slight stretches in social tolerance. In the direction of overconfor-

mity, there are "ideal values." These involve various altruistic actions such as putting a dime in someone's parking meter. Conversely, there are "practical norms," which move in the direction of underconformity, but are not usually seen by society as serious violations of social norms or the law. Still, these may be viewed by many citizens as violations. In essence, these practical norms are how most people in society govern their daily lives. It is common, for example, to see someone stop by a parking meter, run into a store for a minute, and never put money in the meter. Although technically this is a violation of law, it is not one that most people will view as terribly serious. Similarly, more serious excesses of social tolerance than practical norms, while not criminal, may nonetheless be viewed as deviant.

Jerry Simmons (1969) interviewed a cross-section of Americans, and asked them to list

Box 1.1 _____

Continuum of Social Behavior

| Overconformity | | ACCEPTABLE BEHAVIOR RANGE | | Underconformity |

[Extremes] ◄──► [Extremes]

Conformity

Ideal Values   Practical Norms

EXAMPLES OF OVERCONFORMITY
— Putting a dime in someone else's parking meter when the time runs out
— Notifying the post office that mail was delivered with too little postage
— Notifying the Internal Revenue Service of a relative's false claims (and refusing to accept the usual 10 percent reward)

EXAMPLES OF UNDERCONFORMITY
— Not bothering to put money in your meter when just "running into a store for a minute"
— Intentionally sending a letter with no postage affixed by indicating the addressee as the return address
— Claiming the charitable allowance on your federal return, but not really making any contributions

which types of people they classified as deviant. Simmons (1969, 3) found that most lists included expected categories such as homosexuals, prostitutes, drug addicts, and criminals. He additionally found:

> . . . it also included liars, career women, Democrats, reckless drivers, atheists, Christians, suburbanites, the retired, young folks, card players, bearded men, artists, pacifists, priests, prudes, hippies, straights, girls who wear makeup, the president, conservatives, intergrationists, executives, divorcees, perverts, motorcycle gangs, smart-alec students, know-it-all professors, modern people, and Americans.

In short, how one defines an act or actor as deviant relates to a given time and place, and the person(s) making such an assessment (Hagan 1986). Naturally, certain behaviors are defined more frequently than others as beyond the limits of social tolerance and therefore deviant. Vulgar words were not only viewed as deviant and a stretch of social tolerance in 1961 when comedian Lenny Bruce uttered them, but they got him 90 days in a county jail for being obscene. In 1979, the Supreme Court of the United States in *United States* v. *George Carlin* ruled for Carlin. Carlin had brought suit when his record, "Class Clown," was banned in several cities as obscene. Carlin's album contained the routine "The Seven Words You Can Never Say on Television," including words that got Lenny Bruce arrested. The high court ruled that such language, when uttered during a theatrical performance, is acceptable and should not be considered obscene. For some people, comedy performances by George Carlin, Eddie Murphy, Richard Pryor, Richard Belzer, and others are seen as deviant, even by today's standards. For other people, however, the comedic monologues of these performers fall squarely within the limits of social tolerance.

Deviant behavior, then, amounts to a range of activities that does not conform to the expectations of a given group of people. Within the array of possible deviant acts are behaviors of overconformity, such as feeding coins

into someone else's parking meter; social stretches of acceptable behavior, such as profanity used during a comedy routine; and underconformity, which may represent law violations such as theft or even murder. People frequently confuse the concepts of crime and deviance. These terms are not, however, always one and the same.

For instance, smoking marijuana is illegal in most states, but is it actually deviant? According to several research studies, a significant number of Americans has used or is using drugs such as marijuana. In Alaska, it is legal to grow, own, and use up to five marijuana plants in one's own home.

In 1986, the state of Oregon's legislature narrowly defeated a bill that would have legalized marijuana. The bill lost by a single vote. It would be incorrect to argue that all crimes are acts that significantly depart from social norms of society. It would also be inaccurate to assume that most deviant acts are crimes. For example, if one were to observe somebody shoplifting in a department store, but did nothing about it, one would not have broken any law. Some people might view this non-action by the observer as underconformity or deviance. This ambivalent behavior, however, is not a crime. The question, then, may be what exactly are crimes?

Crime and the Law

Although one can certainly find slightly different definitions for **crime,** a stark legalistic view suggests that it is simply a violation of criminal law (Hagan 1986). From this legalistic perspective, regardless of how reprehensible, morally outrageous, or deviant an individual's act, it is not technically a crime unless specifically defined as such in criminal law. Sutherland and Cressey (1974) effectively outline four factors that must exist to classify the violation or omission of a rule as a crime:

1. It is **assumed by political authority.** The state assumes the role of plaintiff or the

party bringing forth charges. Murder, for example, is no longer just an offense against a person, but against the state . . .

2. It must be **specific,** defining both the offense as well as the prescribed punishment.
3. The law is **uniformly applied.** That is, equal punishment and fairness to all, irrespective of social position . . .
4. The law **contains penal sanctions enforced by punishments** administered by the state.

In effect, Sutherland and Cressey suggest a definition for crime that links it to criminal law.

At one time, most people considered crime a private matter. When one person was injured or offended by another, that person sought compensation in the form of revenge. In some instances, these led to blood feuds and the destruction of entire families (Chapter Two will consider this in greater length). As time progressed, crimes became offenses committed against the Crown (a king or queen) and later, against subjects of the Crown (Lee 1971). Eventually, fines levied on behalf of the Crown (or the state) evolved, and the connotation of the state as plaintiff emerged (Hagan 1986).

One type of crime is defined by legislative statute or statutory law. Crime additionally is determined on the basis of **case law** or **common law.** Case law is the use of judicial decisions from previous and similar adjudications to determine the outcome of a subsequent case. Hence, case law's determinations are significantly influenced by previous decisions called **precedents.**

Common law originated, and continues to be the main body of law in England. In early colonial America, residents were subject to the law handed down by English judges, and hence, Common Law. After American Revolution, the colonies in America adapted and changed the English law to fit their particular needs. In many states, legislatures standardized many common-law crimes such as murder, burglary, arson, and rape by putting them

into statutory form or **statutory law.** In other states extensive penal codes were passed, thereby abrogating the common law crimes.

Beyond **common law, statutory law,** and **case law,** crimes are defined by **administrative** or **regulatory law.** Typically, regulatory laws administer civil privileges, such as the privilege to own a gun or drive a car and other licensed activities. Regulatory laws, however, may also encompass criminal charges. An example of a regulatory law that includes criminal charges would be mailing cocaine to someone. This activity certainly constitutes a misuse of the mail as governed by federal mail regulations. It also is a criminal offense to have or distribute cocaine. Another example might be a bartender selling alcohol to minors. Such illegal sale of alcohol is also governed by the Department of the Treasury's Bureau of Alcohol, Tobacco, and Firearms. Thus, crimes are established by provisions contained in statutory law, case law or common law, and administrative law.

According to LaFave and Scott (1972) criminal law can best be understood as defined by three basic elements. First, it prevents harm to society and its members. Second, it specifies what conduct is considered criminal. Third, it identifies prescribed sanctions for criminal conduct.

Let us consider each of these elements in some greater detail. The first element, preventing harm, implies that a central purpose of criminal law is to protect society from various activities that might otherwise injure its members or social institutions. Vandalism, theft of personal property, and assault are examples of harms typically associated with violations of criminal law. The implications of criminal law should be clear. If compliance with these laws is ensured, the result is an orderly, just, and free society. Criminal law, like other laws, provides a formal social control for society.

The second element, specification of what conduct is criminal, refers to the particular act or acts defined as illegal. This articulation of the code provides that every outlawed act is separately detailed and described.

The third and final aspect of LaFave and Scott's definition of criminal law involves prescriptions for punishment. Lay people often assume that punishment assures compliance or at least encourages people to follow certain rules of conduct represented by criminal law. The assumption is that knowledge of what sanctions society may impose, if one is convicted of some law violation, will serve as an incentive to obey the law (Durkheim 1951). In an ideal sense, there cannot be crimes unless there are corresponding penalties. Conversely, one cannot be punished for committing a crime unless one has been convicted of violating a law.

Felony versus Misdemeanor Crimes

Usually, crimes committed in the United States are classified by the justice system as either felonies or misdemeanors. Originally, this distinction was a critical legal one. Under medieval English common law, felonies were crimes for which a person could be required to forfeit all property and often his or her life. Distinctions between felonies and misdemeanors are not always clear-cut. Often, the distinction is made on the basis of the length of sentence imposed for the crime. Although sentences, even for the same crime, vary from state to state, felonies typically are among the more serious and usually carry lengthier sentences than misdemeanors. Felonies, then, contain capital crimes—those crimes for which the death sentence may be imposed—as well as crimes for which the sentence includes imprisonment in a state prison for more than one (or in some states two) years. Misdemeanors are less serious crimes for which fines and shorter county jail time may be imposed. Usually, misdemeanors carry no more jail time than one year. The distinction between types of crimes is important. Later in this book it will become clear that police discretion, what

represents permissible force, rules of evidence, and other police issues frequently revolve around whether the crime was a felony or a misdemeanor.

Mala In Se and *Mala Prohibita* Crimes

Another important distinction between types of crimes used by criminal justice practitioners is mala in se crimes and mala prohibita crimes. Mala in se crimes are inherently bad acts. These involve forbidden behaviors that members of society agree need outlawing. These behaviors include serious crimes such as rape, assault, murder, robbery, and similarly heinous offenses. Mala in se crimes are sometimes referred to as violations of natural law.

In contrast to these natural law violations, mala prohibitum crimes are the breaking of laws created by humans, or the breaking of laws and ordinances passed by legislative bodies. Unlike the more universal and timeless mala in se crimes, mala prohibita crimes reflect a society's current moral temper and values. Mala prohibita crimes periodically are created to control a behavior during a given time, but later removed or modified to reflect changing values and attitudes predominant in society. The recent change in legal drinking age to 21 across the nation represents an example of mala prohibitum. Other examples include laws and ordinances associated with guns, prostitution, abortion, and even traffic laws.

PERSPECTIVES ON CRIMINOLOGY AND LAW ENFORCEMENT

Criminologists and sociologists view society in different ways. Some see the world as a basically stable, harmonious environment. From this vantage, social institutions are viewed as existing and continuing during one generation to the next, and social values and norms are mutually agreed upon and shared.

Some criminologists and sociologists see society as composed of many groups, each with their own system of norms and values. Because adherence to one group's norms may force one to violate another group's norms, there may be conflict between groups. For other criminologists and sociologists, the most interesting aspect of society is how humans interact and respond to one another.

These differing perspectives of society are all ways of examining the same phenomenon. Criminologists and sociologists may use any of a number of theoretical approaches to study values, norms, law, and their enforcement or violation. The three perspectives that are most widely used in criminology and sociology provide an introduction for how various researchers discussed later in this text may have examined various aspects of policing. These are the consensus, conflict, and interactionist perspectives.

The Consensus View of Crime

Most of the preceding discussion derives from a perspective on crime commonly referred to as the **consensus model.** This consensus view of crime is frequently credited as rooted in the functionalist school of sociology (Alexander 1985; Schaefer and Lamm 1989). Functionalism emphasizes how each part of a society and its social institutions contribute to the whole. From this perspective, various parts of society fulfill different societal requirements, but are interdependent. Consequently, a change in one area or institution may exert serious influence over other areas.

Functionalism, as it applies to crime, suggests that members of society agree upon some idealized standard of behavior as represented in a real set of laws. In turn, these rules and laws serve to guide the behavior of most society members. These codified laws also make it possible for people to anticipate and expect certain types of conduct in various social situations and settings. Sociologically, crimes are

defined as violations of these consensually accepted patterns of conduct.

The Conflict Approach

The consensus model of crime, however, is not the only perspective on this issue. For some theorists, crime is explained as various groups and institutions in society vying for power, material resources, and control. This theoretical orientation is referred to as the **conflict** perspective (Chambliss 1976, 1988).

The conflict model describes society as a collection of disparate groups in conflict with one another over a variety of issues. Groups with superior possession of or access to political and economic resources use the law, law enforcement agencies, and the justice system to advance their own causes and interests. From this conflict perspective, then, criminal laws serve a central purpose of protecting the haves from the have nots and maintaining their superior position in society.

Willem Bonger, sometimes credited as the first conflict criminologist, was one of the earliest theorists (1916) to recognize crime's relationship to one's relative economic position in society. Stated in simple terms, unequal access to economic resources leads to a social context in which economic advantage is equated with superiority and economic disadvantage with inferiority. Crime, in this context, is the attempt by persons with limited access to financial resources to obtain money, education, and power. In contrast, those with superior access to income and education strive to maintain this advantage by suppressing the less fortunate.

To illustrate how this appears in society, conflict criminologists often compare the harsh penalties exacted on people for theft of personal property to the fairly minor penalties for illegal business practices. Similarly, proponents of a conflict perspective on crime suggest that in spite of publicly supported legal defenses for indigents charged in criminal cases, they do not receive defenses comparable to wealthy defendants'. As evidence of this, conflict criminologists point to the significantly disproportionate number of poor and non-white felons who were defended by state public defenders and who are now serving lengthy prison terms. Briefly stated, the conflict perspective presents a predominantly socioeconomic rather than legalistic view of the concept and definition for crime. It is wealth and political power, not moral or social consensus, that determines whether a behavior is or is not a crime.

From this perspective it is readily understandable how property crimes might be associated with assuring the power and interest of the upper classes. It is less easy to see the conflict orientation as embedded in crimes such as rape, murder, and assault.

Throughout the 1970s, these kinds of crimes might have been explained by conflict theorists as reflecting political and economic underpinnings. For example, the outlawing of violent behaviors increases the likelihood of social tranquility among the underclasses. In turn, these disenfranchised groups are less likely to direct their anger and frustration at the overclasses who exploit them.

During the 1980s, however, conflict theory began to change in orientation. For modern conflict theory, the focus is no longer directly upon social influences from economic and political organizations and institutions. Rather, the focus is upon the entire political and social system (Chambliss 1988). In other words, the focus is not on social class as a category, but on class relations as created and sustained by a political–economic system. To the initiated, this orientation should be recognized immediately as derived from Marxist theory (Marx 1906).

Similarly, the new focus of conflict theorists is on how people interact with their environments, rather than how behavior is determined. The theoretical orientation is not that people are entirely free to act any way

they choose. Rather, the theory suggests that people inherit various social, economic, and political constraints within which they have choices. In other words, social behavior such as law violation must be understood as people making decisions to break the law under certain circumstances. These circumstances, one may suggest, are significantly affected by how a person defines his or her environment and interacts with others.

The Interactionist Approach

In addition to the consensus and conflict perspectives on crime, another orientation, the **interactionist** view, has received fairly wide acceptance. The interactionist model of crime traces its origin to the symbolic interactionist school of sociology often associated with George Herbert Mead, Charles Horton Cooley, and W.I. Thomas (Blumer 1969).

The interactionist perspective suggests that society is the product of continuous interaction among individuals in various social settings (See Mead 1934). People define their social situations and behave according to these interpretations of reality. By interacting with others, people develop definitions of self and expected patterns of appropriate behavior. Because these expectations are shared with others in society, social life becomes systematic, patterned, predictable, and, in short, orderly.

The interactionist perspective on crime falls somewhere between the consensus and the conflict models. In many ways, the interactionist approach extends both consensus and conflict ways of examining law violations. For example, the interactionist model, in contrast to consensus, perceives crime and law enforcement as independent from an absolute, morally justifiable standard or code. From the perspective of an interactionist, the definition of crime, as with any category of deviance, is determined by persons with sufficient influence to invoke the rules that apply and impose sanctions (Becker 1963). Criminals are individuals who have violated social rules (laws) and who have been identified and labeled as deviants or outsiders (Becker 1963). Interactionists view the definition of crime as the *social response* to certain unacceptable behaviors. Thus, certain rule violations are crimes merely because society defines them as such and not because these acts are bad or inherently evil.

When comparing the interactionist view of crime with the conflict perspective, one finds certain similarities. For instance, both suggest that crimes are the social product of those in sufficiently influential positions to affix the label of deviant and impose sanctions. Unlike the conflict perspective, the interactionist view does not assert that this influence is economically motivated. In other words, laws are not necessarily enforced to preserve the capitalist interests of the upper classes.

Interactionists link their definition of crime with the efforts of "moral entrepreneurs." These individuals use their positions and influence to effect legal process, but are chiefly motivated by a kind of "moral crusade" (Becker 1963). In sum, how interactionists view and define crime is intricately related to how shifting moral attitudes and legal standards in society arouse social reactions to various rule violations. This interactionist view, then, is similar to modern conflict approaches, which view criminal behavior as decisions made by individuals based upon certain social and environmental constraints.

SUMMARY

This chapter conveys the idea that social order and freedom require certain elements of control and constraint. One simply cannot have liberty in the absence of rules, laws, and order. All societies provide an elastic range of acceptable behavior. Behavior that society sees as overconformist, and behavior society sees as underconformist is deviant. Yet, even when behavior may be so odd, bizarre, or repugnant that it stretches the limits of social tolerance, it may not be illegal. Crime is conduct that society classifies as illegal. To qualify as crime, behavior must be specifically defined in the law, be enforced by some political body, and associated with prescribed penalties.

Laws themselves are divided between those that are mala in se, or inherently evil in nature (e.g., rape, murder, assault), and mala prohibitum, or those established strictly by statute or ordinance.

The task of the law enforcement officer, which will be more comprehensively detailed in future chapters, is to enforce the criminal laws (as well as other types) and to provide certain necessary community services. The uniformed police officer serves the important symbolic function of personifying the American criminal justice system.

REVIEW QUESTIONS _____

1. What would society be like if there were only **norms** and **informal social controls?**

2. What is the social role of **deviance?**

3. How might one distinguish between the social definition of **crime** and its legal definition?

4. What are some of the principle differences between **felonies** and **misdemeanors?**

5. Why is there a need to define crimes as mala prohibitum?

REFERENCES

Alexander, Jeffrey, ed. *Neofunctionalism.* Beverly Hills, Calif.: Sage, 1985.

Becker, Howard S., *Outsiders: Studies in the Sociology of Deviance.* New York: The Free Press, 1963.

Blumer, Herbert, *Symbolic Interactionism.* Englewood Cliffs, N.J.: Prentice Hall, 1969.

Bonger, William, *Criminality and Economic Conditions.* Boston: Little, Brown, 1916.

Chambliss, William J., *Whose Law, What Order?* New York: Wiley, 1976.

Chambliss, William J., *Exploring Criminology.* New York: Macmillan, 1988.

Critchley, Thomas A., *A History of Police in England and Wales.* 2d ed. Montclair, N.J.: Patterson Smith, 1972.

Durkheim, Emile, *Suicide.* Glencoe, Ill.: The Free Press, 1966; original 1897.

Hagan, Frank E., *Introduction to Criminology: Theories, Methods, and Criminal Behavior.* Chicago: Nelson-Hall, 1986.

LaFave, Wayne and Austin Scott, *Criminal Law.* St. Paul, Minn.: West, 1972.

Lee, William L. Melville, *A History of Police in England.* Montclair, N.J.: Patterson Smith, 1971 [1901].

Marx, Karl, *Das Kapital* Vol. 1. New York: Modern Library, 1906.

Mead, George Herbert, *Mind, Self, and Society from the Standpoint of a Social Behaviorist.* Charles Morris, ed. Chicago: University of Chicago Press, 1934.

Quinney, Richard, *Criminology.* Boston: Little, Brown, 1975.

Schaefer, Richard T. in collaboration with Robert Lamm, *Sociology.* 3d ed. New York: McGraw Hill, 1989.

Siegel, Larry J., *Criminology.* 2d ed. New York: West, 1986.

Simmons, Jerry L., *Deviants.* Berkeley, Calif.: Glendesary, 1969.

Sutherland, Edwin H. and Donald C. Cressey, *Criminology.* 9th ed. Philadelphia: Lippincott, 1974.

THE SOCIOHISTORICAL EVOLUTION OF POLICING

Modern laws and policing styles have not arisen in a vacuum. Both have roots buried deeply in primitive antiquity and the evolution of social history. Chapter Two traces the social environments and changes that arose in laws and law enforcement strategies as society moved from primitive tribal to more urban stages. This chapter examines important historical antecedents to modern policing in America, including a description of perhaps the earliest form: kin policing. This chapter also examines the historic role of rational laws and the impact on law enforcement of codes such as Hammurabi's and bodies of law such as Mosaic Law.

Chapter Two also considers the role policing played in the development of Anglo-Saxon England. The purpose here is to illustrate the origins of much of American policing.

INTRODUCTION: GOVERNING HUMAN BEHAVIOR

The enforcement of law may be accomplished by brute military force, by some form of less rigorous public censure, police activity, or some combination thereof. As this chapter details, the evolution of law enforcement is marked by elements of each. The literal be- ginning of formal law enforcement is shrouded in a cloak of mystery, mysticism, superstition, and historical romanticism. When one attempts to trace the evolution of law enforcement from antiquity to modern times, it becomes impossible either to completely or absolutely identify the origins of this practice.

During ancient times, social order was chiefly patriarchal—a father figure governed the social organization of the group. This individual was responsible for determining the guilt or innocence of an errant family or clan member and administering any punishments. Tribal customs gradually developed as the basis for behavioral guidelines and evolved into informal modes of conduct. Laws, as one might think about them today, do not appear until considerably later. Let us turn to the past and consider some of the ancient versions of law enforcement and their implications for modern law enforcement.

LAW ENFORCEMENT IN ANTIQUITY

During ancient times members of the clan and tribe were the police and security force. The head of the tribe or clan had executive, legislative, and judicial control. Although the head of the clan might appoint members of the tribe or clan to special tasks, such as assisting the enforcement of his rulings or acting as his personal bodyguard, these appointees still were essentially members of the local community. In other words, these individuals did not represent an organized policing system.

During ancient times, the enforcement of a group's norms and laws was handled primarily by the injured party or by one's family and kin. In turn, crimes committed against the group, such as an attack, typically were handled by the entire clan or tribe. As time progressed, what began to arise was a kind of rule enforcement system based upon individual and kin responsibility. Textbooks frequently refer to this sort of system as a **kin police** system.

The Kin Police

In kin policing, the family, clan, or tribe assumes the responsibility for administering justice. During these ancient tribal periods, justice usually operated under the philosophy of retaliation. Consequently, justice was harsh, brutal, and crude. Branding or mutilation of an apprehended offender was common. One could expect to have a hand cut off for stealing something. Or, one might be branded on the forehead as a criminal. Under kin policing, each member of the group possessed a rudimentary type of official authority and was therefore empowered to enforce the group's code of laws.

The Code of Hammurabi

Around 2100 B.C., informal and customary codes of law fell away. Groups began to establish codified and thus more rational and formal systems of law. Among the earliest was the Code of Hammurabi, the king of Babylon (around 1750 B.C.). The Code of Hammurabi was written on a column of stone and discovered by a French government expedition exploring the Persian Gulf in 1901. The code contained 282 sections that described the responsibilities of each individual to every other individual in the society. It outlined rules for private dealings between individuals, methods for dealing with runaway slaves, reclaiming stolen property, inheritances, return of purchased slaves if they were ill, and a vast array of other circumstances (See Box 2.1). In addition, the code detailed penalties for violations.

Also found in the text of the Code of Hammurabi was what may have been the first recorded representation of the principle of *lex talionis*. Roughly translated, lex talionis means "an eye for an eye and a tooth for a tooth" (Seagle 1947). The code was quite brutal. Many crimes, such as robbery, were punished by death. Nonetheless, many scholars believe that this retributive philosophy was intended to limit the kind of rampant blood feuds that often resulted under kin policing systems. Philosophically, under lex talionis, one could exact no greater penalty than the worth of

Box 2.1 _____

SAMPLE SECTIONS FROM THE CODE OF HAMMURABI

The Code of Hammurabi is believed to be the oldest set of codified laws. It contains 282 sections and provides comprehensive guidelines for most social and civil interactions between people. A small sampling from the code:

1. If a man weaves a spell about another man and throws a curse on him, and cannot prove it, the one who wove the spell shall be put to death.
2. If a man weaves a spell about another man, and has not proved it, he on whom suspicion was thrown shall go to the river, shall plunge into the river. If the river seizes hold of him, he who wove the spell shall take his home. If the river shows him to be innocent, and he is uninjured, he who threw suspicion on him shall be put to death. He who plunged into the river shall take the house of him who wove the spell on him.
3. If a man has accused the witnesses in a lawsuit of malice and has not proved what he said, if the suit was one life (and death), that man shall be put to death.
4. If he has sent corn and silver to the witnesses, he shall bear the penalty of the suit.
16. If anyone harbors in his house a runaway male or female slave from the place or the house of a noble, and does not bring them out at the command of the majordomo, the master of the house shall be put to death.
22. If anyone has committed a robbery and is caught, he shall be killed.

23. If the robber is not caught, the man who has been robbed shall make claim before God to everything stolen from him, and the town and its governor within the territory and limits of which the robbery took place shall give back to him everything he has lost.
185. If a man has taken a small child as a son in his own name and has brought him up, that foster child shall not be reclaimed.
186. If a man has taken a small child for his son, and if when he took him his father and his mother he offended, that foster child shall return to the house of his father.
229. If a builder has built a house for some one and has not made his work firm, and if the house he built has fallen and has killed the owner of the house, that builder shall be put to death.
230. If it has killed the son of the house-owner, one shall kill the son of that builder.
231. If it has killed the slave of the house-owner he (the builder) shall give to the owner of the house slave for slave. (Source: Folley 1980, Appendix C.)

As many of the sample sections of the Code of Hammurabi suggest, a major contribution of this set of laws was the concept of *lex talionis* (an eye for an eye). This notion of retributive justice exacts as remedy a sum equal to, but not greater than, the loss or injury. The Code of Hammurabi marked the symbolic end of blood feuds characteristic of previous centuries.

---

that which had been lost. This ancient principle can be seen as a forerunner of at least two major modern notions of law and justice. First, it suggests the concept of a uniform and prescriptive social reaction to violations of society's laws. Second, it implies a system in which, theoretically, the penalty was intended to fit the crime: the more serious the nature of the crime, the more serious the punishment.

In addition to regulating a wide variety of criminal and civil law violations, the Code of Hammurabi made special provision for the protection of children. If one received certain property from a child without parental consent, one might be guilty of a capital offense (Ludwig 1955, 12). Even family relationships were regulated by the code. In fact, the code specified severe punishment for rebellion and disloyalty among family members. While the code clearly articulated a number of civil and criminal matters, it provided no special treatment of children who violated public law. It is unclear whether children who violated the law were punished by the family or were subject to the same harsh punishment as adults.

Mosaic Law

Mosaic law (ca. 1000 B.C.) emerged approximately one thousand years after the Code of Hammurabi. Like the code, Mosaic law was intended to provide a formal and rational system of law. For the ancient Hebrews, the Torah and the interpretative supplementary sacred traditions served as a normative system that governed behavior in all areas of life. Unlike other legal systems emerging across the Mediterranean during this period, the bearers of this legal system were not a ruling class. In fact, the ancient Hebrews were a pariah people (Weber 1978, 824), a nomadic guest culture within other, larger cultures. Consequently, interactions and dealings with outsiders was a kind of foreign commerce. Because of this, transactions were governed by slightly different ethical norms than those that applied to dealings with insiders (other Jews).

To a fairly large degree, the ancient Hebrews strived to adapt themselves and their ethical laws to their environment (and host culture), provided that such adaptation did not run counter to their own ritualistic scruples. Much of the early Torah was an oral tradition that lasted several hundred years. Given this oral tradition and the pariah nature of these ancient Hebrews, it is little wonder that the later, written version of Mosaic law showed signs of influence and borrowing from Babylonian and later from Hellenistic and Byzantine cultures (Weber 1978, 826–27).

Regardless, Mosaic law, like the Code of Hammurabi, represented important moves toward formalizing and standardizing law into a rational system of enforceable rules of conduct. It was not until the early Greek city–states developed that major innovations in law enforcement and law arose.

Greek and Roman Influences and Contributions

It was chiefly during the development of early Greek city–states that clan or tribal policing (kin policing) fully gave way to community or city policing. Peisistratus (605–527 B.C.), the ruler of Athens, often is credited with creating the first formal system of policing. Peisistratus developed a guard system charged with the responsibilities of protecting the ruler, the watch tower, and highways (Germann et al. 1976). In contrast to the more democratic legal system of Athens, the Greek city–state of Sparta developed a ruler-appointed police force. Since Sparta is sometimes characterized as having had an authoritarian regime, this early police system often is described as the first **secret police** (Germann et al. 1976).

During the early Roman era, social order was maintained primarily through brute military force provided by the legions of the rulers. The Praetorian Guard was created by Augustus, the first emperor of Rome (27 B.C.). This guard unit was composed of handpicked members of Augustus' legion and was charged with the responsibility of protecting the person and property of the emperor. It was also during the reign of Augustus that history saw the creation of a rudimentary city police force, commonly referred to as the urban cohort. A less select military unit of men than the Praetorian Guard but also chosen from the legions, the urban cohort originally preserved the peace of the city. Later, and in the wake of considerable civilian unrest and several major fires in Rome, Augustus formed the *vigiles* (watchmen) of Rome. The vigiles were a non-military unit of several thousand men whose duties included both fire fighting and keeping the peace in the city. The vigiles were armed with staves (clubs) and traditional short-swords and were assigned to various geographic precincts throughout the city. The vigiles were empowered to arrest law breakers, signifying the first formal civilian police force.

EARLY ENGLISH CONTRIBUTIONS

After the Fall of Rome around 395 A.D., Europe witnessed several centuries of turbulent warfare and successive conquests. It was not until around the seventh century A.D. that the history of law enforcement again began to make meaningful strides forward. During this early period in England's history, concepts of community and mutual responsibility became more sophisticated than those practiced by primitive styles of kin policing. Small self-governing villages, or tuns, began to emerge and checker the countryside. Within the tun, history witnesses the strengthening of individual and mutual responsibility for personal and group security, police enforcement, and justice.

Superstition and magic for determining one's guilt or innocence of a crime began to yield to more efficient and rational organized systems of justice and law. Borrowing from *frankpledge,* developed in France during the seventh century, England created the tithing system. The tithing system established the responsibility of each tun member for his neighbor and provided an organized peace-keeping mechanism for the safety and protection of the tun.

Tithings were composed of groups of ten families belonging to freemen. All men over the age of twelve were required to be in a tithing. Each member of a tithing was responsible for his own good behavior, the behavior of his family, and his fellow tithing members. The tithing itself was responsible socially and financially for the behaviors of its membership. Thus, if a tithing failed to apprehend an errant member, the entire tithing might be made to pay restitution to the injured party (Reynolds 1984). As part of their self-government, members of the tun elected a chief tithingman. The chief tithingman was respon-

This painting depicts the pomp and majesty commonly associated with medieval tournaments.

A thane watches a joust in his honor (reenactment).

sible for raising the hue and cry, or call to arms, which mobilized every able-bodied man to pursue an offender. The chief tithingman was further responsible for dispensing punishment to the offender.

As the small villages began to increase in population and geographic size, so too did their law enforcement needs. Eventually, groupings of ten tithings evolved into what were called a hundred. Within the hundred, people elected a head man called a reeve or headborough. The reeve presided over monthly meetings in which members of his hundred discussed their various needs and problems. While the reeve administered the hundred, a constable (from the French *comes stabuli*, meaning officer of the stable) was

placed in charge of supervising and maintaining the hundred's equipment. This position was similar to the modern quartermaster. Interestingly, the early French *comes stablis* also were charged with the task of raising and maintaining armies.

Given the connotation of the French, and the importance attached to horse soldiers (cavalry) during this early medieval period, the concept of a constable becomes somewhat more clear. The advent of the warhorse significantly altered not only styles of military battle, but society in general.

As time passed, high constables emerged and administered both hundreds and petty constables who had begun to take on the more traditional role of peace officer in the towns and parishes of the countryside. Shires, or geographic areas analogous to a modern county, developed as several hundreds came together. These shires were governed by a shire-reeve, appointed by either a nobleman or the king. Shire-reeves were freemen, not vassals. This meant they were not the chattel of a lord. The position of shire-reeve had both quasi-military and judicial authority. A number of contemporary historians suggest that both the title and office of the modern sheriff derives from these early shire-reeves.

The tithing system arose and flourished chiefly between the seventh and ninth centuries. During the latter part of the ninth century, Alfred the Great consolidated England

Knights pay homage before beginning a medieval tournament and joust (reenactment).

and found the tithing system useful in his attempt to unify the people and the nation. The tithing system was further refined under the later rule of William the Conqueror. He established a series of 55 individual military districts and placed an official in charge of each. These officials were responsible directly to the Crown, unlike the more autonomous shire-reeves. The shire-reeves, in fact, soon found themselves replaced. While the position of shire-reeve remained, its role and authority changed. No longer, for example, did the position possess the judicial powers of the earlier office. In place of this, William the Conqueror installed the *vice comites,* predecessor of the circuit judge (See Barlow 1970, Reynolds 1984).

The simple tithing style of mutual responsibility for its members soon gave way to frankpledge. In many ways the frankpledge was a system of compulsory collective bail fixed for individuals. However, this bail was not set after arrest for crime, but as a safeguard in anticipation of it (Critchley 1972). The early history after the Norman conquest of Saxon England in 1066 found two alien cultures living side by side in one land. However, one culture was the conqueror, while the other was a defeated and oppressed people. The Normans increased the restrictions of mutual responsibility remnant in the old Saxon tithing system. They required the newly appointed royal shire-reeves (sheriffs) to supervise a specially held biannual hundred court (See Morris 1968; Critchley 1972). The purpose of this court was to ensure that all eligible men were enrolled in a tithing and had thus pledged their good behavior and that of one another. This view of frankpledge and sheriff's tourn, as the court soon came to be called, also was used to maintain brutal repression. Although the Norman sheriffs were royal officers and thus men of great power, they were also often men of few scruples. In addition to extorting the payments of fines at the least opportunity, they were very brutal in their dispensing of jus-

tice. Several sheriffs were notorious for gouging out eyes, in other ways mutilating, or hanging thieves. These sheriffs were brutal even for the twelfth century!

The coming of the Normans also brought a new version of the old tithing office of **constable.** When the term first arose under the Normans, it was regarded as a welcome and familiar tithing position by the simple peasants. But it was no longer the familiar civil position largely represented by the saxon chief tithingman or reeve. It had become a high military position associated first with the royal court and then with the royal reeves or sheriffs. Thus, constables during the late eleventh and early twelfth centuries represented the fusion of popular and royal government more completely than any other local government position (Critchley 1972). Later, constables would be elected by towns and represent the community's law enforcement responsibilities. However, these constables also were the personification of the royal authority that governed these towns.

By the end of the thirteenth century the constable had acquired two distinct characteristics. First, as the annually elected representative of the town or parish, he was the executive agent symbolizing the collective responsibility established by his predecessor, the chief tithingman. Second, he was the central officer recognized by the Crown as responsible for keeping the king's peace.

The administrative and constitutional importance of the early Saxon tithing system and later the Norman frankpledge seems incontestable. Their blend of policy and tradition throughout the eleventh and twelfth centuries combined to establish a considerable foundation for later policing styles in England.

In spite of the legal refinements and social effects from the frankpledge, it had several serious flaws that led to its inevitable demise. Let us consider some of the problems. The tithing system of mutual responsibility was fairly well suited to deal with emergency situations that might arise in an agrarian setting where inhabitants of the community were relatively stable. As urban society began to encroach upon agrarian life and people moved from their birth homes and into various more urban centers, the tithing system became difficult to keep intact and operative. The shifts and changes in residence as members moved into and out of different tithings encouraged tithing members to conceal crime—even to the extent of perjury. The lies about crimes and member-criminals were attempts to avoid financial liabilities that would otherwise fall upon the tithing as restitution for the wrongful acts.

By the thirteenth century, England was still chiefly a rural and agrarian society. Tuns had gradually grown into small towns chiefly populated by persons still living in manors with strong community life, but weak resources. English society was dominated by a hierarchic, wealthy, and militaristic aristocracy. The majority of England's population was illiterate peasantry. Problems and disputes that arose in the manor community were usually handled by the manor court, presided over by the lord or the manor's steward, although this was not universally true across England. For instance, the northern and northeastern portions of England once were occupied by the Danes. In these locations, the village community itself was charged with resolving problems that affected the manor community. This type of community rule is known as Danelaw.

Throughout most of the thirteenth century, farming was the staple occupation of the English peasantry. Typically, the village was nucleated. Peasant farmers built and grouped their houses together around the large open fields they farmed. The actions of the village and community were, on a modest level, an exercise in self-government.

The manorial court met at regular intervals (approximately every three weeks). The emergence of towns, however, offered an increasingly attractive alternative to the agrarian country life-style of the manor. One could

sell one's products for profit rather than subsistence. Although still basically a hierarchical society, cities and towns offered the added incentive of being more democratic than the manors. Gradually, the entire basis of medieval society shifted from agrarian to urban and from a military aristocracy to an elitist aristocracy of wealth.

The Development of Markets and Cities

The development of towns, markets, and cities signified an important turning point in history. The emergence of these urban centers also forced advances in early law enforcement practices. Early markets and towns were virtually indistinguishable one from the other. In medieval Latin, the word *castrum* is used synonymously to mean a fortress, a castle, or a town (Germann et al. 1976). It is likely—although not certain—that during the late Middle Ages these concepts and locations were inextricably interwoven. It is similarly probable that early towns during the tenth century emerged as centers of refuge where merchants and peasants sought security and where permanent markets incidentally arose. Most early walled cities developed around already established markets in order to provide safety and security for the inhabitants. Although some historians suggest that walled cities did not necessarily indicate market centers, certainly no market could exist for long if it were not very near or contained within the safety of a walled city.

During the thirteenth century, as both the export and domestic cloth market developed, so too did the populations of towns. Soon, small towns began to bulge at the seams, giving way to new towns and eventually cities. Urban centers began to sweep across what previously had been empty space, and suburbs crawled increasingly farther into the English countryside. Along with increasing populations and urban development came major changes in forms of government. These arose in the shape of mayors, councils, and explicit rules set forth in the Magna Carta.

The Magna Carta. The Magna Carta, or "Great Charter" as it is sometimes called, is a cornerstone of both democracy and law enforcement. Under pressure by angry nobles, clergymen, and an increasingly organized citizenry, King John of England signed the Magna Carta in 1215. Similar to the Bill of Rights, the Magna Carta gave the common Englishman due process, the right to a trial by jury, and local governmental control. In short, the Magna Carta eliminated arbitrary edicts by lords and established both the responsibilities of the state and the supremacy of formal law (Critchley 1972).

As previously suggested, the tithing system was better suited for agrarian life than for an urban setting. By the thirteenth century, citizens had grown increasingly unwilling to accept the common responsibility for bringing criminals or errant tithing members to justice. In 1285, with the issuance of the Statute of Winchester, King Edward I attempted to reaffirm the old tradition of local mutual responsibility.

The Statute of Winchester. The Statute of Winchester empowered the dean and high steward of Westminster to punish "all matters of incontinencies, common scolds, common annoyances, and to commit to prison all who offend against the peace" (Germann et al. 1976, 55). In other words, this statute made it illegal to conceal or harbor criminals. In addition, it made everyone in the county in which a crime occurred accountable in order to assure their assistance in apprehending the felon. The statute also declared that "cries shall be made in all counties, markets, hundreds, [and] fairs, so that none shall excuse himself by ignorance," thus reestablishing the hue and cry system of ancient Saxon England (Lee 1971; Germann et al. 1976). In order to assure that the hue and cry could be enforced, the statute further established the assize of arms and a watch and ward system.

The assize of arms required every male between the ages of fifteen and sixty to keep a weapon in his home as a means for keeping the peace. The watch and ward established a patrol that surveyed the city during the night, augmenting the traditional daytime duties of the constable (Lee 1971).

The Statute of Winchester further established several important law enforcement measures. For instance, to safeguard merchants and travelers from the dangers of highwaymen, the statute ordered major roads between towns to be kept clear of brush and growth for a distance of two hundred feet on either side. The intention here, of course, was to eliminate places for highwaymen to conceal themselves and lie in ambush for unsuspecting citizens (Lee 1971). The Statute of Winchester also established the parish constable system in England. The parish constable system remained the primary policing system in England for the next six hundred years.

During this same period, attempts to control vice and crime at local levels also emerged in the cities. To this end, the *police des mouers,* (police of the pouters—prostitutes) was established. This early policing agency kept track of and regulated prostitution. The agency maintained a register of prostitutes, whose activities were confined to certain sections of the city. Thus was created what is today more commonly called the "red light district" (Germann et al. 1976).

Throughout the fourteenth and fifteenth centuries law enforcement gained in size and sophistication. These changes came as a unavoidable consequence of a rapidly growing and increasingly transient industrial society. By the early 1500s, England had become an active participant in world commerce. America had been discovered and England was quickly rising as a leader in the production of wool. Throughout the English countryside, farmers had begun to put down their plows and give up farming. In place of large planting fields, farmers began developing pastures for grazing sheep. As land owners began converting their farms into sheep ranches, fewer and fewer farmers were needed. This enclosure system resulted in a mass migration of one-time farmers into the more urban centers. Since farmers had been largely a peasant class while in the countryside, they quickly developed into a volatile horde of poor but angry city dwellers. Crime inevitably increased as these dispossessed and unskilled farm folk arrived in what were already overcrowded cities.

The merchant class of England quickly grew impatient and dissatisfied with the protection they were receiving from the state. The watch and ward, which had never really operated very effectively, began to crumble as merchants and members of the middle class began to hire surrogates to take their place on what had become increasingly dangerous watches. These hired **deputies,** perhaps fearing for their own safety, failed to perform their duties adequately. Growing still more dissatisfied with the protection afforded them by the state, merchants began to employ their own private police force. This early private police group was known as the "Commercial and Parochial Police," and were the early forerunners of modern private security patrols.

At one point in 1550 the city of London was divided into twenty-six wards. Each amounted to a kind of self-contained unit under the control of an alderman and a small group of common councilmen. The right to elect these officers was limited only to freemen residing in the ward. For the most part, members of the trade and merchant classes had to be freemen, as did businessmen operating in London. Lower offices, such as **beadle, constable,** and **scavenger,** were elected by freemen and non-freemen alike. Each of these lower offices was essentially a strong-arm position, the duty of which was chiefly to arrange that the alderman's orders were followed and to maintain order within the ward (Rumbelow 1971).

Theoretically, ward residents were elected to office through democratic process. In practice, however, offices were filled by appointment or nomination by the alderman. These typically occurred by nominating the oldest non-serving inhabitant householder of the ward to an open officer's position. A householder was defined as anyone rated for a house, paying scot, or bearing lot. The term bearing lot typically referred to certain civic duties each ward required of householders. These included such things as hanging lanterns in winter, sweeping clean the ground in front of the householder's home, keeping a bucket filled with water outside his front door (in case of a fire in the ward), and taking his turn as ward beadle, constable, or scavenger. Paying scot was the payment of a fee to the ward for tasks that should have been performed by a paid employee, but were often undertaken by ward members instead.

Soon, one was able to pay scot in order to avoid his duty to serve as a ward beadle, constable, or scavenger. What this actually meant was that thieves, scoundrels, cutthroats, and other disreputables were hired in place of the householders. Under the guise of their petty offices, these individuals were able to practice their dark crafts as they wandered the poorly lighted streets and alleys of the London wards. These corrupt and largely ineffective watchmen, then, contributed both to the inefficiency of the watch and the loathing of police among Londoners that continued for the next several hundred years.

Crime and the Industrial Revolution

By the beginning of the Industrial Revolution during the eighteenth century, England found itself faced with mass poverty, unemployment, overcrowding, and serious crime problems. The cities began to grow into huge slums. In the absence of child labor laws, many children worked alongside their parents for up to sixteen hours a day. Much of the literary work of Charles Dickens and the socio-economic observations of Karl Marx (1906) quite accurately portrayed the squalor, deprivation, and crime of eighteenth century England.

The cities, which had originally attracted the displaced agrarians seeking jobs as unskilled laborers, changed into hordes of unemployed marauding gangs. Machines, such as the steam engine and the power loom, further devalued the need for unskilled factory workers. Crime in the streets of England was rampant. The crowded cities attracted thousands of pickpockets who plied their trade with enormous agility. Cities also offered an effective and speedy way to dispose of ill-gotten goods. Fences, persons who deal in stolen property, began to surface in most large cities throughout England. Counterfeiting, a longstanding problem for the English, became so prevalent that at one point estimates suggest there was more phony money than real in circulation.

Prostitution, like counterfeiting and pickpocketing, developed as an alternative to unemployment. Numbers of prostitutes grew so rapidly that at one point, 25,000 were believed active in London alone. These lawless conditions led to a variety of attempts to restore order. Among these law enforcement innovations were rewards for the apprehension of criminals, harsh penalties for even minor crimes (at one point death could be imposed for more than 160 different offenses), and citizen groups known as **vigilantes** to combat crime.

Unfortunately, many of these innovations backfired. Criminals began both to inform on one another and to frame innocent people, either for the reward or as blackmail. In short, the reward system created a new, institutionalized form of criminal activity.

Henry Fielding and the Bow Street Runners

It was not until 1748, when Henry Fielding became chief magistrate of Bow Street in lawless London, that any meaningful law enforcement strategies arose. Assisted by his blind half-brother John, who later succeeded John Fielding as magistrate, Fielding eventually established a **mounted officers patrol** to ride the crime-infested roads leading into the city. He further innovated a **foot patrol** to sweep through the congested and heavily populated residential and business areas of the city. In many ways, these patrols were precursors of modern **mobile patrols** (discussed in greater length in Chapter Four).

The Bow Street Horse and Foot Patrol was certainly the most cohesive and effective law enforcement force of its time when it began in 1805. By 1828 it had grown to a mounted unit of 2 inspectors, 4 deputy inspectors, 100 mounted patrol officers, and 127 street patrol officers (Rumbelow 1971). Unfortunately, London's population during this time had grown to more than one million. Excluding the parish watchmen—a motley and unreliable crew—and the Thames police, whose patrol was limited chiefly to the river, fewer than 400 men were involved in enforcing the laws of England and preserving safety and peace in the streets of London.

For the most part, Fielding is remembered for having created the Bow Street Runners. Fielding strongly believed that in order to ensure crime prevention, private citizens should join forces with the municipal police force he was actively creating. He suggested that these citizen-volunteers could swiftly move to the scene of a crime, diffuse an angry crowd, and begin gathering information and facts about the crime. These "running civilian volunteers," then, became the Bow Street Runners. The Bow Street Runners, or thief-takers, as they came to be called, initially numbered only eight and were attached to the court at Bow Street in Westminster. Their numbers were later increased to 12. These runners were markedly different from the other persons involved in police-type activities at this time. The work of these thief-takers seriously altered the contest between professional thieves and the wealthy citizens of London. The Bow Street Runners made a serious study of investigations and locating criminals and quickly became experts in this area. Unlike their more amateur peace-keeping predecessors (such as watchmen, parish constables, and some of the privately employed police officers of the period) the thief-takers did not offer only a perfunctory police service. They actively pursued criminals and were motivated by the prospects of reward money (Lee 1971).

The Bow Street Runners certainly accomplished a considerable amount of good by breaking up the various predatory gangs and apprehending a number of infamous criminals. However, they were also a source of considerable crime themselves. Stimulated by the hope of financial reward more than any sense of civic duty, their methods were often questionable, to say the least. They were only concerned with apprehending those criminals who would bring the largest rewards. In other words, the Bow Street Runners were not particularly interested in pursuing fugitives from justice whose capture was chiefly for the good of the community. Furthermore, prevention of crime was never a concern of the thief-takers. Obviously, such a concern would run contrary to their primary interest in securing rewards for capturing criminals. As a consequence, the services of the Bow Street Runners were available only to persons wealthy enough to post a sizable reward. Too, several of the thief-takers were later found to have been involved in the commission of crime in order to obtain rewards. It has been supposed that this spawned the expression, "It takes a thief to catch a thief."

In spite of their questionable methods, the Bow Street Runners were, in many ways, prototypes for both private investigators and detective divisions in modern municipal police departments.

Sir Robert Peel and the Peelers

Throughout the late eighteenth and into the nineteenth centuries, widespread lawlessness continued in England. The courts had begun to implement longer and longer prison terms, and the jails and prisons soon swelled beyond their capacities. Offenders of even such petty crimes as stealing a loaf of bread were often hanged.

Sir Robert Peel, who served as Britain's home secretary in 1829, had been impressed and inspired by the work of Henry Fielding. Like Fielding, Peel believed that one contributing factor to London's severe problem was poorly trained, undermanned, and overworked policing personnel. Peel also believed that if any crime control was to work, it would require both the backing of a strong body of law and the support and respect of the public. Because of this attitude, Peel worked toward improving the harsh, vague, and frequently arbitrary nature of the laws during his time. Peel managed to have the death penalty abolished for many of the 160 assorted offenses for which it could be implemented. He also believed that agents of the law needed to be a unified body of well-selected, and well-trained men. Additionally, Peel adhered to a rigorous use of a probationary period for his officers.

Unfortunately, by this time there were a variety of diverse categories of police. For instance, there were the **merchant police,** hired to protect the markets, banks, and commercial businesses and who could additionally be hired as private investigators to secure stolen property or merchandise. There were the **marine police,** organized by West India merchants in order to provide security on the docks and to protect shipping on the Thames. There also were the **parish police,** hired by parishioners to protect the lives and personal property of persons residing within the parish. Finally, there was the watch and ward, which remained the basic system of policing and peace-keeping in the city. In addition to these police systems, there were the Bow Street Runners and a number of successive, short-lived vigilante groups (Lee 1971). For Robert Peel, unifying these various disparate policing agencies under a single canopy of administration and coordination was an essential element in establishing an effective police organization.

In 1829, shortly after Peel had introduced a "Bill for improving the Police in and near the Metropolis" to Parliament, his Metropolitan Police of London were organized. The primary organizational purpose of this police agency was the prevention of crime (See Box 2.2).

The police constable who made his appearance on the streets of London in 1829 was a very different kind of officer from his predecessors. Peel had recruited his new police force from the best men he could locate. Individuals who sought entrance into the new police force were expected to be in good physical condition, possess above-average intelligence, and be of high moral character (See Lee 1971; Miller 1977).

Peel was sufficiently committed to his dream of an effective municipal police force that he personally participated in the interviewing of more than 12,000 applicants in order to locate 1,000 suitable officers. Sadly, Peel's desire to orient the police toward crime prevention failed to last very long. Owing to

the potential for financial rewards, these public police officers became more and more active in crime investigations and less concerned with crime prevention. During the initial two years of its operation, the Metropolitan Police force fired (or lost through resignation) nearly 500 of the original 1,000 officers. But the concept of personal integrity and high moral character among officers has been firmly implanted in police organizations ever since.

Unfortunately for Peel, all of his efforts to demonstrate the moral fortitude of his Metropolitan Police force personnel continued to meet with doubt and trepidations from Parliament and public (See Browne 1973). During the first several years, most citizens viewed members of the Metropolitan Police force, or Peelers, with disrespect. Even law-abiding citizens of London continued to view the Peelers as disreputable and referred to them as crush-

Box 2.2

The Peelian Reforms

I SPY BLUE, I SPY BLACK, I SPY A PEELER IN A SHINY HAT. [ANONYMOUS]

Sir Robert Peel desired to establish a body of noble law enforcement personnel, a group of men responsible for safeguarding life and property in London's corrupt and lawless metropolitan area. To assure an effective, organized operation, Peel set forth a 12-point guideline, sometimes referred to as "Peelian Reform":

1. The police must be stable, efficient, and organized along military lines.
2. The police must be under governmental control.
3. The absence of crime will best prove the efficiency of the police.
4. The distribution of crime news is essential.
5. The deployment of police strength by *time* and *area* is essential.
6. No quality is more indispensable to a policeman than a perfect command of temper; a quiet, determined manner has more effect than violent action.
7. Good appearance commands respect.

8. The securing and training of proper persons is at the root of efficiency.
9. Public security demands that every police officer be given a number.
10. Police headquarters should be centrally located and easily accessible to the people.
11. Policemen should be hired on a probationary basis.
12. Police records are necessary to the correct distribution of police strength. (Kirkham and Wollan 1980, 29.)

To a large extent, the essence of policing in modern America and England continues to reflect these basic elements offered 160 years ago by Peel. Peel's orientation was for a consolidated municipal force to overtly patrol the streets of London. Peelers were armed only with truncheons (forerunners of police batons) and were instructed in etiquette so that they would be civil when they confronted citizens (Moore and Kelling 1985, 38).

ers and blue devils (referring to the familiar blue coats of the Day Police, who preceded Peel's Metropolitan Police). Some of the original officers were beaten and thrown into the Thames (Rumbelow 1971). Such public disdain and rigid internal organizational discipline were certainly factors that affected the high rate of attrition during the early years of the agency's operation.

Undaunted by the problems, the Metropolitan Police succeeded in only ten years in winning the approval and respect of the public—and the criminals. The cat-calls and derogatory names used for the officers during earlier years were soon replaced with the more affectionate one of bobbies (after Sir Robert).

In 1839, legislation was passed making it possible for communities outside London to create their own police forces. Laws that created tax-supported police agencies throughout England were passed in 1856. Sir Robert Peel's great experiment had become an overwhelming success.

Peter Manning (1977) has examined the rise of the municipal police officer in England during the early part of the nineteenth century. According to Manning (1977, 90), the English police force grew out of a time of extreme turmoil and crime. It was "conceived, at least in part, as a benign force that would mediate between the people as a relatively unorganized body on the one hand and the elites on the other." In order to accomplish this somewhat odd task, the English police were established as a paramilitary organization, including the wearing of a fairly distinctive uniform.

The transformation of early English policing styles into the early American ones and the various reforms and changes that have led to contemporary policing practices are important issues. All reflect various social circumstances that occurred simultaneously in London and the United States. Of particular interest to modern policing is the evolution of municipal police strategies during the late eighteenth and early nineteenth centuries.

These social and historical events will be examined at the end of Chapter Three, after considering the evolution of policing in colonial and pioneering America.

SUMMARY

As the chapter outlines, the original form of policing may have been little more than family members banding together in order to protect themselves against rival families or marauding groups (kin policing). As society evolved and became more complex, informal norms gave rise to codes and loose configurations of laws. These, in turn, needed more sophisticated and better organized groups to maintain and enforce them.

Although primitive and rudimentary by today's standards, the Peisistratus guards and the urban cohort of the early Greek city-state, were major organizational advances in the ancient history of policing. In fact, significant changes in policing were rather slow to emerge during much of England's early history after the Fall of Rome.

As England developed from an agrarian to an urban industrial society, changes in policing were also emerging. As villages, markets, and towns became cities, population density increased along with poverty, unemployment, and ill health, and an assortment of law enforcement and safety needs arose. Eventually, Sir Robert Peel established the first truly modern police with the founding of the London Metropolitan Police force. This police organization, and the standards Peel insisted upon for his officers, remain an important ideal for policing even today.

As Chapter Three will detail, law enforcement developed in the United States throughout the eighteenth and nineteenth centuries in a fairly haphazard and uneven manner. Southern colonial America adopted much of the English countryside's style of sheriffing, while northern colonial America's policing styles more closely resembled the municipal policing traditions of English cities.

REVIEW QUESTIONS

1. How were kin policing systems responsible for blood feuds?

2. Under the Code of Hammurabi one might lose one's hand for stealing bread. How is it, then, that this code is recognized for its "rationality"?

3. In what ways were tithing members responsible for each other? What was the purpose of this mutual responsibility?

4. How are markets, castles, and walled cities related to law enforcement?

5. What effect did the enclosure system have on urban settings? How was the safety and security of residents of these urban settings affected?

REFERENCES

Barlow, Frank. *Edward the Confessor.* London: Eyre & Spottiswoode, 1970.

Browne, Douglas G. *The Rise of Scotland Yard.* New York: Greenwood, 1973.

Critchley, Thomas A. *A History of Police in England and Wales,* 2nd ed. Montclair, N.J.: Patterson Smith, 1972.

Germann, A.C., Frank D. Day, and R.R.H. Gallati. *Introduction to Law Enforcement and Criminal Justice.* Springfield, Ill.: Thomas, 1976.

Healy, R.J. *Design for Security.* New York: Wiley, 1968.

Lee, William L. Melville. *A History of Police in England.* Montclair, N.J.: Patterson Smith, 1971.

Ludwig, Frederick J. *Youth and the Law: Handbook on Laws Affecting Youth.* Brooklyn, N.Y.: Foundation Press, 1955.

Manning, Peter. *Police Work.* Cambridge, Mass.: MIT Press, 1977.

Miller, Wilbur R. *Cops and Bobbies.* Chicago and London: University of Chicago Press, 1977.

Morris, William A. *The Medieval English Sheriff to 1300.* New York: Barnes and Noble, 1968.

Reynolds, Susan. *Kingdoms and Communities in Western Europe, 900-1300.* Oxford, England: Clarendon, 1984.

Rumbelow, Donald. *I Spy Blue: The Police and Crime in the City of London from Elizabeth I to Victoria.* N.Y.: St. Martin's Press, 1971.

Seagle, William. "Hammurabi: King of Babylon." In William Seagle ed. *Men of Law: From Hammurabi to Homes.* New York: Macmillan, 1947.

Weber, Max. *Economy and Society Vol. II.* Berkeley Calif.: University of California Press, 1978 [1920].

CHAPTER 3

THE HISTORY AND DEVELOPMENT OF LAW ENFORCEMENT IN THE UNITED STATES

When the Pilgrims arrived on the shores of the New World they did not originally seek to establish a new social or political order. They were English, governed by English common law and the monarchy. These early colonists, then, began to use the only form of police protection and law enforcement they knew. This form, as Chapter Three will detail, was largely based upon the watch systems of English cities. As colonial America began to expand geographically, police styles were adapted in order to accommodate the larger and less densely populated areas. Colonial Americans again borrowed from their English tradition and, as Chapter Three will describe, the American sheriff system was born.

Chapter Three also considers the substantial influence that politics and political ideology had on the emergence of policing both in England and the United States. By comparing political orientations in nineteenth century England to those of nineteenth century America, the chapter suggests some reasons for each society's attitude toward police as a social institution.

Finally, Chapter Three considers the emergence of the private security industry in early American history. Much of this early security industry was intertwined with changes in the social and political conditions of the times.

INTRODUCTION: LAW ENFORCEMENT AND SECURITY IN COLONIAL AMERICA

The concepts and law enforcement practices that form the core orientation of modern American policing can be easily traced to their ancient Saxon roots. When the early colonists arrived on the shores of the New World, they carried with them their household goods, their crafts, and their seventeenth century English policing traditions.

At first, colonists naturally banded together for safety and security under a system of mutual protection and accountability not unlike early Anglo-Saxon times. Until the colonies gained independence from England, the protection of early settlers was chiefly the responsibility of the king's representatives. Typically, these were town constables and sheriffs. Colonists also used a night-watch system from their English past.

Because the northern climate and soil were less conducive to farming than southern regions of colonial America, and in part because more of the early settlers of New England came from urban than agricultural backgrounds, towns became the principal governmental unit across most of the north.

As northern towns, counties, and cities developed, early law enforcement styles reflected urban English traditions. In many of the early northeastern colonial settlements, the constable and sheriff were frequently augmented by watchmen. Watchmen patrolled the settlement's streets at night, again following the traditions of late medieval English law enforcement. The watchmen, in fact, remained the principal form of nighttime security in America until the mid-1800s when the first full-time, formal (municipal) police forces were started.

The flat, fertile expanse of southern colonial America naturally attracted settlers with more agrarian backgrounds. These individuals brought with them attitudes, beliefs, and law enforcement styles that had grown up in the peasant-filled countryside of England. This included the county sheriff. Perhaps the earliest of these county sheriffs appeared around 1634 in Virginia. From this early seed grew a tradition of the American sheriff as the most powerful and significant law enforcement figure across the southern United States. In many ways, the distinctive southern and northern law enforcement practices that originated in colonial days continue today.

The northeastern and southern regions of the United States were settled much earlier than most of the western and southwestern regions of the country. The West can be characterized by its adaptation of various orientations from both northern and southern policing traditions. Perhaps by virtue of its more rural and isolated geographic location, the West initially adopted the southern sheriff as its primary law enforcement agent.

In northern colonial America, law enforcement interests and techniques typically maintained pace with the rapid growth and industrialization. Nonetheless, public concern for safety and increasing pressure by citizens for improved protection for themselves and their property led first to a daytime watch to supplement the night watchman and, finally, to a municipal policing system.

As Moore and Kelling (1985) suggest, it is sometimes easy for Americans to forget that publicly supported police agencies are a fairly recent innovation. Much of the early colonial period's law enforcement, particularly in the north, amounted to night watchmen, who also were charged with lighting the street lamps and keeping a wary eye open for fires. Beyond these tasks, colonial night watchmen also frequently found themselves chasing runaway animals and assisting in family disputes or emergencies (Moore and Kelling 1985).

The American Hue and Cry

The principal law enforcement strategy practiced by these early watchmen, like their earlier English counterparts, was to raise a kind of hue and cry if they saw a crime being committed. Criminal sightings were fairly rare, and the number of colonial watchmen usually was small. Serving as a watchman was a civic responsibility, and like its English predecessor, the system was largely ineffective.

Boston organized the first night watch in 1631. This watch was organized in a military fashion with a single commanding officer and six watchmen. Boston's official night watch was augmented by a volunteer citizen patrol (Lane 1967). While the citizen's patrol was voluntary, it was expected that members of the community would either serve or pay scot. A colonist who failed either to serve his watch or to hire a surrogate was fined a stiff penalty. In some instances, the colonial courts might even sentence misdemeanants to serve on the night watch (Costello 1972).

The investigation of crimes when a watchman had not witnessed their commission was the responsibility of privately employed investigators. Victims of crime could investi-gate on their own or employ an investigator to gather evidence against an offender. Once enough evidence had been gathered, the victim could enlist the assistance of the town constable to recover stolen property or to have the culprit arrested (Critchley 1972).

The Rattle Watch and Other Early Systems

The police problems that faced New Amsterdam (New York) during the seventeenth century, under both Dutch and English rule, were less serious than those afflicting London and other English cities of the time. Like the other early colonial towns, New York, owing to its small population, did not experience widespread or organized vice and crime (Richardson 1970). Nonetheless, there were problems related to public order. As a seaport town, sailors on shore leave frequently created disorder in drunken tavern brawls. Occasionally a runaway servant from New England or Virginia would reach New Amsterdam and may well have constituted the colony's first criminals.

New Amsterdam remained under Dutch control until 1664 when, following the English conquest, it became New York (Costello 1972). While still influenced by the Dutch, in 1658 a paid night-watch patrol emerged. This night-watch force, known as the **rattle watch,** had its members carry wooden rattles to announce their presence. The idea was to allow a lawbreaker time to flee before a confrontation with the watchman. These wooden rattles allowed watchmen to communicate with one another while on patrol (Crump and Newton 1935). Duty in this paid eight-man force was imposed upon each citizen by turn, and every household was taxed for its support. In an attempt to ensure that citizens took their turns in the watch, fines were levied for lateness, sleeping on the watch, failure to do a watch, and negligence while on watch.

In 1700 Philadelphia created its own night-watch system, followed in 1712 by Boston with a paid, full-time night watch (Bopp and

Service as a watchman during colonial times was a civic responsibility. Here, "colonial soldiers" reenact preparation for firing a cannon.

Schultz 1972). Boston's paid watchmen received approximately 50 cents a night. In 1803, Cincinnati started a night watch, and in 1804 New Orleans began its nighttime vigil.

The extensive use of volunteers for law enforcement during the early history of America may have some relevance today. Many American police agencies have reserve or auxiliary police units. These units typically serve without pay, but frequently have full police powers (Sundeen and Siegel 1986, Berg and Doerner 1988). Unlike their colonial predecessors, of course, members of modern police reserve or auxiliary units are not fined if they choose not to serve. It is important to acknowledge this distinction between volunteerism of the early history and the true volunteerism today. Notwithstanding this distinction, one still witnesses a long tradition of unpaid police officers.

Night-watch policing continued to the exclusion of daytime patrols until 1833 when Philadelphia began a 23-man daytime force. In addition, Philadelphia expanded its night watch to 120 men and began to fashion a paramilitary organization by appointing a captain to command both day and night forces (Fosdick 1921).

Population growth in early America was steady but gradual. This slow growth, which perhaps owed to settlers' fear of organized police forces (from their English experiences), led to a very slow development of organized police agencies. In spite of law enforcement needs, major changes from early English policing styles did not really emerge in the United States until the early nineteenth century. The first full-time, salaried, consolidated day- and nighttime police force in the United States developed in New York City in 1844.

A number of cities combined their day and night watches throughout the late 1800s. Baltimore and Newark combined their watches around 1847. Boston followed suit in 1850, as did Providence in 1864. Full-time municipal police forces, took a bit longer to emerge, however.

By 1856, eight cities had full-time municipal police departments (New York, Detroit, Cincinnati, Chicago, San Francisco, Los Angeles, Philadelphia, and Dallas). These early police departments were often corrupt and manned by poorly trained personnel. In spite of serious detriments, these early police agencies represented a significant organizational advancement over the earlier watchmen systems.

Demands for Social Control

Throughout the late eighteenth and nineteenth centuries, London and New York were growing into major cities. Both grew in social and industrial complexity—as well as in population. London nearly doubled its population between 1750 and 1820 (Miller 1977). New York was growing even more rapidly and quintupled its population during the period between 1790 and 1830. Naturally, much of this growth stemmed from immigration and not native births. It is, in fact, because of these massive immigrations that police in both cities found it necessary to change. The traditional social controls and watch systems were breaking down as populations expanded. The shifts in population brought with them changes in the neighborhoods. The new immigrants found themselves forced to live in slum districts like London's St. Giles and New York's Five Points. Here, too, were the hiding places for much of each city's criminal element.

The merchant-based middle classes quickly moved from these poorer areas, as had the wealthy. The various new police organizations and strategies that began to emerge were intended to manage the growing spread of more organized vice and crime. However, there were several important differences in the underlying political and social forces that affected policing in England and the United States. The next section will consider some of the more important social situations that altered policing in London and New York.

These are offered as illustrations of how each country's police traditions have been affected by the social milieus in which they emerged.

The Need for Organized Policing in London and New York

With the expansion of evangelical Protestantism during the early nineteenth century, many upper and middle class Londoners pressured the police to increase their enforcement of laws pertaining to moral codes—particularly when breached by the lower classes. The upper and middle classes grew more intolerant of the continuing crime and disorder, which were perceived as perpetrated by the lower class.

Ironically, in the face of this growing desire for increased regulation of petty thefts, drunkenness, brawling, and other morally repulsive crimes, there was also a demand for reducing the severity of punishments for both major and minor crimes. A moral reformation was afoot in England and the United States. Harsh physical penalties were replaced with imprisonment in an effort to allow an offender to repent. The moral overtones were clear. Criminals were expected to reject the influences of their lower class culture and seek ways of becoming upright, righteous citizens. Not many criminals were saved or became model citizens. Yet, the legal reforms that reduced the severity of penalties did encourage citizens to prosecute even petty criminals.

At around the same time as social reform appeared in London, New York, too, began a period of legal and social reform. Between 1814 and 1834 the complaints crossing the desks of New York City justices of the peace soared to a level that exceeded population growth for those years (Miller 1977). Social commentators during this time recognized that these increases did not reflect more crimes being committed in New York. Instead, these additional complaints represented a similar intolerance of criminals by New Yorkers, as

demonstrated in England by Londoners. New Yorkers, too, had begun to demonstrate a willingness to prosecute law violators. This willingness, in addition to America's own evangelical movement, forced legal reforms and a demand for a new kind of policing system.

The rapid urbanization of London and New York was spawned largely by their economic and industrial developments. As the merchant and propertied classes of citizens became more vocal about their concern with crime and disorder, local governments had to become more responsive. Much of London's early urban economy was based upon factories and industrial labor. During the eighteenth century this large group of lower class laborers found that their only effective avenue for protest was rioting. The propertied middle class and wealthy ruling elite were appreciably smaller in number than were the lower classes of London. Riots resulted in great amounts of property damage, financial losses from looting, serious injuries, and deaths.

Some riots, such as the Gordon Riot of 1780, simply could not be controlled by the existing police organizations. To put down the riot, the government had to call in military troops.

In London by the nineteenth century, Parliament had grown sensitive and, in some ways responsive to riots that threatened to topple the ruling minority. By 1820 the wealthy political minority grew uncertain of the effectiveness of using military troops to control riots. In 1823 the Duke of Wellington proposed a civilian-controlled police to "preserve the lives and properties of his Majesty's subjects against domestic insurrection and disturbances" (Miller 1977, 7). The serious need for an organized, well-trained, standing police organization, such as what Sir Robert Peel proposed in 1829, was certainly foreshadowed by the Gordon Riots, and the Duke of Wellington's call for a new police organization.

During the eighteenth and nineteenth centuries New York was not wracked by riots. Among the few serious riots that occurred in the eighteenth century was the Doctors' Riot of 1788. In this instance, angry crowds assaulted New York Hospital to protest the exhumation of bodies for use in the medical school. However, in 1834 New York was faced with what has been called, "the year of riots" (See Costello 1972, Miller 1977). For the first time, New York was confronted with a civil disturbance serious enough to require a call for the military to restore peace in the city. It was during this year that the mayor of the city was elected by the citizens for the first time. Prior to 1834, city mayors had been appointed by the governor and city council. Party strife in the city's Sixth Ward (commonly referred to as "the bloody ould Sixth") led to serious brawls and eventually a riot. Three months after the National Guard put down the election riot, they were required to battle a more formidable nemesis. This time, the guard was called out to intervene between a group of abolitionists and a mob that had attacked their meeting. Throughout the year other riots also occurred. These included the Stonecutter's Riot, the Five Points Riot, O'Connell Guard Riots, and the Chatham Street Riots (Costello 1972). The need for a more formidable police organization became apparent. Business-oriented newspapers and leading citizens began to campaign for reorganization of the New York city police system along lines similar to those of the London police reforms.

Certainly, one impetus for both London and New York to force reorganization of their city police agencies was the effect that riots and social disorder had on developing local economies. Yet, the increases in common sorts of crimes in both cities should not be overlooked as a motivating factor as well.

Social Influences in London. To be sure, London and New York were socially and culturally heterogeneous and increasingly cosmopolitan cities at the turn of the nineteenth century. Both had withstood rapid population and industrial growth, increased crime, and poverty. Similarly, both had met the challenge to increase social control by reestablishing and reorganizing their police agencies. History suggests that both cities had experienced similar growth and development problems and responded to these in similar ways. Less obvious, perhaps are the different underlying political ideologies and social forces that influenced each police force's understanding of its authority and purpose. Nor, for that matter, is it obvious how the public image of each city's police force affected police reform.

Peel's Metropolitan Police Force began operation during England's constitutional crisis over parliamentary representation. The wealthy propertied minority was in control, the lower class was oppressed and exploited, and the merchant middle classes were disenfranchised. To co-opt the middle class, the aristocratic upper class passed electoral reforms that permitted middle class representation in Parliament through the House of Commons.

The working class was a different story. Groups of angry working class Londoners felt excluded from both the aristocratic Parliament and the propertied House of Commons. Their dissatisfaction was voiced in numerous charts and petitions that included demands for universal suffrage, annually elected Parliaments, and the abolition of property qualifications for membership in Parliament. These Chartists, as members of this new movement came to be called, cried out for representation for the wage-earning classes.

Chartism was quickly recognized as a serious challenge to the prevailing constitutional authority. Critchley (1972, 76) suggests that by 1839, the idealism of the movement had already given way to violent extremes that further increased the government's fears. The idealism transformed into a potent evangelical draw for millions of supporters. This was especially true for poor factory workers, many of whom lived in squalor. However, the idealism was quickly transformed again into militancy. Secret meetings were held on the northern moors of London where men drilled and trained to force their demands through violence, if need be (Critchley 1972).

By the mid-nineteenth century, however, middle class commitment to the English social order was firm. This was clearly demonstrated during the Kensington Common Chartist Demonstration of 1848. The riot broke out in London, and middle class shop-keepers turned out in droves as special constables to put down the demonstrating working class (See Miller 1977, Smith 1985).

During the 1850s, political unrest in England took a back seat to economic prosperity. In the 1860s, however, working class groups again cried out for a voice in their government. The workers had by that time organized into trade unions. These trade unions were far less politically militant than the Chartists of the 1840s but represented serious protest groups. In 1867, the efforts of the trade unions were rewarded by reform acts that gave workers the right to vote. Yet, this right was granted without the wealthy ruling minority having to alter the balance of social or economic powers in England.

The various political crises throughout nineteenth century England—in spite of an eventual resolution in 1867—profoundly influenced the development of a police force in London. Throughout the various politically motivated riots and demonstrations, police officers found themselves defending a social order maintained by a ruling minority. They, then, were seen by the oppressed working class as supporters of this unbalanced political order.

Social Influences in New York. The development of a municipal police force in New York occurred in a very different social context. Unlike London, New York was not the nation's center of culture, commerce, or poli-

tics. Most Americans did not regard New Yorkers as setting the country's political tone. The United States' principal political crisis was the breaking up of the Union in 1861 and the subsequent War Between the States, which ended in April 1865. The war and its politics were not argued in the streets of New York City. Rather, they were fought in Washington, D.C., or largely on the battlefields of South Carolina, Tennessee, Virginia, and other states of the Confederacy.

Only infrequently did the disorder that nineteenth century New York police officers faced have anything to do with a national crisis. The backdrop for the development of the New York police was local crises, which were chiefly the result of ethnic conflicts. New York was the gateway to America for huge numbers of immigrants entering the country. As in London, New York's social conflicts were largely class-based. In New York's case, the hostility arose between skilled and unskilled laborers. This was particularly evident in clashes between native-born workers and Irish immigrants. Because these Irishmen were willing to work in the various unskilled trades for low wages, native-born workers regarded them as an economic threat (Miller 1977).

These job rivalries drove wedges between what objectively were all elements of the same working class. As a consequence, the fear and hatred for one another prevented any sense of common political interests. In fact, the fear for job security was so severe that many native-born workers rallied to the propertied and merchant middle classes to raise political support against the foreign intruders. In many ways, American-born tradesmen shared the values and political ideals of their employers. Certainly, one cherished American ideal was a political order based upon a representative, democratic government. Under such a system, even the working man could rise on merit. However, the rowdy Irish immigrants had arrived in the United States entrenched in their own political ideals, the conservatism of the Catholic church. Their beliefs ran counter to the majority of Americans' revered ideals of democracy.

The religious-political splits that arose in New York City never appeared in London. In London workers (and the working class) seldom expressed such institutional faith. Their overriding concerns were geared more toward common class issues. In America, the propertied middle class and the native-born working class shared support of the American political order. Both now felt threatened by these aliens who failed to appreciate the benefits of a free democracy.

It was the task of the New York City police of the nineteenth century to uphold the political order of a representative government. In this case, however, the political and social order were popular forms of government. In other words, the majority of Americans supported both the political order and the police who maintained this government of the people.

This pervasive attitude permitted both native New Yorkers and the police to mistreat a sizable community of immigrants in their city. Unlike London's police problems, the civil disobedience practiced by Irish immigrants in New York did not require officers to act with particular tact or sensitivity. In the United States at this time, it was an uncertain and slightly unstable stock market that forced Americans to press for better police organizations to quell shootings, robberies, and riots. As this chapter will later point out, Irish coal miners throughout western Virginia and Pennsylvania were also treated as outcasts. Their attempt through the Molly Maguires to improve working and salary conditions of coal miners included militant actions that matched or surpassed the Chartists of London. The suppression and eventual hanging of a number of accused Mollies illustrated the pervasive hostility toward Irish working men in the United States.

Writing about New York's old constabulary, Harriet Martineau (1838) ironically captured the principal distinctions between the London and New York police forces during the nineteenth century. According to Martineau (1838, 192) English police were "agents of a representative government, appointed by responsible rulers for the public good." In contrast, American officers were described as "servants of a self-governing people, chosen by those among whom their work lies." Nineteenth century English police, then, represented the public good as defined by the minority ruling class—whose view was chiefly self-serving. The New York police, as symbolic representatives of an emerging American policing style, represented "a self-governing people." In this case, it was "a product of what that government's conceptions of power and the conflicts which divided that people. The result was personal authority" (Miller 1977, 24).

The emergence of municipally supported police departments in the United States did not represent the entire demise of private citizen involvement in policing. Particularly during law enforcement's infancy, the demand for protection of personal property far exceeded the American system's supply of effective police officers. The industrial revolution had not occurred in a vacuum. In a manner similar to England's epidemic of crime, poverty, and unhealthy sanitation, America faced growing incidence of these phenomena. The newly established police forces were inadequately prepared to cope effectively with the demands being placed upon them by their public (Purpura 1984).

An increasing number of American business owners and investors began to recognize the need for increased security to protect their assets and investments. Soon, a new industry began to flourish: private policing.

THE EARLY PRIVATE SECURITY INDUSTRY

During the late 1800s several important events altered the course of American law enforcement practice. In 1848, with the discovery of gold in California, Americans streamed from the East to the shores of California. Boom towns sprang up and dotted the West and southwest as the forty-niners rushed to make their fortunes in the mines, streams, and rivers of California. By 1850 at least 100,000 people had crowded into California. By 1851 the population had grown to more than 300,000 pioneers (Hungerford 1949).

With this sudden and massive growth in population and the enormous stretch in geography came several new industries. Among the many innovations was the transportation of mercantile goods and mining supplies from the East to the West Coast and the safe transportation of gold from the West back East. The express companies solved many of these problems. Express companies brought miners their mail, newspapers, and mercantile goods. These express companies also carried miners' gold dust and nuggets back to assay offices and delivered them to banks.

In 1850, to provide a means of transportation for supplies needed by miners and settlers east of the Missouri River, Henry Wells and William Fargo (See Box 3.1) founded the American Express. Two years later, they established Wells Fargo and Company, which serviced the areas west of the Missouri (Hess and Wrobleski 1982). To protect the goods transported by their companies, Wells and Fargo hired riders equipped with shotguns to protect the cargo, frequently kept locked in the legendary iron-bound, wooden green strongbox. This green strongbox became a trademark for Wells Fargo for many years (Hungerford 1949). Wells and Fargo also employed a small private police unit to investigate robberies and protect cargo.

Railroad Security

The Department of Justice established the Bureau of Investigation in 1908 to investigate federal crimes. It did not become the Federal Bureau of Investigation (FBI), however, until 1924. For the most part, then, public (municipal) police agencies operated strictly at a local level. Throughout the 1800s the United

---

Box 3.1 _____

THE WELLS FARGO AND COMPANY BEGINS

The history of the Wells Fargo Express Co. began even before the discovery of gold at Sutter's Mill in California on January 24, 1848. It began in New York state when several experienced parcel express men came together to consider the nature of the growing and extensive railroad system in America. They heard about the discovery of gold and later read of the admission of California as a state in 1850. Two years later, these men again met in a cramped storage room of a book store in Syracuse, N.Y. During this meeting, these men began to make serious plans for the future of the express industry (Hungerford 1949). These two men were Henry Wells and William G. Fargo.

In 1841 Henry Wells, George Pomeroy, and Crawford Livingston formed the express firm Livingston, Wells and Pomeroy Co. This freight carrier operated between Albany and Buffalo, N.Y. and linked the various towns of western New York.

In 1845 Henry Wells organized another freight moving firm and named it Wells and Co. This second firm operated west of Buffalo to Cincinnati, St. Louis, and Chicago (Hungerford 1949).

In 1849 John Butterfield, one of the pioneer leaders of the express industry, formed Butterfield, Wasson and Co., which operated on the New York Central Railroad. Finally, in 1850, with the growing interest in getting freight into and gold out of California, Wells, William Fargo, and John Butterfield (along with several others) organized and opened the American Express Co.

Two years later, during a business meeting in New York City, the three principals of the American Express Co. decided to form Wells Fargo and Co. Their plan was to compete against the other express companies already operating in the boom towns of California.

States witnessed a truly wild western frontier, where violence, murder, lynchings, and gun fights in the streets were commonplace. Many of the northern cities were faced with similarly lawless activities. Toward the middle of the 1800s, even Congressmen attending sessions in Washington did so with guns strapped to their legs (Hess and Wrobleski 1982). As a consequence, law enforcement beyond the local political boundaries of most cities was supplied chiefly by private police forces.

As the United States expanded West in quantum leaps, the most efficient mode of transportation was the railroad. Track had to be laid before trains could move settlers from the East to the West coasts. Soon, the railroad traversed the United States. In the more sparsely populated locales, there was often little or no form of formal public law enforcement. As railroads roared into these towns and stopped to load, refuel, or take on water, personnel were confronted with considerable lawlessness.

In addition to robberies by gangs of outlaws and highwaymen, cargo thefts, vandalism, and the destruction of tracks, trains also were subject to attacks by savage Indians. In an effort to offer increased security for passengers and clients for freight and cargo delivery services, many states passed railway police acts.

Typically, railway police acts gave full police authority to proprietary forces employed by the railroads. The central purpose of these statutes was to permit the railroad owners and investors a means of protecting their property and investments (Gough 1977).

In 1855, Allan Pinkerton, a one-time cooper (barrelmaker), founded the North West Police Agency. Pinkerton's private police agency provided security for six midwestern railroads. Later, in 1857, Pinkerton created the Pinkerton Protection Patrol to offer protection in the form of a provisional (contract) security service. In essence, Pinkerton established the earliest private guard services in America. For over fifty years Allan Pinkerton's security forces were the only private forces offering interstate protection services, chiefly those purchased by the railroads.

In 1861, following the outbreak of the Civil War, President Abraham Lincoln asked Pinkerton to establish a military intelligence unit for the Union Army. Under the pseudonym of E.J. Allen, Pinkerton conducted intelligence-gathering work for the Union Army. He also foiled an attempted assassination of Lincoln and assisted in the apprehension of John Wilkes Booth. Pinkerton's spy work is more commonly associated today with several federal bureaus of law enforcement and investigations.

Pinkerton Men and the Molly Maguires

In the late 1800s Pinkerton and his Pinkerton Men became embroiled in the growing labor disturbances growing out of the emerging American labor unions. It was, in fact, a Pinkerton man who in the 1870s infiltrated the infamous Molly Maguires. The Molly Maguires were an organization of coal miners responsible for a variety of terrorist acts in the anthracite fields of Pennsylvania and West Virginia. The group had taken their name from a widow who had led a group of Irish anti-landlord agitators during the 1840s.

The articulated purpose of the Mollies was to obtain privileges, rights, and safety codes for coal miners in Pennsylvania. Their overt style, however, included sabotage, assassination, and threats of violence.

Under a contract with the mine owners, Pinkerton's firm obtained information on the Molly Maguires (See Box 3.2) by using an undercover agent. After testimony Pinkerton produced against the organization, 17 men were hanged. Sadly, it was later learned that many were entirely innocent. The Pinkerton firm had suffered a serious blow, as did the fledgling private security industry.

Pinkerton's firm was involved in several other strike-breaking incidents throughout the early days of unionization, but none as devastating as the Molly Maguire mistake. In

1937, Congress formally investigated labor-management relations. Sixty years of bloody battles between laborers and management culminated in an important change in private police practice. In the face of congressional investigations, Robert A. Pinkerton, Allen Pinkerton's grandson, head of the Pinkerton Agency, made it company policy to never again work covertly in union-management altercations (Hess and Wrobleski 1982).

Holmes and Brink

Pinkerton's success, as well as his problems, should not overshadow contributions to law enforcement techniques provided by several

Box 3.2 _____

PINKERTON AND THE MOLLY MAGUIRES

In October 1873, already well-established in his private detective business in Chicago, Allen Pinkerton received a request for him to journey to Philadelphia for a meeting. The request came from F.B. Gowen, president of the Philadelphia and Reading Railroad Co. and the Reading Coal and Iron Co. Pinkerton went to Philadelphia. During this secret meeting with Gowen, Pinkerton learned about the brutal crimes, violence, and murders promoted (and committed) by the Molly Maguires throughout the Pennsylvania coal mining towns. Gowen explained that he wanted Pinkerton to "penetrate the core of the Mollies," and bring the society's leaders to justice (Horan and Swiggett 1951).

Gowen had previously tried unsuccessfully to use conventional tactics and uniformed police agencies to restore order to the mining communities. The unrest and disruptions caused by the Molly Maguires was costing the coal companies and the railroad large sums of money. Pinkerton expressed to Gowen his knowledge of and contempt for the Mollies and said that he had equated them with organizations such as the Ku Klux Klan (Horan and Swiggett 1951). Pinkerton willingly agreed to take on the case.

Pinkerton selected one of his operatives, James Mcparlan, to infiltrate the Molly Maguires. At a meeting with Pinkerton, Mcparlan was simply instructed to "make his way into the Molly Maguires by his own means," and to report in writing daily to a local Pinkerton supervisor, Benjamin Franklin (Horan and Swiggett 1951).

On October 27, 1873, dressed as a tramp, Mcparlan arrived in Port Clinton, Pa. under the name of James Mckenna. He entered the community under the guise of seeking work in the mines. He traveled from town to town meeting various members of the "Sleepers" (the Molly Maguires). He spread a cover story that he was wanted for a murder in Buffalo and that the money that he lavishly spent buying rounds of drinks for locals came from the disposal of counterfeit money.

This cover story, in combination with his personal charisma, and vocal declarations of a hatred for "landlords" (managers) provided Mcparlan both considerable popularity and access to the inner circles of the Molly Maguires. On April 14, 1874, Mcparlan, under the pseudonym of Mckenna, was sworn into the Mollies during a secret ceremony (Horan and Swiggett, 1951).

During the next several months Mcparlan learned of a number of planned assassinations, attacks, maulings, and beatings perpetrated or promoted by the Mollies. Whenever possible, Mcparlan notified Franklin in advance of the assaults. Toward the end of his investigation, the Mollies threatened Mcparlan's life after they began to suspect that he was a detective.

Throughout the late 1870s, James Mcparlan served as the principal witness against seventeen accused conspirators and murders, all alleged to be members of the infamous Molly Maguires. Several months after the seventeen were hanged, many were found to be innocent of most of the capital crimes. Questions were even raised concerning how Mcparlan could have been in possession of certain pieces of information, unless he himself had taken part in various atrocities. It would be many years before the Pinkerton firm lived down the disgrace of their agent's blunder.

other early security companies. For example, in 1858, Edwin Holmes began the first central-office burglar-alarm company. The Holmes system involved a detection device (trigger) at the firm, a communications link to the central office alarm system, and personnel to monitor and respond should the alarm go off. Holmes' original business security firm evolved into Holmes Protection, Inc., a full service private policing agency.

Modern telecommunication technology advanced rapidly. The American District Telegraph Co. (ADT) established itself in 1874 and the use of alarms and electronic detection devices expanded. By 1889, the use of electronic protection for industrial and commercial settings throughout New York City was commonly used and accepted.

In 1859, Washington Perry Brink founded his truck package-delivery service in Chicago, one of America's leading centers of commerce and industry. Brink began as a small, single-wagon operation. In the face of enormous commerce in Chicago, Brink soon discovered there was a significant demand for the safe transportation of payroll monies. In 1891, Brink extended his earlier package trucking business to include the delivery of payrolls. His first account was with the Western Electric Co. During his early days in the payroll delivery business, Brink sought to remain as inconspicuous as possible. To remain incon-

spicuous, Brink used both his usual drivers and standard wagons and buggies even when delivering payrolls. In 1917, however, after two of Brink's men were brutally gunned down, Brink developed the armored car, described as a "bank vault on wheels" (Tozer 1960).

The original concept of an armored car amounted to little more than an average trucking wagon with sheets of steel bolted over its wooden sides and roof. This did, of course, leave the wooden floor of these cars rather vulnerable. In 1926, one of these armored trucks was tossed into the air by an explosion rigged to detonate as the vehicle passed over it. The bomb had been the work of a robber named Paul Jawarski. After he and his gang broke through the shattered wooden floorboards, they made off with the $104,000 the truck had been transporting (Tozer 1960). Shortly after this incident, Brink redesigned his armored truck. In addition to several lesser changes, steel plates replaced wooden floorboards, and steel posts replaced framing studs.

Although Brink had begun humbly as a one-truck operation in 1859, by 1900 his delivery service had grown to a fleet of 85 cars. Today, Brink's trucks are responsible for the safe transportation of almost half the cash moved by private courier service in the United States. It is likely that Perry Brink developed his attraction to the express business after

Washington Perry Brink developed the armored car in 1917 to provide safe transportation of money and valuables. Here, Brink and Wells Fargo armored trucks make deliveries.

witnessing the success attained by other parcel-moving pioneers like Henry Wells, William Fargo, and Alvin Adams. By 1859 there were three major express companies in America. These three companies included the Adams Express Company, Wells and Fargo, and the American Express Co. Collectively, these firms were doing a business amounting to over $6 million a year (Seng and Gilmour 1959, 20). The American Express Co. and the Adams Express Co. dominated the parcel-moving industry in the East, and Wells Fargo dominated the West. Brink, however, had an opportunity to capture the midwest market.

By the turn of the century, several important advances had occurred in law enforcement. In 1909, Baker Industries Inc. established itself as both a fire control and burglary-detection equipment business (similar to the Holmes alarm company). Also in 1909, William J. Burns, head of the newly created Bureau of Investigations, founded the William J. Burns Detective Agency. Although the Burns agency was begun primarily as an investigative agency for the American Banking Association, it rapidly grew to become one of the largest international private guard agencies in the world.

SUMMARY

This chapter began with a description of several leading colonial law enforcement carry-overs from English tradition. Perhaps chief among these was the watch and ward system of patrolling the colonial settlements. This watchman system provided a cornerstone upon which modern policing was built. Remnants of watch systems remained the principal policing style until late into the nineteenth century.

This chapter has also shown how certain geographic and climactic aspects of colonial America influenced early policing styles and practices. For example, the South offered a more rural and agrarian style of living than the North. As in England's countryside, south-

ern sections of colonial America established law enforcement organizations centering around the sheriff. Conversely, northern sections of America, like the urban centers throughout England, developed municipal police organizations.

Next, the chapter drew attention to both similarities and differences in social contours that shaped English and American policing styles throughout the eighteenth and nineteenth centuries. One distinguishing feature of the Victorian London police was that they represented a minority ruling elite. This ruling class, as detailed in the chapter, maintained the police force for their view of the good of the public. Contrasting this development of policing was the New York police force, which symbolized a police force maintained to protect the popular majority interests in democracy.

Throughout the late eighteenth and nineteenth centuries, the boundaries of America and the innovations in policing expanded. Among some of the more critical policing innovations were the creation of full-time salaried police agencies, systematic training of police officers, standards of entrance rather than arbitrary appointments, the emergence of the security and alarm industry, and the development of state and federal agencies to regulate laws beyond local political (and geographic) limitations.

American policing throughout the 1980s has struggled to fight off its past. The historical pattern of uneven development across the northeast, west, and south further contributed to the adverse advancement of American policing. Many of the larger metropolitan police agencies have effectively developed modern policing techniques, hired women and minority officers, and developed efficient administrative and management strategies.

For many police officers and agencies, there remains what Jay Albanese (1988) has described as the "police officer's dilemma." Specifically, this involves the belief among many officers that if only they had more police authority, they could reduce crime in America. Yet, there is growing evidence that little can be done by the police to eliminate crime or apprehend greater numbers of offenders than they already do. As later chapters in this text will illustrate, even in the face of this dilemma, many police organizations continue to strive for innovations and effective policing strategies. In the 1990s, police agencies continue to struggle with the overwhelming problems associated with the sale and distribution of drugs and a wide assortment of crimes that are drug-related. As Herman Goldstein (1990) suggests, "A high percentage of all police business is now affected, in one way or another, by drug traffic and use." Only time will tell how effectively police officers of the 1990s will resolve this dilemma.

REVIEW QUESTIONS

1. What were some of the reasons offered to explain why law enforcement styles differed in the northern, southern, and western portions of the United States?

2. What were some of the evolutionary changes that took place in the English watch system, once it began in colonial America?

3. What impact did the finding of gold in California have on express companies? How does this relate to law enforcement?

4. Who were the "Molly Maguires" and how were they related to Allen Pinkerton? What effect did the encounter between the Pinkerton man and the Molly Maguires have on private policing?

5. Why might public sentiments about the police in England differ from those in the United States?

REFERENCES

Albanese, Jay S. *The Police Officer's Dilemma.* Buffalo, N. Y.: Great Ideas, 1988.

Berg, Bruce L., and William G. Doerner. "Volunteer Police Officers: An Unexamined Dimension In Law Enforcement." *American Journal of Police* 7. (1988):81–89.

Bopp, William J., and Donald O. Schultz. *A Short History of American Law Enforcement.* Springfield, Ill.: Thomas, 1972.

Costello, Augustine E. *Our Police Protectors: A History of New York Police.* Montclair, N.J.: Patterson Smith, 1972 [1885].

Critchley, T.A. *A History of Police in England and Wales,* 2d ed. Montclair, N.J.: Patterson Smith, 1972.

Crump, Irving, and John W. Newton. *Our Police.* New York: Dodd, Mead, 1935.

Fosdick, Raymond B. *American Police Systems.* New York: Century, 1921.

Goldstein, Herman. *Problem Oriented Policing.* New York: McGraw-Hill, 1990.

Gough, T.W. "Railroad Crime: Old West Train Robbers to Modern-Day Thieves." *FBI Law Enforcement Bulletin.* (February 1977):16–25.

Hess, Karen M., and Henry M. Wrobleski. *Introduction to Private Security.* New York: West, 1982.

Horan, James D., and Howard Swiggett. *The Pinkerton Story.* New York: Putnam, 1951.

Hungerford, Edward. *Wells Fargo: Advancing the American Frontier.* New York: Free Press, 1949.

Kelly, W., and N. Kelly. *Policing in Canada.* Toronto: Macmillan/Maclean-Hunter, 1976.

Lane, Roger. *Policing the City: Boston 1822–1885.* Cambridge, Mass.: Harvard, 1967.

Martineau, Harriet. "Morals and Manners." Quoted in Wilbur R. Miller, *Cops and Bobbies.* Chicago: University of Chicago Press, 1977:24 (original publication, 1838).

Miller, Wilbur R. *Cops and Bobbies.* Chicago: University of Chicago Press, 1977.

Moore, Mark H., and George L. Kelling. "To Serve and Protect: Learning from Police History." In

Abraham S. Blumberg and Elaine Niederhoffer, eds. *The Ambivalent Force.* New York: Holt, Rinehart and Winston, 1985.

Purpura, Philp P. *Security and Loss Prevention.* Boston: Butterworth, 1984.

Richardson, James F. *The New York Police: Colonial Times to 1901.* New York: Oxford, 1970.

Seng, R.A., and J.V. Gilmour. *Brinks, The Money Movers: The Story of a Century of Service.* Chicago: Lakeside, 1959.

Smith, Philip Thurmond. *Policing Victorian London: Political Policing, Public Order, and the London Metropolitan Police.* Westport, Conn.: Greenwood, 1985.

Stenning, Philip C. "The Role of Police Boards and Commissions as Institutions of Municipal Police Governance." In Clifford D. Shearing, ed. *Organizational Police Deviance.* Toronto: Butterworths, 1981.

Sundeen, Richard A., and Gilbert B. Siegel. "The Use of Volunteers by Police." *Police Science and Administration* 14. (1986):49–61.

Tozer, E. "Riding with a Million in Cash." *Popular Science.* March, 3–4, 90–91, and 246–247, 1960.

CHAPTER 4

THE ORGANIZATION OF AMERICAN LAW ENFORCEMENT AGENCIES

This chapter begins with an examination of August Vollmer's and O.W. Wilson's major contributions to modern American policing. The purpose here is to set the stage for future chapters that will discuss in greater detail contemporary attempts to modernize and professionalize American policing. Many of the organizational goals proposed by these policing pioneers have only recently begun to gain formal acceptance. This chapter also surveys a representative variety of law enforcement agencies. The purpose here is to demonstrate both the complexity of law enforcement and its diversity.

INTRODUCTION: MODERNIZATION OF POLICING

It was not until the early 1900s that any meaningful attempts were undertaken to create a professional police force. Lane (1967) and Wilson (1977) both note that today's police force grew out of forces of men appointed as parttime watchmen. These early watchmen were expected to keep the streets clear of obstructions, human and material, and to supervise a number of ordinances pertaining to health, lighting, and animals running loose (Wilson 1977). Crime-related law enforcement duties during this era were limited chiefly to

calming raucous behavior and curtailing public lewdness and brawls (Potholm and Morgan 1976). Real crime, theft, robbery assault, and murder were not the purview of the watchmen. Recovery of stolen property, identification of culprits, and apprehension of the offenders were private matters, not the principal function of the watchmen.

Borrowing from Robert Peel's Metropolitan Police Force, early American police forces began moving away from appointed or volunteer personnel and toward selection on the basis of merit (Cole 1983). Better training procedures, the introduction of new policing techniques, creation of juvenile bureaus, and even the use of women officers contributed to innovations and reforms in nineteenth century police styles. Among these innovations was the notion that police should be used to prevent crimes before they occur, as well as to arrest criminals after crime commission. This novel style of policing would later come to be know as **proactive policing.**

During the twentieth century, American policing has emphasized the creation of more efficient, professionally trained enforcement and crime-prevention organizations (Walker 1977). The literature on policing frequently describes a number of people as having contributed enormously. Perhaps most influential was August Vollmer.

August Vollmer's (1876–1955) innovations and contributions as a law enforcement administrator and police officer have received worldwide recognition. For over 32 years, Vollmer served as the chief of police in Berkeley, California. Although Sir Robert Peel is called by many the father of policing, Vollmer is more properly recognized as the father of modern police science. In some circles, Vollmer is referred to as the father of police professionalism (Walker 1983). Vollmer expressed his general philosophy on policing when he wrote:

> *Those authorized and empowered to enforce the laws, rules, and regulations which are intended for the better protection of the public, should have some knowledge of the fundamental principles underlying human action more especially those actions which are commonly designated as criminal or contrary to law and order. (Vollmer and Schneider 1917, 878)*

Vollmer established the first police training school in 1909, innovated the use of bicycles in police patrols (soon followed by motorcycles in 1911), and placed patrol officers in cruisers equipped with radios in 1913 (entirely mobilizing the Berkeley police department by 1917). He is credited with developing the police call box system known originally as the "red light recall system." Vollmer also established one of the earliest fingerprint bureaus in the United States and has been credited for having pioneered the area of **modus operandi files.** Building on the work and innovations of his mentor Vollmer, Orlando Winfield Wilson (1900–1972) moved law enforcement toward a more professional model. Wilson's efforts were not easy. In 1926 he was fired from his first position as chief of police in Fullerton, California after only one year. The community leaders viewed Wilson's attempt to professionalize the town's police department as too radical (Bopp 1977). His next law enforcement position began in 1928 as the chief of police in Wichita, Kansas where he served for 11 years. Although he earned a reputation as an honest, creative, innovative, and effective police administrator, it was this very reputation that caused his downfall in Kansas. Several public officials who desired to return Wichita to the corrupt and vice-filled city it had been prior to Wilson's arrival forced him to resign (Bopp 1977).

In 1939, Wilson returned to his alma mater, the University of California at Berkeley, where he served as a professor of police administration and dean of the school of criminology until 1960. Although he had intended to retire, Wilson received an urgent call from Chicago's Mayor Richard Daley and was invited to chair a citizen's committee searching for a new police commissioner. The former police commissioner had been forced to resign in the wake of the Summerdale scandal, which involved eight police officers arrested for burglary.

When they were unable to agree upon a successor for the commissioner, the citizen's committee persuaded Wilson to take over the job. Although he entered the position with criticism that he could "be gone in six months," he remained seven years until his retirement. During this period, the Chicago Police Department became a model organization. Throughout the 1970s, both law enforcement administrators and lay people regarded the Chicago police system as among the finest in the world.

Wilson's innovations, like Vollmer's, were impressive. A review of even a small portion of his accomplishments includes his having created the Law Enforcement Code of Ethics, developed the first systematic procedure to prevent juvenile delinquency, developed the first American police–college cadet program, hired the first female police captain, invented the idea of roll-call training programs, pioneered early state-run police training programs, and initiated the first battery of psychological tests for police candidates and for veteran officers prior to promotion (Bopp 1977, Cole 1983).

THE BASIC STRUCTURE OF AMERICAN LAW ENFORCEMENT

Law enforcement may occur at a variety of governmental levels. It may occur at the county, state, federal, and even the international levels. In 1988, there were well over one half million (680,638) sworn officers representing all levels of law enforcement in the United States. In addition, best estimates indicate there were an additional 153,892 civilian ancillary personnel working for law enforcement agencies (Uniform Crime Reports, 1989). The following section of this chapter examines each of the governmental levels of law enforcement to draw out the basic structure of policing in America.

County Law Enforcement

Rolling down the highway with your C.B. radio set to Channel 19, you suddenly hear, "County mounty on the move one mile south of the five-mile marker." That "county mounty," of course, is likely to be a deputy sheriff. Although the duties of the county sheriff's department may vary from one jurisdiction to the next, their chief officer remains the traditional law enforcement agent,

the sheriff. Among the several ways to distinguish the various activities of the sheriff's department is to consider the region in which it is located. In the south and major portions of the mid- and southwest, sheriff's departments often serve as the principal law enforcement agency in the area. In many smaller communities the sheriff's department also may be responsible for tax assessing and tax collection, patrolling the local bridges and highway extensions, serving as jail attendants and court room bailiffs, as well as the executioners of both criminal and civil processes (i.e., the serving of warrants, subpoenas, and eviction notices). Conversely, in the northeast the local sheriff's departments do little active law enforcement and considerably more of jail, courtroom and process-serving tasks (Brown 1978).

The position of sheriff holds a unique slot in the American policing system. With the exception of sheriffs in Rhode island and Hawaii who are appointed, the position is an elected one. In a manner similar to its early Norman predecessor, the elected sheriff in America has long played an important role in local politics. In many small, rural communities the sheriff stands out as the most influential political figure in the community. On the one hand, obtaining sufficient political support to win elections may represent the need of a sheriff to repay political favors. On the other hand, because the sheriff is not appointed, he or she is often able to operate with considerably greater autonomy than appointed municipal police chiefs.

Policing the City

Typically, when one thinks about a police officer, a blue uniformed city police officer comes to mind. Municipal police organizations, are, in fact, among the primary types of policing organizations in the nation and include the majority of sworn officers. Municipal police departments differ from their county law enforcement colleagues in several ways. First, most municipal police agencies employ a greater number of personnel (both sworn and ancillary) and offer more extensive law enforcement services than county agencies. Second, because of the added complexities associated with a large work force, municipal agencies frequently have larger financial and equipment resources than county organizations. Third, large metropolitan municipal police organizations may share local law enforcement responsibilities with other municipal policing agencies. For example, New York City operates both a municipal police force and a transit authority police department. Similarly, in Boston one finds a "Registry Police Department," a "Massachusetts Bay Transit Police" force, the "Metropolitan District Commission," an agency similar to other large city parks and recreations police, and the "Boston Metropolitan Police." In fact, Boston may have as many as 26 separate agencies responsible for some aspect of municipal policing.

As in Boston, municipal policing agencies often share their resources, and/or certain services with other municipal and county agencies. In other instances, also partially illustrated by Boston, municipal agencies must compete for or share services because of the overlap.

State Law Enforcement Agencies

The transition of the United States from rural to urban had an enormous effect on municipal policing. As towns grew into cities and cities enlarged both in geography and population density, the need for a larger policing organization was obvious. Eventually, state police organizations began to emerge.

State police agencies have fairly recent origins. Although corruption and ineffectiveness within municipal police agencies may have been motivating factors in establishing state police divisions, these are not the only reasons. Rather, each state was forced to rely upon its municipal forces to administer and enforce all of its state regulations in addition to the local ordinances. When a local sheriff or municipal police chief saw a particular state law as inappropriate, unjust, or just unnecessary, this law was not likely to be enforced. Since local law enforcement agents were drawn from the communities in which they worked, they sympathized more with their fellow community residents than with residents of the state.

Among the earliest state policing agencies were the Texas Rangers. As Samora and his associates (1979) suggest, with the possible exception of the Royal Canadian Mounted Police, there is no police agency more famous the world over than the Texas Rangers. The Texas Rangers were established by the Republic of Texas' provisional government in 1835. Originally, the Texas Rangers included three companies of men and began as a paramilitary force to defend settlers against marauding Indians and to maintain the border between Mexico and Texas.

What is particularly interesting about the Texas Rangers is that, while they are frequently pointed to as forerunners of state police forces, they were not originally designed as such. In fact, during the early period of "ranging men" (as they were known from 1823–35), the rangers did little investigating and no community service. This contrasts with police agencies both of that time and today where officers are responsible to their communities. The concept of range men being public servants simply did not fit their highly independent and semi-autonomous activities.

Ranger companies did not police any given community of colonists as municipal forces did. Texans created the Rangers to secure and maintain the frontier of the Republic of Texas (Samora et al. 1979). Order maintenance and peace-keeping were not the principal tasks of the Rangers. Their functions were to repel Indians and Mexican revolutionaries bent on overthrowing the government of the Republic and retaliating for the cattle-rustling undertaken in Mexico by Anglo-Texas cowboys (Samora et al. 1979).

After 1835 the Texas rangers began refining their activities—although always slightly maverick, they soon came to investigate crimes that occurred in the state. Today, the principal task of the Texas Rangers, in addition to border-patrolling, is crime investigation and assisting other Texas law enforcement agencies in their criminal investigations.

On May 16, 1865, Governor John A. Andrews announced that the state of Massachusetts would open the door at 50 Bromfield Street in Boston as the first headquarters for a "state constabulary." The chief constable would direct the statewide activities of the state police force from this Boston-based office (Powers 1979). Police historians recognize this early state constabulary as the first state police force.

In 1875 the Massachusetts State Constabulary became the State Detective Force. After posting a bond of $5,000, each of the newly appointed 15 detectives was granted statewide policing powers. The central purpose of this new state police was to assist the attorney general and various district attorneys in evidentiary matters and the pursuit of felons. In addition, the governor had the right to call upon the State Detective Force to suppress riots or in other ways preserve the peace (Powers 1979).

In 1876 the responsibilities and policing powers of the Massachusetts State Detective Force were significantly expanded. Their duties then included inspecting public buildings and factories throughout the Commonwealth of Massachusetts. Their mission was primarily to assess conditions that might lead to accidents or fires. In addition, the force was expected to ensure that all laws pertaining to child labor and working hours were adequately enforced.

Massachusetts State Police officers were unarmed. In fact, the force existed, in one form or another, for over fifty years before officers were permitted to carry either badges or weapons. The laws of the commonwealth were enforced largely on the personal integrity and reputation of the organization. In 1906 the Massachusetts legislature passed a law that prohibited the unlicensed carrying of a loaded pistol or revolver. The statute also outlawed the carrying of an assortment of other concealed weapons. In 1908 the commonwealth authorized state detectives to carry badges, revolvers, truncheons, and handcuffs. Soon, the state police organization emerged as the District Police, which in 1920 became the Massachusetts State Police.

While Massachusetts was busy arming its state officers, another significant development emerged in state policing history. In 1905 the Pennsylvania state Legislature enacted a bill that established America's first uniformed state police organization (Powers 1979). Earlier state police agencies had focused their attention on limited frontier problems and enforcement of unpopular vice laws. The Pennsylvania state police, however, were founded with three clear purposes in mind: to establish an executive enforcement arm to assist the governor in carrying out his duties; to restore order in coal mining regions where labor disputes had led to a series of riots and terrorist attacks; and to strengthen law enforcement in the rural areas of the state where county police had been unable to provide adequate police services.

According to Powers (1979, 27), shortly after the legislature established the Pennsylvania state constabulary, Governor Samuel W. Pennypacker, in a state address, underlined his desire to have an enforcement arm:

In the year 1903, when I first assumed the office of chief executive of the state, I found myself thereby invested with supreme executive authority. I found that no power existed to interfere with me in my duty to enforce the laws of the state, and that by the same token, no conditions could release me from my duty so to do. I then looked about to see what instruments I possessed wherewith to accomplish this bounded obligation—what instruments on whose loyalty and obedience I could truly rely. I perceived three such instruments—my private secretary, a very small man; my woman stenographer; and the janitor. . . . So I made the state police.

The rioting among coal miners, was a serious problem for Pennsylvania. The local sheriffs' agencies were unable to control the outbreaks of massive civil disorder and organized violence. A larger, more centralized police organization, which the state police provided, was a necessity.

Like other state policing agencies, the Pennsylvania organization was heavily dependent upon a military model. A system of troop headquarters and substations of mounted officers spread across the state, ensuring uniform implementation of police policies. Mounted officers allowed the Pennsylvania state police to provide law enforcement to even the most remote rural areas. This use of the troop headquarters has been likened to

the deployment of military troops and was later adopted by most state police and highway patrol organizations across the nation.

Other forerunners of state policing organizations developing around this time were the Arizona Rangers (See Box 4.1) in 1901 and the New Mexico Mounted Police in 1905. Like the Texas rangers before them, both were essentially border-patrolling organizations, not policing as in Pennsylvania and Massachusetts.

Federal Law Enforcement Agencies

As the individual states experienced growth and the benefits and problems associated with it (health and sanitation problems, housing shortages, unemployment, crime, rioting, etc.), so, too, did the nation as a whole. The growth of individual states, coupled with the ratification of new ones entering the union, industri-

---

Box 4.1 _____

"BLAZE FORTH A NEW STAR": THE ARIZONA RANGERS

Texas was not the only state with ranging men. In 1901, 11 years before it became a state, Arizona established the Arizona Rangers. During its territorial days, like other western border territories, Arizona faced tremendous problems related to growth and development. Hostility raged as homeless settlers drifted across the land, and outlaws terrorized railroads and settlements and then holed up in stony crags rising from the vast, desolate desert of Arizona (Arizona Highway Patrol 1987).

Under the shade of tall pine trees, outlaws camped and planned their crimes. It was common for them to attack emerging settlement towns and raid livestock from the nearby ranches that were developing with the prospering of Arizona's cattle industry (Wagoner 1970). To establish order and safety, a group of Arizona men donned silver stars and rode the range. Like the Texas Rangers, this Arizona company of men was somewhat unorthodox in its policing style. They wore no uniforms,

carried no banners, but did wear five-pointed stars that signified their authority within the territory of Arizona.

Because of the efforts of the Arizona range men, the cattle industry was able to flourish. As ranches and towns became better established, agricultural and technological strides were also made. Soon, Arizona had established a copper mining industry and, with the development of water pumping and irrigation technology, Arizona joined the ranks of the nation's leading cotton producers.

The five-pointed star and a blue-barreled revolver (to prevent any glint from the sun or moon when chasing down desperadoes) became the trademarks of the Arizona Rangers. Today, the tradition of the five-pointed star lives on, but now is worn by the sheriffs in each of Arizona's 14 counties.

alization, and changes in technology contributed to the need for improved methods of enforcing the nation's legislation. For example, the improvements in road construction and the advent of automobiles brought changes in criminal styles of behavior. One could commit a bank robbery in one state, swiftly drive to a neighboring state, and escape the legal limitations of the local police agency. The disparate arrangement of various local law enforcement agencies simply offered far too inefficient a mechanism for the apprehension or capture of criminals.

The U.S. Constitution gave Congress a solution to the nation's problem. Under Article I, Section 8 Congress is responsible for taking necessary steps to assure the common defense and promote the general welfare of the country's population. Essentially, this article and section authorize Congress to enforce or invoke provisions of the Constitution and its amendments to protect and serve the American people. Folley (1980, 93) offers the following illustrative example:

> . . . the Constitution provides authority to lay and collect taxes (Article XVI) and, therefore, Congress has the authority to establish the Internal Revenue Service as an enforcement agency. The Constitution stipulates that Congress has power to coin money and punish counterfeiters (Article I Section 8) and concurrently, Congress also has the authority to establish an agency to detect and arrest counterfeiters.

Unlike local policing agencies, which originally were given broad policing powers, federal agencies, owing to their highly specific functions, were given much more narrow powers. Americans feared becoming a police state. Consequently, Congress did not immediately impose a systematic development of centralized federal law enforcement agencies. Similarly, as legislation arose, Congress did not concomitantly establish enforcement agencies. The emergence of federal law enforcement agencies was slow, and in many ways their effective operation was much slower

still. Typically, a federal law enforcement agency was not congressionally mandated until the flagrant disregard of law grew so great as to endanger the welfare of the nation.

Within the jurisdiction of the federal government are over fifty law enforcement and regulatory agencies. These agencies are designed to maintain the balance between an individual citizen's ability to act freely in society and the society's need for social order. In keeping with early American concerns over creating, in effect, a police state, no single federal law enforcement agency possesses unlimited or unchecked jurisdictional powers. The Department of Justice and several of its more well-known investigative and enforcement agencies are briefly detailed below.

The Department of Justice

The U.S. Department of Justice is sometimes called the legal arm of the government. The Department of Justice is headed by the attorney general, who is empowered to enforce federal law, represent the U.S. government in federal court actions, and to conduct law enforcement investigations.

The U.S. Marshals Service. The first federal law enforcement agency established was the federal marshal organization created by President George Washington in 1789. In its original form, the Federal Marshals Service more resembled a national sheriff's organization than a federal law enforcement agency. The first appointment of 13 marshals corresponded to each of the first 13 states and represented judicial districts. The U.S. Marshals Service has grown in size as the United States and its judicial districts have expanded.

Although very little scholarly material has been undertaken on the marshals, a considerable number of "pulp paperback" volumes exist. These fictional offerings describe early and colorful legends of the Wild West where the marshals were personified by Bat Masterson and Wyatt Earp. The question that remains, however, is "What exactly do the U.S. Marshals do?"

Created in 1789 with the passage of the Judiciary Act, federal marshals were charged with two basic responsibilities: attending to the needs of the federal courts in each of the 13 judicial districts and executing all lawful precepts issued to them under the authority of the U.S. government ("The National Sheriff" 1982; Berg 1985). Typically, marshals were responsible for discharging many of the law enforcement duties traditionally associated with early American sheriffs in each of these districts.

Like many early policing organizations, the marshals have operated under the auspices of several different federal agencies during their lengthy history. Marshals have served the presidency, the federal court system, the Department of Justice, as well as the departments of Treasury, War, State, and the Interior ("The National Sheriff" 1982). In 1969 the U.S. Marshals Service was established; in 1974 it was elevated to the status of a federal bureau. Although modern marshals continue their tradition as presidential appointees, deputies are hired under competitive civil service procedures. Currently, there are 94 U.S. marshals and approximately 1,800 sworn deputy marshals representing all fifty states and American territories.

Contemporary marshals continue to focus their energies principally toward servicing the federal court system. First, they service the civil and criminal process and execution of arrest warrants. Second, they transport and protect federal prisoners and witnesses and, finally, U.S. marshals provide security for federal court premises and personnel (judges and juries).

During the early 1980s, the marshals service took over responsibility for the Federal Witness Protection and relocation program. This program had previously been operated by the FBI. The Marshals also developed a sting operation called "FIST" (Fugitive Investigative Strike Teams). Under a FIST operation, U.S. marshals and their deputies saturate a single geographic area with warrants and subpoenas. Although these projects last only about 90 days, they average 3,000 warrants each (Safir 1983).

The Federal Bureau of Investigation. The need for a Justice Department, created in 1870, is sometimes attributed to the chaos and lawlessness that followed the American Civil War during the country's period of reconstruction. The need for some type of centralized federal law enforcement agency seemed apparent to many, but abhorrent to others. The persistent fear among many of the members of the Sixtieth Congress was that the attorney general, as the director of the Justice Department, already had become too involved in the use of Secret Service and U.S. marshals as investigators. So strong was this concern that Congress passed a law prohibiting further loans of Secret Service detectives to other agencies.

On July 1, 1908 U.S. Attorney General Charles J. Bonaparte quietly established the Bureau of Investigation, renamed in 1935 the Federal Bureau of Investigation. The Bureau of Investigation was chiefly a detective force that operated under the direction of the attorney general. When reproached by Congress for his actions, Bonaparte explained that Congress had "forced his hand" by forbidding the future use of Secret Service agents as investigators (Lowenthal 1950).

The Investigation Bureau emerged as a separate and more autonomous federal law enforcement agency in 1924 under the direction of J. Edgar Hoover. Throughout its existence the FBI has been subjected to both the acclaims and scoldings of Congress and the American people. Yet, regardless of criticism leveled against the agency or its director of 48 years, Hoover (who died in 1972), the FBI remains among the most respected and efficient law enforcement agencies in the world. Ironically, the FBI is not really a police agency.

Like the Bureau of Investigation, the central function of the FBI is investigative. The jurisdiction of this agency extends to all areas and matters that pertain to the United States as an interested party (See Adams 1973). These matters include violations of federal laws and statutes, espionage, sabotage, treason, violation of federal civil rights acts, robbery of federally insured banks, kidnapping, and interstate transportation of contraband such as drugs, explosives, governmental secrets, or stolen property.

The FBI additionally provides a nationally accessible forensic laboratory, specialized training courses and certification programs, and publishes national crime statistics annually in *Uniform Crime Reports.*

The Drug Enforcement Administration (DEA).

Before the television show "Miami Vice" hit the screens of American television viewers in 1984, few people outside of law enforcement and the illicit drug world had ever heard of the DEA. The Drug Enforcement Administration, once a sister bureau of the FBI known as the Bureau of Narcotics and Dangerous Drugs, is responsible for enforcing all federal drug legislation. Federal interest in drug enforcement can be traced to the Harrison Act (1914), which established federal jurisdiction over the distribution and use of controlled narcotics. Although changing social attitudes and corresponding political interests have contributed to the major functions and goals of the DEA, large-scale drug-smuggling operations have typically been the central targets of this agency. During the 1960s and 1970s, heroin and marijuana received considerable public and political concern and that of the DEA. Throughout the 1980s, the agency focused upon interception and interdiction of marijuana, heroin, and cocaine-smuggling operations. In the mid-1980s, a rapidly growing criminal activity evolved, the systematic synthesis and distribution of *crack.* Crack is a version of cocaine distilled to increase potency and combined with baking powder to

provide a slower, more even burn. The enormous surge in crack operations across the United States quickly attracted the attention of DEA agents.

Immigration and Naturalization Service (INS).

Although not directly an investigative and enforcement agency, the Immigration and Naturalization Service does fall under the Department of Justice. The central purpose of this agency is to control the entrance of aliens into the United States. In addition to the use of border patrols to dissuade illegal aliens from entering the United States, INS is responsible for monitoring those aliens who have already entered (both legally and illegally). In 1987 the task of the INS was made more difficult with the passage of an immigration moratorium bill. In effect, this bill allowed aliens who had illegally entered the United States before 1983 to remain and obtain legal alien status.

The Treasury Department

The U.S. Treasury Department also maintains several enforcement branches among its regulatory agencies.

Federal Postal Inspectors.

Postal inspectors, or "silent investigators," actually owe their creation to America's first postmaster general, Benjamin Franklin in 1775, who hired a postal surveyor. But, it was not until 44 years later that the federal postal inspection agency formally came into existence. The problems of mail fraud and misuse of the federal mail service prompted the creation of a Post Office Inspection system in 1829. It was not until 1936 that the postmaster general was authorized to actually employ postal investigators. These postal inspectors were meant to pursue all regulatory matters related to the Post Office Department.

During the 1960s and 1970s, the postal inspectors directed much of their effort to curtailing the use of the mail for transporting illegal drugs and explosives. Following the passage of the Child Protection Act of 1984, considerable energy on the part of the postal inspectors was directed at apprehending child pornographers, who frequently send their wares through the U.S. mail (See Ball 1987). Although chiefly a regulatory agency, criminal laws related to the mail and covering postal inspectors are covered in Title 18 and Title 39 of the United States Code. These laws include mail-conducted lotteries and pyramid schemes, burglary or robbery of the mail, and use of the mail to distribute obscene or crime-inciting materials (Adams 1973).

Among the interesting aspects connected with the various operations of the postal inspectors is that they are, as mentioned, a regulatory service with police powers. What this actually means is that certain latitudes are permitted them that more traditional law enforcement agencies could not legally undertake. A partial explanation for this is that use of the mail system is a privilege, not a constitutional right.

For example, in order to apprehend someone sending pornography through the mail, postal inspectors can actually solicit material from a known or suspected offender in order to obtain evidence. If a municipal police officer were to ask a potential criminal to commit a crime and later arrest that person, this would constitute **entrapment** (because the crime was officer-initiated). However, since the crime of sending pornographic material through the mails does not occur until the material enters the mail system, courts have ruled that it is not entrapment to solicit this material. The usual explanation runs something like the pornographer "initiates the mailing" of the illegal material and has rationally elected to do so.

Counterfeiting and the Secret Service.   Counterfeiting has long been a weapon used in war to destroy the confidence of a people in their government. As mentioned in Chapter Two, England witnessed a period in the eighteenth century when counterfeiting was widespread. At one point, London was estimated to have had a greater amount of counterfeit currency in circulation than real money. During the American Revolution, the British dumped huge quantities of fake Continental currency into the American economy—effectively destroying public confidence in these private bank notes (Bowen and Neal 1960). Similarly, during the American Civil War, it was estimated that as much as a full third of all money in circulation was counterfeit. While Congress had passed a counterfeiting law in 1842, this legislation had few teeth since local law enforcement seemed unable to contend with rampant counterfeiting. Since the private banks producing paper money across the country were not restricted to any real standards of production or uniformity in design, counterfeiters enjoyed almost unrestrained prosperity.

In 1863 the federal government authorized production of the first national currency, commonly referred to as "greenbacks." Unfortunately, this effort did nothing to inhibit counterfeiting. It was not until July 5, 1865, when William P. Wood was sworn into office as the first chief of the U.S. Secret Service that the manufacturers of phony money had any serious fears about their chosen vocation.

The task ahead of the Secret Service was enormous. The 11 field offices established by the service spread the original 30 agents very thin. Although initially charged singularly with the responsibility of suppressing counterfeiting, this small, inexperienced force was unable to accomplish this enormous task alone. With the assistance of the U.S. marshals, the Secret Service did eventually manage to bring counterfeiting in America under control.

With the discovery by Allen Pinkerton of a plot to kill President Lincoln as he rode a train through Baltimore in 1861, the Secret Service moved into the area of presidential protection, at least partially. For much of its early existence, the Secret Service worked closely with private detective firms such as Pinkerton's and loaned agents to other federal law enforcement agencies. For example, the Department of Justice, which had no force of its own, would frequently borrow detectives from the Secret Service to undertake department investigations. The Secret Service remained principally charged with protecting the interests of the U.S. Treasury, suppressing counterfeit currency. It was not until 1903, in fact, following the assassination of President William McKinley, that the primary operational activity of the Secret Service officially became the protection of the president.

Today, the Secret Service is actively involved in the protection of political figures and visiting dignitaries. In 1989, a unit of uniformed Secret Service officers was assigned to patrol and protect the White House and the president of the United States. The Secret Service also continues to be active in proactive law enforcement duties and, like other federal policing agencies, is involved in the war on drugs.

The Bureau of Alcohol, Tobacco & Firearms (ATF).

At one time ATF agents were better recognized as "the revenuers." Revenuers were depicted in films as ax-wielding G-men (government men) running through backwoods hills ripping up illegal stills. Although it is true that the regulation of liquor production and taxation continues to be a function of ATF, its tasks have been significantly expanded. In addition to regulatory responsibilities associated with sale, transport, and distribution of firearms and explosives, ATF also provides ancillary assistance to state and local agencies investigating cases involving explosives, bombs, and certain incendiary devices. It is chiefly through the Gun Control Act of 1968 and the Organized Crime Control Act of 1970 that the agency receives its jurisdiction over the illegal sale, importation, and criminal use of firearms and explosives.

Bureau of Customs.

The Bureau of Customs attempts to prevent objects and controlled substances from illegally entering the country. In addition to controlled narcotic substances, which television delights in focusing on with regard to Customs, other concerns of the Bureau of Customs include jewelry, fine art works, plant and animal life (which have restrictions), cash, and a number of other items. The work undertaken by Customs agents necessarily brings them into a close working relationship with an assortment of both local and other federal law enforcement agencies.

Internal Revenue Service (IRS).

Perhaps one of the greatest fears in the hearts and minds of many Americans is finding a letter in their mailbox from the IRS asking to come in for an audit. Yet, the IRS is not exclusively composed of dozens of beady-eyed, white-sleeved accountants wearing horned-rimmed glasses and poking calculators with the eraser ends of pencils.

Established in 1862, the Internal Revenue Service has three principal divisions. These include an investigative intelligence division, an audit division, and a collections division. The intelligence division, the smallest of the three, investigates violations of tax laws that come to the attention of IRS. In addition to cases that specifically correspond to income frauds (tax evasions), the investigative unit may also look into cases concerning citizens who own certain types of automatic weapons and machine guns. Several statutes require that owners of automatic weapons and machine guns pay taxes and obtain licenses for these weapons to be lawfully owned.

Among several federally coordinated drug enforcement and interdiction programs developed during recent years are those engaged in by the IRS audit and intelligence divisions. In 1985 a federal banking law was implemented that required that all banks formally notify IRS whenever a patron makes a deposit amounting to $10,000 or more. Bankers refer to this as IRS Form 4789. The intention of this law is to assist in identifying potential large-scale drug traffickers. In addition to the various law enforcement activities outlined above, the IRS is, of course, also involved in disseminating various pieces of information about tax regulations to the American public.

The Federal Law Enforcement Training Center (FLETC)

In 1970 Congress established the Federal Law Enforcement Training Center (FLETC) in Glynco, Georgia. Many law enforcement practitioners affectionately refer to the FLETC as the "Disneyland" of law enforcement training. FLETC offers extensive training for 59 federal agencies and an assortment of semi- or quasi-governmental agencies at both its Glynco campus and its recently added Tucson, Arizona satellite campus. Training at the Tucson campus includes instruction for the security forces used at many of the nation's nuclear power production plants; contract security guards hired to protect the federal courts through the U.S. Marshals Service; the Indian Police for the Bureau of Indian Affairs, and several others.

SUMMARY

Chapter Four began with a description of several important pioneers of modern American policing, August Vollmer and O.W. Wilson. The social history of each man's rise to policing prominence was briefly detailed. A number of their major contributions to modern policing strategies were outlined. Chief among these innovations was an emphasis on professional training and specialized police equipment. Many of their policing strategies and administrative orientations remain in use today.

In order to provide a sense of the diversity of the American police community, this chapter also surveyed a variety of law enforcement agencies at different levels of government. Although none of the descriptions was sufficient to completely describe each agency, they did provide a sense of the basic organizational structure of the American system of policing.

REVIEW QUESTIONS

1. In what ways did August Vollmer and O.W. Wilson move American policing toward a professional model?
2. What were some of the evolutionary changes that took place in the English watch system, once it began in colonial America?
3. Why is it necessary to have so many different federal law enforcement agencies?
4. What are some of the reasons state police agencies evolved?
5. What are some of the principal differences of policing at the county, city, state, and federal levels?

REFERENCES

Adams, Thomas F. *Law Enforcement: An Introduction to the Police Role in the Criminal Justice System.* Englewood Cliffs, N.J.: Prentice Hall, 1973.

Arizona Highway Patrol. *Fifty Years of Courteous Vigilance.* Phoenix, Ariz.: Department of Public Safety, 1987.

Ball, Joanne. "Child Pornography Probe Targeted 12 New England Residents." *The Boston Globe.* Sept. 15 (1987):17, 19.

Berg, Bruce L. "Private Security in the Public Sector: The U.S. Marshals Service as a Case Example." Paper presented at the annual meeting of the American Society of Public Administrators. Cincinnati, Ohio, November 1985.

Bopp, William J. *"O.W.": O.W. Wilson and the Search for a Police Profession.* Port Washington, N.Y.: Kenikart, 1977.

Bopp, William J., and Donald O. Schultz. *A Short History of American Law Enforcement.* Springfield, Ill.: Charles C. Thomas, 1972.

Bowen, Walter S., and Harry Edward Neal. *The U.S. Secret Service.* New York: Chilton, 1960.

Brown, Lee. "The Role of the Sheriff," In Alvin Cohen, ed. *The Future of Policing.* Beverly Hills, Calif.: Sage, 1978.

Cole, George F. *The American Style of Criminal Justice.* Belmont, Calif.: Brooks/Cole, 1983.

Folley, Vern L. *American Law Enforcement: Police, Courts, and Corrections,* 3d ed. Boston, Mass.: Allyn & Bacon, 1980.

Lane, Roger. *Policing the City: Boston 1822–1885.* Cambridge, Mass.: Harvard, 1967.

Lowenthal, Max. *The Federal Bureau of Investigation.* New York: Sloane, 1950.

National Sheriff, The. "United States Marshals Service." (April/May 1982):28.

Potholm, Christian P., and Richard Morgan. *Focus on Policing: Policing in American Society.* New York: Wiley, 1976.

Powers, William F. *French and Electric Blue: The Massachusetts State Police.* Lowell, Mass.: Sullivan, 1979.

Safir, Howard. "United States Marshals Service Fugitive Investigative Strike Teams." *Police Chief.* (1983):34–37.

Samora, Julian, Joe Bernal, and Albert Pena. *Gunpowder Justice: A Reassessment of the Texas Rangers.* Notre Dame, Ind.: Notre Dame, 1979.

Uniform Crime Reports. Federal Bureau of Investigation. Washington D.C.: GPO, 1989.

Vollmer, August, and Albert Schneider. "The School for Police as Planned at Berkeley." *Journal of the American Institute of Criminal Law in Criminology* (March 1917):875–883.

Wagoner, Jay J. *Arizona Territory 1863–1912: A Political History.* Tucson, Ariz.: University of Arizona Press, 1970.

Walker, Samuel. *A Critical History of Police Reform.* Lexington, Mass.: Lexington, 1977.

Walker, Samuel. *The Police in America.* New York: McGraw Hill, 1983.

Wilson, James Q. *Thinking About Crime.* New York: Vantage, 1977.

POLICE PATROLS AND TRAFFIC FUNCTIONS

The police are both a proactive and reactive organization. They are proactive when they become involved in various community crime prevention activities or programs designed to reduce certain types of predictable crime or identify and locate wanted felons. Police are reactive when a crime has been committed and they become involved in an attempt to assist victims and pursue the offender.

As Chapter Five will suggest, organizationally police agencies are geared to be both proactive and reactive. In this chapter the patrol unit is examined in detail. In addition to describing the importance of patrol to policing in general, this chapter considers a number of specific programs and projects intended as experiments and innovations for policing's proactive activities. This chapter also surveys the general array of different kinds of police patrols used by various agencies. The intention here is to offer a glimpse of both the usual and unusual types of specialized patrol activities undertaken by some agencies.

The central purpose of the discussion in Chapter Five is to introduce operational aspects of policing as they relate to patrol and traffic functions.

INTRODUCTION: PATROL STYLES

Traditional criminology textbooks dwell on the causes of crime. Even practice-oriented criminal-justice texts will devote at least a chapter or two to it. Yet, as John Webster (1985, 263) writes, "The process from apprehension through sentencing has until recently been rarely touched." This *process* encompasses much of what occurs when officers patrol the streets.

A number of writers have suggested that James Q. Wilson's *Varieties of Police Behavior* (1968) was the first examination of how police officers operate while handling situations on the street. Literal enforcement of the law might be one way the officer handles a situation encountered on patrol. In another instance, the officer might find it necessary to threaten, coerce, empathize, or joke with parties involved in some dispute or technical crime. In effect, American police officers typically practice a style of policing characterized as *discretionary*.

Although there are certainly circumstances in which a police officer must enforce the law (e.g., when witness to or informed of certain

Police cruisers stop on a highway to assist troubled motorists.

felonies), in the vast majority of officer-civilian encounters the officer simply handles the situation. In the literature on policing, this handling of situations frequently is referred to as **selective enforcement** and is closely related to discretion. Briefly stated, police discretion is the ability of an officer or a police agency to make decisions about their actions within certain limited parameters of the law.

In his book *Discretionary Justice*, Kenneth Culp (1969, 4) similarly defines police discretion. Culp asserts that a police officer or police agency exercises discretion whenever effective limits on power leave the officer or agency free to make choices from several courses of action or inaction.

On the one hand, police officers are expected to make determinations about when and if they should take hard-line approaches (perhaps resulting in an arrest or physical confrontation), when to issue formal (written) warnings or merely admonish citizens, when administering a social sanction is sufficient (such as walking a youthful vandal home and informing the parents); and when taking no action at all may be the most appropriate police action. If the officer makes a poor choice, he or she may have to deal with colleagues, superiors, bad press, unhappy neighborhood residents, and often the scoldings

Police patrols typically account for 60 percent of a department's personnel. Here, a cruiser patrols during nighttime hours.

from the officer's own family. On the other hand, discretion is tightly connected with police agency policies and not exclusively to an officer's judgments. Often, an officer's decision about how or whether to act is influenced by departmental policy set by administrators. In spite of these pressures and the obvious risks associated with police work, patrol officers are truly the backbone of policing.

Police patrols typically account for 60 percent of a department's personnel. While 80 percent of American police departments employ fewer than 20 officers, the principal activity among officers even in these smaller agencies is patrol work (Adams 1985). Many of us grew up watching Andy Taylor, the fictional sheriff of Mayberry (played by Andy Griffith) and his one deputy, Barney Fife (played by Don Knotts), patrol Mayberry. Andy was the sheriff, chief law enforcement officer in the area, and a patrol officer. Like Andy Taylor, in the real world, small police agencies frequently require their chiefs to serve as the local juvenile officers, records clerks, traffic officers, crime investigators, and patrol officers. Certainly, the greatest amount of the chief's time will require patrol.

In this chapter, the central focus is on law enforcement's basic field unit, the **patrol division.** To understand fully the objectives of patrol, it is important to consider the primary orientations of police officers in general. Let us consider the watchwords of most municipal police agencies: "To Protect and Serve."

Protecting and Serving the Public

While a fairly grandiose and encompassing statement, the principal objectives of policing are succinctly summed up by the phrase protect and serve. To be sure, the public expects patrol officers to be crime fighters and crusaders for good and fair justice regardless of how successful they may be at it. Patrol officers are also expected to serve the community. In other words, patrol officers function as

social service, community relations, and public relations agents. They must give directions to lost tourists, help children find runaway pets, educate community members through speeches and public appearances at civic, school, and church or synagogue functions, maintain lines of communication between residents and the police, and so forth.

As research repeatedly demonstrates, a large majority of calls to the police are "service calls." In his study of the Syracuse police, Wilson (1968) found that only about one-tenth of all calls received by the department during an average week were law enforcement-related. More recently, Lundman (1980) found that while police activities may vary in different police agencies, law-enforcement calls among the departments he studied never exceeded a third of any single agency's calls. According to Harry W. More and Fred Wegener (1990), police officers spend no more than 10 or 15 percent of their on-duty time actually enforcing criminal law. The majority of their time is spent providing essential, but non-police calls for service.

Calls for service are distinguished from law enforcement calls in that the former does not lead to situations in which a summary arrest (an arrest made on the spot) can be made. For example, when a husband and wife get into a heated argument, raise loud voices, and neighbors call the police, it is seldom that the officer will make an immediate arrest. The married couple may have begun their argument over one or the other spouse spending too much money on groceries. This unfolds into a debate about whose parents raised more financially wise offspring and an airing of a string of past arguments (most of which have little to do with the current situation). When the officer arrives, the debate is tabled by the shock of the officer's presence.

Calls for service commonly require little more of an officer than to get a cat out of a tree, remind the participants in an argument that their problem is a civil one and that they should try to resolve their differences calmly and amicably. In some instances, of course, an individual may be arrested during a service call.

The local police officer is often expected to be an information resource for the area. Because officers are trusted sources of information, they are frequently called upon to give directions to specific business or residential addresses, local community events, the best place in town for chops or lobster, where to buy tropical fish, how to get into a car when someone locks the keys inside, where the local shopping malls are, where to find a place where one can have film developed in an hour or buy beta format video cassettes. As the most visible representative of local government, municipal police officers must be prepared to answer such non-law enforcement-related questions.

In addition to the direct crime intervention and service function of patrol officers, there is a broader notion associated with patrol. This notion is **order maintenance**. This function becomes a kind of catchall for activities that are legally the responsibility of the force, and also for those tasks that have become traditionally associated with them.

In some cases these include vestiges of old watch systems, such as making sure store keepers keep the sidewalks clear and swept. In other instances, these involve civil activities where there just does not seem to be anyone else to undertake them: directing traffic during peak hours in certain locations, controlling crowds and preventing panic at some disaster, offering emotional support in the aftermath of a serious automobile crash, responding to someone's call about a drowning child in their pool, or removing snakes, bats, raccoons and other wild animals from peoples' homes, and so forth (Adams 1985).

It is impossible to determine precisely how many crimes are committed each year. It is generally agreed, however, that a far greater number of crimes are committed than those that are reported. Victimization surveys, which ask members of households if anyone in the family has been the victim of a crime (regardless of whether it was reported), demonstrate the disparate rates between officially reported and actually occurring crimes.

The inference here, of course, is that whatever it is that patrol forces are doing, it is never enough. Traditionally, police agencies are charged with the responsibility of preventing, repressing, and solving crimes. These responsibilities are hampered by the realities of limited funds and personnel and increasing sophistication among professional law violators.

Good Policing

According to the American Bar Association (1974) and Pugh's description (1986) of "good policing," the central purpose of police patrols is multi-fold. First, police patrols are intended to deter crime by maintaining a highly visible police presence. Second, patrol officers maintain public order (peacekeeping) throughout their beat. Third, officers on patrol provide the police department with a means of responding expediently to both law enforcement and service calls. Fourth, patrol officers are able to prevent crime by identifying and apprehending law violators. Fifth, patrol officers on the beat are able to assist individuals who cannot help themselves. Sixth, patrol officers are able to assure the safe flow of heavy traffic (both people and automotive). Seventh, patrol officers are implicitly charged with improving the welfare of the community through reduction of fear about crime and increasing the community's sense of safety (See Lab 1988).

Securing Scenes and Beginning the Investigation

As the first official person on the scene of a crime, the patrol officer must be prepared to take charge. While the scene is still fresh and victims and witnesses are still present and caught up in the spontaneity of the situation, the patrol officer's job is to preserve the scene. What this actually means is to keep thrill-seekers away and to identify the victims, witnesses, and suspects. Although in most instances the patrol officer will turn the case over to a detective, until then it is the uniformed officer's task to investigate and record as much information about the crime as possible. Later, the officer's notes and reports will be turned over to the detectives assigned the case. These detectives, in turn, will follow up the investigation. Chapter Five will consider the patrol officer's role during an investigation in greater detail.

Law Enforcement Innovations

To accomplish the fundamental requisites of policing, law enforcement agencies are constantly finding new and improved ways to protect and serve their communities. During recent years, several innovations have arisen among law enforcement agencies. Among the more realistic approaches are selective assignment, referral to other agencies, and distribution of patrol units in such a manner as to be the most effective.

In a general sense the assignment of patrols involves the delivery of various patrol-related services to the community. This involves consideration of the number and allocation of officers available for duty, distribution of the officers according to temporal and geographic concerns, the kinds of patrols used by the agency (e.g., foot patrol, mounted patrol, one-officer or two-officer cars), the style of police activities practiced by the agency (e.g., proactive or reactive), and various styles of supervision in the field (See Wilson and Boland 1979; Leonard and More 1987).

Allocation of Patrol Officers

The term *allocation* refers to the proportion of the agency's officers assigned to patrol or other departmental duties. Some large American police departments may allocate as much

as 60 percent of their full complement of officers to patrol duties. One can find considerable variation in the proportion of officers assigned to patrol duties in agencies across the nation. It is usual, however, to find a fairly large proportion of the available officers assigned to patrol.

Distribution of the Patrol. To operate efficiently, the patrol must be distributed effectively both *temporally* (throughout the day), and *spatially* (geographic distribution). Different tours of duty cover a full 24-hour period every day. Personnel and equipment must be assigned to different geographic quadrants in order to carry out patrol duties. The traditional geographic breakdowns are called the **beat, sector,** and **precinct,** (or in some parts of the country, **division** or **reporting district**). The following section considers some temporal allocation concerns.

Temporal Distribution

Although not always obvious, time is a very important element in law enforcement. Some types of crime, for example, are more likely to occur at certain times than at others. For instance, most industrial and commercial burglaries occur during the late night hours when these establishments are closed and when darkness can provide cover for the intruders. Consequently, these areas require increased police patrol during the nighttime hours. Or, in police management terms, these areas at night represent an increased workload. Conversely, residential burglaries, although certainly occurring at night, tend more often to happen during the daytime, when residents are out of their homes at work, school, or shopping.

Traditionally, the 24-hour day is divided into three major **watches** or **tours of duty.** These include:

Day shift	8 A.M. through 4 P.M.
Evening shift	4 P.M. through 12 midnight
Night shift	12 midnight through 8 A.M.

Well-designed patrols will have an unequal number of officers assigned to different shifts, in order to more appropriately cover a given jurisdiction's crime problems. For example, during evening and night shifts, one would intuitively expect a slightly higher number of patrol cars in commercial areas than during day shift. In some departments, shifts are rotated on a regular basis (typically on a monthly basis) among most of the officers. In other jurisdictions, many of the officers are assigned to permanent shifts.

There has been considerable concern about the physical, psychological, and emotional effects upon people who work rotating shifts. To be sure, permanent shifts allow an officer to establish more regular eating, sleeping, family, and social activities. Unfortunately, not all jurisdictions can afford the luxury of hiring enough officers to offer extensive coverage during all shifts on a permanent basis. However, increased coverage may occur during special events or in cases of emergency.

To accommodate a slightly more regular life-style for officers and in keeping with trends in other occupational groups where shift work predominates (e.g., nursing), innovative shifts have arisen. Although still being evaluated in many jurisdictions (See Moore and Morrow 1987) the **four-ten** schedule has become popular in many departments. Put simply, this schedule calls for officers to work a four-day, ten-hour shift in place of the more traditional five-day eight-hour one. In jurisdictions where this schedule has been used, officer job satisfaction and morale have gone up. Explanations for why officer satisfaction increases are related to the officers' additional time off and their ability to catch up with sleep, family activities, and life patterns.

From an administrative perspective, the four-ten shift allows for an overlap of shift coverage simply impossible with the traditional eight-hour shift. So, departments are able to increase their street forces during peak hours of crime activity (8 P.M. through 3 A.M.). In addition, because the patrol force is better rested and more satisfied with its working conditions, its job performance improves as well. A typical four-ten work schedule is set up as follows:

First shift (replacing day shift)
7 A.M. through 5 P.M.
Second shift (replacing evening shift)
4 P.M. through 2 A.M.
Third shift (replacing night shift)
9 P.M. through 7 A.M.

Another benefit of the overlap in shifts under the four-ten plan is that command, administrative, and specialty officers can flexibly alter their schedules to be available to more than one shift during a given workday (Moore and Morrow 1987).

In a number of departments a third shift-structure has arisen and is attractive to officers. This third scheduling scheme is called the **four-two** shift. In this scheduling format, officers are assigned to work eight-and-a-half-hour shifts four days a week, followed by two days off. The seventh day of each week is used as a kind of pivot to move the schedule ahead, thereby alternating which days each week an officer receives as off. Over the course of the month, the pattern that emerges is one that allows the officer to have the same days off for two consecutive weeks. These eight-and-a-half-hour tours typically are:

Day shift
7:30 A.M. through 4 P.M.
Evening shift
3:30 P.M. through 12 midnight
Night shift
11:30 P.M. through 8 A.M.

A typical schedule might look something like Table 5.1.

The four-two scheduling scheme also allows for a slight overlap in patrol. For the most part, this extra half-hour is designed for paperwork and a smooth transition from one shift to the next. As a result, unlike the four-ten schedule, personnel on the streets is not

TABLE 5.1   The Four-Two Work Schedule:

MONDAY	TUESDAY	WEDNESDAY	THURSDAY	FRIDAY	SATURDAY	SUNDAY
OFF	OFF	ON	ON	ON	ON	OFF
OFF	ON	ON	ON	ON	OFF	OFF
ON	ON	ON	ON	OFF	OFF	ON
ON	ON	ON	OFF	OFF	ON	ON
ON	ON	OFF	OFF	ON	ON	ON

meaningfully altered. Since the officers are technically working a full-time shift of only 34 hours, worker satisfaction is high while remaining relatively cost-effective for departments.

Each of the various scheduling formats is an attempt to balance safety on the streets with the cost of these officers. As a consequence, these as well as other scheduling experiments may be seen as attempts to bring police agencies closer to the goal of good policing.

Geographic Distribution.   In addition to the temporal distributional concerns, the necessity for sound geographical distribution of officers on patrol should be obvious. Geographic distribution refers both to the physical deployment of officers and various administrative supervisory concerns. Let us begin this examination of the geographic distribution of officers by considering the basic unit of patrol, the beat.

The Beat.   The basic geographic unit of patrol is the beat. Speaking generally, this encompasses the patrol officers' assigned area of surveillance. Whether the officer is on foot or uses some kind of motorized vehicle, the officer assigned to a beat is responsible for all events and activities——service and criminal ones——that occur in this area during the officer's shift or tour of duty.

The beat is a fundamental element of police patrol. In fact, the effectiveness of the entire police organization can be linked to a properly developed and implemented patrol force. Unfortunately, many police agencies tend to simply assign patrols in an ad hoc and arbitrary fashion or as determined by the amount of space and the number of officers available. As a result, their effectiveness at crime prevention and criminal apprehension is somewhat inconsistent. When carefully designed, beats will vary in size and numbers of personnel, depending upon such factors as population density, type of area (residential or commercial), previous records of crimes in the area, and environmental (topographical) aspects of the area.

The Sector.   Patrol sectors consist of a number of beats combined ostensibly for administrative purposes. Each sector has a supervisor, usually a corporal or sergeant who is called the line supervisor. The line supervisor's function is to coordinate the various activities of officers on the beats in the sector. The line supervisor is also charged with the responsibility of assisting patrol officers in the sector and managing a crime scene when necessary. In addition, line supervisors observe officers in order to assess their performances, and correct errors in police technique (Adams 1985).

The Precinct.   In many of the large cities of the United States, the geography requires that sectors contain many beats or that many sectors be created. To handle such large settings, a larger division of the work area is necessary. The precinct refers to this larger area, which consists of several patrol sectors. In a manner similar to the sector, precincts are geographical divisions intended to improve administrative coordination and supervision of the officers on patrol.

The Fluid Patrol System. During recent years a unique method for the deployment of the patrol force in mid-size and large departments has emerged. Under this version, the conventional beat system is abandoned. The experimental approach is the **fluid patrol system** (Leonard and More 1987). This style of officer deployment provides for the shifting of patrol personnel hour by hour into sections of the community where and when records indicate the greatest need.

Functionally, the city is divided into small grids or reporting districts of approximately one-quarter mile in area. Crime rates and data on demands for calls for service are calculated for each grid. The patrol commander uses this information to determine the personnel needs of each grid before every tour of duty. The patrol force is divided into squads, each under the supervision of a field sergeant.

The sector is patrolled by four squads according to the flow of reports and information from the police records and actual calls coming into the agency. The operative assumption in the fluid patrol system is that officers can more effectively respond to both calls for service and law enforcement calls based upon previous rates of calls to various areas.

TYPES OF POLICE PATROL

Modern policing strategies include both fairly traditional and innovative, aggressive attacks on crime. Regardless of the variations in styles and the ingenious experiments in policing (discussed later in this chapter), there are principally two major types of patrol: walking (foot patrol) and riding (mobile patrol). The foot patrol or beat system is certainly the older of the two. The advances made in automobiles, motorcycles, electric carts, as well as the changes in community life-styles, have necessitated alterations in mobile patrolling. Let us consider the various kinds and styles of patrolling.

Foot Patrol

A vestige, perhaps, of the watchman style of policing, the foot patrol is probably the original type of police patrol. Skolnick and Bailey (1986) suggest that police agencies in a growing number of cities are again walking beats in an attempt to work more closely with their communities in reducing crime and fear of crime. In what has quickly became a highly regarded article entitled, "Broken Windows: The Police and Neighborhood Safety," James Q. Wilson and George Kelling (1982) called for the police to leave the shells of their patrol cars and take to the streets. Wilson and Kelling suggested that walking beats allows officers and citizens to better come to know and support one another. Wilson and Kelling also suggested that primary emphasis should be placed on deploying patrol officers in locations where they can best instill public confidence and inspire feelings of safety—even if these locations are not in areas that receive the highest number of calls for police. Ensuring a sense of community, public safety, and maintaining the order, and not crime fighting, according to Wilson and Kelling, should be the mandate for police officers:

> *Just as physicians now recognize the importance of fostering health rather than simply treating illness, so the police—and the rest of us—ought to recognize the importance of maintaining intact communities without broken windows. (Wilson and Kelling 1982, 37)*

While walking limits the officer to a relatively small area of geography, foot patrol is still among the most effective forms of patrol. Patrol officers walking their beats can deal with special problems associated with preventing and repressing crimes. Two sub-categories of foot patrol can be identified: **fixed foot patrol** and **moving foot patrol** (Adams 1985).

Fixed Foot Patrol.   As implied by the language, fixed foot patrol involves a stationary type of activity. Fixed foot patrols are ideally suited for such activities as traffic direction, surveillance, crowd control at special events, and a showing of police presence. The Atlanta police, for example, frequently employ a fixed patrol in their downtown shopping area to provide a physical showing of police presence, assistance to tourists, and surveillance of what was at one time a rather high crime area. Officers remain at their fixed locations and radio for mobile units to assist them when the need arises.

Moving Foot Patrol.   Moving foot patrol allows the officer to walk a limited area of space (a beat). It is particularly useful in high density pedestrian areas such as business and shopping areas, near bars and taverns, in high crime neighborhoods, by theaters, and in areas where there are many multiple family housing or apartment complexes.

Mobile Patrols

Typically, mobile patrols are associated with the black-and-white units made famous in such television shows as "Adam-12" and "T.J. Hooker." Actually, cruisers come in a variety of colors, but in most jurisdictions they remain two-tone (two shades of blue, brown, black and white, orange and yellow, and so forth). In part, the idea behind these distinctively colored vehicles, like the distinctive uniforms worn by officers, is to draw attention to them. Uniformed police officers and their vehicles are not intended to blend into the background.

Police cruisers are likely the most extensively used and, in many ways, the most effective means of transportation for police patrol. Cruisers are well marked with lights, sirens, and distinctive insignias identifying them as police vehicles. In most cities these patrol cars are late-model vehicles. In typical police use, these vehicles have life expectancies of about two or three years (60,000 to 100,000 miles).

The average patrol car is designed as a kind of mobile police station. It is equipped with the latest in radio gear, various types of rescue and restraining devices, including in many cases first-aid kits and oxygen tanks. As a consequence of the recent AIDS hysteria, many patrol cars now additionally carry surgical masks, air ways, and rubber gloves.

In many of the large or more modern police departments (city size is not always an indicator of the level of its police department's technological sophistication), computer terminals are being added as standard equipment in police patrol cars. These terminals are radio-connected to a base computer, linking the officers in the mobile unit to a wealth of information at a finger tip. Just one of the uses, for example, is the new **911 enhanced computer,** which almost instantly identifies the telephone number and its corresponding residential address when a resident dials in on 911. The Orlando, Florida, municipal police department has been successfully using such a base computer since 1986 and intends to add terminals to its fleet of cars. Several municipal police agencies throughout Massachusetts have slated the addition of car terminals in their projected budgets for the late 1980s and early 1990s.

The use of computers and related communications technology is growing rapidly in law enforcement. Some of the innovations that are becoming standard in many police communications systems include: automatic fleet-monitoring systems, significantly improved hand-held transceivers, computerized logging and recording of dispatch operations, radio scramblers to ensure security during police communications, and a variety of computer-supported dispatching and deployment programs (Leonard 1980). The combination of links of computer networks such as the FBI's National Crime Information Center and dispatchers and mobile patrols may prove to be enormously useful. Also, as detailed in Chapter Fifteen, computer technology has advanced to a stage where fingerprints can be electronically scanned, transmitted to a fingerprint base computer, and a suspect identified in minutes.

Although the marked police car is an ideal vehicle for urban and some rural areas, other types of vehicles are sometimes required for patrol. For example, beach patrols in some West Coast areas and in certain seacoast locations in the northeast are accomplished with four-wheel-drive vehicles such as jeeps or police dune buggies. Regardless of its outward appearance, a police vehicle provides a fast, safe, and effective means for rapidly moving to a crime scene or transporting suspects or victims in a crime to the police station.

Another important issue related to the delivery of patrol services involves the question of one-officer or two-officer cars. For the most part, there are two central views on this. From the point of view of police administrators, the one-officer car is the most fiscally effective. It is the least expensive way to obtain the greatest coverage of a geographic area. Certainly, two one-officer cars can traverse more physical space than one two-officer car. Thus, surveillance of a neighborhood or community is increased. And police cars (even when replaced at regular intervals) tend to be less expensive than officers' salaries. As a result, many police administrators view one-officer cars as a way to increase departmental mobility and surveillance capabilities while not appreciably increasing their budgets.

The other major viewpoint is that of the officers. From their vantage, one-officer cars enormously reduce safety during a poten-

tially dangerous situation. Although research on one- versus two-officer cars does not indicate greater safety is always afforded by two-officer cars, officers' perceptions tend to persist. As Chapter Eleven will detail, police officers' perceptions of risk and danger create a number of somatic problems. Their perceptions should not be discounted.

Nonetheless, and in spite of many police union arguments against the use of one-officer cars, their implementation continues to prevail. The use of two-officer cars (as well as two-officer walking patrols) has been limited during recent years to areas of demonstrated high crime and/or high risk.

Beyond foot patrol and mobile units there are several other, less conventional types of patrols. These include mounted patrol, motorcycle, bicycle, and small vehicle patrol, helicopter and fixed-wing airplane patrol, marine patrol, and K-9 patrol.

Mounted police officers return to the stable after participating in a parade.

Horse Patrols.   Under certain circumstances, horses are used for patrol. In areas of large expanses of land that automobiles cannot easily travel (or may be restricted from traveling), horse patrols may prove useful. For example, one would not expect to see a motorized officer racing across wooded paths in Central Park in New York City or through pedestrian malls in certain parts of Providence, Rhode Island, Columbus, Ohio, Long Beach, California, or similar areas. Horse patrols are also useful when it is necessary to move or control large crowds such as might congregate during a parade or protest. Horses are also used when search-and-rescue operations bring police officers to wild or rough terrain.

Motorcycle Patrols.   Motorcycle patrols have traditionally been associated with traffic control and enforcement. Motorcycles have also been used by some jurisdictions, however, as a general fair-weather patrol vehicle. The motorcycle's speed and maneuverability are outstanding features of its pursuit abilities on the highways, making it an extremely valuable police vehicle.

Motorcycle patrols traditionally have been associated with traffic control and enforcement. Pictured here is a motorcycle officer demonstrating his skill during a Fourth of July parade.

Bicycles and Other Small Vehicles.   The bicycle has long been used by police officers in other countries. In China, for example, where streets are heavily congested with both cars and pedestrians, bicycles provide an effective mode of transportation for patrol officers. In England and Ireland it is fairly common to spy an officer riding along on a bicycle. Recently, American law enforcement organizations have begun to realize the utility of bicycle patrols. A bicycle allows an officer to traverse a greater distance in far less time than walking a beat. Unlike the enclosed cruiser, a bicycle provides a somewhat more personal interaction between community residents and the police officer riding it.

In addition to bicycles, other types of small, motorized, golf-cart-like vehicles have been successfully used by police agencies. These small carts allow officers to patrol regular beats either in addition to foot and/or automobile patrol or in place of them. These carts provide shelter for officers during inclement weather, can be loaded with radio and rescue equipment, and offer a relatively speedy form of transportation. In many ways, these carts are similar to patrol cars, but may be more practical under certain circumstances. During local county or state fairs, such carts allow considerable mobility and effective transportation, whereas a large cruiser would be impractical.

Helicopters and Fixed-Wing Aircraft.   Although very few jurisdictions use fixed-wing aircraft on regular patrols, they do provide a useful means of observing long stretches of highway or inaccessible land masses. There seems little use, however, for fixed-wing aircraft in heavily congested urban areas. Helicopters, on the other hand, because of their ability to hover and to lift off horizontally, have become more popular among metropolitan police departments. In addition to highway patrols, helicopters frequently are used to pursue, spot or observe fleeing persons in automobiles. Helicopters are additionally useful for rescue efforts in inaccessible areas, owing to their agility and speed for transporting severely injured persons to hospitals, specialized burn or trauma units, and similar locations.

During recent years, both fixed-wing aircraft and helicopters have been used regularly to patrol public lands to locate and eradicate domestic marijuana patches. Florida's Department of Law Enforcement, a state policing agency, has been conducting such a Domestic Marijuana Eradication program since the early 1980s.

The first airborne police unit was created in New York City around 1930. Its creation came in response to dare-devil pilots who had begun to fly all around the city, frequently buzzing or crashing into homes in densely populated areas (Potter 1979). The original unit began with a single amphibious plane and three biplanes. This air patrol unit operated until the mid-1950s, when it was upgraded to a fleet of helicopters.

Marine Patrols. Because many cities have large harbors or waterways, the use of boats to patrol these areas may be necessary. In some instances, this may prove a relatively simple task. In New York, for example, the coast is fairly short and straight and offers little need for extensive patrolling outside of the immediate harbor area. North Carolina, Florida, and other Gulf Coast jurisdictions, however, prove more difficult to patrol. Florida is estimated to have over 300 clandestine coves and bays where smugglers can land and unload contraband, chiefly drugs. North Carolina's riverways provide similar concealment and numerous places for smugglers to navigate, hide, and unload cargo.

Maritime police patrols require highly trained officers, commanding what are often extremely specialized boats for patrol. The **cigarette boat** made famous by "Miami Vice," is truly the smuggler's boat of choice. It is also the pursuit boat of choice among maritime police patrols. Unfortunately, its price

tag of about $100,000 places it well beyond the financial means of most municipal police agencies. Several agencies have obtained these boats through the Racketeer Influenced and Corrupt Organization Act (RICO). This statute permits agencies to commandeer drug smugglers' property if it can be reasonably demonstrated the property was obtained with drug profits. (In late spring 1989, the U.S. Supreme Court additionally ruled it criminal for attorneys to be paid by drug proceeds.) In some instances, boats obtained through RICO statutes by one agency are shared by several municipal agencies. This sharing sometimes occurs even when the boat is captured by a state or federal law enforcement organization.

As in Florida, maritime patrols operate in close cooperation with the Coast Guard, various state law enforcement agencies (e.g. Division of State Department of Game and Fresh Water Fish, Florida's Department of Law Enforcement), and both local city and county agencies.

A police dog waits for his handler-partner in the patrol car. Dogs have been used by police to search for lost children, to locate jail or prison escapees, and to assist in locating drugs and explosives.

Canine (K-9) Patrols. Dogs have long been used by law enforcement agencies to search for lost children and to locate jail or prison escapees. In recent years, dogs have additionally found their way into more proactive policing activities, such as searching for explosives and drugs. In some jurisdictions, foot patrol officers are accompanied by a canine partner. These teams typically have trained extensively together, live and play together, and develop extremely strong ties. When a building or dwelling needs to be inspected, the canine usually will enter first, followed by the handler (International Association of Chiefs of Police 1977).

Some observers are concerned that dogs employed in this manner are really being used as decoys in poorly lighted and dangerous places. This is not, however, the intention or purpose of the canine member of a K-9 team. Trained dogs, in addition to their relationship with their partners, cost large sums of money to train and require many months to learn their tasks. No police agency intentionally sends dogs into places because dogs are more expendable than people. In fact, in many instances, it is simply safer for the dog to enter.

Dogs are more agile, swifter, lower to the ground, and can see better in the dark than their human partners. Additionally, a screaming police officer is far less likely to get the attention of an armed felon than a growling or barking trained police canine.

Often the various "other types of patrol" operate temporarily, or in combinations of two or more of these patrol methods, or in conjunction with conventional mobile patrols. For example, the police might use a helicopter to locate a lost hunter from the air, while a K-9 team might search on the ground. By using sophisticated communications devices, air and ground teams can apprise one another of their progress.

Regardless of the kind of patrol, field officers must be constantly available and on the street in order to perform certain routine police activities. These include preliminary investigations of traffic accidents, criminal law violations, civil disorders, and other types of emergencies. Policing agencies can no longer indulge themselves in what has proven to be rather unproductive, watchman-like patrols. The cost of vehicles and their upkeep, along with general operational expenses, simply cannot be justified by a passive or haphazard style of police patrolling. The days when a good patrol unit was one that could demonstrate that half its time was spent physically on patrol, cruising and searching for the unexpected to happen, can no longer be defended as appropriate police work (Adams 1985).

Proactive versus Reactive Policing Strategies

In the face of austerity cuts and budget streamlining in many police agencies, a debate over proactive versus reactive policing has been raging during the past decade. Essentially the problem rests on police organizations' inability to afford the luxury of measuring patrol time by the quantity of time logged by patrolling officers while reacting to calls for police (Adams 1985, 2). The proactive police model includes such activities as selective coverage of roadways during holidays in order to check on the sobriety of drivers, increased patrol coverage of high-hazard collision locations, and increased monitoring of selected high-risk robbery locations.

Many people believe that the major role of police officers is enforcement of laws. But research undertaken throughout the 1960s and 1970s demonstrates that only a fraction of an officer's time on the beat is devoted to "crime fighting." Albert Reiss (1971), for example, examined patrol practices in a number of American cities in an attempt to characterize a typical day's work. He found that patrol work defies all efforts of typification "except in the sense that the modal tour of duty does not involve an arrest of any person" (Reiss 1971, 19). Using statistics reported in *Uniform*

Crime Reports, Egon Bittner (1980, 127) found that patrol officers average only a single arrest of any kind each month and only three index crimes (a category of crime) during an average year.

More recently, Mark Moore, Robert Trojanowicz and George Kelling (1988, 6) reported that police "fight serious crime" by developing a capacity to intercept it, to be in the right place at the right time during a given patrol, or to arrive so quickly after a crime is committed that the offender is captured. Although this kind of reactive policing may be appealing, it remains unclear how effective it actually is at reducing crime. During the past several decades, confidence in a reactive approach to policing has waned in the face of growing empirical evidence suggesting it is limited.

It is inaccurate to suggest that the sole role of the police officer is crime-busting. In fact, crime reduction often results from a heightened awareness of safety and security needs in one's home, place of business, and community. Additionally, law enforcement tasks are not exclusively directed toward strict enforcement of laws and apprehension of criminals. In modern police organizations throughout the 1980s, strategies for combating crime have turned to an examination of precipitating causes (Moore et al. 1988). This approach has required police departments to build closer relationships with their communities and to enhance the communities' self-defense efforts. The underlying theory is that existing police strategies can be strengthened through increased contact with citizens. This includes both individuals residing in the community and various neighborhood groups.

Research by Greenwood, Chaiken, and Petersilia (1977), Eck (1979), and Skogan and Anutunes (1979) suggests that the use of information gathered by patrol officers is among the most effective means for police agencies to increase their ability to apprehend offenders. In the following section several strategies used by police patrols to decrease crime and fear of crime are examined.

The Kansas City Preventive Patrol

Among one of the earliest studies designed to measure the effectiveness of high-visibility random patrol by uniformed officers was the Kansas City Preventive Patrol Project.

The study arose within the Kansas City Police Department in 1971. Under the administrative guidance of Chief Clarence M. Kelley, the Kansas City Police Department had already developed considerable sophistication in various aspects of police technology (Kelling, et al. 1985). The department included a number of young professionally motivated officers, and the concept of both short- and long-range planning had become institutionalized in the agency's organizational style. Kelley also was quick to explore the utility of various new police methods and procedures. Kelley was open, therefore, to the idea of conducting a study to determine the effectiveness of one such new procedure. The basic strategy of the Kansas City project has been outlined by Kelling and his associates (1974). Briefly, the project began in 1972 and concluded in 1973. The project identified fifteen beats and matched them for such items as crime rates, calls for service, ethnicity, and income levels. All fifteen beats were located in the South Patrol Division of Kansas City and were sub-divided into three groups of five beats each and labeled as follows:

1. *Reactive*—No preventive patrols (that is, no randomly assigned marked cars patrolling the area). Instead, officers entered these areas only when responding to calls for service.
2. *Proactive*—Assigned two or three times the usual number of patrol vehicles (sent through at random times)
3. *Control*—Assigned their usual number of police patrol vehicles (one each beat), which cruised the areas in their normal manner.

Contrary to expectations, the results of the Kansas City project suggested that variations in the level and visibility of police patrols made little difference in any of the areas tested.

More directly stated, no significant differences were found in the rates of crime among reactive, proactive, and control beats. Nor, for that matter, were the community members' levels of fear reduced among any of these experimental sectors.

James Q. Wilson (1977) cautions that observers of the Kansas City project should not be misled by the findings. Wilson (1977, 99) explains:

The [Kansas City] experiment does not show that the police make no difference and it does not show that adding more police is useless in controlling crime.

All it shows is that changes in the amount of random preventative patrol in marked cars does not, by itself, seem to affect, over one year's time in Kansas City, how much crime occurs or how safe citizens feel.

Box 5.1

Baltimore County's Citizen-Oriented Police Enforcement Unit (COPE)

The Baltimore County Police Department has begun to implement problem-oriented policing. Let us look at how these agencies diagnose problems and try to resolve them.

Two sensational murders within a week brought fear of violent crime among Baltimore County residents to a head in August 1981. The incidents were unrelated and unlikely to be repeated, and the murderers were soon caught and eventually imprisoned for their acts. Still, the public's concern did not subside. In response, the Baltimore County Council provided its police department with 45 new officers.

Realizing that these officers would be spread very thin in a 1,700 officer department, Chief Cornelius Behan and his command staff decided to concentrate them into a special, 45-officer unit to combat fear of crime—the Citizen-Oriented Police Enforcement unit (COPE).

In 1981, no one knew much about fighting fear of crime. As a result, COPE officers confined much of their activities in target neighborhoods to directed patrol, motorcycle patrol, and community crime prevention. Despite some modest successes, COPE managers were dissatisfied with their efforts. Chief Behan had given them a charge to be innovative; so far, they had done little that had not been done many times before.

Gary Hayes, the late Executive Director of the Police Executive Research Forum and a friend of Chief Behan's was asked to help. Hayes arranged for Herman Goldstein, a well known Police Specialist, to train COPE supervisors in the theory and practice of problem solving. Almost immediately,

COPE began to take on a sense of direction it had lacked in its first year of operation.

COPE's approach to problem solving relies heavily on a unique combination of creativity and standard procedures. A problem is usually referred to COPE by another unit of the police department, or another county agency. An initial assessment of the nature of the problem is made, and one officer is assigned to lead the solution effort. COPE officers then conduct a door-to-door survey of residents and businesses in the problem neighborhood. The officers also asked for other opinions: patrol officers, detective, and officials from other agencies are often important sources of information. The results are used to define the problem more specifically, and to identify aspects of the problem the police never see.

The COPE officers assigned to solve the problem then meet to consider the data they have collected, and to brainstorm possible solutions. Next they designed an action plan, which details the solutions to be attempted and a timetable for implementing them. Once the solutions are in place, COPE officers often conduct a second survey, to see whether they have been successful.

Three years after its inception, these procedures have become the COPE unit's primary approach to reducing fear.

From John E. Eck and William Spelman, "Who Ya Gonna Call? The Police as Problem-Busters," *Crime and Delinquency* 33 (1987): 38-39, copyright 1987 by Sage Publications, Inc. Reprinted by permission of the author and Sage Publications, Inc.

But the findings of a single study should not be taken as an absolutely accurate depiction of the effects of preventive patrols. Furthermore, the findings of a single study of one kind of preventive strategies should not be construed as meaning all preventive patrol strategies may be unsuccessful.

Some proactive programs have adopted high intensity selective approaches to the apprehension of street criminals (Martin and Sherman 1986). One example of a proactive policing program that targets street criminals is the Metropolitan Police Department of Washington, D.C.'s "Repeat Offender Project" (ROP, pronounced *rope*). The project began in 1982 with a special task force of 88 officers (later reduced to 60). The program was geared toward creating a selective identification and apprehension strategy. The basic strategy was to locate and apprehend individuals believed to be highly active criminals (Martin and Sherman 1986). The project planners slated two groups of individuals for apprehension: those persons already wanted by the police who had one or more arrest warrants already issued, and those persons believed to be criminally active, but who were not already wanted (no warrants had been issued). The first group was called "warrant targets," and the second "ROP-initiated targets."

The ROP experiment was found to increase the likelihood of arrests among targeted repeat offenders. By many measures, ROP appears to have succeeded in its manifest goal of selecting, arresting, and contributing to the incarceration of active repeat criminals. Nonetheless, evaluators of the ROP experiment are cautious of too strongly recommending such a strategy (Martin and Sherman 1986). They warn about the potential dangers inherent in a program that singles out not only fugitives, but others as well for surveillance and close monitoring.

Policies concerning law enforcement and crime prevention practices have resulted in an expanded concept (See Box 5.1) of community relations. In addition to maintaining open lines of communications and a good public image for police officers (a traditional public relations concept), recent community relations efforts include **community-oriented policing.**

COMMUNITY POLICING EFFORTS

Chiefly as the result of several major riots during the 1960s—notably, the Watts riots during the summer of 1965 and the Miami Riot in 1968—police agencies began to reevaluate their links and lines of communication with the communities they serviced. Urban riots, while certainly not a new phenomenon, were new for the police personnel of the 1960s. Black and Hispanic communities grew more and more concerned over the way police officers interacted and used excessive force when dealing with minority residents.

During the 1970s Dade County, Florida became a focal point for many racial disturbances and several riots. Between 1970 and 1979 Dade County experienced 14 outbursts of racial violence (Alpert and Dunham 1988). These major incidents, along with a great many minor clashes between minority groups and police officers, culminated in 1980 with

Community policing efforts have included an assortment of programs and strategies. The "Safety Bug," shown here, was used in an Officer Friendly program for elementary school children.

what have come to be called the McDuffie riots. The McDuffie riots resulted in an enormous amount of violence and damage, ending after three days with eighteen people dead, $80 million in property damage, and over 1,100 people arrests.

Police during the past three decades have been equally concerned about diffusing growing tension and dissension among minority community residents and restoring the legitimacy and image of police in the eyes of the public. Certainly, the police cannot operate effectively if they do not have the respect and legitimacy bestowed upon them by their community. The police were faced with a serious challenge. They had to quell the riots, while at the same time minimize property damage, injury and loss of lives, and to reduce their already growing negative public image.

The discharge of police duties simply cannot be undertaken in the absence of the authority given to police officers by both the government (in the form of their sworn status and legal authority) and by their local community (in the form of their compliance, based upon acknowledgment of the officer's authority).

Some of the early attempts by the police to improve their image and legitimacy in the eyes of the public involved alterations in the police organization's bureaucratic structure. For instance, community relations units were created, and civilians were drawn in through their inclusion on civilian review boards. Yet, both of these early efforts were fairly limited in their scope and effectiveness. Community relations units had virtually no effect on how street officers behaved when interacting with residents. Similarly, street officers strenuously resisted the idea of outsiders or civilians sitting in judgment in police matters.

Civilian Review Boards

Civilian review boards are civilian-dominated committees independent of the regular police agency administration. Their purpose is to facilitate, investigate, and hold hearings on complaints against police officers levied by residents. The police departments, however, reserved the right to discipline offending officers. Civilian review boards concentrated chiefly on four categories of complaints: brutality or excessive and unnecessary force, misuse or abuse of police authority, including violation of a resident's civil rights, abusive language or discourteous treatment, and racial discrimination by officers.

Police departments continue to have detailed procedures for recording, processing, and investigating citizen complaints. However, most civilian review boards were dismantled or rendered impotent almost as quickly as they arose (Goldstein 1977). One surviving community relations strategy that arose during the 1960s, however, was the notion of "team policing."

Team Policing

Many American police organizations have strived to improve the effectiveness of their patrols. One such approach frequently associated with community-oriented policing is team policing. In its most elemental form, team policing brings together groups of officers and a supervisor who are given complete responsibility over a specified community area (Martin and Sherman 1986, Belknap et al. 1987). The team typically develops its own strategies for patrol and deployment, its working hours, and its methods and procedures (within the confines of agency policy). The central purpose of most team policing schemes is to increase the police–community partnership in repressing crime and to involve community residents in policing efforts. A secondary purpose, related incidentally to the first, is the reduction of fear of crime in a given community.

Storefront Policing

Storefront policing sub-stations were an innovation that placed officers in the communities that appeared to need them most.

Imitating an earlier Japanese storefront policing experiment, Detroit was among the original cities to create mini-stations during the
mid-1970s (Holland 1985). In a short time, a
number of cities were experimenting with
variations on the Detroit mini-station format.

In some instances, in addition to staffing
these storefronts with uniformed officers, it
was common for off-duty officers to stop by,
assist in locating stolen bicycles and lost dogs,
help local residents with various social service and utilities problems, and visit with
local residents. Typically storefront stations
were located in high-crime areas or areas
populated by large proportions of welfare
recipients and elderly persons—prime crime
targets. The operative assumption was that
community residents would be more willing
to walk into a police station located in an
unpretentious and convenient setting such as
their own neighborhood (Eck and Spelman
1987). These storefront police stations were
well received by communities and did serve
to improve communications between local
residents and the police. There was even some
evidence that the presence of these storefront
stations served to reduce the fear of crime
(Brown and Wycoff 1987). Unfortunately, officers who were not assigned to these stations
frequently saw them as public relations units
and not real police work.

The Flint, Michigan Neighborhood Foot Patrol

Joanne Belknap and her associates (1987) describe a recent attempt to carry out a community-oriented program of policing, the Flint,
Michigan Neighborhood Foot Patrol Program.
In a drastic departure from both the mini-
stations and traditional foot patrols, Flint's
Neighborhood Foot Patrol Program based officers so they would be accessible to residents
from all socioeconomic backgrounds. Patrol
officers were placed in community centers
and public schools. Officers were expected to
go far beyond the limitations of assisting
neighborhood watch groups and to serve as

catalysts in the formation of neighborhood
associations and links to governmental social
agencies (Belknap et al. 1987). In short, the
Flint foot patrol was charged with both the
responsibility of full law enforcement service
and was expected to concentrate seriously on
the social service aspect of their promise to
protect and serve their community.

Reducing the Fear of Crime

Recent research has led to the conclusion that
fear of crime may lead to neighborhood de-
moralization, which in turn may lead to higher
crime rates (Brown and Wycoff 1987). Fear
reduction programs, consequently, fall under
the purview of proactive policing strategies.
Naturally, not all programs designed to fight
fear in communities fall under the auspices of
the local police agency. Nor, for that matter,
are all studies on reductions in fear of crime
necessarily accurate, owing to variations in
their styles of measurement (Ferraro and
LaGrange 1987). Nonetheless, when there is
fear in a particular community, and as we
have already seen police have moved steadily
toward community-oriented policing, fear reduction programs do frequently fall into the
hands of the police and offer some degree of
reassurance. During the 1970s, many municipal agencies sought to improve community
relations by developing Officer Friendly programs. In these programs, officers attended
elementary school assemblies, provided demonstrations in local shopping centers and, in
general tried to get youths to feel safe and
comfortable interacting with police officers.

The increased interest in fear reduction and
the benefits it seems to have for improving
social order within communities have once
again forced both police and the public to
rethink their image of the police officer.
Throughout the past twenty years, society
has witnessed a vast array of proposals and
strategies intended to draw the police and the
communities they serve closer together. Increased responsibilities for police–community
relations units, team policing, mini-stations,

a return to foot patrols, and Officer Friendly programs are only a few of the innovations and experiments carried out during the last two decades (Eck and Spelman 1987; Rosenbaum 1987). These attempts may be understood as a trend toward creating, or perhaps more accurately, reestablishing, a closer working relationship between the police and their community (the public).

These efforts have led to the evolution of neighborhood watch groups, along with the other community-oriented policing programs mentioned above. Most neighborhood watch organizations instruct both local residents and merchants to watch more closely the activities around them and the neighborhood and to contact police whenever they observe suspicious circumstances or persons.

The "Big Three" Community Crime Prevention Strategies

While the police obviously cannot be everywhere at the same time, their omnipresence can be felt in communities where the law enforcement consciousness of residents has been raised. Typically, what this means is that local residents have realized that the police simply cannot effectively operate in the absence of a working partnership with the people they serve. Dennis Rosenbaum (1987, 104) identifies what he and Feins (1983) call "the big three" community crime prevention strategies and suggests that policing has entered "the heyday of community crime prevention." According to Rosenbaum (1987) these "big three" crime prevention strategies include **block watches,** (neighborhood watch organizations) **operation I.D.** (personal property engraving for identification purposes), and **home security surveys.**

Block Watch.   Block watch has enjoyed widespread and enduring use by communities and the police. Steven Lab (1988, 37) has described the neighborhood block watch as follows:

> *The basic goal of neighborhood watch is increasing community awareness and problem solving. This*

can be accomplished through a variety of methods. Foremost among these is the bringing together of neighbors and residents of an area. Often, the resulting groups and activities are referred to as a neighborhood watch. Mutual problems and goals among participating individuals lead to increased feelings of communal needs and, possibly, joint action.

Neighborhood watch programs have received considerable public support in opinion polls, and national policy has encouraged block watch types of organizations with the "Community Anticrime Program" and the "Urban Crime Prevention Program" (See Debow and Emmons 1981, Gallup 1981, Feins 1983, Roehl and Cook 1984, and Cunningham and Taylor 1985).

The popularity of neighborhood watch programs has recently taken on international proportions with its increased use in Great Britain.

Neighborhood crime watch signs dot the nation's roads and warn criminals not to work the area.

In October 1982, after the appointment of Sir Kenneth Newman as commissioner of the London Metropolitan Police, *The London Times* published an article outlining his sincere interest in neighborhood watch programs as part of his overall proactive policing policy (Bennett 1987). Since 1982 the use of neighborhood watch programs has spread across much of Britain.

Block watch programs may well be regarded as the zenith of community policing activities since they receive repeated claims of success at reducing crime and fear of crime both in the United States and Great Britain (See Rosenbaum 1987, Mawby 1987). In many modern American neighborhood watch programs, the use of various media sources (newspapers, radio, and television) augments crime prevention and fear of crime reduction efforts. The fairly well-recognized cartoon character "Officer McGruff" (a bloodhound dressed in a trench coat and a deerstalker hat) and his favorite statement, "Take a bite out of crime," serve as an example of media campaigns related to neighborhood watch programs (See Surette 1985).

In addition to the use of media, a recent innovation has been the inclusion of a kind of victim assistance program as part of the neighborhood watch organization's duties (See Box 5.2).

Operation I.D. Programs. Operation I.D. programs have received considerable local and national support. Frequently, such property identification programs are undertaken and coordinated jointly with the local neighborhood watch organizations and the police. Essentially, these programs involve marking personal possessions with an identification mark or number. In many jurisdictions, local law enforcement agencies will provide an "electric pencil," which can be borrowed and used to engrave identification marks on one's television, stereo, personal computer, typewriter, and so forth. Many people use their Social Security numbers as their "personal identifications number." Police agencies pre-

fer citizens to use their driver's license numbers, since they are easier to use to locate an owner of the recovered item. It is also frequently recommended that residents photograph their possessions, particularly small items such as jewelry, in order to increase the likelihood of its identification if recovered after being stolen (Purpura 1984).

Home Security Surveys. Home security surveys borrow heavily from the tradition of business risk-management (See Purpura 1984). In some instances, local law enforcement agencies will provide a security checklist for a resident to use to survey his or her home or business. In other jurisdictions, usually as part of the agency's community relations program, an officer will actually come to the resident's home or business and survey the premises (Hess and Wrobleski 1982). The

All items of value on these premises have been marked for ready identification by Law Enforcement Agencies.

OPERATION I.D.
A Project Of Your Local Law Enforcement Agency

This window sticker notifies would-be burglars that the homeowner has marked and registered valuables with the local police.

Box 5.2 _____

BLOCK WATCH IN ACTION: THE PHILADELPHIA EXAMPLE

An emergency call sends police officers rushing to the scene of an assault, where they find a young man who has been savagely beaten by a gang of thugs. They rush him to the hospital, talk to witnesses, and set off to catch the criminal who did it.

The criminal justice system knows its job: find the suspect, charge them, prosecute them, punish them if convicted. A corps of highly trained professionals—police officers, attorneys, judges, probation officers, corrections officials—stand ready to do its part.

The victim and his family need help, and they need more than medical attention and a sympathetic interview. Police and prosecutors have come to recognize this need in recent years, but often their agencies are not equipped to do much about it.

When a crime like this occurred in Philadelphia recently, the victim's family received a telephone call from someone in the neighborhood offering to help. The caller was a member of the block watch (sometimes called town watch, block watch, or neighborhood watch) in which local residents band together to keep an eye on their neighborhood and to alert police whenever they see something suspicious. In most communities, block watch members play no role after a crime has been committed, but in Philadelphia many members have trained to provide crucial assistance to victims.

The call from the block watch neighbor was simple: "How are you getting along? Is there anything I can do to help?" When the neighbor found that the victim's mother was distraught, she comforted her and helped her get information about her son.

Eventually, the young victim began to express a commonly held fear—that his attackers would assault him again if he pressed charges. The block watch neighbor reassured him. When it came time to go to court, the neighbor escorted the victim and sat through the proceedings.

Such neighbor-to-neighbor involvement is common in northwest Philadelphia. It is the result of a pioneering partnership among police, a victim assistance program, and neighborhood block watch organizations. Together, they help victims with short-term, immediate needs and with the long-term goal of making the neighborhood safer.

SOME BASIC ELEMENTS OF THE PHILADELPHIA BLOCK WATCH

— Reassuring the victim. Let victims know that neighbors are concerned and ready to help. This may involve nothing more than saying, "How are you getting along?" "I just wanted to say we're around the corner if you need some help." "Call me if you get scared."

— Stay with victims for an hour or two after a crime. Many people are afraid to be alone after a traumatic event. Having someone there is particularly helpful with elderly men and women, who sometimes become virtual recluses after being victimized.

— Listening. Let victims express their fears, retell what happened, and reveal their worries about the future. Often neighbors are better listeners than friends and family who may be impatient with the victim's anxieties or contribute to the victim's feeling at fault for letting the crime occur. Neighbors may even be more effective than trained counselors because some victims trust only people they know and are intimidated by "professionals."

— Providing practical assistance. When a neighbor came home one night to find that burglars had ransacked her house after pushing in the skylight, a couple of agile block watch members temporarily boarded up the roof to prevent anyone from returning. When another family had all their money, major appliances, and food stolen, the block watch lent them money from its treasury and collected food from the neighborhood. Block watch members sometimes baby-sit when victims make trips to the doctor or court.

— Accompanying victims to court or to local services. A mugging victim who ignored two court summonses to appear at a line-up agreed to go only when a block watch captain arranged for three neighbors to accompany her. One block watch captain pleaded to get permission from a badly bleeding—but uninsured—victim to call an ambulance but ended up driving the injured man to the hospital to spare him the $100 ambulance fee.

— Helping victims obtain other help. This might include filing with the crime victim's compensa-

tion program or requesting financial assistance from a community safety program, or seeking local professional counseling.
— Helping victims make informed decisions. One block watch captain strongly encouraged a mugging victim who was reluctant to report the crime to telephone the police. The volunteer had learned in training that reporting helps victims regain a feeling of control over their lives. He also explained to the victim that insurance compensation often depends on reporting the crime to the police within 48 to 72 hours.
— Explaining the criminal justice system. Let vic-

tims know what to expect when police arrive and what will happen in court.
— Providing liaison with police and prosecutor. When victims are afraid to leave their homes, a block watch can persuade the police to increase local street patrol or persuade the prosecutor to ask the court's warrant unit to make an extra effort to locate a defendant who may have jumped bail.

From Peter Finn, "Block Watches Help Crime Victims in Philadelphia." *National Institute of Justice Reports.* Washington, D.C.: NIJ Printing (November-December 1986):2, 5

---

checklist contains questions about the type of doors (solid or hollow), windows, locks, alarms, lighting, and shrubs. In addition to identifying points of potential risk, officers frequently will sit down with the resident and discuss ways to correct these security weak points.

TRAFFIC

As you go rolling along the highway at 75 miles per hour and glance in your rearview mirror just in time to see the police car behind you switch on its lights and siren, a moment of terror comes over you. Okay, so you were speeding—a little. But the real question or rationalization that runs through your head is, "What's this guy doing chasing down poor, honest speeders when there are serious criminals out there?" Of course, when you have just been cut off by some other dare-devil speeder doing 75 and you are forced to slam on your brakes to avoid crashing into their back, the words that flash through your mind are different. Now it runs something like, "So where are the police when you need them?" Certainly, in the last instance you would gleefully laugh as you whirled by watching the officer ticket that reckless driver. The difference, of course, is that in the first case it is you and in the second case it is someone else.

The streets and roadways of America are inextricably linked both to automobiles and

the crimes connected with cars. In addition to the literal traffic laws that govern the highways, expressways, and local streets, every conceivable category of crime regularly involves cars. Cars and roadways are used to reach and escape targets of crime, to transport ill-gotten goods and criminals, to smuggle guns, drugs, illegal aliens, and to move rape, murder, and ransom victims. It has become commonplace for officers to encounter serious felons while making routine traffic stops. Once stopped, even for a minor violation, it may be found during a routine check that the motorist is wanted by the police for some serious crime.

In addition, during a traffic stop, drugs or other illegal contraband frequently may be observed on the seats or the floor of the vehicle. For instance, during one week in June 1987, the Massachusetts State Police arrested nine individuals on drug charges resulting from three separate traffic stops. These nine arrests added to the 130 drug-related arrests that had occurred during traffic stops made by Massachusetts State Police between January 1987 and June 1987 (Tan 1987).

The traffic function in policing (See Box 5.3) includes two basic duties: traffic control and accident investigation. As in other aspects of policing, who is involved in each activity is an organizational decision based upon personnel numbers and cost-effectiveness. In smaller departments the patrol division is responsible for all police operations, including traffic. In such cases all three traffic duties belong to the patrol officers. Larger departments in large urban centers typically have units that specialize in traffic control and accident investigations. In these cases, only when enforcing traffic laws are officers engaged in an activity shared with the regular patrol officers. Even under these circumstances, traffic officers are seldom excluded entirely from all other patrol functions. Naturally, a traffic officer would intercede if he or she observed a crime or assist when called to back up another officer. However, these officers will spend the majority of their time in traffic-related activities.

Traffic Control

The traffic control function of patrol officers, of course, is likely the most obvious and familiar role for the public to relate to. Certainly, at one time or another each of us has witnessed an officer directing traffic on some busy street corner or when a signal light has broken down. To be sure, some of us have received traffic citations for having passed through a stop sign or traveled faster than a posted speed limit or for driving a vehicle that has not been correctly maintained (with broken lights, a defective muffler, improper registration, etc.). We may have resented receiving these citations. In a more rational moment it may be possible to realize what the actual purpose of these traffic laws are: safety. The most important element involved in all traffic control and traffic laws is the prevention of traffic accidents and serious injuries to drivers and pedestrians.

Because traffic control is such a necessary, but complex task, and also because of the enormous numbers of automobiles on the roads, it would be impossible to stop every violator of a traffic or vehicle safety law. As a result, traffic divisions in police departments, as with other aspects of police work, practice selective enforcement.

Box 5.3

"The Problem of Bad Laws"

"THIS IS A 35 MILE AN HOUR ZONE? YOU'VE GOT TO BE KIDDING!"

If you are a driver of any experience you have driven on roads where posted speed limits were obviously too slow, where the pace of normal traffic regularly exceeded posted speeds by 10 or 20 miles per hour, and where, you hope, police exercised necessary discretion in not enforcing the legal limits. The lesson of this experience is a very general one: The law is not infallible.

Legislatures sometimes enact laws that make sense and receive wide-scale support in some communities at some times and in some situations but are wholly inappropriate in others. In part at least, this is so because of the way lawmaking works. Often laws are made in response to a crisis that mobilizes public sentiment and puts pressure on law makers to "do something"—a mandate legislators often interpret as passing a law against it. This whole country is littered with unnecessary stop signs and stop lights that traffic authorities were forced to install following some tragic accident. Likewise, political pressures can force legislators to enact what they know are bad laws as a way of satisfying local interest groups. What legislators also know is that when and where the interest for enforcement of laws is absent, police will not enforce them. Such laws may eventually be repealed. For reasons I am sure you will appreciate, legislators usually prefer to let them die a slow quiet police discretionary death.

From Carl B. Klockars, *The Idea of Police* (Beverly Hills, Calif.: Sage Publications, 1985): 101, copyright 1985 by Sage Publications, Inc. Reprinted by permission of the author and Sage Publications, Inc.

The traffic function in policing includes two basic duties, traffic control and accident investigation. Here, an officer directs traffic during rush hour.

Stated simply, based upon research or experience over time, a police department will identify areas within its jurisdiction where traffic violations or accidents appear to occur most frequently. At these locations, the department will detail heavier concentrations of traffic patrols. Some officers will employ a wide latitude in their discretion (which will be elaborated in Chapter twelve) on whether to issue a citation or not. Other officers, however, will hold motorists to the letter of the law and issue citations for any violations they witness.

During recent years, there have been attempts to increase the proactive nature of the traffic function of patrol work. For example, in a growing number of states, road barricades are set up during holidays in order to stop cars systematically and check motorists who may be driving under the influence of alcohol or drugs.

Accident Investigation

Traffic safety programs and safe roadways are extremely important aspects of the police traffic function. Accident investigations involve the collection and assessment of facts surrounding automobile collisions. This in-

formation can be tabulated and used both directly in a given investigation and to demonstrate that certain activities by motorists contribute to continued safety or problems on the road—seat belt usage or drinking by drivers involved in accidents.

In many ways, the accident investigation amounts to little more than data collection and reporting. Although skid marks and other physical evidence are recorded by the officers, little investigation beyond the accident scene is usually accomplished.

SUMMARY

This chapter has examined patrol work. As presented, patrol can be understood as a complex function within police organizations. Patrol encompasses not only crime-busting, but also a variety of social service and public relations tasks. The patrol division is in many ways the core around which all other policing revolves.

Because police agencies are among the very few official representatives of local government that operate on a 24-hour basis, they are often called upon to perform tasks that one would not typically associate with law enforcement. As a partial response to this call for service, as well as in an effort to improve and increase the patrol's presence on the street, experiments in scheduling have been undertaken.

Changes in styles of criminal activity and advances in technology have resulted both in an alteration in styles of policing from reactive to proactive, but also in modes of patrolling. Foot patrol has given way to a variety of more expedient modes of motorized patrolling, although a revitalization of foot patrols has also recently occurred.

Similarly, innovative strategies and experiments in community policing have increased the feeling of confidence in police agencies, while at the same time decreased the fear of crime in many communities.

REVIEW QUESTIONS —————————————————————————————

1. Exactly what is meant by the commonly used motto among police, "To Protect and Serve?"

2. What is the purpose of having shift overlap?

3. What are some of the various kinds of patrols that police departments use? What are the different reasons or circumstances for an agency's relying more heavily upon one type of patrol or another?

4. What is meant by the "big three" community crime prevention strategies? How does each operate?

5. What was the purpose of the Kansas City Preventive Patrol Experiment? Did it achieve its desired goal(s)?

REFERENCES —————————————————————————————

Adams, Thomas F. *Law Enforcement: An Introduction to the Police Role in the Criminal Justice System.* Englewood Cliffs, N.J.: Prentice Hall, 1973.

Adams, Thomas F. *Police Field Operations.* Englewood Cliffs, N.J.: Prentice Hall, 1985.

Alpert, Geoffrey P., and Roger G. Dunham. *Policing Multi-Ethnic Neighborhoods.* New York: Greenwood, 1988.

American Bar Association. *Standards Relating to Urban Police Function.* New York: Institute of Judicial Administration Standard, 1974.

Belknap, Joanne, Merry Morash, and Robert Trojanowicz. "Implementing a Community Policing Model for Work with Juveniles." *Criminal Justice and Behavior* 14, (1987):211–45.

Bennett, T. "Neighborhood Watch: Principles and Practice." In Robert I. Mawby, ed. *Policing Britain.* Proceedings of a conference in the South West Social Issues series. Conference II: Policing Britain. Plymouth Polytechnic: April 1987.

Bittner, Egon. *The Function of Police in Modern Society.* Cambridge, Mass.: Olegeschlager, Gunn, and Haine, 1980.

Brown, Lee P., and Mary Ann Wycoff. "Policing Houston: Reducing Fear and Improving Service." *Crime and Delinquency* 33, (1987):71–89.

Culp, Kenneth. *Discretionary Justice: A Preliminary Inquiry.* Baton Rouge, Louisiana: Louisiana State University Press, 1969.

Cunningham, W.C., and T.H. Taylor. "Private Security and Police in America." Report for the National Institute of Justice. McLean, VA.: Hallcrest, 1985.

DeBow, F., and D. Emmons. "The Community Hypothesis." In D. Lewis, ed. *Reaction to Crime.* Beverly Hills, Calif.: Sage, 1981.

Eck, John. *Managing Case Assignments: Burglary Investigation Decision Model Replication.* Washington, D.C.: Police Executive Research Forum, 1979.

Eck, John, and William Spelman. "'Who Ya Gonna Call' The Police as Problem-Busters." *Crime and Delinquency* 33, (1987):31–52.

Feins, J.D. *Partnerships for Neighborhood Crime Prevention.* Washington, D.C.: Department of Justice, National Institute of Justice, 1983.

Ferraro, Kenneth F., and Randy LaGrange. "The Measurement of Fear of Crime." *Sociological Inquiry* 57. (1987):10–101.

Finn, Peter. "Block Watches Help Crime Victims in Philadelphia." *NIJ Reports.* Washington, D.C.: National Institute of Justice (November-December 1986):2, 5.

Gallup, George H. *The Gallup Report #200.* Princeton, N.J.: Gallup Poll, 1981.

Goldstein, Hermann. *Policing a Free Society.* Cambridge, Mass.: Ballinger, 1977.

Greenwood, Peter W., Jan M. Chaiken, and Joan Petersilia. *The Criminal Investigation Process.* Lexington, Mass.: Heath, 1977.

Hess, Karen M., and Henry M. Wrobleski. *Introduction to Private Security.* New York: West, 1982.

Holland, Lawrence H. "Police and the Community: The Detroit Mini-stations Experience." *FBI Law Enforcement Bulletin* 54, (February 1985):1–6.

International Association of Chiefs of Police *The Patrol Operation*. Rockville, Maryland: IACP, Bureau of Operations and Research, 1977.

Kelling, George, Tony Pate, Duane Dieckman, and Charles E. Brown. The Kansas City Preventive Patrol Experiment: A Summary Report. Washington, D.C.: Police Foundation (October 1974).

Kelling, George, Tony Pate, Duane Dieckman, and Charles E. Brown. "Kansas City Patrol Experiment." In W. Clinton Terry III, ed. *Policing Society*. New York: Wiley, 1985.

Klockars, Carl B. *The Idea of Police*. Beverly Hills, Calif.: Sage, 1985.

Lab, Steven P. *Crime Prevention: Approaches, Practices and Evaluations*. Cincinnati, Ohio: Anderson, 1988.

Leonard, V.A. *The New Police Technology—Impact of the Computer and Automation on Police Staff and Line Performance*. Springfield, IL.: Thomas, 1980.

Leonard, V.A. and Harry W. More. *Police Organization and Management* 7th ed. Mineola, N.Y.: Foundation Press, 1987.

Lundman, Richard J. "Police Patrol Work: A Comparative Perspective." In Richard J. Lundman, ed. *Police Behavior: A Sociological Perspective*. New York: Oxford, 1980.

Lurigo, A.J., and Dennis P. Rosenbaum. "Evaluation Research in Community Crime Prevention: A Critical Look at the Field." In Dennis P. Rosenbaum, ed. *Community Crime Prevention: Does It Work?* Beverly Hills, Calif.: Sage, 1986.

Martin, Susan E. and Lawrence W. Sherman. "Selective Apprehension: A Police Strategy for Repeat Offenders." *Criminology* 24, (1986):155–74.

Mawby, Robert I., (ed.) *Policing Britain*. Proceedings of a conference in the South West Social Issues Series. Conference II: Policing Britain. Plymouth Polytechnic, April 1987.

Moore, Daniel T., and J. Glen Morrow "Evaluation of the Four/Ten Schedule in Three Illinois Department of State Police Districts." *Journal of Police Science and Administration* 15, (1987):105–109.

Moore, Mark H., Robert C. Trojanowicz and George L. Kelling "Crime and Policing." *Perspectives on Policing* series, Washington, D.C.: National Institute of Justice, U.S. Department of Justice, 1988.

More, Harry W., and W. Fred Wegener *Effective Police Supervision*. Cincinnati, Ohio: Anderson, 1990.

Potter, Joan. "Aviation Units: Are They Worth the Money?" *Police Magazine* 2. (1979):22.

Pugh, George M. "The Good Police Officer: Qualities, Roles, and Concepts." *Journal of Police Science and Administration* 15, no.1(1986):1–5.

Purpura, Philip P. *Security and Loss Prevention*. Boston: Butterworth, 1984.

Reiss, Albert J. *The Police and the Public*. New Haven, Conn.: Yale, 1971.

Roehl, J.A., and R.F. Cook. *Evaluation of Urban Crime Prevention Programs*. Washington, D.C.: Department of Justice, National Institute of Justice, 1984.

Rosenbaum, Dennis P. "The Theory and Research Behind Neighborhood Watch: Is It a Sound Fear and Crime Reduction Strategy?" *Crime and Delinquency* 33. (1987):103–34.

Skogan, Wesley G., and George E. Antunes. "Information, Apprehension, and Deterrence: Exploring the Limits of Police Productivity." *Journal of Criminal Justice* 12, (1979):217–42.

Skolnick, Jerome H. and David H. Bailey. *The New Blue Line: Police Innovation in Six American Communities*. New York: Free Press, 1986.

Surette, Raymond. "Video Street Patrol: Media Technology and Street Crime." *Journal of Police Science and Administration* 13. (1985):76–85.

Tan, Kim L. "Police Cracking Down on I–95 Drug Traffic." *The Boston Herald* (June 1987):6.

Webster, John. "Patrol Tasks." In W. Clinton Terry III, ed. *Policing Society*. New York: Wiley, 1985.

Wilson, James Q. Varieties of Police Behavior: *The Management of Law and Order in Eight Communities*. Cambridge, Mass.: Harvard University Press, 1968.

Wilson, James Q. *Thinking About Crime*. New York: Vantage, 1977.

Wilson, James Q., and Barbara Boland. *The Effect of the Police on Crime*. Washington, D.C.: U.S. Department of Justice, 1979.

Wilson, James Q., and George Kelling. "Broken Windows: The Police and Neighborhood Safety." *Atlantic Monthly* (March 1982):29–38.

CHAPTER 6

POLICE OPERATIONS: INVESTIGATIONS, JUVENILES, AND SPECIAL UNITS

Police services to the public are numerous and varied. In order to accomplish policing tasks effectively and efficiently the police agency must be organized. Toward this end larger police agencies have grown more and more bureaucratic in their administrative systems. Consequently, tasks related in purpose or method tend to be grouped together and coordinated by a hierarchy of supervisory personnel. What results, then, are a collection of specialized units, each expected to contribute to the overall task of police protection of residents. Even in smaller police agencies, specialized tasks are allocated to personnel or during specified time frames so as to operate in an orderly, organized fashion.

The purpose of this chapter is to describe a number of the major, specialized units one might expect to find in modern municipal police agencies. The intention is to introduce some of the basic operational elements of contemporary police organizations and to sketch out a brief description of each.

INTRODUCTION: POLICE ORGANIZATION AND OPERATION

The police have been organized around a military model since the days of Henry Fielding in England. A structure of ranks from patrol officer to sergeant, through lieutenant and captain and up to chief indicates the authority and responsibility with which each position in the organization is charged. As with other bureaucratic institutions, police organizations designate hierarchical relationships in order to establish chains of command, communication sequences, control, and accountability. In an ideal sense, the organizational structure of police agencies serves an important purpose. Owing to methodical record-keeping, formalized rules and regulations, specialized divisions of labor, and both internal and external checks and balances, the structure of police agencies ensures that laws are enforced but, theoretically, not at the expense of Americans' civil liberties.

Law enforcement agencies vary in size and in their number of personnel. In larger departments, the division of labor exceeds mere allocation of tasks by the same officers during different portions of the day (the small department's "Andy Taylor" kind of arrangement). In larger departments the operational tasks are divided into different divisions or units that specialize in a given function or set of activities. Thus, the "operations bureau" may contain separate patrol, traffic, investigations, narcotics and vice, and juvenile divisions. In Chapter Four traffic and patrol were extensively considered. In this chapter, the focus will be on investigations, narcotics and vice, and the juvenile details.

The Investigations Division

The investigations division is a specialized unit primarily involved with identifying and apprehending violators of fairly serious crimes. Less serious criminal offenses tend to remain under the purview of the uniformed patrol officer. Although a kind of split appears to occur between patrol and investigative units, this tends to be more artificial than real. The investigative unit will likely concentrate on crimes such as murder, rape, major robberies, and serious aggravated assaults. But, the patrol unit often shares in the re-

sponsibility for apprehending the perpetrators of these serious crimes, as well as the responsibility for handling lesser crimes. In fact, a very large number of cases that originate in the patrol unit are resolved by patrol officers and never reach the desks of investigators.

Although there is a considerable amount of shared responsibility, there is a certain amount of resentment between officers in patrol and investigative units. Most of this resentment derives from the "special privileges" and autonomy exercised by investigators. Intensifying this antagonism is the tendency of both the public and the media to assume that investigators are solely responsible for breaks or apprehensions in big crime cases. Frequently, patrol officers perceive their efforts as the real police work, for which investigators take undeserved credit. One may certainly question why investigators seem to enjoy this position of privilege—if indeed they do. Let us consider the role and function of the **police detective.**

The Police Detective

Detective, as a noun, makes its first appearance in lay parlance in the 1840s in order to identify the police organizational position of an investigator (Klockars 1985, Kuykendall 1986). The central function of early detective work in police organizations was apprehension. The early history of the detective, both in England and colonial America, was filled with controversy. Kuykendall (1986, 175) details seven general perceptions of early (chiefly private) detectives:

1. [They] investigated only either difficult and serious or easily solved cases;
2. worked primarily for profit and usually only for middle and upper classes;
3. spied on citizens to acquire information about their actual and possible political and criminal activity;

4. acted as agent provocateurs or thiefmakers to incite crime and entrap citizens;
5. used secrecy, deceit, treachery, coercion, and brutality to acquire information;
6. participated with criminals to both create and cover up illegal behavior; and
7. used and manipulated informers.

In England these perceptions of early detectives were perhaps more pronounced than in early American versions. Yet, the slow development of investigative agencies, such as the Federal Bureau of Investigation and the covert activities of Allan Pinkerton in the Molly Maguire incident (See Chapter Three), certainly affected American attitudes about detectives. The slow move toward formal and organized detective bureaus in America, in fact, may reflect public mistrust and fear of detectives. The romanticism of contemporary detectives, in turn, may have been an attempt to compensate for these feelings of distrust and apprehension. Today, merely mentioning the word *detective* and some mysterious trench-coated sleuth springs to mind. Because of television, some people may envision the sleuth as a dashing fellow driving a flashy red Ferrari.

A survey by the Rand Corp. indicates that virtually all mid-size American cities (those with populations of about 250,000 people) have officers specifically assigned to investigative duties. This same study indicates that 90 percent of the smaller cities similarly designate officers to detective tasks (Greenwood et al. 1977).

Investigative units frequently are separated from the regular patrol chain of command. In large measure, they possess an autonomous parallel chain of command that works hand in hand with other divisions of the police department (e.g., patrol, narcotics, etc.). The image of detectives enjoying higher prestige than other categories of police officers may rest on the fact that they frequently receive higher pay, more regular work hours, greater control in what they do, and less supervision.

It is not unusual, for example, for a detective sergeant to receive a higher salary than a patrol sergeant and for this detective sergeant to work a regular non-rotating shift.

In many jurisdictions, detectives within a given unit are organized around a particular type of crime: homicide, robbery, forgery, and so forth. In some other jurisdictions, detectives are assigned to cases according to their geographic area of occurrence. Along similar lines, Thomas Reppetto (1985) describes the overall organization of American police detective work as having historically fallen into two basic orientations, territorial generalists and headquarters specialists. The former were typically attached to a local precinct and worked directly or indirectly with local patrol officers. These detectives investigated a wide assortment of large and small cases. In the case of headquarters specialists, investigators were organized into squads (much like today's) specializing in particular categories of crime.

Most large metropolitan police departments organize their detective units around three central details. These include a unit specializing in various crimes against people, a unit designated to investigate crimes against property, and a unit of detectives to handle general investigative assignments. Detectives assigned to the crimes-against-persons unit investigate cases in which people have been physically harmed, abused, violated, or threatened. Examples of such crimes include murder, aggravated assault, rape, and armed robbery.

Officers in the crimes-against-property unit pursue criminals who have in some manner stolen or severely damaged material goods and objects. Thus, property-unit detectives may find themselves searching for car thieves and "boosters" (professional shoplifters) one day, and burglars or "dips" (professional pickpockets) the next.

Or, property detectives might be assigned to locate youths believed to be vandalizing and destroying car windshields or systematically "clouting" cars (stealing items out of cars) in parking lots.

In partial contrast to crimes-against-persons and crimes-against-property units, the general assignment unit is less specific in the categories of crime it handles. To some extent, this third unit receives cases that fall between the cracks of the other two units. General assignment officers are likely to deal with flim-flam and confidence games, keeping an eye on Gypsies as they migrate through a given city or jurisdiction, forgery (signing someone else's name, typically to a check), **uttering** (intentionally issuing bad or worthless checks), and **kiting** (intentionally writing checks for more than a balance will cover).

In some police departments detective divisions are further subdivided into speciality units or task forces. Task forces, by definition, are usually established as temporary squads of detectives to accomplish a specific, limited task.

In 1986, for example, the Tallahassee, Florida police department put together a small task force of both detective and patrol officers. The central purpose of this task force was to identify and apprehend persons involved in sales and distribution of crack, the cocaine derivative. Similar task forces were also established in many larger cities like New York and Boston, where the use of crack was seen as potentially growing to epidemic proportions.

Similarly, special anti-crime squads or task forces assigned to expose organized crime and racketeering have a long history in investigative work. During the 1920s, the Los Angeles police department had its "Crime Crusher" squads and during the 1930s there were the various FBI "Get Dillinger" and "Public Enemy Number One" squads (Reppetto 1985).

The use and existence of such highly specialized detective units is quite literally akin to the proverbial double-edged sword. On the one hand, these kinds of task forces tend to pull together the best skilled and frequently

most energetic investigators, and by nature usually possess strong support and often financial backing from their administrations. As a consequence, these special task force units customarily achieve dazzling results.

On the other hand, since these units do put together the best officers and spend increased amounts of department funds on time and equipment, there may be a drain on these resources in other units. More mundane crimes—the bulk of the case loads—are likely to be underinvestigated or unsolved.

Another potential problem one might associate with these special task force arrangements is overemphasis by police managers, supervisors, and administrators of solving what might be called **high-fear** crimes. Recent illustrations of these high-fear crimes include the serial murders in New York, Los Angeles, central Ohio, and Atlanta. The murder sprees have been attributed respectively in the media to the "Son of Sam," the "Hillside Strangler," the ".22-caliber Killer," and the "Atlanta Child Killer." All of these cases created instant fear fever among members of each community. This fear was all the more damaging to people in these communities because the killers remained at large for long periods of time. Although the detectives who worked on these cases certainly made every effort to capture the culprits, many Americans could not understand why it was so difficult. Using their television images of such notable detectives as Kojak, Columbo, and Cagney and Lacey, Americans found it difficult to accept that in the real world, crimes are not always resolved in a neat, sixty-minute format.

It may well be that a portion of the mystique that surrounds detective operations is the impression that a detective has certain, hard-to-gain skills and intellectual prowess; that investigating a serious crime requires enormous scientific knowledge; and that detective work is more important and much more exciting than uniformed street patrol. It may come as a surprise to many people, but detective investigations, as with a considerable amount of all police work, involve routine, rather tedious chores. Often, detectives find themselves knee-deep in paperwork (see Box 6.1), form-processing, and various tasks that are much less exciting than activities many patrol officers undertake daily.

Although some true detection can be associated with detective work, it is usually proportionately less than television and the movies would have the public think. It is similarly debatable whether a detective necessarily requires significantly greater skill or knowledge than patrol officers possess. Certainly, it is undeniable that a considerable amount of detective work amounts to little more than luck and checking out a lead on a hit-or-miss basis. It is only in fictional accounts of detective investigations that bank robbers, drug dealers, and bunco artists are

regularly apprehended and successfully prosecuted.

In the real world of cops and robbers, and with the exception, perhaps, of murder, most crimes go unsolved. As shown in Table 6.1, between 1972 and 1984 less than half (about 47 percent) of all violent-crime investigations resulted in arrest. By comparison, less serious crimes (various property crimes) averaged arrests in only 17 percent of the cases during this time period.

One logical explanation for this phenomena rests upon our society's attitudes about life and property and the relative social value placed upon human life compared to property. Although the public may be angered by thefts and robberies, they are outraged by the taking of another person's life. As a result, police agencies frequently expend more effort and personnel power to investigate a kill-

---

Box 6.1 _____

"Who Loves Ya Baby?": The Kojak Syndrome

Detective stories and books bulge America's library shelves and television is filled with detective programs and movies. Although periodically a program about uniformed police officers, such as "Hill Street Blues," attracts the attention of American viewers, such programs are not nearly as numerous or successful as detective shows. The extent to which the police detective has been popularized in books, television, and in the movies has a profound effect upon the way real-life detectives operate. Some of the sophisticated forensic equipment used by television detectives may only be used by a few large city agencies. But there is a tendency for real detectives to attempt to use television detectives' investigative techniques, rather than rational strategic plans to solve crimes (Goldstein 1977).

Sometimes, life does imitate art. The fictional television character of Kojak, for example, not only further promoted the image of detective as supersleuth, but actually affected police organizations and management styles. In June 1981, Sam

Souryal wrote an article entitled, "The Kojak Syndrome: Meeting the Problem of Police Dissatisfaction through Job Enrichment." In this article, Souryal identified the "Kojak Syndrome" as increasing dissatisfaction among police officers with their agency's policies, working conditions, misguided supervision, political interference, and a long list of other grievances. Lt. Theo Kojak, although a fictional character, idealized the police detective for many officers as well as the public. Kojak simply would not allow red tape to interfere with his investigations. Often against the advice of his superiors, Kojak cut through red tape and pushed his investigations to the limit—regardless of whose toes he had to step on. This "Kojak Syndrome"—although certainly present among detectives for a long time—has only recently begun to be addressed administratively. The result is that a number of changes and adaptations in police policy have emerged in order to improve police managerial styles (Souryal 1986).

TABLE 6.1 Percent of Offenses Cleared by Arrest, by Type of Offense 1972–84

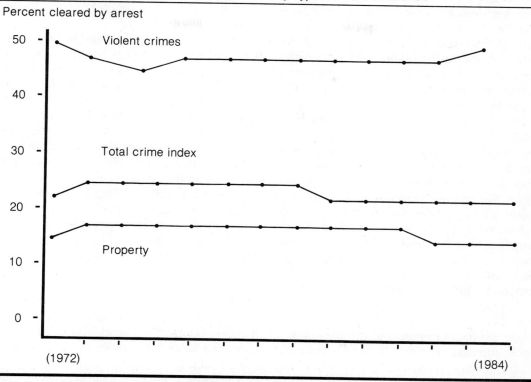

Violent crimes include murder, forcible rape, robbery, and aggravated assault.

Property crimes are burglary, larceny-theft, and motor vehicle theft. Data exclude arson.

Adapted from Flanagan and McGarrell, eds. *Sourcebook of Criminal Justice Statistics.* U.S. Department of Justice, Washington, D.C.: Government Printing Office. Figure 4.2, page 438.

ing than they do typical cases of burglary or robbery. The public seldom balks when huge amounts of personnel and money are spent on special efforts to apprehend serial murderers like David Berkowitz (the Son of Sam killer in New York during the 1970s). If, however, like amounts of money were spent on robberies and similar property crimes, the public would strenuously object.

Investigation

Detectives principally are involved with law enforcement activities after a crime has been committed and identified, either by police or a resident's complaint. Typically, by the time detectives receive the case, it has already received preliminary investigation by the uniformed officers who responded to the initial call. The uniformed officer's detailed notes may provide important leads and clues the detective can use to solve the case.

Certainly, it is possible for detectives to enter a case at different points, depending upon such factors as the seriousness of the crime, the time at which the crime occurs, their physical proximity at the time the crime is identified, or the personal interest a given detective may have for a particular case. Although some large departments do provide 24-hour investigative coverage by assigning detectives to each shift, many mid-size and smaller departments do not. In these smaller agencies, detectives may be formally scheduled for day shift (8 A.M. to 5 P.M.) Monday through Friday and share in the **on-call** responsibilities during other shifts and during the weekend. If a serious crime occurs, investigators may get called in, even if they are not officially on call.

Many of the crimes that occur, such as residential burglaries or commercial break-ins, simply can wait until morning or until Monday when the detectives come in to the office. Until then, uniformed officers responding to the call are responsible for the case. Again, owing to television portrayals, many victims of such crimes as a residential burglary are disappointed to learn that a forensic team is not rushing to the scene. Although the science of criminal investigations or **forensics** is quite advanced technologically, it is also very expensive. In the real world, it would be enormously costly to bring even a single forensic technician to the scene of every residential burglary. It is often pointless to send forensic technicians to the scene until after a detective has had an opportunity to assess the situation. In many cases, there would be no benefit.

In some Florida jurisdictions, uniformed officers carry small forensic kits in their patrol cars. When summoned to a burglary call, they will routinely dust for prints if there are obvious points of entry (a jimmied window or door). For the most part, this activity is undertaken as a public relations endeavor rather than a real law enforcement one. Although any prints lifted are sent along to the detectives, it is infrequent that these prints are actually used. In a few cases, these prints do provide additional evidence after a felon has been captured, but provide little assistance in identifying the culprit. Fingerprinting and its use in identifying suspects will be more fully discussed in Chapter Sixteen.

Perhaps the easiest way to demonstrate the way detectives investigate a case is to follow one through the system. Allowing for

certain variations of agency policy or local ordinance, there is a general pattern, as can be seen in Figure 6.1.

First, a crime must occur and be brought to the attention of the police. For the purpose of our example, let us consider a home burglary. After the homeowner calls in the report, a patrol officer in the vicinity is notified and goes to the scene. Once there, the officer will take careful notes about the burglary and fill out an **incident report** as part of the preliminary investigation. This initial report will be sent to the investigative unit, where one of the detectives will be assigned to conduct a follow-up investigation. To begin, investigators read through their assigned cases and sort them into what amounts to three different priorities: routine cases, common offenses, and special attention cases.

In routine cases, the circumstances indicate the next obvious step to take. These cases are straightforward, although perhaps requiring long hours of leg work and even longer hours of interviewing witnesses, victims, and/or suspects.

The second category is those cases that are straightforward, but less promising. These cases will be checked against an officer's personal file as well as the department's. But, because of their rather common characteristics, the investigator does not view them as likely to be readily solved at this time. A symbolic investigation will be undertaken and the victim contacted to see if any additional information might be added to the report. Following this, the investigator will file the case as unsolved (open).

Finally, cases may be viewed as serious, regardless of how few leads and clues seem readily available. These cases will require the investigator to examine the existing evidence as well as the crime scene in order to locate any leads or clues missed by the responding officer. Investigators will additionally canvass the neighborhood actively seeking information and/or witnesses to the crime. In serious cases, investigators may additionally call in a

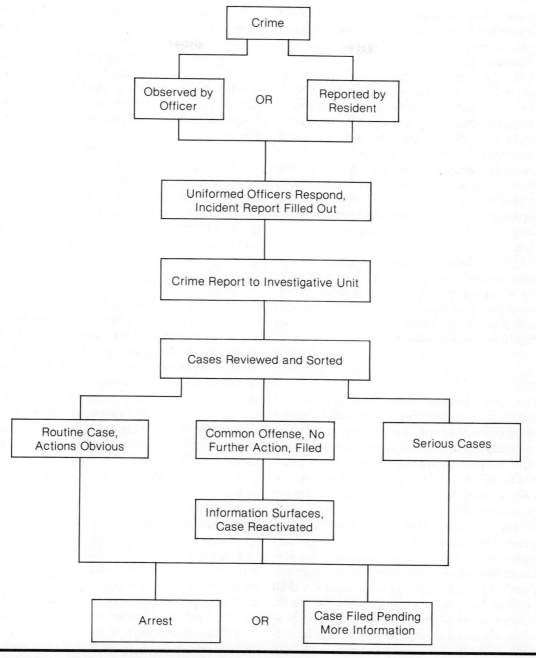

FIGURE 6.1   Typical Crime Investigation Sequence

forensics team and use other kinds of laboratory techniques that may be available (local or state crime laboratories, or even the FBI's laboratory facilities).

In the burglary example, it is likely that the case will be viewed as either routine or common. As a routine case, the investigator might recognize something reminiscent of a similar recent burglary. In this situation, the other case file will be sought and comparisons may lead to sufficient information for an arrest. Or, nothing may come from the comparison. In this event, and following a perfunctory investigation and perhaps adding some notes from the follow-up investigation, the case is filed.

Unlike television, where virtually every case is satisfactorily resolved by at least an arrest, in the real world it just does not always end happily ever after. There are several elements about resolving or **clearing cases** that bear consideration.

Clearing Cases

The type of crime under investigation will certainly affect whether a case will be cleared by an arrest or simply filed away (to be cleared clerically at a later date). Homicides, although not the most common crime that police must deal with, do tend to have the highest rate of cases cleared by arrest. The national rate for homicides cleared by arrest averages 75 to 85 percent annually (*Sourcebook* 1985, *Uniform Crime Reports* 1983). Conversely, and as illustrated in Table 6.1, the annual clearance rate (from arrest) for most property crimes is appreciably lower, usually between 15 and 20 percent. Similarly, clearance rate by arrest for violent personal crimes, such as rape and assault, also tend to approach or exceed 50 percent annually.

To a large measure, this disparate clearance by arrest rate reflects how police tend to invest a greater amount of their time and resources in serious crimes. Implicit in this rate of clearance is the social attitude of a greater priority being placed on human life—

both the injuring and taking of it—than on monetary or property losses from thefts.

Finally, it is important to note that clearance is not synonymous with **conviction**. Whether or not each offender arrested is later convicted is a decision of the courts, not the police. As a result, many more cases may be cleared by arrest than will actually result in conviction.

As suggested at the beginning of this chapter, investigative divisions are frequently composed of several specialized units. Among the more common specialty units are the **vice** (or **morals**) squad and the **narcotics unit** (frequently a single combined squad). In the next section, this unit is described in detail.

Vice and Narcotics Squads

Vice laws may be summarized as those statutes that reflect the morals of a community's residents. Because of their social significance, vice laws, perhaps to a greater extent than most other laws, come under frequent community and law enforcement debate and negotiation. Although somewhat less controversial than questioning whether prostitution should be illegal, laws against illicit drug use are also reflective of changing social values.

In a broad sense, vice laws encompass an array of "victimless crimes" associated with prostitution, gambling, and drug use. Vice and narcotics officers often set themselves up as customers in order to apprehend persons actively involved in these law violations. For example, in response to residents' complaints, undercover detectives might begin frequenting some public men's rooms in order to be solicited by a male prostitute, who will subsequently be arrested. In the face of increasing concern over the spread of AIDS through homosexual contacts, male prostitutes have been charged not only with prostitution, but also attempted homicide if they know that they are active AIDS virus carriers.

In some instances, policewomen pose as prostitutes and await propositions to perform sexual acts for money. In all of these situations, the investigators must be careful not to initiate the solicitation and thereby entrap someone. Similarly, officers must not actually engage in any sexual contact with the individual they are arresting. Occasionally, in an effort to get charges dropped, a perpetrator may accuse the arresting officer of having engaged in sex just prior to the arrest. Such accusations, along with substantiated cases of corruption on the part of some officers, have led to criticism of covert police operations that might violate personal rights of residents.

Undercover Police Work

As a result of the continued necessity for clandestine investigations, vice and narcotics officers must take elaborate precautions to avoid discovery by the law violators. To this end, and to some degree because of the serious risk of becoming corrupted by the very elements they are attempting to police, vice and narcotics officers frequently report directly to the chief of the department. By shortening the links in the chain of command, vice and narcotics officers are afforded both increased insulation against accidental or intentional departmental leaks about operations and increased autonomy in the field.

Much of law enforcement heavily relies upon the authority vested in the role of the officer. Traditionally, this has come to be represented by the uniform, badge, squad car, and other outward symbols of police authority (Wilson 1978, Miller 1987). But for obvious reasons, these outward symbols of police authority can also limit an officer's ability to collect information and evidence covertly.

The term *undercover* can be used as a kind of generic label to identify decoy work, sting operations, and police intelligence-gathering efforts (Marx 1980). Regardless of the exact nature of the assignment, undercover officers are only effective if their activities remain secret.

According to George Miller (1987), there are two types of undercover work, **light cover** and **deep cover.** Jay Williams and L. Lynn Guess (1981) have similarly distinguished between "partial" and "deep" cover with approximately the same meaning as Miller. Officers assigned to light cover typically work a regular tour of duty. These officers may assume different names and identities and wear plain clothes during their work shift. But, at the end of their shift, these disguises comes off, and they go to their homes and families.

In contrast, deep-cover is elaborate. Officers assigned to a deep-cover operation must entirely submerge themselves in their disguised identities. To a large measure, these officers must temporarily become the individuals they pretend to be. Officers must remain in character twenty-four hours a day. In fact, as Michel Girodo (1984) observes, deep cover operations are often open-ended in duration and last several months or even years.

Because by definition deep cover requires a more complete immersion in some criminal group or organization, one might expect that the officer must be highly experienced, skilled, and trained in police work. Ironically, more often than not, undercover officers are selected immediately after their graduation from the police academy.

In many jurisdictions, persons with no police training—or affiliation—at all are hired as undercover officers. The logic here, of course, is that to be effective, undercover officers must not be known to the groups they plan to infiltrate. George Miller (1987, 31) quotes one of his subjects as stating:

> I had no academy training. The Personnel Officer offered me the undercover assignment after I submitted my application. I took the civil service exam alone . . . and received mailed notification a week later that I had passed. I met the Chief and [my supervisor] in a hotel room to get sworn in.

Frequently, police administrators select undercover officers on the basis of some particular need in a specific case. These may refer to the requirements of a certain ethnic type, language requirement, age, gender, or special skill or knowledge. Obviously, having a black officer attempt to gain information about the activities of several Ku Klux Klansmen would be preposterous. By the same token, asking a white officer to infiltrate a Haitian cocaine smuggling ring would have disastrous results.

The nature of both vice and narcotics investigations is highly sensitive, and the chief or supervisor must be kept apprised of all facets of an investigator's activities nearly all of the time. Yet, it is difficult to supervise or communicate with deep-cover officers, since direct contacts with the officer would jeopardize the cover. Consequently, the deeper one's cover, the more limited and infrequent are supervisor-contacts (Williams and Guess 1981, Miller 1987).

As Gary Marx (1985) indicates, the enormous effect of isolation from other, more legitimate contacts while in deep cover can have serious and unintended consequences. "Playing the crook," as Marx describes it (1985, 109), may amplify an officer's already-existing feeling of cynicism about the effectiveness of law enforcement and the role of a police officer. The officer may begin to find it just as easy to employ illegal tactics as legal ones, even to accomplish departmental goals. In time, a officer under deep cover may become the very felon the officer set out to apprehend.

One illustration of the dangers of deep-cover operations is that of a northern California police officer who spent eighteen months investigating the Hell's Angels. Although he was ultimately responsible for a number of arrests for serious felonies and received high praise from his superiors, the officer paid a heavy price. His carousing with the Angels while undercover led to both alcohol and drug dependency. These, in turn, resulted in the break-up of his family, loss of his position through forced resignation, and sentencing to prison after a series of bank robberies (Linderman 1981).

Ironically, in the face of what may be the most dangerous segment of policing, undercover work, officers frequently describe their task as a game (Hicks 1973, Miller 1987). It is described as a matching of wits of the officer and the felons, a contest of skill and ingenuity. But, it is a contest the officer cannot really afford to lose. For the officer, a loss might mean death.

Adding to the general dangers of undercover work is the fact that officers sometimes find it impossible to carry a gun while undercover. Miller (1987) points out that many undercover officers have never received any training in the use of weapons. This being the case, what is a problem for some may be a benefit for others. In recent years, youths have become increasingly involved with violent criminal activities and drug dealings. As a result, undercover narcotics officers often find themselves dealing with children. "Narcs," as they are sometimes called, find it necessary to infiltrate adolescent groups on high school and college campuses. In many instances, these officers are not permitted to carry weapons. Unfortunately, nobody has shared these rules with the youthful bad guys who continue to carry and use weapons.

Internal Affairs: Policing the Police

It has been suggested that for a democratic society to operate effectively, the public must be protected from arbitrary practices of public officials (Redford 1969, Bent and Rossum 1976). The police, as a governmental agency with both legal and symbolic authority, must ensure that their policies and practices offer sufficient control over law violators, while not jeopardizing the liberty of law-abiding citizens.

As Sir Robert Peel (See Chapter Three) suggested, some amount of police misconduct and corruption can be avoided by careful screening of recruits, followed by effective, standardized training and proficient supervision. Unfortunately, despite police entrance examinations, psychological screenings, local and state level standards of training, and most recently a national move to certify qualifying police agencies (to be discussed in greater length in Chapter Eleven), police malpractices continue to occur.

Most large police departments have formal mechanisms for investigating allegations of police malpractice. These departmental investigations generally are handled by a specialized unit of detectives commonly referred to as **internal affairs.** Although it is safe to say that most internal affairs units make earnest attempts to ferret out corrupt and disreputable officers, it would be naive to think this can be accomplished completely.

The efforts of internal affairs units are sometimes hampered by the media. For example, television and newspapers may hear about allegations of police wrongdoings and, in their zeal to report the facts, inadvertently turn allegations into fact—regardless of the actual outcome of the investigation. Further inhibiting the responsibility of internal affairs detectives is the cloak of secrecy that is immediately drawn over a department when accusations of improper conduct arise. Curiously, as leery of outsiders or non-police affiliated persons as police officers are, they are more suspicious of internal affairs detectives. No one in the police organization is more feared, and at the same time more despised, than the "head hunters" or internal affairs officers. The President's Commission on Law Enforcement (*Task Force Report* 1967, 194) made special note of this attitude when it wrote: "Policemen all too often, because of misplaced loyalty, overlook serious misconduct by other officers." Although it is now more than twenty years later, this attitude continues to persist.

The hostility leveled at internal affairs officers results, in part, because these detectives have sometimes used questionable practices during their investigations. But, in part, other officers are suspicious because they either do not understand the purpose or disagree with the need for such an investigative unit (Territo and Smith 1985). What, then, is the goal and purpose of internal affairs units?

Realistically, no police department will ever be immune to some officer's misconduct at some time or another. It is, however, the civic as well as legal responsibility of each department to make concerted efforts to assure that police integrity and behavior is exemplary. If police officers are to maintain public trust and continue representing, both in a real and symbolic sense, American ideals such as liberty and freedom, they must remain detached from corruption, misconduct, and malpractice. The manner in which a department deals with residents' complaints about unacceptable police conduct strongly reflects on that agency's capacity to maintain the public's trust. An open system, where residents neither fear reprisal nor anticipate cover-ups, is essential for reliable law enforcement operations (Carter 1986).

Juvenile

During the past several years, police have found it necessary to become involved with juveniles with increasing frequency. Recent surveys indicate serious and violent crimes being committed by juveniles at an alarming rate. Delbert Elliot and his associates (1983), for example, conducted a national panel study and reported that many youths commit illegal acts multiple times daily. According to the *Sourcebook of Criminal Justice Statistics* (1987, 479), nationally, 49,322 youths were detained or committed to juvenile correctional facilities in 1985. In addition to their involvement in violent crimes and property crimes, juveniles are rapidly committing increasing numbers of alcohol, narcotics and drug-related offenses. Occasionally, undercover officers discover a case they are working involves a juvenile. In most instances, the department's **juvenile** unit is notified and sometimes actually drawn into the investigation.

The enormity of juvenile crime in the United States has necessitated increasingly stringent actions on the part of the police. The juvenile unit, or juvenile detail as it is sometimes called, is an attempt to curb delinquency. As a general rule, the juvenile detail is a specialized unit within the detective division. The responsibilities of juvenile officers typically include handling any case that relates to children or adolescents. Consequently, juvenile officers may work with youths who have committed crimes or who have themselves been victims.

A youthful offender's status as a juvenile is established by each state's statute. Among several relevant factors usually used in statutes is a youth's age. Many state statutes include as juveniles all persons under the age of 18. Other states may set the upper limit at 17, and still others at 16 years of age. Even when a youth falls under the age provision for juvenile status, however, he or she may be handled as an adult under certain circumstances. For example, if the nature of the crime is sufficiently violent and premeditated, the courts may handle the youth as they would an adult after transferring jurisdiction through petition.

In some jurisdictions, officers working in juvenile detail receive cases solely on the basis of the age of the perpetrator, or victim, regardless of the nature of the crime. In other jurisdictions, cases are distributed on the basis of specific types of criminal activity. For example, statutory crimes such as running away, being incorrigible, or possession of alcohol, may be handled exclusively by a juvenile officer.

Overall, the nature of the investigators' work in the juvenile detail is no different than in other units. For the most part, police investigations undertaken by juvenile officers include gathering data about the child involved in the crime (whether the child is the victim or the perpetrator). Interviewing relevant parties in a crime involving a juvenile actually serves a dual purpose.

First, the details of the alleged law violation can be clarified. Second, especially in serious criminal cases, officers have an opportunity to advise children of their rights under the *Miranda* and *Gault* rulings (Thornton et al. 1987).

In addition to enforcing laws that may be violated by youths, these units frequently must provide counseling and maintain liaison relationships with various juvenile agencies and organizations. These may include links to juvenile probation departments, alternatives-to-prosecution programs, various community councils, and crime prevention groups. In many instances, it is the recommendation of the juvenile officer that determines whether a youth is referred to juvenile court, probation, or an alternative, community-based program (Berg 1986).

Beyond the more mundane law enforcement tasks and certain liaison activities, some juvenile details require officers to make public appearances in local schools and community youth centers. It is also usually the juvenile unit that sponsors the department's safety and/or Officer Friendly programs. In short, juvenile investigators frequently become involved in an assortment of preventive and community relations programs.

Among the most-well known prevention programs sponsored by the police is Project DARE in Los Angeles. DARE is an acronym for Drug Abuse Resistance Education and is a joint project by the Los Angeles Police Department and the Los Angeles Unified School District.

The basic intent of the project is to offer children the skill to resist peer pressure regarding drug-taking. The program is built around a number of experienced officers who teach a seventeen-session classroom program. The sessions include instruction on such topics as "Practices for Personal Safety," "Drug Use and Misuse," "Consequence from Drug Use," "Resisting Pressures to Use Drugs," "Resistance Techniques: Ways To Say No," "Alternatives to Drug Abuse," and "Role Modeling" (DeJong 1986).

In the face of soaring delinquency and juvenile misbehavior rates, the police have become an important resource for battling juvenile delinquency. Today, it is usual for police officers to have a considerable amount of contact with a large number of young people in the community. The importance, of the juvenile police officer should not be underestimated.

The Dispatcher and Communications

The communications unit is responsible for supervising all departmental communications activities. These may include the two-way radios or mobile digital and computing systems used by officers in the field, telephones at the department, the complaint desk, the 911 telephone-computer systems, and any message or messenger service used within the department. In addition, the communications unit is also typically responsible for maintaining communication devices used between the department and other police agencies. These may include teletypes, Speed-Photos, facsimiles (FAX), computer network systems, or even television links.

Teletypes, or automatic teletypewriters as they are sometimes known, use telephone lines to transmit written information among different locations and agencies. At one time, teletypes were the fastest method of transmitting written information among agencies or record-keeping centers such as the FBI. Today, while teletypes are still widely used, many of the larger city police agencies have shifted to computers, electronic photo reproduction devices (facsimiles), and computer-supported information centers such as the National Crime Information Center (NCIC).

The National Crime Information Center was established by the U.S. Department of Justice in 1967. It was intended to serve as a centralized national clearinghouse for storing and retrieving crime-related information. Today, NCIC is used by the FBI field offices in all fifty states, the District of Columbia, and by Canada (Adams 1985). In addition,

dozens of municipal law enforcement and federal agencies access this computerized file system daily. The stored files include information on fugitives, stolen vehicles, license plates stolen and used in crimes or by wanted persons, firearms and explosives transactions, assorted lists of identifiable stolen property, securities files, and information on stolen aircraft, boats, and recreational vehicles. NCIC additionally stores criminal history files that provide a national means for communicating information about personal descriptions and dispositions of fugitives and arrested persons.

Transmitting Images. The use of various image transmission devices has allowed law enforcement agencies to share photographic records and other documents (ransom notes, forged contracts or checks, and so forth) quickly and effectively. As a result of recent technological break-throughs, several agencies can now transmit and receive copies of computer-generated fingerprints almost instantly. Other agencies can rely upon receiving facsimiles of latent fingerprints, or of a suspect's original fingerprint card (to be discussed in greater detail in Chapter Sixteen) in a matter of minutes.

Television transmissions and video tapes have recently begun to capture the attention of law enforcement agencies. A number of police organizations use video tapes during **roll-call training** programs. These roll-call training sessions involve brief, instructional seminars held during the roll call preceding each shift. Since television can be transmitted to many locations simultaneously, this capability also allows police chiefs or instructors to reach diverse jurisdictions from a centralized point.

Television also makes it possible to offer a line up in one location, while witnesses who may be unable to travel to view the suspect at some other location (Adams 1985). Video cameras have also been used in connection with street sobriety tests, to record the physical impairments of subjects and create a kind of visual field note. In June 1990, the U.S. Supreme Court ruled that the use of video-taped sobriety tests is legal, even if the suspected drunk-driver has not been informed of his or her constitutional rights.

The Dispatcher.   Perhaps the least discussed, yet more important element in the communications unit is the dispatcher. Although seldom a high-ranking officer, in fact, frequently a civilian, radio dispatchers issue orders with the authority of a commander. The authority of dispatchers is chiefly vested in their critical role as the police officer's lifeline to headquarters.

As suggested above, communications by various mechanical means can be extensively used in law enforcement. In fact, in many ways, a centralized radio communications system is an absolute necessity if officers in the field are to operate effectively. Police departments are, beyond all else, geared for emergency operations. But, if a dispatcher is ineffective, the agency loses its ability to handle emergency conditions.

When a call comes in to a police department, it is usually a dispatcher who must decide what action should be taken. At one time, only experienced police officers were permitted to serve as dispatchers (Bittner 1980). In some jurisdictions, policewomen found their way into these positions as a means of escaping victim-assistance work or other, more mundane clerical tasks. Today, many law enforcement agencies employ civilians as dispatchers. These individuals, although lower paid than regular officers, are highly skilled and specially trained for their work.

The work of police radio dispatchers has been compared to that of air traffic controllers. Both are extremely stressful occupations that require careful, split-second decisions.

For example, a dispatcher in Miami, Florida recently received a telephone call from a woman who indicated that she heard a prowler. The dispatcher kept the woman on the phone while sending a patrol car to the scene. Tragically, the woman was correct and the prowler strangled her to death as the dispatcher listened. The patrol unit, which arrived in minutes, although too late to save the woman, arrested two suspects. One was the fourteen-year-old daughter of the victim and the other the girl's seventeen-year-old boyfriend. Investigators later learned that the daughter had arranged for her boyfriend to kill her mother. The boyfriend was abetted by his cousin, who had escaped out the back door when police arrived.

Dispatchers have been more successful on other occasions, but one can well imagine the pressure under which these people operate. In addition to handling emergency situations themselves (poisonings, drownings, murders, etc.), dispatchers must separate out the false alarms and determine a priority of responses for the remaining cases. Since dispatchers are the people who handle the telephone calls, they are also the people who must deal with the complaints of residents when response time is slow.

Computer technology has also assisted the dispatcher. Many cities now possess computers that immediately identify the address and telephone number of the call and may even offer the dispatcher information on the nearest available patrol car. A growing number of police agencies are now equipping their patrol cars with computers that allow dispatchers to notify and deploy officers "on screen." These computer terminals also allow the officers to request various pieces of information on vehicles, suspects, and the like. Direct access to these computerized bits of information increase officer response time. While remaining in the patrol car, an officer need only type in certain codes and virtually instantly will receive the requested information.

Records.   Law enforcement agencies accrue and use an enormous amount of information. Everything from personnel reports to capital costs (the expenses used to run the agency), information on crimes and criminals, traffic accidents and citations, fingerprints, evidence and property, and operational plans must be recorded and stored. These various bits of information are used to determine the need for increases or decreases in personnel numbers, purchases of new equipment, planning special operations such as stings and task forces and, of course, solving run-of-the-mill crimes.

At the heart of any record-keeping system is the idea of safe and effective storage with quick and efficient retrieval. As the size of files and needs of departments grow, law enforcement agencies are rapidly turning toward computerized systems and away from manual files. With the advances in microchips and the impending emergence of non-metallic conductors, the cost of computing has dropped radically. As a result, even small police departments are finding it both financially feasible and necessary to enter the computer age.

Special Weapons and Tactics (S.W.A.T.) Teams

One final specialty unit that has become increasingly popular among larger municipal police agencies are the "Special Weapons and Tactics" or S.W.A.T. teams. These squads of specially trained officers are regarded both by civilians and police personnel as elite teams of highly skilled law enforcement agents (Alpert and Dunham 1988).

Typically, S.W.A.T. teams are called to the scenes of ongoing, dangerous situations after more conventional strategies have failed, or when serious and imminent threats to peoples' lives exist (a sniper on top of a roof top, a hostage held in a store by robbers, a husband wheeling a shotgun while keeping his family locked in their apartment, etc.).

Members of S.W.A.T. teams have received firearms and strategic training, as well as training in climbing and rapelling, handling high-

jackings and other hostage situations, and riot-control tactics. During the 1960s and 1970s, S.W.A.T. teams emerged to assist regular patrol officers faced with increasingly angry crowds during the turbulent anti-Vietnam War era and racial unrest in many large cities.

In the 1980s, S.W.A.T. units grew increasingly useful for, among other things, gaining access to "crack houses." Crack houses are well-fortified residences where crack cocaine is sold. These homes frequently have steel-reinforced doors and windows with only small gun-slits for defensive purposes. In an effort to combat these fortress-like houses, one S.W.A.T. team in Los Angeles converted the gun turret of a surplus military tank into a battering ram and added it to its arsenal.

SUMMARY

In Chapter Four the general impression was that uniformed officers were the thin blue line that separated order from disorder in society. This chapter, however, sought to move beyond this image of the uniformed officer and examine contributions by a number of specialized police units. Chapter Six began with a discussion of the investigative division and police detectives. Included in this examination of detectives and their work was an attempt to debunk some of the fictional accounts of detection from books, films, and television. But, it was also the purpose of this chapter to demonstrate the impact that fictional accounts of detective work may hold for real detectives as suggested by the "Kojak Syndrome."

This chapter additionally illustrated a typical crime investigation sequence. In this instance, the intention was to show some of the ways investigators handle cases.

The vice and narcotics squads and undercover work in general were discussed in light of their dangers and risks for corrupting officers. Along similar lines, internal affairs units were considered with regard to their purpose as watch dogs of the public trust as invested in police officers.

The juvenile detail was examined in this chapter in order to relate it to both investigative work and community relations. It was suggested that crimes committed by juveniles are among the most costly and numerous in America today.

Finally, this chapter examined the role of the communications unit and the radio dispatcher. The significant strain under which dispatchers operate was discussed, as was their importance to effective police operations.

REVIEW QUESTIONS

1. The investigative division is charged with which responsibilities?
2. How are deep cover and light cover differentiated?
3. What are some of the things that hamper internal affairs investigations? Why are these investigations necessary?
4. Some people have described the communications unit as the backbone of policing. Why might this be said?
5. Why is it that some crimes are given greater importance and, consequently, a more thorough investigation? Which crimes are the most important?

REFERENCES

Adams, Thomas F. *Police Field Operations.* Englewood Cliffs, N.J.: Prentice Hall, 1985.

Alpert, Geoffrey P., and Roger G. Dunham. *Policing Urban America.* Prospect Heights, Ill.: Waveland, 1988.

Bent, Alan E., and Ralph A. Rossum. Police, Criminal Justice, and the Community. New York: Harper and Row, 1976.

Berg, Bruce L. "Arbitrary Arbitration: Diverting Juveniles into the Justice System." *Juvenile and Family Court Journal* 37(1986):31–42.

Bittner, Egon. *The Function of the Police in Modern Society.* Cambridge, Mass.: Oelgeschlager, Gunn and Hain, 1980.

Carter, David L. "Police Abuse of Authority." In Thomas Barker and David L. Carter, eds. *Police Deviance.* Cincinnati, Ohio: Pilgrimage, 1986.

DeJong, William. "Project DARE: Teaching Kids to Say 'No' to Drugs and Alcohol." *National Institute of Justice Report* (March 1986):1–5.

Elliot, Delbert S., et al. *The Prevalence and Incidence of Delinquency Behavior: 1976–1980.* Project Report No. 26. Boulder, Colo.: Behavioral Research Institute, 1983.

Flanagan, Timothy J., and Edmund F. McGarrell, eds. *Sourcebook of Criminal Justice Statistics.* U.S. Department of Statistics, Washington, D.C.: Government Printing Office, 1985.

Girodo, Michel. "Entry and Re-entry Strain in Undercover Agents." In Vernon L. Allen and Evert van de Vliert, eds. *Role Transitions.* New York: Plenum, 1984.

Goldstein, Herman. *Policing a Free Society.* Cambridge, Mass.: Ballinger, 1977

Greenwood, Peter W., Jan M. Chaiken, and Joan Petersilia. *The Criminal Investigation Process.* Lexington, Mass.: Heath, 1977.

Hicks, Randolph D. *Undercover Operations and Persuasion.* Springfield, Ill.: Thomas, 1973.

Klockars, Carl B. *The Idea of Police.* Beverly Hills, Calif.: Sage, 1985.

Kuykendall, Jack. "The Municipal Police Detective: An Historical Analysis." *Criminology* 24(1986):175–201.

Linderman, Lawrence. "Undercover Angel." *Playboy,* (July 1981):134–136, 142, 220–235, 244.

Marx, Gary T. "The New Undercover Police Work." *Urban Life* 8(1980):399–446.

Marx, Gary T. "Who Really Gets Stung? Some Issues Raised by the New Police Undercover Work." In Frederick A. Elliston and Michael Feldberg, eds. *Moral Issues in Police Work.* N.J.: Rowmon and Allanheld, 1985.

Miller, George I. "Observations on Police Undercover Work." *Criminology* 25(1987):27–46.

Redford, Emmette S. *Democracy in the Administrative State.* New York: Oxford, 1969.

Reppetto, Thomas A. "The Detective Task: State of the Art, Science, Craft?" In Abraham S. Blumberg and Elaine Niederhoffer, eds. *The Ambivalent Force.* New York: Holt Rinehart and Winston, 1985.

Sourcebook of Criminal Justice Statistics. U.S. Department of Justice, Bureau of Statistics. Washington, D.C.: Government Printing Office, 1985.

Sourcebook of Criminal Justice Statistics U.S. Department of Justice, Bureau of Statistics. Washington, D.C.: Government Printing Office, 1987.

Souryal, Sam. "The Kojak Syndrome: Meeting the Problem of Police Dissatisfaction Through Job Enrichment." *Police Chief* (June 1981):60–64.

Souryal, Sam. "Reversing the Kojak Syndrome in Police Agencies: A New Managerial Challenge." *The Justice Professional* 1(1986):96–110.

Task Force Report: The Police. President's Commission on Law Enforcement. Washington, D.C.: Government Printing Office, 1967.

Territo, Leonard, and Robert L. Smith. "The Internal Affairs Unit: The Policeman's Friend or Foe?" In Harry W. More, Jr., ed. *Critical Issues in Law Enforcement.* Cincinnati, Ohio: Anderson, 1985.

Thornton, William E. Jr., Lydia Voigt, and William G. Doerner. *Delinquency and Justice.* 2d ed. New York: Random House, 1987.

Uniform Crime Reports 1983. FBI. Washington, D.C.: Government Printing Office, 1983.

Williams, Jay R., and L. Lynn Guess. "The Informant: A Narcotics Enforcement Dilemma." *Journal of Psychoactive Drugs* 13(1981):235–245.

Wilson, James Q. *The Investigators.* New York: Basic, 1978.

CHAPTER 7

CONSTITUTIONAL REGULATIONS AND POLICING: LIFE, LIBERTY, AND THE PURSUIT OF CRIMINALS

Permission to use coercive force or even deadly force if necessary is a tremendous power, which is necessary for the police to perform their daily functions properly. Our society has vested the American peace officer with this enormous power to provide a means for ensuring freedom and liberty. For police officers to live up to these ideals, rather than abuse their power, they must operate under the restrictions set forth in the U.S. Constitution. The Constitution outlines basic, fundamental rights of citizens, which often center on due process. *The observance of citizens' constitutional rights are viewed by some as creating unreasonable obstacles for police officers. Others see the restrictions as fundamental to the philosophy on which the Constitution is based.*

The Bill of Rights of the U.S. Constitution contains a number of provisions that are important for understanding the restrictions placed on police officers. But, the provisions of the Bill of Rights are not absolutes and require interpretation. Over the years, the U.S. Supreme court has heard and decided many cases involving the basic rights of American citizens. At the same time, legislative branches of government have produced laws intended to enforce basic rights and restrictions as interpreted by the high court. It would not be possible in the confines of this book to consider all the decisions, interpretations, and statutes that bear on police officers' behavior. It is, however, possible to highlight some of the more important constitutional limitations on police powers, and it is the purpose of Chapter Seven to accomplish this task.

In subsequent chapters, when appropriate, constitutional amendments and Supreme Court rulings will be mentioned and discussed. In this chapter the primary concerns are with the limitations placed on police officers in the arrest, interrogation, and search processes. This will include consideration of **Miranda** *warnings, stop and search restrictions, the exclusionary rule, and police jurisdictional issues.*

INTRODUCTION: THE AMERICAN PEACE OFFICER

This chapter will examine in some detail a number of constitutional limitations on police officers to ensure liberty and personal privacy for citizens. Chapter Seven will address elements involved in processing through the criminal justice system a person charged with a felony.

Earlier chapters have alluded to the concept of law enforcement agents as peace officers. Peace officer is a generic term that includes persons employed by some branch of the government and sworn to uphold the laws of the United States and the state, county, or city that employs them. Peace officers are typically divided according to their level of governmental employer. Federal officers are employed by the federal government, whereas state officers are employed by a given state. The sheriff and his or her deputies are employed by the county or parish, and the municipal police are employed by cities or incorporated counties (Stuckey 1986).

Customarily, one thinks of the principal tasks of peace officers as including maintenance of public order, deterring criminal activity, and apprehending those who violate the law. But the modern American peace officer has an expanded role in society. Peace officers must actively work with communities not only to deter crime, but also to relax fear of crime among community residents (See Chapter Four). Peace officers serve as extensions of public welfare and public health agencies by diverting juveniles, alcoholics, and drugs addicts from deeper penetration of the judicial system. In many police agencies, peace officers have moved into areas of criminal pattern research and planning. Peace officers assure that emergency conditions such as floods, hurricanes, riots, or other natural disasters do not result in civil disorder, looting, or other socially dysfunctional activity.

In many ways the American peace officer is the most visible component of the criminal justice system. He or she is charged with the responsibility of preserving the liberty of Americans, often at considerable personal risk both physically and emotionally. It is interesting to note that much of what we think of today as justice originated in the writings of Plato. This is somewhat ironic because in Plato's original formulation, he located guardians (enforcers of the state's laws) near the top of his ideal society's social structure.

In fact, Plato maintained that rulers could only be successful after they served as guardians. As guardians, potential rulers were understood to gain wisdom, valor, courage, and

Massachusetts State Police officers serve as a color guard during a parade.

temperance—the four cardinal virtues of Plato's ideal society. The irony, of course, is that police officers today find themselves at the lower end of the social structure of society, but aspire to preserve justice through only slight variations on the original four cardinal virtues.

It is important to recognize that temperance or moderation that affect control over police actions and behaviors is embodied in both the U.S. Constitution and Supreme Court decisions. Yet, controversy has long accompanied various Supreme Court decisions that affect police practice. On the one hand, there are outcries that certain decisions have handcuffed the police and provided an officially sanctioned way for felons to be set loose on society. On the other hand, many maintain that Supreme Court reviews of legal cases assure that liberty is maintained for citizens and integrity upheld for the law enforcement community.

It would be incorrect to insist that criminals have never been released on some technical error made by either the judicial system or the police. But, it is similarly inaccurate to elevate mistakes made in particular situations to the level of institutionalized permission to commit crime. Furthermore, it is critical to keep in mind the fact that whenever constitu-

tional rights are maintained, all in society benefit. In the United States, the encroachment on the rights of individuals by the police or other governmental agencies historically has not been tolerated.

With regard to constitutional provisions, five amendments principally deal with civil liberties relevant to police and policing. These include the First, Fourth, Fifth, Sixth, and Fourteenth Amendments. The full content of each is shown in Box 7.1. From these amendments and the various Supreme Court decisions that modify and affect their application, guidelines for the performance of law enforcement officers and the law are established.

Citizen's Arrest

Speaking generally, an arrest occurs when an authorized person seizes and restrains another person. But one may certainly question what constitutes being authorized. In fact, all private citizens possess certain rights regarding the ability to arrest law violators under certain circumstances. Arrests made by private persons are frequently referred to as **citizen's arrests,** although an individual need not be a citizen in order to make the arrest. In most states, the conditions and circumstances under which private persons are permitted to make arrests are rather restricted. These restrictions are geared to discourage private persons from actually undertaking the task of making arrests.

One frequently occurring restriction is that the person conducting an arrest have been present during the commission or attempted commission of the crime. Some state statutes, however, do permit private citizens to make arrests, even when an individual was not physically present during the occurrence of the crime. In these circumstances, the restriction typically is that a felony has been committed and that the arresting party has probable cause to believe that the person being placed under arrest committed this felony. Some statutes, such as those referring specifi-

Box 7.1 _____

Selected Amendments to the U.S. Constitution

AMENDMENT 1

·(THE FREEDOMS OF RELIGION, SPEECH, AND PRESS; RIGHT TO ASSEMBLY:)

Congress shall make no law respecting an establishment of religion, or prohibiting the free exercise thereof; or abridging the freedom of speech, or of the press; or the right of the people peaceably to assemble, and to petition the government for redress of grievance.

AMENDMENT 4

·(LIMITING THE RIGHT OF SEARCH:)

The right of the people to be secure in their persons, houses, papers, and effects, against unreasonable searches and seizures, shall not be violated, and no warrants shall be issued but upon probable cause, supported by oath or affirmation, and particularly describing the place to be searched, and the person or things to be seized.

AMENDMENT 5

·(GUARANTEE OF A TRIAL BY JURY; PROTECTION FROM DOUBLE JEOPARDY AND SELF-INCRIMINATION; PRIVATE PROPERTY TO BE RESPECTED:)

No person shall be held to answer for a capital, or otherwise infamous crime, unless on a presentment or indictment of a grand jury, except in cases arising in the land or naval forces, or in the militia, when in actual service in time of war or public danger; nor shall any person be subject for the same offense to be twice put in jeopardy of life or limb; nor shall be compelled in any criminal case to be a witness against himself, nor be deprived of life, liberty, or property, without due process of law; nor shall private property be taken for public use, without just compensation.

AMENDMENT 6

·(RIGHTS OF THE ACCUSED:)

In all criminal prosecutions, the accused shall enjoy the right to a speedy and public trial, by an impartial jury of the State and district wherein the crime shall have been committed, which districts shall have been previously ascertained by law, and to be informed of the nature and cause of the accusations; to be confronted with the witnesses against him; to have compulsory process for obtaining witnesses in his favor, and to have the assistance of counsel for his defense.

AMENDMENT 14

·(CITIZENSHIP DEFINED [FEDERAL AND STATE]:)

Section 1. All persons born or naturalized in the United States, and subject to the jurisdiction thereof, are citizens of the United States and of the State wherein they reside. No State shall make or enforce any law which shall abridge the privileges or immunities of citizens of the United States; nor shall any State deprive any person of life, liberty, or property, without due process of law; nor deny to any person within its jurisdiction the equal protection of the laws.

·Explanations of Amendments. Subheads (indicated by ·) not included in the Constitution.

---

cally to shoplifting, may provide certain guidelines and circumstances under which civilians may make arrests.

Lawful arrests by private citizens are as binding as those by sworn officers. On the other hand, when a private citizen makes an "unlawful" arrest, any information gained through the arrest (e.g., a confession) and all evidence accumulated during the course of this unlawful arrest become inadmissible in court (Stuckey 1986).

It is interesting to note that historically, most federal law enforcement agents derive their arrest powers from this basic citizen's arrest power. Nowhere in the Constitution is the federal government directed to authorize persons with arrest powers beyond those citizen powers already described. Nonetheless, through repeated court decisions and based upon widely established protocols, federal law enforcement officers are regarded as authorized to make lawful arrests. Let us consider arrests by other authorized peace officers.

Arrest by the Police

In a manner identical to citizen's arrest, sworn officers must make lawful detentions if courts are to regard these arrests and any accumulated evidence as legitimate. The police officer has the ability to make two different types of valid arrests: with and without an arrest warrant.

A warrant of arrest is a document ordering a police officer to arrest the person named and to deliver that person to the court or magistrate issuing the document. The warrant of arrest is deemed executed once the named person is taken into custody.

On some occasions, the actual identity of an offender may not be known by the police. Although investigations may have secured relevant evidence and information to identify a suspect, the real identity may be unknown. Under such circumstances, and provided the information and evidence is sufficiently compelling, some courts will permit a complaint to be filed under the name of John or Jane Doe or, for record-keeping purposes, any pseudonym selected by the police agency.

In most jurisdictions a warrant remains valid until successfully executed or withdrawn by the issuing court. In some states the warrant may be executed only in the county of the court issuing the warrant. In most states, however, the warrant may be executed throughout the issuing court's state.

Arrest with a Warrant.   When an arrest with a warrant occurs, it means that a complaint has been duly filed and placed before a magistrate. If after reading the complaint the magistrate finds probable cause, an arrest warrant

---

Box 7.2 _____

Example of an Arrest Warrant

The People of the State of [Any State] vs.

[Arrestee's Name] Defendant(s)

CASE NUMBER
0000000

ARREST WARRANT

In the County of _____ [Any County] _____
The people of the State of _____ [Any State] _____ to any police officer of this State:
A complaint on oath has this day been laid before me that the crime of [designation of crime] was committed and accuses [the arrestee's name] thereof. You are therefore ordered to arrest the accused forthwith and bring him before a judge of this court.

ENDORSEMENT FOR NIGHT SERVICE
For good cause shown to this court, I direct that this warrant be served at any hour of the day or night
Dated at _____ (place) this _____ day of _____, 19___

_____
[Signature of judge or magistrate]

will be issued. In most situations an arrest warrant is lawful even when the arresting officer does not have the warrant in possession at the time of arrest. However, upon request, warrants must be shown to the arrested person as soon as possible. A sample arrest warrant is shown in Box 7.2.

Arrest without a Warrant. In contrast, arrest without a warrant may occur under certain conditions. For example, a lawful arrest can be made without a warrant whenever an officer has probable cause to believe that a person has committed a felony. In such an instance involving a felony, it is immaterial whether the officer was actually present during the commission or attempted commission of the crime. Police officers may also make arrests without warrants when a crime (either a felony or a misdemeanor) has actually been committed or attempted in the officer's presence. Historically, the authority to make such warrantless arrests derives from the English common law tradition (discussed in detail in Chapter Eight). In the case of common law, peace officers were permitted to make an arrest if they had probable cause to believe a felony had been committed. In most jurisdictions today, peace officers are authorized to make warrantless arrests on the basis of court decisions and/or state statutes. How certain court decisions arose and affect today's policing practices will be discussed below. Among these court decisions, perhaps the most heralded, yet controversial, the right not to incriminate oneself.

Protection from Self-Incrimination: *Miranda* Warnings

An officer is to use the *Miranda* warnings whenever an individual has been taken into custody. One standard rule of thumb by many street officers is to "Mirandize" whenever the conversation with a person moves from an interview to an interrogation.

A suspect who has been taken into custody by an officer must be warned—at the time of arrest—of their protection under the Fifth and Sixth Amendments. These include one's right to be safe from self-incrimination and the right to have the assistance of counsel in one's defense. These constitutional rights were established as national doctrine in the landmark case of *Miranda* v. *Arizona* (1966).

Ernesto Miranda, a twenty-five-year-old mentally impaired man, was arrested in Phoenix, Arizona. He was charged with kidnaping and rape. Miranda had been arrested in his home and was taken to a police station where he was identified by a complaining witness. Following a two-hour interrogation, Miranda signed a written confession and was later convicted and sentenced to twenty to thirty years in prison. This conviction was affirmed in his appeal to the Arizona Supreme Court. Miranda continued his appeal, eventually heard by the U.S. Supreme Court. The appeal's argument rested heavily on the fact that Miranda had never been warned that any statement he made could be later used against him and that he had been unaware of his right to have legal counsel present during interrogation.

The *Miranda* case was one of four similar cases heard simultaneously by the Supreme Court. Each case dealt with the legality of confessions obtained by the police from suspects being held incommunicado and without benefit of full warnings about their constitutional rights. The other cases included *Vignera* v. *New York* (1966); *Westover* v. *United States* (1966); and *California* v. *Stewart* (1966).

The major constitutional issue decided by the Court in all four cases was the admissibility of statements obtained from suspects questioned in custody (or otherwise denied freedom). Under the provision of the Fifth Amendment, "no person . . . shall be compelled in any criminal case to be a witness against himself." Taken literally, this means that a defendant cannot be required to testify in court. It also means that a suspect cannot be physically or psychologically coerced to confess nor be made to confess under fear or duress. In the opinion of the Supreme Court, Miranda had given in to psychological pressures from the "third-degree method" employed by the police. Miranda's conviction was overturned and the Court established specific procedural guidelines for the police to follow before attempting to interrogate suspects. These procedures are more generally referred to as *Miranda* warnings.

Most people—at least those who have seen any television police shows during the past twenty years—are rather familiar with the *Miranda* warnings. Although variations on the warnings exist in different jurisdictions, all share several basic characteristics. Before being questioned you are entitled to be advised of certain rights:

1. You have the right to remain silent. You are not required to make any statement or answer any questions. Anything you say will be taken down and can later be used against you in a court of law.
2. You have the right to speak with an attorney and to have a attorney present during questioning.
3. If you cannot afford an attorney, but desire to have one present during questioning, one will be provided by the court at no charge.
4. If you want to answer questions now, without an attorney present, you will still retain the right to stop answering at any time.

The *Miranda* decision has been hailed by many legal scholars as the most significant legal case of the twentieth century. For others, the *Miranda* case has been seen as a serious impediment to carrying out the task of maintaining justice in America.

Shortly after the *Miranda* decision in 1966, several studies sought to examine its impact on police officers' behavior. Among the most systematic studies were those conducted by Michael Ward and associates (1967) in New Haven, Connecticut, Pittsburgh, Pennsylvania, and Washington, D.C.

Each found that while *Miranda* warnings were routinely given to suspects in custody, there was little effect on the law enforcement process. Ward et al. (1967) suggest that *Miranda* warnings reduced the ability of police to obtain confessions during interrogation in relatively few cases. Often, confessions occurred later during interrogation, once plea negotiating had begun. Thus, Ward et al. indicate that confessions during interrogation were largely unhampered by *Miranda*.

In several studies that examined court decisions in relation to *Miranda*, few cases were actually lost directly as a result of *Miranda* errors (See Wasby 1970, 156–157). Thus, the impact on convictions from *Miranda* was largely negligible.

During the past several years, the *Miranda* decision has again been the subject of public attention. It has even been described by members of the Supreme Court as a straitjacket (Kilpatrick 1986). Yet, the trend of restricting information gained prior to apprising suspects fully of their *Miranda* rights began to shift in 1980 with the case of *Rhode Island* v. *Innis*.

The *Innis* case bears an eerie similarity to another case (*Nix* v. *Williams*, 1984) which occurred in 1984 involving Robert Anthony Williams and the kidnapping and murder of Pamela Powers (the facts of this case are detailed later). In the *Innis* case, a Providence cab driver was found slain. He had been killed by a shotgun blast to the back of his head. Police investigations soon resulted in the arrest of Thomas Innis. While in custody, Innis was read his *Miranda* warnings four times. Eventually, Innis asked to speak to an attorney. Police immediately discontinued their interrogation. But as officers were driving Innis to an appointment with counsel, they passed a school for handicapped children. One of the officers in the cruiser remarked, "God forbid one of them (referring to the children) find a weapon with shells and they might hurt themselves." Innis immediately instructed the officers to turn the car around, and led them to where he had hidden his weapon.

When the U.S. Supreme Court reviewed the *Innis* case, it ruled 6–3 that no violation of the suspect's rights had transpired. Innis, at the time of his disclosure, was not in the process of an interrogation within the meaning of *Miranda*.

Not long after *Innis* (1980), several other cases emerged that seem to loosen the constraints imposed by the *Miranda* doctrine. In *California* v. *Prysock* (1981), for example, Randall Prysock, a youthful killer, was read his *Miranda* rights, and he informed police Sergeant Byrd that he did not want to talk to him. Later that day, in the presence of Prysock's parents, Sergeant Byrd carefully went through each of Prysock's rights under *Miranda* and elaborated on each in order to assure the juvenile understood the meaning of his rights. When asked, "Now, having all these legal rights in mind, do you wish to talk to me at this time?", young Prysock responded, "Yes."

The exchange was tape-recorded, but was briefly interrupted at this point by Prysock's mother. She asked if her son would be permitted an attorney at a later time, even if he made a statement now. Sergeant Byrd assured her he could and that he was entitled to have one present now, if he desired, as well.

Prysock's statement, made after the lengthy explanation of his rights, was used against him during his murder trial. When the Supreme Court reviewed the case, it held that the *Miranda* warnings were valid even when not given word for word, as decreed by Chief Justice Earl Warren in *Miranda* v. *Arizona* (1966).

In 1984, another exception to the rigid rules of *Miranda* arose. In *New York* v. *Quarles* (1984), the Court voted 5–4 to create an exception when "overriding considerations of public safety" are at stake. The *Quarles* case involved

a rape suspect, armed with a .38-caliber revolver, running into a crowded supermarket as he fled the scene of an assault. A patrol officer named Kraft, notified by the victim of the attack, pursued the suspect into the market. When Officer Kraft cornered the suspect, he noticed the man's shoulder holster was empty. Without reading him his rights, the officer shouted, "Where's the gun?" The suspect pointed toward where the gun lay. The recovered weapon was subsequently used as evidence in the man's trial. The Court's decision was to allow the gun's admission as evidence and to uphold the conviction of Quarles. The Court stated:

> We conclude that the need for answers to questions in a situation posing threat to the public safety outweighs the need for the prophylactic rule protecting the Fifth Amendment's privilege against self-incrimination.

As another example of the High Court's recent trend toward diluting the Miranda doctrine, consider the case of *Moran* v. *Burbine* (1985, 1986). On March 10, 1986, speaking through Justice Sandra Day O'Connor, the Court held that Brian Burbine's constitutional rights had not been violated. Burbine, a robbery suspect, had been twice informed of his *Miranda* rights and had made no effort to obtain a lawyer before or during questioning. While Burbine was still in custody of the Providence R.I. police, officers learned that he might have been responsible for a local slaying a year earlier. Burbine's sister contacted the public defender's office to obtain counsel for her brother. Shortly thereafter, an attorney from the public defender's office contacted the police and advised them that she would act as Burbine's counsel if they desired to question him. The police did not inform the public defender of Burbine's new status as a homicide suspect.

In the interim, Providence police conducted several interviews with Burbine who, not knowing his sister had arranged counsel, had waived his *Miranda* rights. Statements he made during these interviews were later used against him at trial, and he was convicted on the murder charge. The Court held in a 6–3 decision that it did not believe that "the level of the police's culpability in failing to inform [the] respondent of the telephone call [from the attorney] has any bearing on the validity of the waiver [of his *Miranda* rights]." The High Court, by majority, simply "declined to further extend *Miranda*'s reach" (Kilpatrick 1986, 60).

Finally, consider the similar latitude extended to police officers in the case of *Colorado* v. *Spring* (1987). In this instance, the defendant Spring and a friend shot a man to death while on a hunting trip in Colorado. Shortly after buying stolen firearms from an undercover agent, Spring was arrested. He waived his *Miranda* rights and was interviewed about both the purchase of illegal guns and the killing. Statements he made during these interviews were later used against him, and he was convicted on the murder charge. In his appeal, Spring maintained that his waiver of *Miranda* rights was invalid because he thought he was only going to be questioned about the purchase of illegal guns and not the slaying. The Court, however, ruled that the mere silence by law enforcement officials as to the subject matter of an interrogation is not "trickery" sufficient to invalidate a suspect's waiver of *Miranda* rights.

In spite of empirical investigations of the *Miranda* decision, which show it to have little effect on police work, the Supreme Court seems intent on allowing police greater latitude in their application of the strict language in the *Miranda* finding.

Probable Cause: Searches, Seizures, and Arrests

It will become apparent that the issue of reasonable or **probable cause** is relevant to both searches and lawful arrests. Thus, the question of what constitutes probable cause for search and arrest warrants requires some consideration. Courts have generally held that

probable cause, also characterized as reasonable suspicion, is evident if a person of average intelligence and foresight (ordinary prudence) would be led to believe that a crime has been committed. In other words, probable cause may exist even when there may be some doubt. But, for the arrest to be lawful, more than mere suspicion of a crime being committed is necessary (Stuckey 1986). The next question that naturally arises is "How is probable cause established?" As illustrated in Chapter Three, occasionally, officers making routine traffic stops will sometimes notice contraband in plain sight. In most instances, this observation will provide sufficient probable cause for a summary arrest.

Similarly, the tradition of warrantless searches concurrent with an arrest are usually permissible. In other words, if a lawful arrest of a fleeing bank robbery suspect is made at a bus terminal and the suspect is carrying a suitcase, a search of the suitcase would be proper. But, as one might suspect, there are certain restrictions. First, the arresting officer(s) must make the search of the offender's person immediately upon arrest; and second, the search of the area beyond the offender's person is limited to the area within the offender's *immediate control*. Immediate control typically has been given to mean approximately within one arm's reach. The reasoning behind this limitation is to restrict the search to a location where the felon might reasonably have concealed a weapon or contraband prior to arrest.

The restriction placed on the scope of a search that is **incident to an arrest** (occurs immediately after arrest) can be traced to the Supreme Court case of *Chimel* v. *California* (1969).

Before this case, police officers had been permitted to search all areas in the immediate vicinity of the arrested party. Following the *Chimel* case, officers were not permitted to search an entire house without a duly authorized search warrant (See Box 7.3). In short, the scope of the search is limited in its physi-

Box 7.3 _____

Search Warrant

TYPE - OR PRESS FIRMLY WITH BALL POINT PEN

REORDER FROM **Garlits** INDUSTRIES, INC.   30 N. PENNSYLVANIA AVE., MORRISVILLE, PA 19067-1110 (215) 736-2660

Commonwealth of Pennsylvania COUNTY OF _____	**SS: APPLICATION FOR SEARCH WARRANT AND AFFIDAVIT**

WARRANT CONTROL No.

J 09993

DATE OF APPLICATION

_____
(Name of Affiant)   *(Police Department or address of private Affiant)*   *(Phone No.)*

being duly sworn (or affirmed) before me according to law, deposes and says that there is probable cause to believe that certain property is evidence of or the fruit of a crime or is contraband or is unlawfully possessed or is otherwise subject to seizure, and is located at particular premises or in the possession of particular person as described below.

INVENTORY No.

IDENTIFY ITEMS TO BE SEARCHED FOR AND SEIZED *(be as specific as possible):*

SPECIFIC DESCRIPTION OF PREMISES AND/OR PERSONS TO BE SEARCHED *(Street and No., Apt. No., Vehicle, Safe Deposit Box, etc.):*

NAME OF OWNER, OCCUPANT OR POSSESSOR OF SAID PREMISES TO BE SEARCHED *(If proper name is unknown, give alias and/or description):*

VIOLATION OF *(Describe conduct or specify statute):*

DATE OF VIOLATION

PROBABLE CAUSE BELIEF IS BASED ON THE FOLLOWING FACTS AND CIRCUMSTANCES *(See special instructions below):*

ATTACH ADDITIONAL PAPER (5) COPIES IF NECESSARY ☐ CHECK HERE IF ADDITIONAL PAPER IS USED.

PLEASE READ AND FOLLOW THESE INSTRUCTIONS CAREFULLY

1. If information was obtained from another person, e.g., an informant, a private citizen, or a fellow law officer, state specifically what information was received, and how and when such information was obtained. State also the factual basis for believing such other person to be reliable.
2. If surveillance was made, state what information was obtained by such surveillance, by whom it was obtained, and state date, time and place of such surveillance.
3. State other pertinent facts within personal knowledge of affiant.
4. If "nighttime" search is requested (i.e., 10 P.M. to 6 A.M.) state additional reasonable cause for seeking permission to search in nighttime.
5. State reasons for believing that the items are located at the premises and/or on the person specified above.
6. State reasons for believing that the items are subject to seizure.
7. State any additional information considered pertinent to justify this application.

_____   _____ | Badge No. | District/Unit |
Signature of Affiant   *Address of Private Affiant*

Sworn to and subscribed before me this _____ **day of** _____ 19__ . Office Address

_____ (SEAL) Mag. Dist. No. _____
Signature of Issuing Authority

AOPC 410-80   ORIGINAL APPLICATION

BOX 7.3   Continued

TO LAW ENFORCEMENT OFFICER: WHEREAS, facts have been sworn to or affirmed before me by written affidavit(s) attached hereto from which I have found probable cause, I do authorize you to search the premises or person (described on the reverse side), and to seize, secure, inventory, and make return according to the Pennsylvania Rules of Criminal Procedure, the items described on the reverse side.

* ☐ This Warrant should be served as soon as practicable but in no event later

than _____ ☐ A. M. ☐ P. M. _____ , 19 _____
and shall be served only during daytime hours of 6 A.M. to 10 P.M.

Issued under my hand this _____ day of _____ ,

19 ___ , at _____.M. o'clock. *(Issue time must be stated)*

(SEAL) _____

_____
(Signature of Issuing Authority)

Mag. Dist. No. _____ Office Address _____

Date Commission Expires _____

** ☐ This Warrant should be served as soon as practicable but in no event later

than _____ ☐ A.M. ☐ P.M. _____ , 19 _____
and may be served anytime during day or night.

Issued under my hand this _____ day of _____ ,

19___ , at _____.M. o'clock. *(Issue time must be stated)*

(SEAL)

_____
(Signature of Issuing Authority)

_____ Phone No. _____

Title of Issuing Authority _____

**The issuing authority should specify a date not later than two (2) days after issuance. PA. R. Crim. P. 2005(d).*
***If issuing authority finds reasonable cause for issuing a nighttime warrant on the basis of additional reasonable cause set forth in the accompanying affidavits and wishes to issue a nighttime search warrant, only this section shall be completed. PA. R. Crim. 2006(b).*

Printed by Garlits Industries, Inc.

cal extension to an arm's length from the suspect.

But what about searches without warrants that may occur when not incident to an arrest? Does the average resident have the right to expect the privacy of home, for example, to be maintained under the Fourth Amendment? Can one refuse entry to duly sworn officers who want to come in and look around, but who do not have a warrant in their possession? These concerns were addressed in the case of *Mapp* v. *Ohio* (1961) and have established a doctrine commonly referred to as the **exclusionary rule.**

The Exclusionary Rule

Perhaps the major way limitation upon searches and seizures have come about has been the exclusionary rule. The exclusionary rule is founded in the Fourth Amendment of the Constitution. It is intended to assure that individuals are protected from any illegal searches and seizures. In practical terms, this means that the police must follow certain guidelines when searching for and seizing material as evidence.

Under this rule, evidence illegally obtained is excluded from the judicial process. Typi-

cally, this results when a motion to suppress the illegally seized evidence is granted by the court. In making such determinations, the courts consider the facts surrounding the identification or collection of evidence and whether the seizing of this evidence was lawful. Related to this, of course, are concerns about probable cause in cases of frisks (discussed below) and searches. The exclusionary rule long has been viewed as controversial since it is applied to a case *post factum* (after the fact). In other words, when the motion to suppress is requested, the justice system has already identified the suspect and located evidence that incriminates this suspect. When a judge grants a suppression motion, the illegally obtained materials may not be used against the defendant. Thus, without sufficient evidence, an apparently guilty murderer-rapist may walk out of the courtroom free, simply because the very evidence that indicates his guilt cannot be used against him. In fact, it can be suggested that the public outrage from such an instance has given rise to a dangerously increasing vigilante mentality. Many people have begun to take the law into their own hands, at least partially, because they fear the justice system is incapable of effectively punishing criminals.

For instance, in the highly publicized case of Bernhard Goetz, New York City's subway vigilante, he repeatedly told the press, "If you break the law you're a criminal, if you obey the law you're a victim. I'd rather be a criminal than a victim" (Associated Press 1987). Allegedly fearing for his personal safety and that his assailants would walk freely from any courtroom, Goetz shot four youths on December 22, 1984, when they allegedly tried to mug him on a New York City subway platform. Bernhard Goetz was subsequently acquitted of assault and manslaughter charges, but found guilty and sent to jail for unauthorized carrying of a firearm. It is as yet unclear what message has been sent to others regarding taking the law into one's own hand.

The exclusionary rule, of course, does serve an important role in the judicial process. The role concerns placing important restraints upon the authority of the police to intrude in the private lives of residents. Furthermore, if the police violate the laws of the land in order to obtain evidence against criminals, they have themselves become lawbreakers. The Supreme Court has suggested that when this occurs, it is *de facto* (in effect) the government that becomes the outlaw, and that such activities breed contempt for law (*Olmstead* v. *U.S.*, 1928). In effect, such contempt for the law on the part of police breeds the vigilante attitude evident in Bernhard Goetz' words and deeds. After all, if the police are above the law, why not the average resident? The obvious and ultimate extreme of this attitude, of course, is anarchy.

The application of the exclusionary rule has been one of the most controversial aspects of controls placed on the behavior of police officers. Its opponents argue that the exclusionary rule provides guilty persons with a technical loophole to gain their ill-deserved freedom. From this perspective, the safety of society is jeopardized and the basic principles of the justice system undermined. In contrast, proponents point to the exclusionary rule as among the most important cornerstones of

freedom. They maintain that it protects American citizens from becoming subjects in a police state where officers are willing to use any means to investigate a crime. Without the provisions of the exclusionary rule, homes could be broken into, phones arbitrarily tapped, individuals strip-searched, and cars stopped and impounded, all in the name of law enforcement. In many ways, the exclusionary rule stands as an important demarcation between democracy and totalitarian governments.

In spite of the necessity to maintain the rights of residents, the exclusionary rule is frequently attacked. In fact, during recent years, several exceptions to the exclusionary rule have emerged in the decisions of the Supreme Court. The **good faith exception** to the exclusion rule, for example, suggests that illegally obtained evidence should not be excluded if it can be shown that the evidence was obtained in good faith. What this really means is that officers in the performance of their duties believed that they were acting in accordance with the law when they obtained the evidence. Although both the American Bar Association and the American Civil Liberties Union oppose the widespread adoption of this doctrine, many states have nonetheless endorsed its use. In 1984, the Supreme Court adopted the good faith exception in its ruling in *Massachusetts* v. *Sheppard*. The Court held that when police conduct searches in good faith, even when the technical search warrant is defective, seized evidence will not be excluded from acceptability as evidence (See Wagner 1987).

Critics of the assault on the exclusionary rule suggest that these cases foretell a new era of weakening the rule in general (Misner 1986). There seems little question that the nation's courts are moving in the direction of granting police and other agencies greater leeway in their law enforcement practices. This is apparently true even if it means restricting the rights of criminal suspects and jeopardizing the rights of residents in general.

For instance, in 1984, the Supreme Court adopted the **inevitable discovery** exception to the exclusionary rule. The Court ruled in the case of *Nix* v. *Williams* that evidence the police may have obtained illegally, but that would eventually have arisen through legal means, may be admitted as valid evidence in court.

Briefly, the case involved Robert Anthony Williams and the murder of ten-year-old Pamela Powers. On Christmas Eve 1968 in Des Moines, Iowa, Powers was abducted and killed. From witnesses, the police managed to identify and arrest Williams in Davenport, 160 miles away. He was read his *Miranda* rights and escorted back to Des Moines by two police officers. These officers had agreed not to question or interrogate Williams during the trip back, and they did not.

Almost offhandedly, one of the officers remarked during the drive home about the sadness that the little girl's body would lie buried somewhere under the snow and that she deserved a Christian burial. Williams was touched with remorse at the officer's words and voluntarily led them to where the child's body could be found. By a vote of 5–4, the Supreme Court ruled that the officers' behavior had violated Williams's rights under the Fifth Amendment.

After two appeals of the case, the Supreme Court reversed in June 1984. The High Court concluded that search parties would eventually have found the little girl's body, even if Williams had said nothing. The Court had, in effect, incorporated the doctrine of inevitable discovery into the more common understandings of exclusion and *Miranda*.

The question that arises is how much will these various exceptions actually affect police practices and the justice system? Studies conducted by the National Institute of Justice and by scholarly researchers indicate that exclusionary rule violations occur very infrequently (Forst et al. 1977, Krantz et al. 1979, U.S. Department of Justice 1982). These studies indicate that only about one or two percent of all criminal cases were rejected because of technical errors related to the exclusionary rule. In fact, it is only in narcotics-related cases that any significant number of exclusionary-rule violations seem to arise. However, even in these cases the number of cases rejected by the courts remains less than three percent.

While expansions in the ability of police officers to work beyond the limits of the exclusionary rule may have little effect on the justice system, the rule itself is very important. The exclusionary rule offers a vital, symbolic expression of the basic protections guaranteed to all American citizens. In fact, its existence may be the explanation for why most police officers do not violate the right of privacy afforded to citizens.

Vehicle Searches

The question of scope during a lawful search following an arrest is again the focus of concern when considering automobiles. Discussion of the practices of searching vehicles is usually begun with consideration of *Carroll* v. *California* (1925). In this case, the Supreme Court established a clear distinction for searches of people, vehicles, and premises. Essentially, the Court held that a warrantless search of a vehicle was legitimate, provided the police had probable cause to believe the vehicle contained evidence or contraband. As with lawful searches in general, warrantless searches of automobiles have been a problematic procedural area for the police. For instance, while the *Carroll* case provided a doctrine for permitting police to search a vehicle, it did not specify the extent to which this search was permissible. If a vehicle was stopped, did the police have the right to inspect the trunk? What if a package were found in the trunk? Could the police lawfully open it for inspection? Could the police lift the rear bench-seat to search below it? Could they enter a locked glove compartment? Was it permissible to search passengers in the car?

Even with more recent cases, one finds procedural problems and confusion over the permissible scope of a search. For instance, in *Chambers* v. *Maroney* (1970), the High Court ruled warrantless searches of vehicles are lawful, since cars are movable and, once alerted, occupants of a vehicle could certainly destroy or conceal evidence. Yet, little attention is paid to the scope of the search in this ruling. Further clouding the waters were later cases, such as *Robbins* v. *California* (1981) and *United States* v. *Ross* (1982).

In the first case, a police officer observed a car weaving and driving erratically on a California highway. Upon stopping the vehicle, the officer smelled marijuana smoke as the car's door opened. A search of the vehicle located two wrapped packages. These packages were opened by the officer, inspected, and found to contain marijuana. The California Supreme Court, however, held that the opening of the sealed packages for inspection without a warrant exceeded the legitimate scope of the vehicular search.

In the second case, *United States* v. *Ross* (1982), scope of a vehicular search was finally addressed. The U.S. Supreme Court reversed the decision of a District of Columbia lower court concerning the warrantless search of a narcotics dealer's car trunk and later location of drugs therein.

In this case the police received a telephone tip (tips are discussed later in this chapter) from a reliable informant about a man known as Bandit selling narcotics from the trunk of his car (Katz 1983). The informant further indicated that he had just seen Bandit complete a drug deal and that he had been told by Bandit that more drugs remained in the car's trunk. The informant described Bandit, his car's location, and the vehicle itself. When the police arrived, they found the car, but no one matching Bandit's description. A computer check of the vehicle's license revealed that it was registered to a man named Albert Ross. Ross matched the physical description of Bandit given to the police by their informant.

The officers drove off to avoid alerting the suspect. When they returned, they observed the vehicle being driven from its parking spot. The officers ordered the driver to pull over and observed a man matching the description of Bandit. The officers searched Ross and observed a bullet on the front seat in the automobile. Upon searching the interior compartments of the car, they found a gun in the glove compartment. Ross was handcuffed and arrested. The officers next took Ross' car keys and opened the trunk. They found two containers. One was a closed but unsealed brown paper bag, and the other a zipped red leather pouch. In the paper bag, the officers found glassine envelopes containing a white powder, later determined to be heroin. The leather pouch was left undisturbed. The paper bag was replaced in the trunk and the vehicle transported to police headquarters (Katz 1983).

At trial, Ross' motions to suppress the heroin discovery were denied, and he was convicted of possession of heroin with intent to distribute. The Court of Appeals for the District of Columbia heard the Ross case twice, but did not reverse the findings of the lower court.

When the case reached the U.S. Supreme Court, the Court ruled that police officers who have legitimately stopped an automobile and who have probable cause to believe that contraband is concealed somewhere within it " . . . may conduct a search of the vehicle that is as thorough as a magistrate could authorize in a warrant particularly describing the place to be searched." The automobile exception established by *Ross* now stands as a general exception to the search warrant requirement for vehicles. It has been suggested that the widening of automobile exceptions to the Fourth Amendment limitations on privacy intrusions have been in the name of law enforcement expedience. But the Supreme Court defends against such claims by stating that the Fourth Amendment guarantee against unreasonable searches and sei-

Box 7.4

New York v. *Class*: Searching for Elephants in Glove Compartments

The question of whether police officers making routine traffic stops can justifiably search the glove compartment of the vehicle (without a warrant) touches upon important Fourth Amendment rights to privacy. Whether the officer's need to intrude outweighs the resident's expectation of privacy are usually the key issues in these controversies. The case of *New York* v. *Class* (1986) provides an opportunity to examine this issue in detail.

In the *Class* case, two New York city police officers, Lawrence Meyer and William McNamee, observed a 1972 Dodge driven by Class exceeding the speed limit by ten miles an hour and having a broken windshield. Meyer and McNamee, driving in an unmarked police car, turned on their lights and siren and ordered Class to stop, which he did. After stopping, Class got out of his car and approached Officer Meyer. He offered the officer the vehicle's registration certificate and proof of insurance. Meyer then learned that Class was unlicensed.

At the same time, Officer McNamee (who had neither seen the automobile documents nor learned of Class' unlicensed status) went to the vehicle to inspect the car's vehicle identification number (VIN). He first opened the driver-side door, since this is where the VIN is often placed on older vehicles. When he found no VIN, and while still outside the vehicle, he looked at the left-hand corner of the front windshield. In many vehicles made after 1969, the VIN is located on the dashboard and visible from outside the car. Still unable to locate the VIN because papers on the dashboard obscured his view, McNamee entered the vehicle to move the papers he believed could be covering the VIN plate.

Once inside the vehicle, however, Officer McNamee observed the handle of a .22-caliber pistol protruding from beneath the seat. The officer seized the weapon, and Class was arrested for possession of the gun. He was issued summonses for driving without a license and for driving a vehicle with a broken windshield. A search of Class additionally found he was in possession of .22-caliber ammunition.

At trial, Class moved to suppress the finding of the gun, but was denied the motion. Justice William Holland of the Bronx Supreme Court ruled that the search for the VIN had been reasonable and that McNamee's intrusion into the vehicle was justified, notwithstanding any lack of probable cause to believe the car had been stolen because the defendant's conduct (exiting the car and approaching the officer and his being unlicensed) made the officer's actions quite reasonable. Class was convicted of the weapons charge and was sentenced to a period of probation not to exceed five years.

On appeal, a four-justice majority of the appellate division affirmed the conviction without opinion. The New York Court of Appeals, however, concluded that the police intrusion was without adequate objective justification and reversed the decision (*People* v. *Class*, 1984). Writing for the court, Judge Kaye noted that one does not have a legitimate expectation of privacy in locations observable by a passerby. But, there are locations inside the car, including the area beneath the seat, "which cannot be viewed from the outside and which an individual legitimately expects will remain private."

The case reached the U.S. Supreme Court, where the Court reinstated the guilty verdict 7–2. In its ruling, the Court indicated that because of its physical characteristics, transportation function, and pervasive regulation, the automobile has been traditionally viewed as possessing a lesser degree of privacy than a private home. The Court also acknowledged that a "car's interior as a whole" is subject to the some degree of Fourth Amendment protection. But, in the situation presented in *Class*, if he stayed in his car and acceded to a request to remove the paper obstructing the VIN plate, Officer McNamee "would not have needed to intrude into the passenger compartment."

The Court further explained the dilemma confronting Officer McNamee. On the one hand, if he allowed the defendant Class to return to the car to remove the obstructing papers, Class could have reached the pistol under the seat (or any other potentially hidden weapon) and caused injury to the officers. On the other hand, and as the officers did act, McNamee could continue to detain Class outside the vehicle and move the papers himself without fear of potential risk.

From this, Justice O'Connor noted that warrantless searches were permissible in certain law enforcement contexts, in spite of their substantial intrusiveness. Under the doctrine derived from *Terry v. Ohio* (1968), the constitutionality of a warrantless search is to be judged by balancing the need to search against the intrusion the search entails. Three important factors existed to justify McNamee's search. First, the safety of the officers was served by the intrusion. Second, the intrusion was kept to a minimum, and third, the search stemmed from at least some probable cause created by suspicious behaviors on the part of the individual affected by the search, namely Class. When weighed against the governmental interests, Class' own reasonable expectation of privacy was simply not as compelling. This is particularly true, since there is no reasonable expectation of privacy concerning the VIN plate and since Class had committed two traffic violations.

---

zures mandates "that searches conducted outside the judicial process, without prior approval by judge or magistrate, are per se unreasonable . . . " (Katz 1983, 185).

It is important to note the manner in which the *Ross* ruling addresses the scope of a search. First, it does provide that when an officer has probable cause to search an automobile, he or she may do so without a warrant in every part of the vehicle where the contraband could be concealed. This includes containers and packages wherein the contraband or evidence could conceivably be hidden. One cannot irresponsibly search places in the vehicle where the suspected contraband simply could not be. This has given rise to the rule of thumb that officers may not search glove compartments if they are looking for an elephant. In other words, it would be impossible to conceal an elephant in the small confines of a glove compartment. Consequently, the officer has no authority—without a warrant—to examine those areas of the vehicle where the contraband or evidence could not conceivably be concealed.

Recently, however, even this maxim of not seeking elephants in glove compartments has come into question in the case of *New York* v. *Class* (1986). In this situation, a New York city police officer entered the vehicle he and his partner had stopped for a traffic violation. The full details of the case are described in Box 7.4. In brief, one of the officers, while looking for the vehicle's identification number, found a gun, and the driver of the car was arrested. The case eventually reached the Supreme Court, where the officer's actions were ruled necessarily intrusive and justifiable under the circumstances (See Box 7.4).

Putting aside for a moment the actual case of *Class*, the actions of the Supreme Court suggest several important implications for law enforcement. First, the ruling expands usual understandings of the Fourth Amendment exception for automobiles. In effect, the Court may have opened a door through which police officers can be granted *carte blanche* to search automobiles they have lawfully stopped (Maclin 1987, 19ff). For example, could a police officer open a glove compartment in order to look for a vehicle registration certificate or proof of insurance? How about when a lawfully conducted roadblock has been set up? Can the officers involved willfully open the car door or the car's hood in order to look for the vehicle identification numbers or to check that engine heads match the dashboard's numbers? If, in the course of these activities, the officer happens to observe contraband, is its seizure legal? Naturally, no single Supreme Court decision answers all questions that arise. But, it remains important to think about some of the implications that may yet surface from this particular ruling. As Kilpatrick (1986) indicates, it is important to recognize that Supreme Court decisions are not intended to make police (or public) policy. Indeed, it should be readily apparent that while Supreme Court decisions may provide vague guidelines for officers' performing warrantless searches, there are really no explicit rules.

Most law enforcement agencies do provide their officers with ad hoc or departmental limits on conducting searches. But, it is certainly conceivable that an overzealous police officer will exceed the scope of a lawful search, particularly with regard to an automobile. The two central reasons for this, of course, are the mobility of cars and the potential risk for the officer.

Stop and Frisk

The vagueness associated with rules for searching vehicles also directs us to a more general concern and exception to the laws requiring warrants, frisking a suspect. At this juncture it would be useful to consider how stopping and frisking suspects may also intrude upon the privacy of residents.

The questioning of a suspect or potential suspect on the street does not necessarily occur exclusively during an arrest situation. In fact, simply stopping a suspicious-looking person and questioning him or her is likely to happen fairly frequently without ending in an arrest. Similarly, in the course of a lawful traffic stop, when an officer is given reason to feel suspicious about the driver of a car, this officer may pat down the driver.

Usually, the police are not required to have sufficient evidence or probable cause for an arrest when they merely stop people to question them briefly. Sometimes questioning will lead to the required probable cause to arrest the individual or someone else.

Hypothetically, if police officers could only stop and question those persons they were arresting, serious problems could arise. For example, an extraordinary number of people might find themselves being placed under arrest. Or, conversely, the police might find it so difficult to obtain necessary information that many dangerous felons might never be brought to justice. In either situation, the usefulness of being permitted simply to stop and question people should be clear.

Connected with the police officer's ability to stop and question people on the street is the necessity to do so safely. As a result, there is the further need for authorization to frisk suspects.

Most frisking is conducted quite casually and involves patting down the outer garments of a suspect with the palms of one's hands. This patting down is usually undertaken to search for weapons. Although one might technically assume that police officers should frisk an individual only when the officer has reason to fear for his or her safety, such an assumption is extremely naive.

Usually, when an officer stops someone for questioning, it is because something about the individual has provoked suspicions or the individual may be believed to be in possession of certain bits of information relevant to a case, or because the officer has observed or been notified of a violation of law. Certainly, then, what is unknown about the individual being stopped may mean that a frisk for safety reasons is advisable. The appearance of the suspect should not override the need to frisk. A tragic illustration of this need is offered by a recent shooting of two Boston police officers and the eventual death of one from his wounds.

It was 1:10 A.M. Friday, October 2, 1987 when two police cruisers responded to a radio call about a woman screaming. The screams, it would be later learned, were part of a domestic quarrel unrelated to what happened to patrolmen Roy Sergei, Jorges Torres, and their respective partners.

When the officers arrived, Sergei and his partner went to the front of the building, while Torres and his partner moved to the building's rear (Stewart and Feeney 1987). Torres and his partner, Chris Rogers, were first to observe a small man scaling a fence. The officers ordered him down and placed him against the building's wall with his hands raised. As they were about to frisk him, the man reached into his coat pocket and fired a shot through his coat that missed Rogers, but wounded Torres. He fired several more shots that also missed Rogers, before turning to again shoot Torres. The suspect then fled up the alley toward the street and the front of the building where he was confronted by Sergei and his partner, William Kennedy. The suspect fired three times, striking Sergei with each shot. Kennedy fired several rounds at the gunman as he ran down the street.

A nationwide search for a suspect, Ted Jeffrey Otsuki, was undertaken and a reward of $25,000 established by the Boston Police Patrolmen's Association. It was not until almost a year later, in the fall of 1988, that Ted Jeffrey Otsuki was arrested and charged with homicide. On October 27, 1987 Officer Roy Sergei died as a result of complications from his wounds that led to a heart attack.

The delicate balance between the rights and liberties of citizens and the government's need to abridge these constitutional guarantees is tested daily in the course of police work. Among the most often cited doctrines connected with appropriately maintaining this balance is the case of *Terry* v. *Ohio* (1968).

In this case a Cleveland detective, Martin McFadden, observed John Terry and another man, Richard Chilton, standing on a streetcorner. McFadden watched as they walked back and forth along a strip of the block and paused each time to look inside the same store's window. Following each promenade past the store window, the men stood on the corner and chatted. McFadden grew suspicious and suspected that they were casing the store for a burglary. Suddenly, a third man, Katz, appeared but left almost immediately. Detective McFadden followed Terry and Chilton as they walked several blocks and again met up with Katz.

McFadden approached the three men, identified himself as a police officer, and asked their names. The men mumbled something fairly inaudibly, which led the officer to spin Terry around and pat him down. Keeping his frisk to the outer garments, McFadden detected a gun in the pocket of Terry's overcoat, but was unable to remove it. He ordered all three men to face a wall with their hands raised over their heads, and removed the gun. McFadden next proceeded to frisk each man,

which resulted in the seizing of another revolver from the pocket of Chilton. No weapon was found on Katz.

Terry and Chilton were each charged with carrying concealed weapons, but the defense moved for a suppression of the evidence of the weapons. While the trial court did not accept the prosecution's claim that the guns had been seized incident to a lawful arrest, it did permit the guns as evidence. The court justified the inclusion of these guns as evidence by indicating that while the officer did have probable cause to be suspicious of these men given their behavior, he did not have probable cause to make an arrest. However, given his suspicions, McFadden was justified in frisking these men for his own protection, since he had probable cause to believe they might be armed.

In effect, the *Terry* case established a distinction between an investigative stop for questioning and an arrest. The case also distinguished between a frisk of outer clothes (for the protection of the officer) and an intensive search for evidence. The defendants Terry and Chilton were found guilty. The case was appealed and was subsequently heard by the Supreme Court, which upheld the convictions.

Voluntary-Consent Searches

Warrantless searches may also be lawfully undertaken if the party in immediate control of an area gives **voluntary consent.** In effect, when one consents to allow the police to search one's premises or person, one waives one's constitutional rights under the Fourth Amendment. Again, because the restrictions on police behavior are established to assure the safety and privacy of the average innocent citizen, there are limitations.

The question of consent, of course, remains questionable. For example, imagine being a marijuana farmer several miles from the nearest town or city when a knock comes at your door. You open the door and are confronted by ten or twelve law enforcement agents brandishing badges and pointing their guns at you. Now assume the officers have sufficient probable cause to arrest you: They know you own the land, and they have observed sixty acres of marijuana growing between your corn stalks. For the officers to lawfully search your home a quarter of a mile from the fields still requires a warrant—or consent. A large, unfriendly officer asks, "May we come in and look around?" The likelihood is you will not say, "Excuse me, but no, I'd really rather you did not." Thus, the question of exactly how voluntary the consent may have been can be raised.

In most cases, courts are reluctant to accept the uncorroborated word of an officer who maintains that a voluntary waiver has been obtained. As a result, individuals who do waive their rights may be asked to verbalize consent in the presence of several officers as witnesses or to first sign statements indicating they have consented to the searches without warrants. Similarly, courts may view voluntary consents to search as legitimate, provided that the individual has been informed of the prerogative to refuse consent. But, even with these restrictions, and as illustrated in the above example, voluntary consent could be obtained through duress and later may be challenged in court.

The Open Field Doctrine

Related to the searches of private property are the **open field** and **abandoned property** doctrines. Both provide exceptions to the requirement of a search warrant. For the most part, the singular controversy has been at what point the yard ends and the open field begins. In other words, where domiciles protected from unreasonable searches assured by the Fourth Amendment end and open fields begin (Albanese 1988).

The open field doctrine was established in the case of *Hester* v. *United States* (1924). The case involved an investigation by ATF officers who suspected that Hester was manufacturing alcohol illegally in his home. When

Hester realized that the officers were approaching his house, he and a confederate fled across a field adjacent to the house—both carrying bottles. The two men were pursued by federal officers, one of whom fired his weapon. Hester and his associate dropped the bottles they were carrying, which were later found to contain illegally produced liquor. The officers, who did not have any search warrants, arrested Hester and his companion, who were later convicted.

On appeal, the conviction of the two men was overturned on the grounds that the officers had made an illegal search and seizure. Eventually, the case reached the U.S. Supreme Court, which reversed the appeal decision and reinstated the conviction. In its decision the High Court stated:

> The defendant's own acts, and those of his associates, disclosed the jug, the jar, and the bottle—and there was no seizure in the sense of the law when the officers examined the contents of each after it had been abandoned . . . the special protection accorded by the Fourth Amendment to the people in their "persons, houses, papers and effects," is not extended to the open fields. The distinction between the latter and the house is as old as the common law.

Since this Supreme Court decision, the definition for what constitutes a house or domicile and where the property legally viewed as a portion of this domicile ends has been fairly well established. Stated simply, all of the area and buildings in that area commonly used by the persons dwelling there are considered part of the domicile's curtilage. The protection of the Fourth Amendment assured to a person in his home, therefore, extends to this curtilage as well.

The 1984 case of *Oliver* v. *United States* illustrates both the concept of yard, or curtilage, and the general understanding its limits. In the *Oliver* case, two narcotics agents with the Kentucky State Police went to Oliver's farm to investigate allegations that marijuana was being grown. When they arrived, the officers drove past Oliver's house to a locked gate with a "no trespassing" sign on it. A small footpath visible to the officers led around one side of the gate. The officers walked around the gate and down a road for several hundred yards. The two officers passed a barn and a parked camper truck. At about this point, someone stepped out from behind the camper and shouted, "No hunting is allowed, come back here." The officers identified themselves as Kentucky state police and moved toward the camper. When they arrived no one was there. The officers renewed their investigation of the property and soon located a field of marijuana about a mile from Oliver's house. Oliver was subsequently arrested for manufacturing a controlled dangerous substance.

Later, during the trial, it was brought out that the officers had searched the property without a search warrant, and Oliver was not convicted. The Court of Appeals reversed the decision, and the U.S. Supreme Court accepted a petition to hear the case and upheld the conviction.

The High Court ruled, "The rule of *Hester* v. *United States,* that we reaffirm today, may be understood as providing that an individual may not legitimately demand privacy for activities conducted out of doors in fields except in the area immediately surrounding the home." The Court, therefore, found the two officers' search of the property lawful—even in the absence of a warrant. As the Court expressed it, "It is not generally true that fences or no trespassing signs effectively bar the public from viewing open fields in rural areas" (*Oliver* v. *United States,* 1984).

Informers and Probable Cause

Another controversial area in the establishment of probable cause and its use to obtain warrants is the use of tipsters or informers. Many crimes would never be solved were it not for some informer tipping the police about some clandestine meeting, planned murder, or the like.

Some informers are solid citizens who have stumbled across relevant information and

turned it over to the police. More often than not, however, tips come from disgruntled girlfriends or employees of underworld figures. As a result, many informers have lengthy criminal histories. Because of this, informers may sometimes provide information to police, but remain anonymous. The question of whether the police can actively pursue a case and make arrests strictly on the basis of anonymous tips has recently drawn considerable fire.

The events surrounding the Supreme Court case of *Illinois* v. *Gates* (1983) are as follows. The police received a letter from an anonymous sender. The letter detailed information about a husband and wife alleged to be involved in illegal drug sales and smuggling. The letter also indicated that on a specific date, the wife would drive the family car, loaded with drugs, to Florida. The letter indicated that her husband would fly to Florida and meet her. The letter also stated that approximately $100,000-worth of drugs were already stored in the couple's basement in their Illinois home.

After receiving the letter, the police placed the couple under surveillance as they made their respective trips to Florida. The couple was observed as they met in Florida, checked into a hotel, and began their drive north the next morning on a highway frequently used by travelers to Illinois.

Equipped with these facts, the police secured a search warrant for the Illinois residence and the couple's car. When the couple drove into the driveway of their home, the police were waiting. Upon searching the house and car, the police found drugs they later attempted to use as evidence against the couple. The attorney for Mr. and Mrs. Gates was successful at suppressing this evidence at their trial, resulting in their acquittal. Later, on appeal by the state, the Illinois Supreme Court upheld the lower court's decision. But, the U.S. Supreme Court was not as easily convinced that the constitutional rights of the Gateses had been violated. The Supreme Court established a new test, commonly referred to as the **totality of circumstances test.** The Court ruled that in the *Gates* case, independent police verification of the anonymous allegations provided sufficient information on which a magistrate could have probable cause to issue warrants.

The Supreme Court's *Gates* case is extremely important. The police frequently receive anonymous tips about criminal activity. Although these tips continue to represent leads and not probable cause in themselves, information collected as a result of these tips now can be clearly used to develop probable cause. The establishment of probable cause is obviously an important restriction with regard to arrest, as well as for the preservation of personal liberties. The various confusions and ambiguities commonly associated with establishing probable cause, in fact, have not entirely been resolved by the *Gates* case.

Before the Supreme Court's ruling in *Gates*, most jurisdictions employed doctrines of probable cause based upon two earlier cases. These cases are *Spinelli* v. *United States* (1969) and *Aguilar* v. *Texas* (1964). In the first case, *Spinelli* (1969), the Supreme Court had ruled that evidence needed to be corroborated if it was to serve as the basis for probable cause sufficient for issuance of a warrant. Importantly, the corroboration did not necessarily have to be independent of an informer, provided that the informer had personal knowledge of the facts of the crime and had previously supplied reliable and truthful information.

In the earlier case of *Aguilar* v. *Texas* (1964), the High Court had established a two-part test of credibility with regard to hearsay evidence (first-hand information provided by a party other than a participant in the crime). First, the police were obligated to show *why* they believed the informant's information. Second, the circumstances by which the informant came to have personal knowledge of a crime had to be investigated.

The *Gates* case offered a new, less restrictive test of probable cause and has likely per-

mitted many officers to obtain search and arrest warrants. Nonetheless, some states continue to employ the older, more specific doctrines of the *Spinelli* and *Aguilar* cases. For instance, the Supreme Court of the Commonwealth of Massachusetts recently ruled that the *Gates* case was unacceptably shapeless and permissive and consequently lacked necessary precision. Instead, the court employed the older *Aguilar* and *Spinelli* doctrines when it decided it was improper for a police officer's use of a telephone tip as probable cause to obtain a warrant (*Commonwealth* v. *Upton*, 1985).

The importance of establishing probable cause has long been a necessary element in the lawful pursuit of searches and seizures. But the role played by police officers continues to be controversial. The laws and Supreme Court decisions regarding lawful search and seizures have unmistakably moved in the direction of increased acceptance of police decision-making, whether more neutral magistrates have issued warrants or not (Atkinson 1985).

There are additionally several other relevant restrictions on a police officer's ability to make lawful arrests. Among these, several important factors are jurisdictions and special conditions of immunity from arrest.

POLICE JURISDICTION

In addition to certain legal and constitutional conditions related to lawful arrests, there are necessary procedural restrictions as well. One central issue related to procedure is the question of whether an officer possesses the jurisdictional authority to conduct the arrest. In most states, the territorial jurisdiction of the municipal police is confined to the city limits. Territorial limits of the sheriff are usually restricted to the county, parish, or unincorporated sections up to the city limits. Officers who have been granted state police powers find themselves restricted only by the limits of the state borders. Courtesy dictates, however, that state officers notify the local jurisdictional agency whenever possible before beginning any operation in the area.

If the officer exceeds his or her territory of jurisdiction, the arrest may be ruled unlawful. Any evidence collected in association with the arrest will be ruled inadmissible in court. The limitations imposed by territorial jurisdictions have not been without some problems.

Hot Pursuit

When the West was wild and woolly, it was generally accepted that if an outlaw could outrun a pursuing sheriff to the county line, he would escape arrest. The reasoning, of course, was that the pursuing sheriff's authority to make lawful arrests stopped at the county line. In an effort to prevent the escape of fleeing outlaws, the **hot pursuit** rule evolved. Loosely interpreted, the rule of hot pursuit assures that if an officer is in "hot" or "fresh" pursuit of an outlaw, the officer can chase this offender, even into another jurisdiction, to make a lawful arrest.

Exactly what was meant by hot pursuit was given to interpretation. Customarily, hot pursuit came to mean that an officer had managed to keep the outlaw in sight or, at minimum, could see the dust kicked up by the offender's horse. With the advance of paved roads and the automobile, some necessary modifications to this interpretation were in order. Today, the usual understanding of hot pursuit is that the officer has been chasing the felon continuously and with no interruptions. Burt Reynolds' highly successful "Smoky and the Bandit" films of the late 1970s capitalized on this idea of hot pursuit. Jackie Gleason, who portrayed the southern sheriff chasing Reynolds (the Bandit) across one state line to the next, repeatedly shouted from behind his "Billy-Bob," mirrored sunglasses, "Get out of my way, I'm in hot pursuit."

Originally, even the policy of hot pursuit did not authorize police officers to cross state lines to apprehend fleeing criminals. It is only during the past several decades, in the face of increased automotive technology and speed, that rules and regulations have been modified. Among these regulatory advances is the "Uniform Act of Fresh Pursuit." According to Stuckey (1986, 44), "This act provides that a peace officer of one state may enter another state in fresh pursuit to arrest one who has committed a felony in the state from which the offender fled." Several states extended this act to include certain misdemeanors related to violations of acceptable morals, codes, and honesty.

The Uniform Fresh Pursuit Act does not articulate any specific limitation on the distance a pursuing officer may roam out of jurisdiction in order to effect the arrest. The convention, however, has been to keep both the duration of time out of one's own jurisdiction and geographic distance to a minimum. In other words, unlike the movies, pursuing officers, when unable to capture the felon expediently, are expected to discontinue the pursuit. In some cases, pursuing officers may turn over the pursuit to officers in the new jurisdiction.

The Uniform Fresh Pursuit Act also provides that an officer making an out-of-jurisdiction arrest must take the offender before a local magistrate immediately after taking the lawbreaker into custody. The hearing before a magistrate is intended to assure that the arrest was lawfully made. If the magistrate rules that the arrest was unlawful, the accused is released. If the magistrate rules that the arrest was legitimate and lawful, the magistrate may commit the offender, pending extradition (legal transference of the felon to the jurisdiction where the initial crime occurred). As with any criminal detention, the magistrate may consider the request for release on bail (to be discussed in Chapter Eight) until extradition proceedings are undertaken. Obviously, the nature of the crime and any available pertinent information about the accused will be weighed by the magistrate before deciding on bail.

Mutual Aid

In a number of larger cities and in states where many small counties cluster together, local law enforcement agencies develop policies of mutual aid. For example, in Boston, where approximately twenty-six separate municipal police agencies operate within various restricted partitioning, it is common for officers from one agency to offer assistance to officers from another as they dash into and out of the various jurisdictions. Similarly, when a state police officer is in hot pursuit of an offender on the interstate highway, he or she may request assistance from a local city police cruiser that may happen along, although the highway may not fall under the city officer's jurisdiction.

Limited Arrest Powers

In some jurisdictions, peace officers have been granted limited official police powers. In Florida, for example, the state university system is policed by officers with limited state police warrant. This means that while on university property during a tour of duty, the officer possesses full police power. Off-campus and during off-duty periods, these officers technically possess only civilian authority. Yet, in the spirit of mutual aid, if a lawbreaker commits a crime on campus property and flees off campus, these officers typically are permitted to pursue and effect a lawful arrest.

Another sort of limited police jurisdiction accompanies the status of special police officer. Governors in several states, including New York, can warrant an individual with limited police powers through award of the status of special police officer. Typically these individuals work in the private sector as store detectives. As with the state university campus police in Florida, special police officers are restricted in their authority. Their police authority is limited to the premises of the stores and hours of their shifts.

In some jurisdictions, store detectives and college campus police are afforded police authority through deputization. The right to deputize derives from the *posse comitatus* right of the sheriff. In Anglo-Saxon England, the shire-reeves possessed the right of posse comitatus, which allowed them to summon able-bodied men to assist in the duties of the shire-reeve. In the early American West, this right allowed the sheriff to organize posses to chase outlaws. In several western states today, shopping mall security guards are granted limited police powers through deputization and are also active members of the local jurisdiction's posse.

While derived from essentially the same root, deputization and membership in a posse today are not always synonymous. Powers vested by the posse comitatus usually are more temporary than those afforded by deputization.

Immunity from Arrest

Under several circumstances, certain categories of persons are immune from arrest because of statutory regulations. For the most part, these categories are restricted to representatives of foreign governments, but may additionally include American legislators and state or federal witnesses in exceptional situations. Immunity from prosecution has become a popular plot device on many television police programs. On television, some ambassador or consul commits a rape or murder or is shown smuggling drugs into the country. When they are found out, they hide behind their diplomatic immunity. But, what is **diplomatic immunity?**

Diplomatic Immunity. In an effort to offer both the symbolic olive branch of peace and to ensure the effective performance of their diplomatic missions, official representatives of foreign countries are granted immunity from arrest and prosecution. The provision of diplomatic immunity is governed by international law as well as various treaties and agreements between the United States and other sovereign nations. Although not all foreign dignitaries enjoy blanket immunity from arrest, some diplomats do. Foreign ambassadors, ministers, their assistants, and attachés, for instance, possess unlimited immunity from arrest, detention, and prosecution. For the most part, this diplomatic immunity extends to include the family members of each of these foreign delegates as well.

While diplomatic immunity offers foreign representatives a considerable amount of freedom, it is not intended as a license to ignore American law. In fact, most diplomats are instructed by their governments that it is their duty to respect the laws of their host country. With perhaps the exception for espionage, members of foreign diplomatic corps avoid petty conflicts that could become internationally embarrassing. When foreign representatives do commit law violations, their offense is directed to the U.S. Department of State. If the crime is serious, and again with the exception for espionage, the home country will be asked to recall the diplomat.

Legislative Immunity. In several instances, American citizens may also be granted immunity from arrest and prosecution. Members of state legislatures, for example, are frequently granted a limited immunity. This immunity traditionally pertains only when the legislature is in session and is designed to permit representation of the legislator's constituents in a democratic society. In this case, immunity is offered only as it relates to arrests arising from some civil matter related to legislative activities. Typically, state legislators are not granted immunity from criminal actions brought against them.

Witness Immunity. Under certain circumstances, federal courts find it necessary to grant immunity to witnesses in important criminal cases. When this occurs, the courts can invoke the Uniform Act to Secure the Attendance of Witnesses from without the State. According to Stuckey (1986, 51):

> This act provides that if a person goes into a state in obedience of a subpoena to testify in that state, he shall not be subject to arrest in connection with any crime committed in the state prior to his entrance into the state to testify.

In many ways, this immunity may be understood as a moratorium rather than a comprehensive and permanent exemption from arrest and prosecution. After offering testimony, the witness is usually allowed a reasonable amount of time to exit the state without fear of arrest. If the witness returns or lingers too long, an arrest and prosecution can be lawfully made. In addition, witnesses protected under this act are not excused from arrest or prosecution for any new crimes they might commit while in the state awaiting their appearance as witnesses.

Although certainly a controversial issue with the Justice Department, the granting of this immunity is sometimes necessary. Often, law enforcement and prosecuting attorneys must weigh potential losses against potential gains when prosecuting major criminal cases. If officers of the court determine prosecution of some crime figure is more important than immediate prosecution of the witness and that the witness could improve their chances of conviction, their decision seems clear. Realistically, there are also occasions when in exchange for strong testimony, a state's prosecutor will grant full immunity from prosecution to a witness for all cases that arise prior to the offering of his or her testimony. Occasionally this will include immunity from prosecution from any involvement in the case at hand as well.

SUMMARY

The chapter began with a brief re-examination of the social and law enforcement role of the peace officer. Included in this exploration was a consideration of the nature of arrest (both by civilians and sworn officers), constitutional concerns regarding advising of rights (*Miranda*), probable cause, and exclusion of evidence for violations of law or citizen's rights, police jurisdictional limits, limited policing powers, and immunity from arrest.

Throughout the discussion of these various restrictions and limitations on the authority of police officers, an attempt was made to express the necessity for preserving constitutionally guaranteed rights, including those of the accused. Plato's concept of temperance seems to best capture the essence of what the Constitution and Supreme Court decisions do for the American style of policing.

The purpose of this version of temperance is not to provide avenues of escape for guilty parties. Rather, the intended purpose for preserving constitutional rights is to protect those who may be wrongfully accused of a criminal offense.

REVIEW QUESTIONS

1. What are the major reasons for restricting a police officer's ability to search people and their homes? How is the case of *Terry v. Ohio* (1968) involved in this question?

2. What are the intentions of the *Miranda* warning, and what are its components?

3. What does the phrase "searching for elephants in glove compartments" have to do with constitutional regulations on search and seizure?

4. How can informants be both an asset and a liability to law enforcement investigations?

5. What are some of the essential elements in a lawful hot pursuit? Why must these guidelines be followed by police officers?

REFERENCES

ABC. "Getting Tough." An ABC "Chronicle" special. Nov. 22, 1987.

Albanese, Jay S. *The Police Officer's Dilemma: Balancing Peace, Order and Individual Rights.* Buffalo, N.Y.: Great Ideas Publishing, 1988.

Associated Press. "Goetz Says He'd Rather Be Criminal than Victim." *The Boston Globe.* (Oct. 21, 1987):11.

Atkinson, David, N. "The Supreme Court and the Police: Constitutional Searches and Seizures." In Abraham S. Blumberg and Elaine Niederhoffer, eds. *The Ambivalent Force.* New York: Holt Rinehart and Winston, 1985.

Berg, Bruce L. "Private Medical Care in the Correctional Setting: The Case of Florida." *International Journal of Offender Therapy and Comparative Criminology* 31(1987):21–30.

Berg, Bruce L. and Jill P. Berg "AIDS in Prison: The Social Construction of a Reality." *International Journal of Offender Therapy and Comparative Criminology* 32(1988):17–22.

Bureau of Justice Statistics. "Report to the Nation on Crime and Justice: The Data." Washington, D.C.: U.S. Government Printing Office, 1983.

Chang, Dae H. and James A. Fagin. *Introduction to Criminal Justice: Theory and Application.* Geneva, Ill.: Paladin, 1985.

Chute, Charles L. and Majorie Bell. *Crime, Courts and Probation.* New York: Macmillan, 1956.

Forst, Brian, Judith Lucianovic, and Sarah Cox. *What Happens After Arrest.* Washington, D.C.: Inslaw, 1977.

Galvin, James. "Setting Prison Terms." Bureau of Statistics. Washington, D.C.: U.S. Government Printing Office, 1983.

Katz, Lewis R. "*United States v. Ross*: Evolving Standards for Warrantless Searches." *The Journal of Criminal Law and Criminology* 74(1983):172–196.

Kilpatrick, James J. "*Miranda v. Arizona*: Twenty Years Have Not Improved It." *Criminal Justice Ethics* 5(1986):2, 59–60.

Krantz, Sheldon, Bernard Gilman, Charles Benda, Carol Rogoff Halst, and Gail Nadworny. *Police Policymaking.* Lexington, Mass.: Lexington, 1979.

Maclin, Tracey. "*New York* v. *Class*: A Little-Noticed Case with Disturbing Implications." *The Journal of Criminal Law and Criminology* 78(1987): 1–86.

Misner Robert. "Limiting Leon: A Mistake of Law Analogy." *Journal of Criminal Law and Criminology* 77(1986):507–545.

Neubauer, David W. *America's Courts and the Criminal Justice System,* 2d ed. Monterey, Calif.: Brooks Cole, 1985.

Powers, Edwin. *The Basic Structure of the Administration of Criminal Justice in Massachusetts.* Boston: Massachusetts Correctional Association, 1973.

Stewart, Richard H., and Paul Feeney. "Police Look to Vests in Wake of Shooting." *Boston Globe* (Oct. 3, 1987):1, 19.

Stuckey, Gilbert B. *Procedures in the Justice System,* 3d ed. Columbus, Ohio: Merrill, 1986.

U.S. Department of Justice. *The Efforts of the Exclusionary Rule: A Study in California.* Washington D.C.: U.S. Government Printing Office, 1982.

Wagner, Allen E. "The Good Faith Exception to the Exclusionary Rule: Some Implications for the Police." *Journal of Criminal Justice* 15(1987): 75–85.

Ward, Michael, Richard Ayres, David W. Hess, Mark Schantz, and Charles H. Whitebread II. "Interrogations in New Haven: The Impact of *Miranda.*" *Yale Law Journal* 76(1967):1530–1538.

Wasby, Stephen L. *The Impact of the United States Court: Some Perspectives.* Homeward, Ill.: Dorsey, 1970.

CASES CITED IN TEXT

Apodaca v. Oregon, 406 U.S. 404 (1972).
Aguilar v. Texas, 378 U.S. 108 (1964).
Ballew v. Georgia, 435 U.S. 223 (1978).
California v. Prysock, 453 U.S. 355, 101 S. Ct. 2806, 69 L.Ed 2d. 696 (1981).
California v. Stewart, 384 U.S. 436 (1966).
Carroll v. U.S., 267 U.S. 132 (1925).
Chambers v. Maroney, 399 U.S. 42,51 (1970).
Colorado v. Spring, 107 S. Ct. 851 (1987).
Commonwealth v. Upton, 363, 476 NE 2d 548 (1985)
Hester v. United States, 44 S.Ct. 445 (1924)
Illinois v. Gates, 462 U.S. 213 (1983).
Johnson v. Louisiana, 406 U.S. 356 (1972).
Mapp v. Ohio, 395 U.S. 643, 644 (1961).
Massachusetts v. Sheppard, 104 S.Ct. 3424 (1984).
Miranda v. Arizona, 384 U.S. 436, 86 S.Ct. 1602, 16 L.Ed. 2d 694 (1966).

Moran v. Burbine, 54 U.S.L.W. 4265 (1985); 106 S. Ct. 1135 (1986).
New York v. Class, 106 S. Ct. 960 (1986).
New York v. Quarles, 467 U.S. 649 (1984).
Nix v. Williams, 104 S.Ct. 250 (1984).
Oliver v. United States, 104 S.Ct. 1735 (1984).
Olmstead v. U.S. 277 U.S. 438, 485 (1928), Justice Brandeis, dissenting.
People v. Class, 63 N.Y. 2d 491, 472 NE 2d 1009, 483 N.Y.S. 2d 181 (1984), rev'd 106 S. Ct. 960 (1986).
Rhode Island v. Innis, 446 U.S. 291 (1980).
Robbins v. California, 453 U.S. 420 (1981).
Terry v. Ohio, 392 U.S. 1 (1968).
Vignera v. New York, 384 U.S. 436 (1966).
Westover v. United States, 384 U.S. 436 (1966).
Williams v. Florida, 399 U.S. 78 (1970).

CHAPTER 8

THE POLICE AND
THE JUSTICE SYSTEM

The police are part of several overlapping social institutions that collectively are referred to as the criminal justice system. A social system can be defined as a pattern of continuing social relations among individuals or groups. A social system, in an ideal sense, is a harmonious arrangement of parties operating in an orderly fashion and functioning as a unified whole. This definition clearly contains an idealized view of social systems. When applied to the real criminal justice system, the positive and cooperative aspects of this definition seem to fall away.

Social systems are, after all, based upon human interactions. Humans interact differently depending upon the circumstances of the encounter, the quality or duration of the activity, and according to the outcome of the interaction. As a result the quality of relationships among participants in the system may vary. In the American criminal justice system some forces and factors exist that create among participants organizational and professional chauvinism. In many ways this chauvinism is counterproductive and tends to work against the overall justice system's ability to operate effectively. Yet, the individual social institutions that compose the justice system are dependent upon one another. For example, there are some who believe that police officers are specialists in law enforcement and criminal apprehension. Since crime continues and the number of criminals does not seem to be decreasing, it is tempting to blame police officers. Yet, once the police have apprehended a suspect, it falls upon the courts to adjudicate, and it becomes the task of corrections to punish and/or rehabilitate.

Police officers obviously depend upon and must cooperate with other social institutions. Police work can not occur in isolation from the courts, corrections, or probationary efforts. In order to better understand the role played by these various other institutions, this chapter offers a basic foundation for examining the justice system's components and its links to police work.

INTRODUCTION: POLICE, COURTS, AND CORRECTIONS

As previous chapters have described, police traditionally have been charged with the responsibility of preserving the peace, maintaining public order, and enforcing the laws of the land. But the police are not alone in their efforts. They are merely one segment of a larger configuration commonly referred to as the criminal justice system. Practically speaking, the criminal justice system is composed of several loosely aligned clusters of agencies arranged around law enforcement organizations, the courts, and correctional institutions. This chapter will begin with a brief description of each of these major components. Following this, the chapter will examine in some detail a number of elements involved in processing a case through the criminal justice system.

The Criminal Courts

For many people, the criminal courts represent the dominant component of the criminal justice system. In its purest sense, the judicial process of the criminal courts represents the American ideal of justice. The usual expectation of American justice is that the guilty will be convicted and punished and the innocent set free.

The criminal court system is formally charged with the responsibility of seeking truth regardless of who the parties involved may be. Once truth has been established, the outcome of the case becomes apparent: either

the accused has been found guilty and will be sentenced, or the individual will be returned to family and community.

Under the American system of justice, the entire operation is understood as occurring without usurping or undermining any of an accused person's legal rights. In fact, every effort is undertaken to protect the personal safety as well as the civil rights of an accused person. Many an accused person has been spared a beating or lynching by an angry crowd because a sheriff managed to disperse the mob or was protected by being spirited to another county to be jailed until arraignment.

In terms of social implications, one must consider any harm done to an accused person

Courts in America represent the justice system in its purest sense. This is a rural courthouse in Massachusetts.

as itself deviant and perhaps illegal behavior. Short-cutting the judicial process through some act of vigilante behavior or violation of a constitutionally guaranteed right weakens the social fabric that binds a community and society. Thus, society must protect itself by protecting those who are accused of crimes. In theory, protection of an accused's rights is the task of the judiciary. In practice, however, it is often the police officer's responsibility to ensure that the safety and rights of suspects are protected.

Some critics of the judicial process suggest that the preservation of these legal rights often creates the appearance of protecting criminals at the expense of their victims. This is not, of course, the purpose of these legal safeguards. Rather, it must be acknowledged that innocent people are sometimes accused of crimes. Under the American judicial system, all people are innocent until proven guilty. Because of this legal principal, all persons accused of crimes continue to be protected by the law, usually the police.

Among the fundamental tenets that protect the accused are the right to counsel by a qualified attorney, the right to a speedy trial, the right of a trial by a jury of one's peers—in short, the right to due process. Due process encompasses certain basic aspects of fairness for the accused. These may include the right to be present at trial, to be informed of the charges being brought by the state, to be given an opportunity to face one's accuser(s), to hear and confront hostile witnesses, to have favorable witnesses speak on one's behalf, and the right not to make self-incriminating statements.

These issues of rights and due process are the cornerstones of the judicial process and are assured by the Bill of Rights of the U.S. Constitution. The preservation of these constitutional provisions, as drawn out in Chapter Seven, assures that when a criminal trial concludes and a defendant is found guilty, he or she may receive sentence and/or appeal the findings of the case.

Corrections

Assuming that a criminal trial has resulted in a verdict of guilty and the offender is sentenced to prison, the offender enters the realm of corrections. The police actually play little or no direct role in the correctional process. This is because state prisons are usually administered by a state department of corrections. The day-to-day operation of the prison is the job of correctional officers who are responsible to the department of corrections. On the other hand, police play a significant role in the operation of jails. County jails are typically under the jurisdiction of the sheriff's department; the municipal police run the city jail.

Ordinarily, state prisons house convicted felons whose sentences exceed a year or, in some jurisdictions, approximately two years. Persons convicted of crimes with penalties of less than this duration are sentenced to jail time. Jails also house persons accused of crimes and awaiting trial. Because of serious overcrowding in state prisons, many inmates must be housed in jails. For example, in 1986, 12,025 prisoners were housed in jails due to overcrowding in state facilities (*Sourcebook* 1988, 483).

Thus, what occurs in the correctional phase of the justice system is of concern to many police officers. In most state correctional facilities there are various rehabilitative, vocational, and educational programs. Jails, however, seldom have such programs for inmates. The responsibility for rehabilitation and custodial care of jailed inmates, then, rests largely in the hands of county and municipal police officers.

In its most ideal sense, the American correctional system is designed to separate criminal offenders from general society. Once separated, various elements and agencies within the correctional system supervise and guide offenders toward the goal of reintegrating in society as productive members. Toward this idealized goal, the correctional system operates a variety of incarceration (restrained separation) styles. Typically, when one thinks about the correctional system, one thinks of jails and prisons.

Corrections, however, may also include attaching special bracelets to offenders' ankles or wrists and placing them under electronically monitored house arrest (See McCarthy 1987). In addition, corrections may represent no physical restraint, but merely a type of community control represented by a probationary status. Again, police officers are not directly involved in the operation of probation. The police may, however, be indirectly involved. Under probation, a convicted offender remains in the community, but is subject to certain conditions imposed by the court. The probationer is supervised by a probation officer who assists the offender in securing and maintaining a job, provides counseling, and seeks various community resources as they may become necessary. The police are interested in probationary trends since they affect jail and prison population levels and place potential law violators back in the community.

Probation

Technically speaking, probation is a judicial action that allows an offender convicted of some crime to remain in the community. But, in order to obtain this privilege, the offender must agree to certain contractual stipulations, including various levels of supervision from a probation officer. Essentially, traditional probation allows the offender to remain at home, continuing working or locate work, and avoid the dangers, debilitation, and stigmatization of incarceration. While in the community, the offender is expected to abide by all conditions of probation, which may include group and/or individual counseling, drug–alcohol rehabilitation programs, work or education requirements, and non-violation of any laws.

Many innovative probation and early prison release strategies can be understood as the direct response to prison overcrowding and the growing costs both of administering prison populations and building new facilities to house them. The estimated costs for new prison construction range between $30,000 and $60,000 per maximum security cell (Ward and Schoen 1981). When one multiplies this per-cell cost by several hundred cells and adds to it the cost of purchasing property to build on and subsequent maintenance costs, the figures become staggering.

As a result, many states have sought alternatives to new prison construction. A number of states have begun to use "accelerated release" programs and intensive probation strategies to ease crowding. In 1983 fifteen states reported a total of 21,420 accelerated releases, and in 1984 fourteen states authorized the early release of 17,365 prisoners (Bureau of Justice Statistics 1985).

The impact on police is two-fold. First, research on recidivism repeatedly demonstrates that as many as two-thirds of all inmates released from prison will commit additional crimes within one year. Hence, many of these released inmates will become the focus of attention for the police soon after their return to the community.

Second, there is potential impact on officer morale. Many officers already feel disenchanted with a criminal justice system that may permit accused persons to slip through the system on various legal technicalities. The reduction of sentences for felons who are convicted, then, further compounds officers' dissatisfaction with the judicial process.

To better understand the interplay of the police and the other segments of the justice system, a more detailed consideration of the criminal justice process seems warranted.

The Criminal Justice Process

As suggested in Chapter Six and Seven, entry into the justice system begins when a crime comes to the attention of some police organi- zation and a suspect is apprehended. Yet, merely entering the system does not mean one will necessarily continue through the entire process. For an assortment of reasons, accused law violators may slip out of the justice system and return to society. For instance, in 1985 1.5 million felony cases were filed and disposed of by the nation's felony courts. The disposal of these cases was by conviction, acquittal, or dismissal. Only 69 percent of these cases were disposed of through conviction, and the majority of these were reported as felonies reduced to misdemeanors prior to conviction (Bureau of Justice Statistics 1989, 48). Several reasons for these reductions and dismissals will be discussed during the following consideration of the justice process.

The following section begins where Chapter Seven left off, with arrest of a suspect. The progression beyond investigation and arrest has been diagrammed in Figure 8.1. Let us begin by booking the suspect.

Booking the Suspect

After the police have made an arrest, the usual procedure is to take the suspect to the local stationhouse for booking. Booking involves making an entry in the police records indicating the suspect's name, time of arrest and the offense(s) involved. During this period, suspects usually are fingerprinted and photographed, and a search for additional fugitive warrants is undertaken.

Following booking, the suspect will be placed either in a large holding facility, sometimes referred to as a holding cage or a jail cell. If the offense is immediately bailable, and the accused can post bail, he or she will be released. If the accused cannot meet the posted bail, or the charge is not immediately bailable, the suspect will be locked up to await appearance before the magistrate, known as the **initial appearance.** While waiting for the initial appearance, the suspect is entitled to a telephone call.

Because television and movies commonly show someone placed in a cell shouting "I know my rights, I get a phone call!" civilians have come to believe that this "right to a call" is immediately, rigorously, and consistently applied throughout the nation. It is not. The right to a call was incorporated in the laws to protect Americans from being held indefinitely and incommunicado (held without anyone knowing). But, how this right is administered varies from one state to the next. These differences include the number of calls one is permitted, who may be called, how soon after an arrest one is permitted to make calls, at whose expense calls are placed, whether calls can be monitored, and whether an arrested party must be advised about the right to make calls.

In most jurisdictions, arrested persons are permitted to make a phone call within a short time after being booked. Although the rule of thumb is a single, completed phone call, some jurisdictions will permit several. The rationale behind several calls is to allow the individual to notify both a relative and an attorney or **bail bondsman** (discussed in Box 8.1). Typically, local calls are made at no cost to the suspect, but toll and long distances calls only at his or her expense. While there are no firm rules about whether a law enforcement agency must inform an arrested person about phone call rights, the right is a continuous one. Consequently, failure on the part of the arrested person to exercise the calling right immediately after booking does not alter one's right to a call later.

Preliminary Hearing or Arraignment before the Magistrate

Following booking, most state statutes require that an arrested person be brought before a magistrate or comparable individual without unnecessary delay. This initial appearance consists generally of the accused person appearing before the court's representative and being advised of the charges and his or her

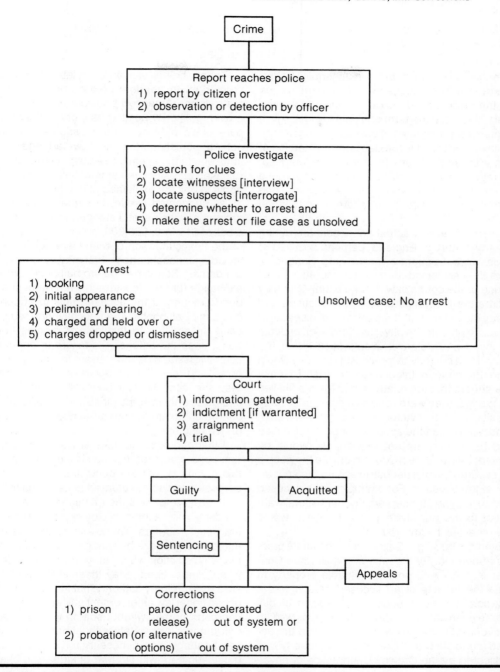

FIGURE 8.1   Simulation of the Criminal Justice System Process

Box 8.1 _____

The Right to Bail

The origins of the term *bail* are uncertain. Gilbert Stuckey (1986, 65) suggests that the term may be from the French word *baillier*, meaning to deliver. Others claim that the term originates from English common law procedures of bailments. Under common law, a bailment is the deposit of something of value with another party for a particular purpose. With regard to bail, the deposit was for the purpose both of gaining the release of the accused, and assuring his or her return at a later time to stand trial.

Given the lack of actual penal concern during the early history of England, persons accused of crimes were frequently thrown into dungeons, where they remained for extended durations until the king or the courts saw fit to hold trial. Often, by the time the trial rolled around, the accused had already died of malnutrition, exposure, disease, or plague. To prevent the physical debilitation or death of a loved one, relatives would seek his or her release from custody by promising that they would assure the return of the accused for trial. To make more certain that the relatives and friends fulfilled their pledge, they were required to post a security deposit of chattel or valuable objects (jewels, gold, deeds, etc.). If, on the specified date, the accused failed to appear, the security deposit would be forfeited. Efforts were made to motivate the people who secured the bail deposit to assure the appearance of the accused. For example, if the accused failed to appear, these security depositors were subject to the punishment that this felon would have received if convicted.

Even during Anglo-Saxon times, bailment practices abounded. By the time of the Norman Conquest in 1066 A.D., posting valuable property to obtain the release of an accused person was a fairly common occurrence. The tradition of bail became financially important to the king as well. In the event that charges were serious and the accused found guilty and executed, the property was confiscated by the Crown. The practice of physically punishing those who posted the bond when an accused person did not return for trial fell away. But, their forfeiture of secured property and objects persisted.

Today, bail is viewed as related to the traditional right to freedom before conviction, which rests on the American principal of innocent until proven guilty. By posting bail, one is free to prepare one's defense, and it assures that undeserved punishment is not leveled against the innocent. In the event that a suspect has not been released on bail by the time of initial appearance, rights to bail are explained at that time.

As suggested above, in some cases the bail amount may be set at a staggering amount. Since a bail of $10,000, $20,000, or $50,000 may be out of the financial reach of many average people—including innocent ones—bail may be posted by a bondsman. Bondsmen put up bail bond money in exchange for fees (customarily ten percent of the bond amount). If the accused fails to appear for court, the bail bond is theoretically forfeited to the court. In addition to the loss of monies held in bond, upon the defendant's failure to appear the court will issue a bench warrant for the immediate arrest and return of the accused. Following rearrest, the accused will be tried on the original charge(s) and, in some jurisdictions, an additional charge of "failure to appear" (skipping out on bail, or "jumping bail").

When the accused does arrive at court on the appropriate date for trial, bail is *exonerated.* What this means is that the bond has now served its purpose and can be returned to its depositor.

In order to protect their financial interests, bail bondsmen sometimes employ *skip tracers,* or modern bounty hunters. These skip tracers have the authority to retrieve bail jumpers and return them to the jurisdiction where they have been charged with a crime. Even today these skip tracers possess extraordinary authority that far surpasses that of traditional law enforcement officers. Skip tracers can enter homes without search warrants, arrest bail jumpers in any state without benefit of extradition hearings, use necessary force to arrest and detain jumpers without fear of kidnaping charges and, in general, ignore various aspects of due process.

The authority of these modern bounty hunters derives from a U.S. Supreme Court decision, *Tay-*

lor v. *Taintor* (1873). In this decision the High Court outlined the common law authority of a bondsmen or agent of a bondsmen:

> When bail is given, the principal is regarded as delivered to the custody of his sureties. Their dominion is a continuance of the original imprisonment. Whenever they chose to do so, they may seize him and deliver him up to their discharge; and if it cannot be done at once, they may imprison him until it can be done. They may exercise their rights in person or by agent.

They may pursue him into another state; may arrest him on the Sabbath; and if necessary may break and enter his house for that purpose. The seizure is not made by virtue of due process. None is needed.

The authority vested in bondsmen and their agents as a consequence of *Taylor* v. *Taintor* is now almost 120 years old. During this time the Supreme Court has never altered its decision on the authority held by a bondsmen or skip tracers working for a bondsmen.

---

rights. This includes a reiteration of the *Miranda* warnings and the information that if he or she is indigent (impoverished), counsel will be provided by the court at the expense of the state or the attorney through an agreement with the court to provide annually a certain amount of free legal service to the community (*pro bono*).

In some states, the suspect is permitted to enter a plea at this initial appearance, and the disposition of the case is decided by the magistrate. Typically, cases disposed of by magistrates are misdemeanors. If the case is not readily disposed of during this appearance, the accused will either be returned to jail or released. Whether the accused is released on his or her own recognizance or required to post a sum of money (a **bail bond**) to assure his or her return depends upon a number of factors. Among these factors are indication of family and home stability, previous criminal record, whether the suspect is steadily employed, demeanor during arraignment, and similar factors. The amount of bail required is determined by the court and usually corresponds loosely with the seriousness of the criminal charge(s). Petty crimes usually have low bail requirements, such as $50 or $100. More serious crimes such as rape or murder may have bail set as high as one million dollars. Because of the enormity of drug profits, persons accused of large-scale drug dealings often have bail set at several million dollars.

The Preliminary Hearing

In most jurisdictions, following the initial appearance in court, the next judicial step is the **preliminary hearing.** This hearing usually occurs within one or two weeks after the initial appearance. Between initial appearance and preliminary hearing, prosecutors may change or drop charges owing to the discovery of greater or lesser amounts of evidence. Also during this period, the defendant may be called in to take part in various witness identification proceedings, such as a **line-up.**

For the most part, a line-up involves a suspect being placed among a group of individuals who are then viewed by a witness. If the witness is able to identify the suspect accurately, a positive identification has been made. On occasion, a witness may be asked to select the suspect from a group of photographs (mug shots) in what is termed a **photo line-up.**

A suspect also may consent to or volunteer for a polygraph test or a lie detector test. While the results of polygraph examinations are not admissible as evidence in court, the findings of examiners increasingly are used during courtroom proceedings. The threat of a polygraph examination is sometimes used to assure a witness is not lying. Frequently, even the suggestion of a polygraph examination motivates lying witnesses to tell the truth.

The preliminary hearing establishes the nature of the evidence identified by the state and determines whether there is probable cause to continue prosecution of a defendant. In many states, preliminary hearings are not required. In these jurisdictions, a grand jury represents the state's interest in determining whether to pursue prosecution of a defendant.

The Grand Jury Process

In the United States, the official accusation that a resident has committed a crime begins in one of two ways. First, the prosecuting attorney, in some states the state attorney, may initiate the process by filing an **information** with a criminal court. This initiates the process leading to the preliminary hearing. The second way a person can be officially accused of a crime is by having a **grand jury** consider the facts and evidence in a case and hand up a **bill of indictment.** The bill of indictment formally charges the defendant with a specific crime or crimes.

Traditionally, grand juries are composed of private citizens, usually twenty-three, although some states have reduced the number. At one time, a majority of votes from the panel was required to bring an indictment. Today, partially as a reflection of the reduction in grand jury panelists, more than a simple majority may be required by statute. The origins of the grand jury can be traced to twelfth century England, where it served as a buffer between the state and the citizen. Its responsibilities included overseeing the prosecutor, evaluating the merits of cases brought before it, and serving as an independent investigative body in certain cases.

In its modern incarnation, the grand jury has become largely a rubber stamp for a prosecutor. In most cities that continue to use a grand jury system, it indicts as many as 80 percent of the cases it reviews. In addition, when a grand jury undertakes a special investigation of some case, it frequently becomes a hunting expedition, rather than a search for truth. Because of the flaws in this system, the National Advisory Commission on Criminal Justice Standards and Goals (1973) recommended that the grand jury system cease to be required in criminal prosecutions. The commission did, however, recommend that the system remain an option for investigating exceptional cases.

Several elements distinguish the grand jury procedure from the initial hearing and preliminary hearing, which it effectively replaces. First, in a grand jury proceeding, only evidence presented by the prosecution (the state) is considered. The accused does not possess a right to present contradicting evidence, refute testimony, or even be present during the hearing. When the accused is invited to be present, the accused is not entitled to have counsel in the actual grand jury hearing room. Further, the grand jury is not bound by all the evidentiary rules that restrict admissibility in a criminal court trial; deliberations of the grand jury are secret.

The central purpose of the grand jury, like the preliminary hearing, is to review evidence presented by the state and determine whether there is probable cause to pursue prosecution. If the grand jury finds sufficient probable cause and evidence, it will return an indictment (sometimes called a *true bill*). The grand jury indictment usually occurs only in the case of felonies. Misdemeanors and petty offenses are generally begun simply by the prosecutor filing information.

After an indictment or information is officially filed, the case will be scheduled or docketed for **arraignment.** At the arraignment, the judge or comparable representative for the courts formally reads all charges, asks if the accused understands the nature of these charges, and also once more informs the accused of constitutional rights. Finally, the judge will ask the accused to enter a plea to the charges. The defendant now has the option of entering one of a number of possible pleas or answers to the charges.

Types of Pleas

Although there are several variations and additional pleas, essentially three major pleas occur during an arraignment. These include guilty, not guilty, and *nolo contendere*. Each plea offers a slightly different effect on the next stage of the process.

First, a defendant can plead not guilty, and a date will be set for trial. Occasionally, defendants refuse to enter any plea and stand silently before the court. History reveals that under early common law, when this occurred the accused was returned to prison. In prison, the accused would be stripped naked and forced to lie on his back, whereupon he was "pressed." Like the pressings of witches during the seventeenth century Salem witch hunts, great weights would be placed on the chests of these prisoners. They were then alternately given stale bread and stagnant water daily until they either died or entered a plea (Stuckey 1986, 77). Later, during periods of judicial reform, when defendants stood mutely before the bench, a plea of guilty was entered on their behalf. Today, on the occasion of a defendant refusing or being incapable of uttering a plea, the state enters the plea of not guilty, and the case goes to court.

The accused can also plead guilty, and a date will be set for sentencing. In some instances sentencing can occur immediately, during the arraignment hearing. At one time, defendants were not permitted to enter guilty pleas. It was believed that justice could only prevail if a fair and judicial process determined the guilt or innocence of an accused. Even today, some vestige of this exists in capital crimes. It is not uncommon, for example, for defendants captured with the fabled "smoking guns" still in their hands or when several eye witnesses have observed the crime, to still enter a not guilty plea. The

reasoning here is generally to permit discussion of various mitigating circumstances during trial.

For example, although a woman may have shot her husband to death, it may have occurred after she had been severely beaten or threatened with death herself. A number of states do not permit pleas of self-defense (the charge of murder in self-defense does not even exist in some states' statutes). In place of a self-defense plea, one must plead not guilty. Other mitigating circumstances may include insanity or accident.

Finally, the defendant may choose to plead nolo contendere (sometimes identified as *non vult contendere*), which literally means "no contest," to the charges. The effect of a plea of nolo contendere is identical to that of guilty. The court will move to set a time when sentencing can be rendered. The principal benefit to a defendant of a plea of nolo contendere is that this plea cannot be used against him or her in any subsequent civil case that may arise from this criminal event.

Pretrial Negotiations

Police may be actively involved in negotiating bargains between accused parties and the state's prosecuting attorney. These negotiations may involve trades of information about other suspects who conspired with the accused or about other crimes they know about, or incentives to testify in some case. In exchange for these pieces of information, the accused may have charges reduced or be offered other types of considerations. Many prosecutors favor negotiating with accused persons during this less formal period before trial. Later, during the trial, negotiations are less flexible and become more competitive.

During the last several years, pretrial negotiations have greatly expanded in the hope that this will allow courts to keep pace with their overburdened dockets or case loads. The sheer number of cases a prosecutor has to contend with has forced many to accept a plea of guilty to a lesser offense, even if the prosecutor might have preferred going to trial.

Not everyone, however, is enamored with pretrial negotiations or plea bargains. Critics maintain that the large number of incentives available to the police and the prosecutor, and to some extent even the defense counsel, encourage a plea of guilty. The accused is given reason to believe that a particular outcome will result from a plea of guilty. Thus, the accused is motivated to plead guilty to a negotiated lesser crime rather than take the chance of being convicted of a more serious offense. Some members of the legal profession believe that judicial process would collapse if substantial use of plea negotiations was discontinued. Yet, as critics are quick to point out, Alaska's courts have managed to operate effectively, in spite of state laws making plea bargaining illegal. Although it would be difficult to demonstrate empirically, estimates suggest that 85 to 90 percent of all prosecutions in criminal courts nationally are disposed of through negotiated pleas of guilty (Bing 1987).

TRIAL

The trial of a criminal case affects many other interfacing segments of the criminal justice system. If due process is not observed, an appellate court may reverse the guilty verdict in a case. The consequences of this can be serious. In addition to increased costs to the community (often soaring to the millions for some major criminal cases), there is the potential threat to safety if the defendant was objectively, albeit not legally, guilty. It is extremely important, therefore, that the trial process proceed with all due speed and proprieties. The other side of this coin, of course, is that the trial process must not be propelled so speedily that prosecutors make serious errors or omissions because of haste. Errors might result in the acquittal of a guilty party or the conviction of an innocent but legally

guilty person. Neither situation can be viewed as desirable.

The accused in a criminal case possesses the right to determine whether the trial will be undertaken before a judge or a judge and jury (the traditional jury of peers). This decision is assured the accused by the Sixth Amendment to the U.S. Constitution, which provides for the right to a trial by jury. As with all rights, one is entitled to waive it, although in some cases the defendant's request for a bench trial may need the concurrence of the prosecutor. Not surprisingly, many misdemeanants choose to waive their right to a jury trial. This typically results in a much speedier trial date and resolution of the case.

The Jury

Let us consider the trial process by first examining the jury system. Many Americans are familiar with the general idea of a jury of peers. Some are familiar from personal experience, having served on a jury, while others recognize the notion from having watched countless hundreds of "Perry Mason" television show reruns. Far fewer Americans, however, are aware of the many nuances associated with the history and practice of the jury system.

Just as law enforcement practices differ from one jurisdiction to the next, so, too, do procedures related to selecting jurors. But, there are certainly some basic points on which all jurisdictions agree. First, no citizen can be excluded as a potential juror on the basis of race, color, religion, sex, national origin, or economic status. Beyond this agreement, however, specific selection procedures may vary significantly. Regardless of specific variations, the overarching idea is to create a large, fairly inclusive listing from which to draw names of jurors.

For instance, in some locations, a pool of potential jurors is created by non-repetitively combining names of registered voters with lists of civil servants, union members, and similar public listings of names. From this list, names can be randomly selected to create the pool of jurors.

Typically, once a potential juror's name has been selected, a brief questionnaire or qualification form is sent. After receiving completed forms, a court administrator will begin to determine which potential jurors are qualified to serve, which have legitimate reasons to be excused (either permanently or temporarily), and which are not qualified to serve (e.g., non-citizens, illiteracy, mental impairment, physical incapacitation, police officers and other members of the justice system). Naturally, persons who initially qualify may later be disqualified when interviewed by both the defense and prosecuting counsels during *voir dire* (discussed later).

Qualified potential jurors will receive notification by **summons** that they have been selected. A summons is an official document issued by the court informing the individual of the court's need to have them appear for some particular reason. In this case, the reason is to serve on a jury. The summons, in effect, orders the person named on it to appear in a specified court on a particular date and often for a minimum specified duration of time (four days, five days, etc.). The duration of time does not necessarily coincide with the length of time a trial may take. Rather, the duration is typically the time a potential juror is required to sit and wait to be called or picked for a jury. In some instances, a potential juror may be called immediately, land on a quick case, and finish up his or her responsibilities that day. In other cases, a person may sit for nearly the duration of their waiting period, only to be called for a case that continues for several additional days.

Voir Dire.   Potential jurors are also subject to questions from the defense and prosecution attorneys in order to determine their fitness as jurors. This challenging of jurors is commonly referred to as voir dire, derived from the French meaning "look, speak." It is a period for each counsel to look at the prospective jurors and ask them questions about various issues, attitudes, and beliefs.

There are two categories of challenge during voir dire. The first challenge arises when either counsel asks that a prospective juror be **excused for cause.** These causes are enumerated in the various statutes of a given jurisdiction. They may include clearly identified bias, implied bias, or other factors that suggest the juror will be unable to offer a fair and impartial verdict.

The second challenge that may be made by either counsel is a **pre-emptory challenge.** In this instance, counsel is not required to explain motives for dismissing a juror nor to show cause. Pre-emptory challenges allow each counsel an opportunity to remove potential jurors merely because the jurors look like they may be difficult to convince. The precise number of challenges (both for cause and pre-emptory) varies from one jurisdiction to the next and usually according to the seriousness of the case to be tried as well. In some jurisdictions "for-cause challenges" are limitless while "pre-emptory challenges" are always limited.

Jury Size.   The average person thinks of a jury as twelve people sitting in a mahogany jury box. While the construction of the jury's box may be accurate, the size of the jury may not. Historically, twelve has been the number of jurors in criminal court cases. During recent years, appreciably smaller juries have been permitted. The size of a jury, of course, becomes relevant because of the rights and assurances of the U.S. Constitution. It was previously mentioned that the right to a trial by a jury is assured by the Sixth Amendment to the Constitution. However, there is no mention of jury size in this amendment.

In 1970, the question of jury size was vividly brought to the forefront in the case of *Williams v. Florida* (1970). On appeal, the U.S. Supreme Court ruled that the six-person jury used in the *Williams* criminal trial for robbery did not deprive Williams of his constitutionally guaranteed right to a trial by jury. The Court made it clear that the size of a jury was not the necessary ingredient to ensure a constitutional "trial by jury." The majority opinion in *Williams* v. *Florida* explains the Court's logic:

> We conclude, in short, as we began: the fact that a jury at common law was composed of precisely twelve is historical accident, unnecessary to effect the purposes of the jury system and wholly without significance "except to mystics." [399 U.S. 78, 90 S.Ct. 1893, 26 L.Ed. 2d 446, (1970, 102–3)]

In essence the High Court is saying that while juries should be composed of persons similar to the defendant and representatives of the community, their exact number is not restricted to twelve.

Yet, in 1978, in the case of *Ballew* v. *Georgia*, the High Court's decision was slightly different. Ballew, a theater manager, had been convicted of distributing obscene materials (several misdemeanors) by a five-person jury in a Georgia county court.

The High Court ruled that smaller juries are less objective and held that juries of fewer than six (the number established *Williams*), are constitutionally unacceptable. According to the Bureau of Justice Statistics (1983, 67), five states allow juries of fewer than twelve for felony and misdemeanor cases (Oregon, Utah, Arizona, Louisiana, and Florida). An additional ten states provide for juries of fewer than twelve in misdemeanor cases alone (Idaho, Wyoming, Colorado, Oklahoma, Iowa, Tennessee, Mississippi, New York, Connecticut, and Virginia).

Unanimity.   One final word on juries is in order: **unanimity**. Traditionally, a verdict in a criminal case had to be unanimously decided among the twelve jurors. The Supreme Court, however, altered this historical tradition in 1972 in two separate decisions (*Johnson* v. *Louisiana* and *Apodaca* v. *Oregon*). In the first case, the High Court permitted a 9–3

verdict, and in the second case a 10–2 guilty finding was upheld.

In the *Johnson* case, the appeal maintained that the prosecution had failed to prove its case beyond reasonable doubt, as evidenced by the fact that three jurors would not find him guilty. The argument, therefore, was over a due process issue. The High Court, however did not agree and stated:

> We conclude that as to the nine jurors who voted to convict, the State satisfied its burden of proving guilt beyond reasonable doubt. The remaining question under the Due Process Clause is whether the vote of the three jurors for acquittal can be said to impeach the verdict of the other nine and to demonstrate that guilt was not in fact proved beyond such doubt. We hold that it cannot.

In *Apodaca*, Robert Apodaca, Henry Morgan Coopers, Jr., and James Arnold Madden were convicted, respectively, of assault with a deadly weapon, burglary in a dwelling, and grand larceny, each before a separate jury. Like the *Johnson* case, Robert Apodaca's case raised the questions of the sufficiency in reasonable doubt and due process when juries split but find a defendant guilty. Among other things, the High Court's statement included the following:

> Like the requirement that juries consist of 12 men, the requirement of unanimity rose during the Middle Ages and had become an accepted feature of the common-law jury by the 18th century. Our inquiry must focus upon the function served by the jury in the contemporary society. As we said in Duncan, [referring to Duncan v. Louisiana 391 U.S. 145, 149 (1968), which concerned denial of his right to a trial by jury] the purpose of trial by jury is to prevent oppression by the Government by providing a safeguard against the corrupt or overzealous prosecutor and against the complaint of biased, or eccentric judges. Given this purpose, the essential feature of a jury obviously lies in interposition between the accused and his accuser of the common sense judgment of a group of laymen. A requirement of unanimity, however, does not materially contribute to the exercise of this commonsense judgment as long as it consists of a group of laymen representative of a cross section of the community who have the duty

and the opportunity to deliberate, free from outside attempts at intimidation, on the question of a defendant's guilt. In terms of this function we perceive no difference between juries required to act unanimously and those permitted to convict or acquit by votes of 10 to two or 11 to one. *Requiring unanimity would obviously produce hung juries in some situations where nonunanimous juries will convict or acquit [emphasis added].*

Although non-unanimous verdicts are not unusual in civil matters, they remain highly controversial in criminal cases. The rationale behind non-unanimous jury votes is the idea that even in the event that a juror does not agree with the decision of all the others, the jury is not "hung." In other words, a decision and verdict can be rendered, reducing the expense and time of conducting a second trial. Opponents of non-unanimous juror decisions argue that "the conservative majority of the Burger Court misread the history of the jury, with the result that a basic constitutional right is being sacrificed" (Neubauer 1985,287). Currently, the unanimous verdict remains the main rule in most state jurisdictions and in the federal court system.

Presentation of the Case

Following the selection of a jury, the prosecution and defense counsels are permitted, although not required to, make an opening statement. Customarily, the prosecution is allowed to present its opening remarks first. The central purpose of the open statement is to orient the jury by acquainting it with various pieces of information about the case. The pieces of information include a description of the offense and charges and some description of the evidence that will be used in the case later. Technically, mere opinions and conclusions not anchored to evidence to be presented during the trial are out of place. When offered, the opposing counsel may literally spring to his or her feet with the haunting phrase made famous by countless television programs, "Your Honor, I object!"

Although officially viewed as inappropriate and objectionable, opening statements are nonetheless frequently an opportunity for each counsel to make veiled innuendos about the guilt or innocence of the defendant—unrelated to any evidence that may be produced later. Some, however, suggest that opening statements can be tactical errors because information may be provided by the defense that the prosecution might otherwise have found it difficult to bring out under the rules of evidence. Others, of course, argue that the failure of a defense counsel to offer an opening statement may be construed by the jurors as implying a weak defense or an admission of guilt.

Following each counsel's opening statement, the prosecution presents the evidence alluded to in the opening statement. This may include physical evidence (photographs, fingerprints, imprint castings, weapons, and so forth) or witness testimony. Witnesses, who have been summoned to the court, are called to the witness stand, sworn in (asked to place their hand on a Bible and swear that what they are about to say is the truth), and questioned. This is commonly referred to as **direct examination.** Typically, after the prosecutor has asked questions, the defense is entitled, although not required, to question the witness as well. In some situations, the defense counsel's cross-examination uncovers material the prosecutor had not anticipated. Under such circumstances, the prosecutor may redirect questions to this witness a second time for purposes of clarity or to re-emphasize previously stated facts that incriminate the defendant. Naturally, the defense is entitled to question this witness again in what is called recross-examination. It is usual that this question-and-answer exchange will not proceed further than a single redirect and recross-examination.

Following the prosecution's presentation of its case, the defense is permitted to offer its argument and refute evidence through witness testimony of its own. The witness questioning will occur as described above, but in reverse. That is, the defense will begin with direct examination of the witness, followed by the prosecutor's cross-examination, and so forth. Once again, the defense is not obliged to offer any counter-argument. In other words, and as previously stated, the defendant is innocent until proven guilty. This is to say that the prosecutor in a criminal trial must demonstrate to the judge and jury (or judge alone) that the defendant is guilty beyond reasonable doubt. If the prosecution has failed to produce any substantial evidence, it may be in the best interest of the client for the defense counsel to merely move for dismissal of charges. Strategically, the defense counsel might not present a full defense. Rather, the defense may go to its closing statement. In such a circumstance, the counsel will likely emphasize how the prosecution has failed to present its case adequately and has not demonstrated beyond reasonable doubt the defendant's guilt.

Jury Deliberation and the Verdict

Although the American court system is based upon the premise of a fair and impartial consideration of facts, and not on emotionality and sentiment, jurors are only human. Consequently, many modern American law schools engage drama coaches to train law students in various dramatic elements of presentation. These may include body language, tone of voice, appropriate pausing for effect, and so forth.

As a partial reflection of lawyers becoming far more schooled in dramatic presentation, their opening and closing statements may be very convincing, irrespective of the facts in a case. It has become fairly common, therefore, for a judge to instruct the jury prior to its deliberation. This instruction is typically a brief explanation of the law related to the crime with which the defendant has been charged and what options, if any, the jury has regarding finding the defendant guilty of lesser included charges. The jury also may be

specifically instructed to ignore emotional statements by either counsel that do not bear upon the facts and to rely only upon those facts in their deliberation.

Jury deliberations are conducted in secret, and jurors are not legally obligated to explain or justify their votes, regardless of the verdict. If the jury finds the defendant guilty, the result is he or she is convicted of the charges. After rendering their verdict through an elected foreman, the jurors may be polled at the request of the defendant, either individually or as a group. Many of the old James Cagney movies illustrated such polls when, after hearing the jury's verdict, the judge would inquire, "So say you all?" and receive the response in unison, "So say we all."

Following the conviction of a defendant and depending on the nature of the offenses, the court will either order the defendant committed to custody or released on bail pending imposition of sentence.

Sentencing and Corrections

Sentencing, or the formal pronouncement of judgment and remedy (punishment), follows conviction of a criminal offense. For many, sentencing marks both the end and beginning of justice sub-systems. Obviously, it marks the initial end of the judicial process, although appeals may certainly continue during the felon's incarceration. Sentencing additionally marks the beginning of the correctional process.

The pronouncement of sentence is generally imposed without unreasonable delay. Many states provide a specific time frame between the guilty verdict and sentencing. This time period, usually ranging between two to four weeks, is intended to provide probation officers with sufficient opportunity to prepare a pre-sentence investigation report for the judge. This report, along with recommendations from the jury, the prosecutor, and the defense counsel, is taken into account in the judge's determination of a fair and appropriate sentence.

The specific sentence for various crimes varies according to jurisdiction. Some states operate under fairly strict **presumptive sentencing guidelines.** These guidelines are established by the state legislature and carry the full weight of the law. Philosophically, sentencing guidelines derive from the demands for greater determinancy in sentencing that arose during the 1970s. Although these demands were grounded in a variety of political and penal ideologies, all shared the common goal of objectifying and neutralizing judicial sentencing discretion (See Greenberg and Humphries 1980, Travis 1982). An example of one kind of sentencing guideline is offered by Florida and shown in Box 8.2. It should be noted, however, that variations in how sentencing guidelines operate do exist in other states.

As suggested in Box 8.2, the guidelines used in Florida sentences are sometimes referred to as presumptive sentences, since there is a presumed sentence associated with every category of crime. Variations in these presumed sentences, as suggested, result from different total scores.

North Carolina, California, and an number of other states provide their criminal judiciary with specific **determinate sentencing guidelines.** Somewhat more rigid than Florida's, many of the predetermined sentences established by other legislatures are linked to specific categories of crime and, when prison is appropriate, contain a fixed duration for incarceration rather than a scored matrix of various elements.

Since the mid- to late 1980s, several other states have begun to consider determinate sentencing plans (Maine, Massachusetts, New York). In spite of a push toward presumptive and determinate sentencing, there are two additional sentencing strategies used by various states. These include **indeterminate sentences** and **mandatory sentences.**

At the federal level, the Comprehensive Crime Control Act of 1984 eliminated indeterminate sentences. Instead, the act established a sentencing commission charged with establishing guidelines and abolishing federal parole (See the Comprehensive Crime Control Act of 1984). The new federal guidelines went into effect in 1989, but it is too soon to evaluate their effectiveness.

Indeterminate sentences involve legislatively specified ranges of incarceration (five to ten years, ten to twenty years, etc.). Typically, these provide the judge with a significant amount of discretion in determining the actual range (the minimum and maximum) of time the offender will serve. In its most extreme form, the range may extend from zero through life. This means that one may be released after serving a customary minimum of time. This duration varies state to state between seven and fifteen years and assumes the felon receives parole. Of course, the offender may just as easily never secure a release and serve out the life sentence.

Because the resurgence of determinate sentencing is relatively recent, little evaluation of its effectiveness has been documented. One notable exception to this is the Minnesota felony sentencing guidelines. The Minnesota sentencing guidelines are regarded by many observers as among the most rigorous in the United States (Moore and Miethe 1986). Minnesota's felony guidelines went into effect on May 1, 1980. These guidelines offered significant improvement in making prison sentences more uniform and neutral during their first year of operation. The Minnesota Sentencing Guideline Commission, along with independent researchers, claimed that this uniformity and neutrality arrived without escalating penal sanctions or prison populations (See Knapp 1982, Blumstein et al. 1983).

More recently, evaluations of the Minnesota sentencing guidelines suggest that there is some degree of inevitable departure from the uniformity originally sought. In other words, presumptive sentencing systems must include permissible exceptions to the rigid imposition of sentences. These exceptions involve various mitigating circumstances. But it is also necessary to assure that these departures from the guidelines are not used by judges as avenues to avoid the guidelines entirely. According to Charles Moore and Terance Miethe (1986), some judges in Minnesota have found ways to adjust sentencing. While these departures occurred in only small number of cases, Moore and Miethe recommend such exceptions should be closely monitored.

In addition to the scattered efforts by 26 states to create sentencing guidelines, legislation has recently been enacted to create a determinate sentencing system at the federal level. The major problem that remains, however, is whether these guidelines actually accomplish what they intend. For example, in one recent study two researchers asked inmates their views on presumptive sentencing (Berg and Larson 1989). Several earlier studies found that inmates desire the objectivity and neutrality associated with presumptive sentencing (McNeece and Lusk 1979, McGinnis and Carlson 1981, Goodstein and Hepburn 1985). Berg and Larson found the opposite to be the case. Berg and Larson report that only about a third of the 58 inmates they interviewed in a Massachusetts maximum security prison favored presumptive sentencing. The larger proportion of inmates spoke ambivalently or of their distrust for the judicial system. Inmates also offered a perception that sentencing guidelines would be used to simply "warehouse convicts and throw the key away on them" (Berg and Larson 1989).

One relevant explanation for the disparity between Berg and Larson's findings and those offered by earlier research involves the time lag and changes in correctional ideologies. In other words, during earlier studies, sentencing in general was not as punitive or lengthy as it has become during recent years. Certainly, along with objectivity and neutrality, the argument for presumptive sentencing has followed from a desire for deterrence. Penal policy and research on sentencing historically are linked to underlying theories of deterrence as a result of clearly articulated sen-

Box 8.2 _____

An Example of Sentencing Guidelines: Florida

In Florida, sentencing guidelines provide a means by which to score categories of crime, as well as their seriousness. The Florida strategy includes nine "offense categories" for scoring purposes. According to the Florida Sentencing Guidelines Manual (1983, amended 1987:4–5), these are:

Category 1: Murder, manslaughter
Category 2: Sexual offenses
Category 3: Robbery
Category 4: Violent personal crimes
Category 5: Burglary
Category 6: Thefts, forgery, fraud
Category 7: Drugs
Category 8: Weapons
Category 9: All other felony offenses

The purpose of organizing the offenses into nine felony categories, according to the manual, is that the offense and offender characteristics considered by the court vary in relative importance according to the type of offense. To provide a fair and impartial sentence, the offenses in categories one through eight have been arranged in descending order of severity. They begin with the most serious and heinous crimes of murder and manslaughter and decrease in order of severity to various weapons offenses. Category nine is designated to contain "all other felony offenses" represented in Florida statutes and not specially indicated in categories one through eight. This is not intended to diminish the seriousness of these felonies, but is a practical catchall.

In addition to the scoring of a primary offense (the most serious offense and multiples of this offense with which the defendant is charged), the sentencing guidelines include a scoring process for additional offenses. For example, if an individual who, in the process of burglarizing someone's home, fought with and killed a resident of this home, his *primary* offense would be manslaughter, and his *additional* offense burglary. The number of previous offenses an individual has (their prior record), is also scored. Once a score has been calculated, the total is compared against a points chart that translates the total number of points into a recommended length of sentence. The points chart and a sample of a scoring sheet for (Category 3) robbery are shown here:

Box 8.2

Sample Scoring Sheet for Florida's Sentencing Guidelines

Rule 3.988(c)
Category 3: Robbery   [PART I]
section 812.13

1. Docket No. (Primary Offense)	3. County	4. Judge	5. Date of Sentence		
2. Docket No. (Additional Cases)	6. Name		7. Date of Birth	8. SEX __ M __ F	
	9. Date of Offense	10. Primary Offense At Conviction		11. Degree	
	12. __ Probation Violation __ Community Control Violation	13. __ Plea __ Trial	14. __ Guideline Sentence Imposed __ Departure From Guidelines		

I. Primary Offense at Conviction

	Number of Counts				Points
Degree	1	2	3	4	
Life	102	122	133	148	___
1st punishable by life	82	98	107	119	___
1st	70	84	91	101	___
2nd	50	60	65	75	___
3rd	34	41	44	54	___

Primary offense counts in excess
of four (from back)   ___

II. Additional Offenses at Conviction

	Number of Counts				Points
Degree	1	2	3	4	
Life	20	24	26	28	___
1st pbl	17	20	22	24	___
1st	14	17	18	19	___

Guideline Sentence:

Sentence Imposed, indicating
length and type:

_____
_____
_____
_____
_____
_____

FOR OFFICE USE ONLY

Offense Code _____
T.S. _____
S.P. _____
Prob. _____
C.C. _____
C.J. _____

(continued)

BOX 8.2   Continued

[PART II]

2nd		10	12	13	14	_____
3rd		7	8	9	10	_____
MM		1	2	3	4	_____

Additional offense counts in
excess of four (from back)   _____

III. A. Prior Record

Degree	Number of Counts				Points
	1	2	3	4	_____
Life	100	210	330	460	_____
1st pbl	80	168	264	368	_____
1st	60	126	198	276	_____
2nd	30	63	99	138	_____
3rd	10	21	33	46	_____
MM	2	5	8	12	_____

Prior convictions in excess of
four (from back)   _____

B. Prior convictions for
   Category 3 offenses:

Number of Prior
Convictions __ × 25 =

                                               _____

IV. Legal Status at time of offense
    No Restrictions   0   _____
    Legal Constraint   17   _____

V. Victim Injury (physical)
    None   0   _____
    Slight   7   _____
    Moderate   14   _____
    Death or Severe   21   _____
                    TOTAL =   _____

_____
Sentencing Judge

_____
State Attorney

_____
Defendant/Defense Counsel

_____
Scoresheet Preparer

Reason for departure: _____

_____

_____

Sample Point Score Chart
For Category 3: Robbery

[PART III]

POINTS	RECOMMENDED RANGE
34–53	Any non-state prison sanction
54–65	Community Control or 12–30 months incarceration
66–81	3 Years incarceration (2½–3½)
82–101	4 Years (3½–4½)
102–121	5 Years (4½–5½)
122–151	6 Years (5½–7)
152–183	8 Years (7–9)
184–229	10 Years (9–12)
230–295	15 Years (12–17)
296–357	20 Years (17–22)
358–417	25 Years (22–27)
418–453	30 Years (27–40)
454 +	LIFE

[Adapted from *Florida Sentencing Guidelines* (amended text effective July 1, 1987). Tallahassee, Fl.: Sentencing Guidelines Commission.]

With the exception of mitigating or aggravating circumstances, the judge in a Florida criminal case is restricted to using the recommended range of sentence time from these presumptive sentencing guidelines. Mitigating circumstances may include relevant factors in the individual's background, mental state at the time of the commission of the crime, and so forth. Aggravating circumstances refer to the manner in which the crime may have been committed (the level of violence or cold-bloodedness of the act) or whether the felon is a career criminal who has repeatedly committed aggravated felonies (sometimes referred to as a habitual criminal).

Since the scoring guidelines are responsive to several factors (prior offenses, multiple counts of current offenses, and so forth), the actual length of incarceration may vary for different felons serving time for the same category of offense. In fact, even with all things being equal regarding the initial sentence and offenders receiving identical initial sentences, the actual time one serves in a Florida state prison may vary. The variation results from a subtraction of days from an offender's full sentence called *good time.* In Florida, for example, a maximum of approximately six days each month may be earned through good behavior. Consequently, an offender can potentially cut almost a full week each month from the total sentence. An additional maximum of ten days may be earned by each inmate as administrative good time (day earned based upon the length of time served without incidents).

The other side of this coin, it should be noted, is that eight years ago, Florida discontinued its parole system. Thus, there are no early releases other than from the good-time programs, a verdict reversal upon appeal, or an official pardon, which is extremely rare.

tences affixed to categories of crime. Sentence duration in Massachusetts has steadily increased during the past several years. It is therefore conceivable that Berg and Larson may have simply tapped into an artifact of the already punitive sentencing structure's effects.

Mandatory Sentences

Many think about mandatory sentences as interchangeable with determinate sentences. This is inaccurate. A mandatory sentence represents a penalty that must be imposed upon conviction. In their purest sense, mandatory sentences leave no measure of discretion for the judge. The judge cannot alter the duration of the sentence, convert it to probation, or suspend the sentence altogether. Many states possess mandatory gun-possession sentences. For example, as of 1983, only thirteen states in the United States did not include in their criminal code statutes mandatory sentences of imprisonment for illegally carrying guns (Galvin 1983).

In Massachusetts, for instance, the penalty for illegally carrying a firearm is a minimum of one year for first offenders, a minimum of five and maximum of seven and one-half years for second offenders, and a minimum of ten years with a maximum of twenty years for third-time offenders (Massachusetts Criminal Code 269.9). In Massachusetts, sentences that exceed two-and-a-half years of incarceration must be served in the state prison.

In addition to incarceration as a sentence, several other potential sentencing sanctions exist. These may be issued by the court in addition to incarceration or in lieu of jail or prison time. In a generalized sense these alternative sentences include fines, restitution, and community service, traditional probation, and experimental shock and intensively supervised probation programs.

Fines.   Fines are economic sanctions that require the offenders to pay a specified amount of money to the state (either in addition to or instead of jail/prison time). Most people who drive cars are familiar with this sort of penalty if they have received a parking ticket.

Restitution and Community Service.   The imposition of a restitution penalty requires the offender to reimburse the victim financially for losses from the crime. In some instances, restitution is imposed along with fines and/or incarceration. In other instances, restitution may be among other provisions agreed upon by the offender in order to obtain probation. Although one immediately associates monetary compensation with restitution, this may not always be the case. Frequently, some work assignment for the actual victim, a letter of apology to the victim, or working on some community service project may be considered just restitution. Community service projects have included innovative assignments to coach Little League teams, tutor high school students, and restore damaged cemetery headstones. They have also involved more mundane clean-up assignments such as washing local police and fire vehicles, picking up litter alongside highways, and raking leaves in local parks.

SUMMARY

In a manner similar to the symbolic representation of peace officers as standardbearers of justice, the courts represent the mechanism (both real and symbolic) through which justice is mediated. This chapter has demonstrated that law enforcement is but one segment in the larger whole of the criminal justice system. In large measure, this chapter moved from the previous specific law enforcement focus to a broader judicial one. Included in this effort, at least partially, was the discussion of certain correctional efforts. This consideration draws us further toward seeing the criminal justice system as various subsystems operating in concert.

This chapter described some of the more relevant aspects of the criminal court process and some of the elements one might typically encounter. These elements included the nature of jury trials, how juries are selected and jurors challenged (voir dire), the ways a defendant might plead, and potential sentencing schemes that result when defendants are found guilty.

Throughout the discussion of these various justice sub-systems and elements, an attempt was made to express the necessity for preserving constitutionally guaranteed rights, including those of the accused.

REVIEW QUESTIONS

1. What does the right to due process, assured by the U.S. Constitution, represent with regard to the American justice system?

2. What are the reasons for permitting an accused felon to be released on bail?

3. What are some of the key features of the grand jury process? How is this process distinguishable from jurisdictions that do not have a grand jury system?

4. It has been suggested that juries are not necessarily composed of a defendant's peers. Why might this be the situation?

5. What might some of the arguments be for replacing indeterminate sentencing systems with determinate sentencing? What advantages might such a switch offer? What disadvantages might one expect from such a switch?

REFERENCES

Berg, Bruce L. and Calvin J. Larson. "Inmates' Perspectives on Determinate and Indeterminate Sentencing." *Journal of Behavioral Science and the Law* 7(1989):127–137.

Bing, Robert L. III. "Plea Bargaining: An Analysis of the Empirical Evidence." (Ph.D. dissertation. School of Criminology, Florida State University, 1987.)

Blumstein, Alfred, Jacqueline Cohen, Susan E. Martin, and Michael H. Tonry, eds. *Research on Sentencing: The Search for Reform.* Vol. 1 Washington, D.C.: National Academy, 1983.

Bureau of Justice Statistics. "Report to the Nation on Crime and Justice: The Data." Washington D.C.: Government Printing Office, 1983.

Bureau of Justice Statistics. "Prisoners in 1984." *Bureau of Justice Statistics Bulletin.* Washington, D.C.: Government Printing Office, 1985.

Bureau of Justice Statistics. *BJS Data Report, 1988.* Washington, D.C.: Government Printing Office, 1989

Florida Sentencing Guidelines (amended text). Tallahassee, Fl.: Sentencing Guidelines Commission, 1987.

Galvin, James. "Setting Prison Terms." Bureau of Statistics. Washington D.C.: Government Printing Office, 1983.

Goodstein, Lynne and John Hepburn. *Determinate Sentencing and Imprisonment: A Failure of Reform.* Cincinnati, Ohio: W.H. Anderson, 1985.

Greenberg David F., and Drew Humphries. "The Cooptation of Fixed Sentencing Reform." *Crime and Delinquency* 26(1980):206–225.

Knapp, Kay A. "Impact of the Minnesota Sentencing Guidelines on Sentencing Practices." *Hamline Law Review* 5(1982):237.

McCarthy, Belinda. *Intermediate Punishments: Intensive Supervision, Home Confinement and Electronic Surveillance.* Monsey, N.Y.: Willow Tree, 1987.

McGinnis, J.H. and K.A. Carlson "Offenders' Perception of Their Sentences." *Journal of Offender*

Counseling, Services, and Rehabilitation 5(1981):27–37.

McNeece, C. Aaron, and Mark W. Lusk. "A Consumer's View of Correctional Policy: Inmate Attitudes Regarding Determinate Sentencing." *Criminal Justice and Behavior* (December 1979):383–389.

Moore, Charles A. and Terance D. Miethe. "Regulated and Unregulated Sentencing Decisions: An Analysis of First-Year Practices Under Minnesota's Felony Sentencing Guidelines." *Law and Society Review* 20(1986):253–277.

National Advisory Commission on Criminal Justice Standards and Goals, The Courts. Washington, D.C.: Government Printing Office, 1973.

Neubauer, David W. *America's Courts and the Criminal Justice System,* 2d ed. Monterey, Calif.: Brooks Cole, 1985.

Sourcebook of Criminal Justice Statistics—1987. Washington, D.C.: Government Printing Office, 1988.

Stuckey, Gilbert B. *Procedures in the Justice System,* 3d ed. Columbus, Ohio: Merrill, 1986.

Travis, Lawrence F. III. "The Politics of Sentencing Reform." In M.L. Forst, ed. *Sentencing Reform: Experiments in Reducing Disparity.* Beverly Hills, Calif.: Sage, 1982.

Ward, David A. and Kenneth I. Schoen. *Confinement in Maximum Custody: New Last Resort Prisons in the U.S. and Western Europe.* Lexington, Mass.: Lexington, 1981.

CASES CITED IN TEXT

Apodaca v. Oregon 406 U.S. 404 (1972).
Ballew v. Georgia 435 U.S. 223 (1978).
Johnson v. Louisiana 406 U.S. 356 (1972).

Taylor v. Taintor 83 U.S. 66 (1873).
Williams v. Florida 399 U.S. 78 (1970).

CHAPTER 9

WOMEN AND MINORITIES
IN LAW ENFORCEMENT

INTRODUCTION: WOMEN AND
LAW ENFORCEMENT
    From Matron to Police Officer
    How Do Female Officers Compare
    to Male Officers?
    Promotion of Policewomen:
    Moving up through the Ranks
    Defeminization of Policewomen
    Theoretical Explanations for
    Gender-based Occupational
    Stereotyping

    The Police Personality and
    Policewomen
    Institutionalized Discrimination
    in Policing
    Minority Officers in Policing
    The Black Police Officer
    The Impact on Minority Hirings
    of Affirmative Action

Throughout the past several decades American police departments have made increasingly concerted efforts to recruit women and members of minority groups. Yet, the numbers of women and minority police officers working in police departments have grown very slowly. Also, the ratio of white male officers to either women or minority officers remains at a low level.

    Chapter Nine examines the historical efforts of women and other minority police officers as they become fully integrated members of American police departments. Included in this examination is consideration of various impediments, such as gender bias, institutionalized discrimination, and the role of affirmative action.

INTRODUCTION: WOMEN AND
LAW ENFORCEMENT

Recruiting and attracting women and other minorities to police work has been an important item facing police administrators for several decades. Although in general terms the empirical literature on minority police officers is scant, recent years have seen a rise in this literature base. For the most part, research on minority police officers focuses on the police subculture and related police personalities, the police organization, including bureaucratic and structural concerns, and police–community relations. Often, findings in these areas have not been taken to heart by police organizations unless public pressure or legal challenges have forced an issue. Among the more controversial areas of police research during the recent past are the roles and impact of hiring women and other minority police officers. This chapter will examine these issues in some detail. Let us begin with a review of the history of women in policing.

From Matron to Police Officer

Many historians suggest that women first entered the business of law enforcement around 1845 when the New York City police department hired two police matrons (Milton 1972, Berg and Budnick 1986). Yet, it is not until 1893, forty-eight years later, that Chicago's metropolitan police department appointed Marie Owens a police officer (Higgins 1951). In 1910, Los Angeles hired a woman police officer, Alice Stebbins Wells. Her hiring received considerable fanfare and publicity— most of it negative. Throughout America at that time, the public's strong displeasure with police officers has been based upon the belief that no "self-respecting women would want to work with debauched women and criminals" (Feinman 1986, 84).

When women began entering police work in the nineteenth century, it was chiefly in response to increased concern by society over social problems involving women and children, especially young girls. Many of these problems were beyond the interest of male police officers or other distributors of public services. Fundamental changes in social living, rapid urbanization, immigration, and increases in technological requirements in the work place all contributed to vast increases in unemployment. The nineteenth century witnessed a steady increase in the number of women arrested and incarcerated for drunkenness, prostitution, disorderly conduct, theft, and vagrancy. As the incidence of crime by females and child-related crimes increased, police departments felt the need to have matrons present in the station to handle these cases. Thus, the presence of women in police work chiefly arose from a social work basis and not one of law enforcement or crime investigation.

Partially as a residual from this ingrained social-worker orientation of police matrons, women officers continued to operate in police forces in this general capacity until the late 1960s. Their police work was typically limited to assisting in cases involving women, children, and teen-age girls (Talney 1969, Hamilton 1971, Feinman 1986). Although the hiring of Alice Stebbins Wells set off a nationwide series of hirings of women throughout the 1920s, female officers were not permitted to involve themselves in what male officers would call "real police work." Real police work, to them, involved patrol work, investigating all sorts of crime, and apprehending suspects.

As with other male-dominated occupations, World War I brought women into the labor market, including operational areas of law enforcement. By the close of World War I, women were employed in some police capacity in over 220 cities. Frequently, women operated in separate **women's bureaus,** such as New York's famous women's precinct, established in the spring of 1921 (Hamilton 1971). Clarice Feinman (1986) outlines the specialized duties of early women police officers in New York's and other cities' women's bureaus. These duties included handling cases involving juvenile delinquency, female victims of sex offenses, women criminal suspects, abandoned infants, missing persons, vice squads, matron duty, and clerical work. Although there were additionally a few women assigned to units involved in active police work such as detective bureaus, these were very few. Even when a policewoman did find herself working in the role of a more traditional law enforcement officer, she was paid an appreciably lower salary than men in her unit and typically was restricted to the rank of patrol officer throughout her career.

By the end of World War I, various social reform movements, spearheaded by an assortment of women's organizations, had concluded that a significant need existed for women in policing. Throughout the war years, female officers had filled an important gap in law enforcement dealings with children and women. Policewomen of this era had argued that they should maintain the social service orientation they had been limited to. In a manner of speaking, female officers projected a fairly consistent false consciousness that supported their role as nurturing social workers and not traditional police officers. In Mary Hamilton's own words (1971, 183), "The policewoman has been likened to the mother. Hers is the strong arm of the law as it is expressed in a woman's guiding hand."

This maternal social-service role of women officers extended beyond merely working with juveniles. The attitude and belief that arose was that women officers were somehow better-suited than men when it came to dealing with women offenders and victims, runaway girls, and children of assorted ages.

Box 9.1

GENDER IDENTIFICATION AND OCCUPATIONAL STEREOTYPES

When Americans turn on their television sets and see a neatly dressed man carrying a brief case as he walks into a court room, they easily accept his portrayal as a lawyer. When a similarly neatly dressed woman walks into the same television courtroom, there may be pause to wonder whether she is a client or an attorney. Even after learning (through plot development) that she is, in fact, the prosecuting attorney, the viewing audience may be dubious. Although television portrayals by women of demonstrative lawyers have increased during recent years, they continue to occur much less frequently than such portrayal by males. When it does occur, a portrayal frequently depicts the woman lawyer as a stereotypic overzealous, aggressive, overachiever. Interestingly, these are characteristics which we revere in men, but when displayed by women many people immediately consider these negative qualities. In such cases, many see these character portrayals as the projection of "male-egos," rather than portrayals of dynamic women.

Although women have been portrayed as forceful police detectives (consider, the long and successful run of "Cagney and Lacey"), these programs too are few in number and, like most cop shows, tend to promote the image of the police as supercops. These depictions of policewomen often reinforce the belief that "successful" policewomen need to project macho images.

Sociological literature frequently distinguishes between occupations that have been stereotyped as either masculine or feminine. Masculine occupations are commonly associated with high levels of competency, competition, assertiveness, managerial skills, and technological proficiency (Shiner 1975; Schaefer and Lamm 1989). Conversely, feminine occupations are stereotypically associated with caregiving, clerical skills, subservience, and generally soft and emotional characteristics (Kanter 1979; Schaefer and Lamm 1989).

In 1979, 43 percent of the total labor force in the United States were women, and by 1986, over 47 percent of all laborers were female (Bureau of Labor and Statistics Bulletin, 1980, 1987). Yet, in 1979 only 3.5 percent of all municipal police officers were female, and by 1988 only 7.5. One could suggest that the proportion of women officers has doubled in America during the past 18 years. One should also recognize that while other occupations have radically increased their proportion of women workers, municipal police agencies have only increased by 4 percent. The table below illustrates the growth of women in policing during the past 18 years.

(continued)

BOX 9.1   continued

PERCENTAGE OF FEMALE POLICE OFFICERS FROM ·1971–88

MUNICIPAL	TOTAL NUMBER OF OFFICERS	NUMBER OF FEMALE OFFICERS	PERCENT TOTAL
1971	··225,474	3,156	1.4
1972	269,420	4,041	1.5
1973	276,808	4,705	1.7
1974	286,973	5,739	2.0
1975	292,346	6,139	2.1
1976	287,448	6,898	2.4
1977	293,019	7,911	2.7
1978	294,579	9,426	3.2
1979	296,332	10,371	3.5
1980	294,181	11,178	3.8
1981	297,324	13,082	4.4
1982	298,334	14,021	4.7
1983	304,012	15,504	5.1
1984	309,960	17,357	5.6
1985	312,713	19,388	6.2
1986	318,484	21,338	6.7
1987	320,959	22,788	7.1
1988	325,095	24,382	7.5

·All figures derive from the FBI Uniform Crime Reports for the respective years. The starting year of 1971 was selected because prior to this data no distinction was made between the total number of police employees (both civilian and sworn) and exclusively "sworn" officers. In addition, prior to 1971, total employee figures failed to distinguish between the number of male and female officers.

··Prior to 1980, figures were offered for only municipal agencies. Beginning in 1980, figures for both municipal and "all other" agencies (e.g., any sworn officer position) were included. To assure consistency, all figures used represent totals from municipal police agencies only.

Unlike her male counterpart, whose policing tools were his gun and baton, female officers used the tools of counseling and report writing, and assumed a maternal role. "As mothers of the next generation," Mary Hamilton ([1924] 1971) once said, female offenders must be viewed as a threat to society. Hamilton also stated:

> A policewoman who corrects a vicious environment is saving boys and girls from lives of crime and this is exactly what a policewomen does do. There are anti-social dangers, backwardness, truancy, incorri-

> gibility and asociability, which if not detected during early childhood become definite causes of crime. To correct these before they become fixed is the duty of the public schools today. If our children are to be saved for the good of society everyone must join together—the parents, the teachers and all community workers. To this group belongs the policewoman. [Mary Hamilton 1971, 153]

To a large measure, comparing the work of policewomen to social workers and other community workers increased the acceptance of women in law enforcement. In this role, women were not a threat to male officers. Even in today's law enforcement community, female officers frequently face a similar "Catch–22" (Berg and Budnick 1986). As they report:

> On the one hand, women may choose to assume traditional feminine roles while working in law enforcement (that is, caretaking, nurturing, and matronly roles). Certainly, these traditional female roles pose no threat to male officers. . . . On the other hand, female officers who do emulate male officers are frequently seen as a career threat by these male officers (these female officers are on patrol and may be considered for command positions just as the male officers are). [Berg and Budnick 1986, 317]

During the early days of women in policing, the assertion was that women's abilities were different from male officers'. This allowed them to fill a unique position in policing rather than a duplicative one and further led to tolerance of policewomen. Although some female officers did desire to be real peace officers and enter the realm of patrol, invariably they performed their tasks in fashions consistent with their presumed natural abilities (Feinman 1986). In most instances, women officers were deployed as decoys in vice raids and continued to investigate rape, abortion, and prostitution cases. It was not until the 1960s that any really significant changes emerged in the roles and functions of American policewomen.

Throughout the 1960s various federal equal employment laws assisted women and other minorities in their attempts to gain parity with white men in the labor force (Townsey 1982, Berg and Budnick 1986, 1987). For example, both the Equal Pay Act of 1963 and Title VII of the Civil Rights Act of 1964 banned the gender-based discrimination previously practiced by labor unions and various non-governmental employers. Similarly, in the 1970s, additional federal actions and legislation laid the foundation for increased equality for women and other minority police officers. For instance, in 1971, the U.S. Supreme Court in *Reed* v. *Reed* declared that any state law

discriminating on the basis of sex violates the equal protection clause of the Fourteenth Amendment (Milton 1972, Feinman 1986). This decision was buttressed in 1973 in the case of *Frontiero* v. *Richardson*. In this case, the Supreme Court ruled that sex, like race, is a characteristic that must be justified if used as a classification of people for legislative purposes (Milton 1972, Feinman 1986).

It was not until the 1964 Civil Rights Act was amended under Title VII of the 1972 Civil Rights Act that women in policing began to achieve a social and functional status even remotely similar to their male colleagues'. This amendment, commonly referred to simply as Title VII, prohibited employment discrimination on the basis of race, creed, color, sex, or national origin (Charles 1982). In addition to increasing the regulatory powers of the Equal Employment Opportunity Commission, Title VII's passage meant that women could negotiate identical terms and compensations for work similar to that performed by men.

In what may have been informally a situation related to Title VII, Pennsylvania in 1972 became the first state to offer both male and female state troopers identical work responsibilities. A number of other states fell in line behind Pennsylvania, and by 1984 all but South Dakota and Wyoming had women functioning as peace officers in their state police forces (*UCR* 1985). In the wake of these civil rights achievements, other legislation followed. The Revenue Sharing Act of 1972, the 1978 Pregnancy Discrimination Act, and the 1979 Justice System Improvement Act had significant impact on the advancement and growth of women and other minority groups in the labor market. These acts made it more difficult to continue to institutionally discriminate against women and other minorities.

How Do Female Officers Compare to Male Officers?

There has long been a research interest regarding the question of whether women make effective police officers. There is additionally a considerable amount of interest directed toward the question of how great an impact, if any, policewomen are making on police organizational structures and policies (Homant 1983, Homant and Kennedy 1985).

In a review of nine major evaluations of women in policing, Merry Morash and Jack Green (1986) indicated that women were found to be less capable then their male counterparts only in a single study. However, Morash and Green raised serious objections to all of these studies because each suffered from a host of methodological problems. For example, they all failed to examine differences within same-gender groups and to take into account that indexes used to assess male and female officers represent many areas of variation. Variance and distribution scores were often ignored so that when female and male officers' scores differed widely, it was impossible to determine whether this represented a majority of females differing significantly from males or that a few extreme scores had skewed the results.

Morash and Green additionally indicated that these studies each defined positive attributes for the police officer in terms of stereotypic *masculine qualities* (e.g., assertive, aggressive). These studies also often measured qualities that had little or nothing to do with actual police work. Finally, there was confusion among these studies as to whether arrests were always the most desirable outcome in a police–citizen encounter (See Whitaker and Phillips 1983), in other words, whether arrests accurately measured police effectiveness. Morash and Green concluded that collectively the nine evaluations of policewomen suggested that while gender differences do not immediately disqualify women from policing, they do have implications for police employment. In other words, one could interpret the findings as suggesting that only a limited number and certain type of woman should be in policing.

Robert Homant and Daniel Kennedy (1985, 30) indicated that, "any research that attempts to compare policewomen with policemen threatens to raise more problems than it answers." For example, because of the disparate numbers of women in policing, it is rather difficult to obtain large, representative samples of them. Even were one to attempt a matched sample, there are countless variables that might be employed to match the two groups of men and women, none of which would necessarily represent accurately either male or female officers. At least as problematic as sampling problems is the question of how one goes about interpreting differences between policemen and policewomen (Homant and Kennedy 1985). Does one attribute identified differences to a cultural socialization process, such as the one that promoted the false consciousness manifest in the 1920s; are differences the result of gender-based differences; are they an artifact of police training or the style of research; might differences between male and female officers result from life experiences that create certain attitudes, values, or motivations, and did these occur prior or subsequent to joining the force; finally, how does one explain similarities? Then again, how does one explain the highly likely overlap that may result from all the factors as explanations for differences?

Early research on women police officers tended to be directed to the question of whether women were suited for police work because of their emotional temperament and mother image. Later research, particularly that undertaken in the face of the various pieces of legislation of the late 1960s and 70s, began to consider the rigors of physical endurance and agility required of policemen and women who wanted to be police. In spite of adversities, research repeatedly indicated that women performed their policing tasks, even physically demanding ones, as well as men (Block and Anderson 1974, Sherman 1975). One traditional belief has been that women officers are less effective than male officers in making felony arrests. In an examination of 2,293 officers in Texas and Oklahoma, James David (1984) convincingly established that the arrest rates for male and female officers were almost identical.

Robert Homant and Daniel Kennedy (1985) found that female police officers were more frequently sympathetic to the victims of spousal abuse than male officers. They additionally found that policewomen, more frequently than policemen, referred abused spouses to special shelters for their safety and counseling. These findings were comparable to conclusions Homant and Kennedy (1984) had previously identified and continue to support the notion that women officers contribute positively to police work.

Policewomen have regularly been shown in research to accomplish their police functions in satisfactory ways, often in ways superior to their male colleagues. Van Wormer (1981) found the question actually became whether *men* should be permitted to be patrol officers.

Men traditionally have been deployed in patrol functions because of alleged superiority over women in physical strength, ability to handle night work, and assumed aggressiveness when confronted with violent situations. According to Kathrine Van Wormer (1981), however, there are some serious disadvantages to using men. For instance, male officers, to a greater extent than female officers, are apt to provoke violence during a given citizen–police officer encounter. Similarly, men are more likely than women to use unnecessary physical force to effect an arrest. In addition, many demographic profiles suggest that male officers often have a lower level of education than female officers, who additionally tend to be better at writing reports and keeping records. By their own admission, men are not believed to be as good as women at handling female victims or perpetrators, juveniles, and runaways. Although many of these male deficiencies likely can be overcome by special training, they certainly do suggest some of the impact that female officers are having on the organizational aspects of policing.

Promotion of Policewomen: Moving Up through the Ranks

Although a number of policewomen achieved the rank of detective during the 1930s and 1940s, few were ever able to move higher than the rank of patrol officer. In part, the discrimination was justified along the lines of educational qualifications. Since policewomen did women's work they were not trained in a comparable manner to male officers and, consequently, could not pursue the same promotion schedules. In 1952, several New York City policewomen applied to take the competitive examination for promotion to the rank of sergeant, but were refused because New York City's civil service agency had no job description for women above the rank of officer (Feinman 1985). In 1961 another New York City policewoman applied to take the sergeant's examination and was denied. But in this case, Officer Felicia Shpritzer took the case to court. Two years and three court cases later, Officer Shpritzer was permitted to take the examination, which she passed (Shpritzer 1959, Milton 1972, Feinman 1986).

Another early leader in the promotion effort was Gertrude Schimmel. Officer Schimmel had met and worked with Felicia Shpritzer during their early years in New York law enforcement. Schimmel had also taken and passed the sergeant's examination in 1964. In 1971, Schimmel made law enforcement history by being the first woman to obtain the rank of deputy inspector, the highest uniformed position in the New York Police Department (Milton 1972).

Although there have been increasing numbers of women officers successfully gaining rank in the nation's police forces, they have also been described as less qualified and less efficient than male officers. Women officers may receive lower performance evaluations from their male evaluators for several reasons, chief among them, perhaps, the fears of male officers of increased competition for a small number of promotions (Wexler and Quinn 1985). Harriman (1985) asserts that while effective women managers have been found to differ little from effective male managers in their attitudes, motivations, and behaviors, their careers, nevertheless, progress more slowly than those of males.

Susan Martin (1989) reported that in a review of studies on leadership, no differences in behavior between sexes were found after controlling for situational and other demographic variables. Martin also notes, however, that several studies tend to link effective leadership traits with stereotypical, masculine traits and consequently regard women as less effective leaders (See Schein 1975, Harriman 1985).

Although there have been apparent increases in the numbers of women entering law enforcement careers, most police agencies continue to underrepresent female officers. In 1980 Marcia Greenberger observed that many police agencies had failed to comply with various federal directives (such as Title VII). In particular, these agencies had not dealt adequately with gender-based employment barriers. Also, a large number of police agencies had not expanded the duties of female officers to make these duties comparable to those of males. Similar observations about disparities between federal employment guidelines and hiring practices have been offered by Daniel Bell (1982), Rachel Braun (1984), and William Heffnernan and Timothy Stroup (1985).

Possibly as a response to obstacles and criticism levied against them, many women officers appear to feel a need to abandon femininity to compete with male officers and advance in the police ranks (Berg and Budnick 1986).

This has been described as the defeminization of policewomen and has been the subject of considerable debate and research (Heffner 1976; Martin 1979, 1980; Gross 1981; Berg and Budnick 1986, 1987).

Defeminization of Policewomen

Put simply, defeminization may be seen as the acceptance and emulation by women of traditional male gender-role behaviors, attitudes, and traits. These attributes may be understood to include being active, authoritative, assertive, autonomous, and daring. In other words, defeminized policewomen are described as having taken on what sociology texts call traditionally masculine characteristics (See Schaefer and Lamm 1989). Heffner (1976) and to some extend Van Wormer (1981) indicate that masculine characteristics are perceived as beneficial for patrol officers, regardless of their possessor's gender.

Some research has suggested that defeminization is the result of tokenism and results from policewomen attempting to gain acceptance of their male peers by outdoing them (Martin 1979). Unfortunately, this attempt by some policewomen to become super-cops frequently works against them. Instead of being embraced by their fellow officers, they are perceived as serious threats to the careers of male officers. After all, these women demonstrate not that they are capable police officers, but better than most. Possibly as a response to the perception that policewomen pose a career threat, it is not uncommon for male officers to demean or ridicule defeminized female officers. Although all police officers are subject to a certain amount of off-color, locker-room humor, defeminized officers find themselves characterized as bitches, castrating, or even lesbians (Gross 1983).

Similarly, recent research suggests that many male officers believe that they must be "chivalrous" and protect policewomen when they are partnered with them. Quoting one of their subjects, Bryant and his associates (1985) state:

. . . The thing is, a lot of men are still very protective toward women. I've been crewed with policemen before, when we had an incident car, and if it is a rough situation they'll say, "Stay there" because

Box 9.2

MR. AND MRS. OFFICER: POLICEWOMEN AND THEIR HUSBANDS

The following excerpt originally appeared in a 1974 *New York Times* article. The original ran the day after the announcement of Gertrude Schimmel's appointment to full inspector, making her (at the time) the highest ranking policewoman on the New York city police force. Although this article is now almost seventeen years old, many of the attitudes and practices it describes continue to be accurate of today's police.

The man in the life of a woman in blue is often another police officer. Officers Cataldo and Acha are members of two sets of "cop couples." There is the professional one: Sharon Cataldo works with different male partners, but Dina Acha, because she is on the Youth Squad detail (mainly looking for truants), has had a steady radio car partner, Vincent Lanzante, for several weeks.

Asked how he liked working with a woman, Officer Lanzante, a round faced 31-year-old, replied: "I like working with this particular officer." "Is my wife jealous? My wife wasn't waiting for a policewoman to come along for me to fool around," he said. "We've been married for ten years."

Off duty, the women have other partners in uniform. In their Staten Island home, Police Officer Frank Cataldo of the 67th Precinct in Brooklyn beams fondly at his wife and tells about her coming to the door in curlers—"Yeah, a cop in curlers."

Frank Cataldo, 18 years on the force, says he believes police women are here to stay, but feels they belong in less dangerous spots: plainclothes work, decoy work, narcotics or vice.

"Girls are capable of doing the same job except in a fight," he said. He has never refused to work with a woman, but he feels that the idea of a woman on patrol is "lousy." "I know what the street is like," he continued. "I worry more about her."

Is he jealous of his vivacious wife, looking very natty in her well-fitted slacks and blue shirt, her shoulder-length hair tucked under her hat?

"Sure," he said, "but I trust her definitely. If a guy and a girl are going to do anything, they'll do it. But a cop who puts his job on the line for a girl is stupid."

His wife agrees, but adds that gossip in the precinct is rampant. "So far," she said, ticking off numbers with a hand flashing a diamond wedding ring, "I'm supposed to be having an affair with one lieutenant, one sergeant and another police officer. Can you imagine a lieutenant risking his job for me?"

"He's a pro," says Dina Acha of police officer Carlos E. Acha of the Ninth Precinct on the Lower East Side known as "Fort Apache South."

"He knows you're too busy in a car to get into a personal thing. Sure you talk, but mostly about the job."

The Achas met at the Police Academy—"He was my company sergeant, he ordered me to marry him." They were married, in uniform, during a recess in Criminal Court a year ago and are looking forward to a belated honeymoon in Tahiti soon.

The 13th, on East 20th street, with its close proximity to the Academy, is considered a model precinct. It has a woman captain, two women sergeants (superior officers get ma'am instead of sir) and 15 women in the ranks.

Source: Angela Taylor, "Women Police Officers," *The New York Times,* November 2, 1974:34. Copyright © 1974 by The New York Times Company. Reprinted by permission.

they really do protect you—they protect you like their wives!

The kind of situation Bryant et al. (1985) described placed policewomen in a serious double-bind. On the one hand, if the officer remains in the car, she fails to provide back-up for her partner and may both increase his danger and set herself up for a charge of cowardice. On the other hand, if she gets out of her car to do the job she was trained and hired to do—which even the greenest male rookie would be expected to do—her male partner may become injured due to his preoccupation with protecting her.

Several studies during the 1980s concluded that policewomen may be forced to sacrifice at least some of their femininity if they desire to be accepted by male officers, as well as seriously considered for advancement beyond the rank of sergeant (Kennedy and Homant 1981; Gross 1983; Berg and Budnick 1986).

In one study, Sally Gross (1983) assessed data collected in a study of 288 trainees attending the Southeast Florida Institute of Criminal Justice during 1982–1983. In her preliminary findings, Gross found that the more successful female academy recruits displayed a number of masculine mannerisms:

Women who show masculine behavior rather than feminine ones will get along better with academy classmates. This is consistent with previously reported findings that women's acceptance is a function of peer relations and fitting in, which in this environment means exhibiting masculine traits . . . [By the end of eight weeks of training] . . . the more feminine they [recruits] were, the worse they felt about themselves.

Confounding her preliminary findings, in later more thorough examinations, Gross (1986) began to observe that other females (those exhibiting at once both masculine and feminine characteristics) tended to gain the greatest success during their time in the academy.

Many people in society may look at these masculine characteristics as detracting from policewomens' *expected* feminine role as women. As a consequence, many police-women themselves may be faced with certain role strains. Their confidence and self-image as wives, mothers, sisters, friends, as well as police officers, may invoke serious emotional conflicts and stress for some policewomen. In some cases, the only alternative may be leaving the police force. For some others the resolution may come from defeminizing at least during the working hours. In many cases, some compromise, either in terms of restricted advancement or the type of assignments, may allow a policewomen to cut a niche in her department.

The possible career pathways of police-women are graphically displayed in Box 9.3. As suggested in the diagram, some women may join the police already predisposed to conducting themselves in a masculine manner, in short, already defeminized. Other women may enter the field of law enforcement with no predisposition. Finally, a third category of women may enter the academy as androgynies.

Perhaps the singular most important function of the police academy beyond basic training in a state's codes is the development of uniform behavior within a department to establish objective, rather than subjective, decision-making skills in the field (Harris 1973, Bittner 1980). Standardized behavior has several compelling advantages. First, it reduces the likelihood of public antagonism from disparate behavior. Second, it offers a consistent, externalized protocol for officer behaviors: formal (written) rules and procedures, report forms, and so forth. Third, standardized behavior offers a means for administrators to plan and coordinate systematically the activities of those under their command.

As suggested in Figure 9.1, women, unlike men, are faced with several recurring dilemmas throughout their careers. Early during their academy training, female recruits must decide whether they will accept or reject the

Box 9.3 _____

A MODEL OF THE POLICEWOMEN'S CAREER PATH CHOICES

[TYPES OF FEMALE POLICE RECRUITS ENTERING THE ACADEMY]

Masculine Women   Androgynous Women   Feminine Women

[WHILE ATTENDING THE POLICY ACADEMY]

Potential For:
Simple change of mind about career decision
Role Strain
Role Conflict
Occupational Stress

Options:

Quit the Academy
Defeminize (adopt masculine characteristics)
Maintenance of Original Gender Characteristics
(Masculine, Androgynous, or Feminine)

- -
[AFTER ATTENDING THE ACADEMY]
- -

Rookies Now Confronted With Increased Probability of:
Role Conflicts
Role Strain
Stress . . . . [Rookies Unable to Adapt]
EXIT POLICING

[Successfully Adapting Rookies]
CONTINUE A POLICE CAREER

MASCULINE AND ANDROGYNOUS ROOKIES	ROOKIES MAINTAINING THEIR FEMININITY
[FIELD POSITIONS] Fair Potential for Command (Self-Assessment of Job Satisfaction)	[NON-FIELD POSITIONS] Low Potential for Command (Self-Assessment of Job Satisfaction)

[TOO LOW] EXIT POLICING	[High Satisfaction] ORIENT TOWARD CAREER STATUS	[TOO LOW] EXIT POLICING	[Adequate Job Satisfaction] ORIENT TOWARD CAREER STATUS

Adapted from Berg and Budnick. "Defeminization of Women in Law Enforcement: A New Twist in the Traditional Police Personality." *Police Science and Administration* 14(1986):318.

traditional, subordinate role for women in policing. Conversely, female recruits must decide if they are willing to adopt various masculine characteristics that will provide them greater access to command police positions. Naturally, throughout their law enforcement careers, women, like men, make vacillating decisions about whether any of it is worthwhile.

Theoretical Explanations for Gender-Based Occupational Stereotyping

As stated in Chapter One of this text, criminologists and sociologists often regard aspects of the criminal justice system from various theoretical perspectives. In the case of the role played by women in police work, there are several possible theoretical constructs. These include structural functionalism, conflict theory, and a perspective in symbolic interactionism commonly referred to as labeling theory. Each of these approaches can be used to express a plausible explanation for the predominance of the subordinate role of women in policing.

From a structural functional perspective, society can be understood as a complex composite of many interrelated parts, each performing some function individually that collectively maintains the entire system. From this orientation, women can be seen as meaningful because they perform an important function for society by bearing and raising children, as well as for teaching them basic social values, and by maintaining the home (cleaning, food preparation, etc.). In addition, women might be seen as providing an emotionally supportive role as mother and caretaker of the husband and family (Parsons and Bales 1955, Jaggar and Rothenberg 1984). While these functions are certainly crucial contributions to society, they usually remain outside the marketplace and labor force, since they do not traditionally require a salary. Therefore, a relatively low economic value is placed on this role when it does become part

of the paid labor force. Extending this to policing, it would follow that insofar as nurturing and caregiving remain the major career outlet, the female officer will find herself desirable. For instance, policewomen continue to excel in matron work, victim assistance, and juvenile units such as run-away programs, but must struggle to demonstrate even satisfactory performance in regular street patrol.

The second construct that offers a possible explanation for gender disparities in occupational settings is conflict theory. According to this paradigm, women hold lower status because they have been exploited by men who have traditionally held power positions in society (Hartman 1977, 1981). Men made the laws, regulated the rights of women with regard to their political efficacy (the right to vote and hold office), income, property ownership and the right to inheritance, and even rights surrounding birth control. Men forbade women from entering the work force, joining unions, entering certain professions, and gaining educations either legally or by tradition (Eshleman and Cashion 1983, Schaefer and Lamm 1989). Extending this image to policewomen, and as represented in Figure 9.1, men regulate the femininity and, in turn, career pathways open to women in policing.

Finally, the third general theoretical construct is gender labeling or, as it is sometimes called, gender identification. According to this perspective, individuals are labeled at birth as male or female, usually by family members. Throughout early childhood, society tends to reinforce these original labels. For instance, little boys are given baseballs, trucks, and G.I. Joe Action Figures to play with, while little girls are given Barbie dolls and cooking toys. Certainly, considerable improvements have been made throughout society with regard to secondary reinforcement of such gender identifications. Put simply, most elementary school textbooks no longer identify certain types of occupations with only boys or only girls. Yet, just as most of the

American labor force once was dominated by men, law enforcement as an occupation continues to cling to the institutional idea that policing is really men's work.

According to Susan Martin (1980) and following a gender-labeling model, by affixing the label feminine, society continues to condition women. Martin also indicated that this sort of labeling presents many women who might otherwise consider law enforcement careers or other male-dominated occupations with insurmountable obstacles:

Many occupations, particularly those offering the greatest income, prestige, and power, call for qualities that are antithetical to the female role and femininity. Most women resolve the potential normative conflict between "appropriate" occupational role and sex role behavior by engaging in jobs in which the tasks involve service to or nurture of others and in which they are subordinates of men. [Susan Martin 1980, 17]

For some women, the prospects of being involved in police work are so inviting that they are willing to overcome aspects of their personalities that might otherwise run counter to career success. In many cases, there may actually be nothing to overcome but the misbelief that there is. In any event, women considering careers in law enforcement are repeatedly faced with role conflicts, stress, and self-reflective reevaluations of their goals in life.

The Police Personality and Policewomen

Regardless of various conflicting social roles and pressures, women continue to make advances toward equality in the ranks of policing. One major obstacle that policewomen still need to overcome, and one that is not generally associated with other occupations, is the "police personality." It remains controversial whether one enters policing already in possession of a police personality or if one adapts to the police subculture by fostering this stereotypic persona.

The police personality is thought generally to be a combination of characteristics and behaviors that have come to be commonly used to stereotype police officers. Often these characteristics are given to include a desire to be in control of situations, assertiveness, cynicism, an authoritarian attitude, a wish to be aloof from civilians, an increased solidarity with other officers, and a tendency to be physically aggressive.

In part, this type of personality may have grown out of profiles of police recruits of the past. Until the mid-1970s, police officers entering the nation's police academies were predominantly white males, ranged in age from 21 to 25, and had both military and combat experience. Perhaps as a consequence of this kind of recruit, it is understandable that the civilian image of police officers was one of an authoritative, para-military, perhaps violent, take-charge guy. Add to this the various violent police–civilian encounters during the antiwar protests and sit-ins of the 1960s (the 1968 Democratic convention in Chicago) and the idea of a police personality becomes rather vivid.

Although the concept of a police personality is very easy to identify, its actual existence is not as easily demonstrated empirically. As Daniel Kennedy and Robert Homant (1981, 347) indicate, " . . . Numerous studies reach essentially the opposite conclusion and tend to suggest that policing contains the same range of personality types likely to be found in any occupation." The police personality will be more extensively considered in Chapter Ten, along with issues of police subculture in general.

Several researchers have argued that the token representation of women on police forces is insufficient to hasten changes in attitude among the majority group of white male officers. Certainly, in spite of many advances in progressive departments, women in policing have not risen appreciably beyond token representation in American policing nationally (See Martin 1989, 323–324). One explanation for this token status may be that access to police positions has been systematically denied to women. This systematic denial, or **institutionalized discrimination,** is detailed in the next section.

Institutionalized Discrimination in Policing

Each of us has at some time or another felt discrimination. Perhaps it was a teacher who chose another student because he or she liked that student better, an aunt who preferred your brother and lavished him with gifts while ignoring you, the captain of the sand-lot baseball team who selected his or her best friend over you to fill the last spot on the team, or maybe some employer who chose another candidate because that person was not (or was) a particular religion, race, age, or gender. This kind of individual discrimination, although unkind, operates chiefly on a one-to-one basis. But there is additionally a more systematic and encompassing type of discrimination: institutionalized discrimination.

Institutionalized discrimination is defined here as denial of opportunities and equal rights to individuals and groups that results from the habitual operations of an organization or institution in society.

For example, in 1966, the streets of Chicago's Puerto Rican neighborhoods were repeatedly filled with rioters. As with other minority communities during the 1960s, Chicago's Puerto Rican residents voiced complaints of police brutality, harassment, and unprovoked assaults. When the dust had cleared and media and federal investigations began to emerge, it was discovered that the Chicago Police Department did not have even a single Puerto Rican officer on the force. Inquiries found that the department had been adhering to a height requirement that exceeded the average height of most Puerto Ricans.

The use by police agencies of height or physical agility requirements to restrict entrance by women and other minorities, while meeting the physical stature and abilities of white males, has been called institutional racism (Locke 1980). In essence, institutional racism may be understood to exist in policing when agency procedures create or perpetuate situations of advantage for the dominant group (white males) to the exclusion or restriction of minority groups (Chesler 1976, Locke 1980, Townsey 1982).

The type of institutionalized discrimination experienced by minorities has been eliminated in most police departments. Nonetheless, there continue to be instances where minority police officers suffer prejudice and various kinds of institutionalized discrimination. In the following section of this chapter, the effects on policing of the influx of minorities are considered.

Minority Officers in Policing

During the past thirty years, American police departments have been changing with regard to racial and gender composition. Since the 1970s, most police agencies have made efforts to recruit and hire women and other minority members. Of course, not all departments have undertaken these efforts willingly. Some agencies have only moved to increase the number of minority officers in their agencies in the face of numerous blue-ribbon national commissions advocating such changes and following legal battles that resisted these changes. In some cities, Hispanic and black officers were not hired until sufficient political pressure was levied by local black communities. Jack Kuykendall and David Burns (1980) state that in some departments the hiring of black officers came after church and civic groups created enough political pressure.

The increased hiring of Hispanic officers, which occurred during the 1980s, is of fairly recent origin. So, too, is the rise in hirings among Asian officers. This surge in minority-officer hiring arose in the late 1980s after police departments recognized the growth of Indochinese neighborhoods in many of

America's large cities. Because Hispanic and Asian officers have only recently entered American police work, little empirical research has examined the impact of their hirings. Black police officers, however, have been serving on municipal police forces since 1872, when Chicago hired its and the nation's first black officer. By 1894, there were approximately twenty-three black officers serving in Chicago (Walker 1980, 61).

Yet, in spite of a rather long historical affiliation with police work, black officers continue to be underrepresented on police forces of even several of the country's largest city police departments (Kuykendall and Burns 1985).

The Black Police Officer

In the late 1950s and 1960s, some agencies recognized specific reasons for bringing black and other minority officers into the ranks. These departments believed that in order to represent community interests more effectively, the force needed to be better represented by community members. Frequently, however, this translated into hiring black officers to patrol black neighborhoods, where they were permitted to arrest only black suspects (Sullivan 1989).

In his book *Black Police, White Society*, Stephen Leinen (1984, 166) states:

> *Over time, white police have come to share a set of occupational values and beliefs about minority groups that set them [referring to the police as an aggregate] apart from significant segments of the black community. The recruitment of greater numbers of blacks into the lower ranks in the early 1970s was part of a larger effort designed to narrow this distance.*

Leinen suggests that police agencies assumed that the new black recruits, by virtue of their natural cultural links to the community, would re-establish both the police role and image in those neighborhoods.

These assumptions, although viewed as progressive for their time, failed to consider how black community residents viewed black police officers. Since white officers were viewed as the enemy, as much for their symbolic position in the system as for their being white, it was the police who were the real enemy, not only the white police officers. Similarly, police departments failed to weigh the response of their new black officers. Many of these black police officers resented the department's efforts to restrict their assignments to what were high-crime, dangerous, slum precincts (Alex 1969, Leinen 1984).

An odd type of institutionalized discrimination arose. Chiefly because they were black and presumed to have a greater affinity for black community problems, these officers found themselves working in far more hazardous areas than most of their more seasoned white colleagues.

Even as black officers were increasing in representation in some police departments, their role in police work remained restricted. Typically, black officers were denied high profile positions or liaison roles between the department and other elements of the justice system or public. Activities such as honor guards in parades, public relation positions, head of special task forces, and other specialized assignments were seldom offered to black officers.

Similar to the discrimination evident in evaluations of female officers, black officers too were institutionally discriminated against during their performance evaluations. In turn, these low-scoring evaluations were used to determine raises, promotions, and specialized assignments. Stephen Leinen reports that by the mid-1960s only twenty-two law enforcement agencies had black officers ranking above patrol officer. Even when black officers were granted raises or promotions in rank, these promotions seldom placed them in command positions. Even black lieutenants were expected to walk beats (Alex 1969). Again, questions concerning their effectiveness on the job often inaccurately addressed their minority status, rather than the more objective problems of this type of an assignment for any inexperienced officer. One might even question whether black officers might not have been placed on such hazardous duty because they were viewed as expendable by white commanders.

Nicholas Alex (1969) has indicated that during the early push for black officers, these men suffered from what he termed **double marginality.** On the one hand, black officers were perceived by their white colleagues as likely to give blacks encountered in the field a break. On the other hand, black officers were frequently subject to overt racism and discrimination by white officers.

In his examination of conditions, Alex (1969) found that the manner in which black police officers interacted with other blacks ranged from those suggesting that black suspects should be treated differently and better than white ones, to black officers responding more harshly to black offenders (Alex 1969, Leinen 1984).

Perhaps the single most difficult barrier to encouraging minority members to apply for police positions is the image that police officers have in minority communities (Hochstedler and Conley 1986, Sullivan 1989). In many minority communities the police are viewed as the enemy. In recent years, among immigrant members of some Hispanic communities the image of police officer carries the additional stigma of police from their home countries, who were politically repressive, brutal, and frequently murderous.

Young people from minority communities may never even consider careers in law enforcement because of the stigma. As a result, even if a young person toyed with the idea of becoming a police officer, peer pressure or family response might dissuade the person.

The Impact on Minority Hirings of Affirmative Action

The implementation of affirmative action standards, various employment discrimination litigations, and a growing number of pro-

gressive and informed police administrators have all contributed to increased minority hiring trends of today (Potts 1983, Walker 1985, Mastrofski 1990). While the overall number of minority hirings nationally have increased, growth in general is slow and, in some areas, has actually declined (Walker 1983, 1985; Hochstedler, Regoli, and Poole 1984).

In the famous case of Alan Bakke, a white man who claimed he had been the victim of reverse discrimination during his application to medical school, Justice Lewis Powell wrote the majority opinion for the U.S. Supreme Court. This opinion, however, left public administrators in a renewed state of uncertainty. In essence, Justice Powell suggested that racial quotas cannot be the sole factor for admission to medical school, yet race can be used as a criterion. The *Bakke* case had been closely watched by the police administrative leadership in America—as it was by college administrators and business leaders. The Supreme Court's 5–4 decision in *Bakke* was indicative of a political climate urging imminent change.

In February 1987 the Supreme Court ruled against the Alabama Department of Public Safety (state police) in the case of *U.S.* v. *Phillip Paradise.* In the case, the U.S. District Court had imposed a quota on the Department of Public Safety. The quota required that one black officer for every one white officer be promoted to corporal. The Supreme Court ruled that this quota was acceptable. Justice William Brennan stated, "It is now well established that government bodies, including courts, may constitutionally employ racial classifications essential to remedy unlawful treatment of racial or ethnic groups subject to discrimination."

Employment discrimination litigation has challenged virtually every aspect of police personnel practices throughout the past twenty years (See Walker 1985). Various traditional forms of institutionalized discrimination, such as height or agility tests, have for the most part been eliminated. A fair number of large metropolitan police agencies have been forced by court orders to actively recruit or promote minority officers—frequently with strict quotas and timetables. As in Alabama, quotas in Detroit's voluntary affirmative action plan were unsuccessfully battled by white officers on the grounds of reverse discrimination.

Samuel Walker (1985) points out an interesting irony regarding discrimination litigation. Walker indicates that there is little empirical research on the effectiveness of this strategy. In fact, the time spent in litigation may even work against reducing discriminatory practices by a police department. In other words, one may reasonably question just how effective a remedy litigation is in employment discrimination. Walker (1985) identifies only a single study that addresses this question directly, Ellen Hochstedler's in 1984. Hochstedler found that court-imposed hiring quotas were the single most important variable in explaining employment patterns. In fact, according to Hochstedler, the absence of a hiring quota generally spelled affirmative action failure within a department.

Walker states that the case of Philadelphia casts serious doubts on the efficacy of litigation as a viable remedy for hiring discrimination. The suit charged the Philadelphia police department with discrimination against black officers and was delayed in the federal court system for thirteen years. During this period, a sex discrimination suit was filed against the agency and settled by consent decree. In addition, a suit charging discrimination against Hispanics was averted and settled. While this litigation was awaiting its hearing in the federal courts, the department made almost no progress in its employment practices regarding black officers—in some respects, it may actually have worsened. Walker (1985) also suggests that the eventual affirmative action plan negotiated from the litigation probably reflects a more relaxed political climate than it does any direct result of pressures brought

by the litigation itself. In fact, it could be argued that the litigation may have impeded progress in hiring practices regarding black officers, by promoting the attitude that no action should be taken by the agency until the case is resolved in the courts.

In addition to problems with minority hirings, police relations with minority groups have become controversial and sensitive. Accusations and allegations of misconduct flare from both law enforcement officers and community residents (Carter 1985). There have been longstanding complaints by minorities of great abuse at the hands of police (Radelet 1987). Conversely, police officers frequently believe that minority groups unfairly target the police as scapegoats for their frustrations, since the police offer a readily available symbol of the "oppression by a white power structure" (Joyner 1977, 112; Carter 1985; Radelet 1987). At least partially in a voluntary effort to reduce these police–minority tensions, many police agencies began focusing their recruiting on hiring women and minorities. Hiring women and minority police officers also contributed to dissolving the view of police departments as bigoted, violent, and insensitive organizations.

For example, Spanish-speaking officers were deployed in Hispanic neighborhoods, officers versed in Asian culture and language in Oriental communities, and similar ethnic and cultural special skills or knowledge were used. Policewomen, as suggested above, found themselves particularly used in areas such as victim assistance, and rape and vice details.

Another explanation for increased hirings of women and minority police officers is federal mandates. Hiring quotas emerged in the 1970s in response to a series of legal suits brought by minority representatives and women, along with various federal guidelines for hiring. In addition, height requirements and entrance examinations were re-evaluated and led to gateways for women and minority recruits.

Changes have occurred in the content of written and physical requirements of police entrance examinations. Many police administrators, however, view these changes as too relaxed. It is understandable, then, that questions have arisen about whether standards may have been lowered at the expense of public safety. Various wrongful-death and police corruption cases have emerged during the past decade and drawn further attention to public safety concerns. Headlines such as "Miami Police Scandal Raising Questions on Minority Recruits" (*New York Times* 1986), "The Police Exam That Flunked," (*New York Times* 1985) and the 1986 arrest and prosecution of Louis Alverez, an Hispanic officer accused and later acquitted of having shot an unarmed black youth to death, and the resulting community unrest certainly have caused more than a few raised eyebrows.

But the question may be asked whether it is the minority status of officers that has created problems or forced hiring practices. Staying a moment with Miami, Florida, one finds that their hiring of a large number of minority officers during the early 1980s was in direct compliance with federal guidelines. Unfortunately, these hirings were restricted to the county rather than the nation and resulted in a limited applicant pool. This applicant pool was largely composed of recent Cuban immigrants who, as the chief who hired them stated, "met minimum standards although they were not the best officers available" (*New York Times* 1986). In addition to an initial weak recruitment pool, and because of federal pressure to hire and retain minority officers, several recruits who might have technically washed out under other circumstances were permitted to repeat segments of their academy training, such as gun qualification, in order to graduate.

Ironically, what may have developed to replace an older, institutionalized discrimination process is a modern version. In this latter day situation, poor quality recruits, but those who meet both affirmative action criteria and minimum standards, are hired. Then,

in a kind of self-fulfilling prophecy, these minimum-level officers, like time bombs, begin to detonate. Charges and allegations of malfeasance, misconduct, and corruption are hurled, along with a few comments of "I told you so!" by old-line, prejudiced officers and administrators. It remains questionable, however, whether minority status is responsible for the "minimum standard level" officers who reach the streets or uneven and ineffective institutional strategies for hiring and training.

Another problem black and other minority officers encounter is that they are seen by white colleagues as additional competitors for choice assignments, promotions, and command positions. Because of this, white officers view affirmative action hirings and racial or gender quota promotion programs as a threat to their own job security (Jacobs and Cohen 1978).

Even with the push to hire more women and minorities in policing and several recent promotions of women and persons of color, it remains difficult to assess how much progress has actually been made (Hochstedler 1984). Since women and black officers have been involved in policing since the mid-1800s, the fact that a handful now possess command positions is unimpressive.

For example, it was not until 1976 that Detroit promoted from the ranks its first black chief of police (William Hart). Houston waited until 1982, when it hired Lee Brown, to have a black chief; New York City did not have a black chief until 1984 when Benjamin Ward was promoted to that rank. Similarly, it was not until 1976 that Captain Victoria Renzullo became the first woman placed in command of a New York City police precinct (Feinman 1986); it was not until 1985, when Vikie Hensley was promoted to commander of Dayton, Ohio's fifth police district, that Dayton had a woman in a command position (Batz 1985).

It was also in 1985 that Indianapolis, Indiana and Dallas, Texas added women to command positions. In Indianapolis this occurred when Charlene Lawrence, a seventeen-year veteran of the force, was promoted to the position of captain (Hallinan 1985). In Texas, the Dallas police department promoted Pamela Walt, a ten-year veteran, and Deborah Melancon, an officer for nine years, each to the rank of captain (Henneberger 1985). Finally, although possessing among the oldest policing histories in the nation, it was not until 1986, with the promoting of Ann Marie Doherty to deputy superintendent, that the Boston, Massachusetts police department had a woman in a key command position (Ford 1986).

Certainly, some progress has been made regarding entry by minority officers to police work. But, it is equally certain that police departments remain largely composed of white males, and that this is particularly true of upper-level command positions (See *Who Is Guarding the Guardians* 1981, Leinen 1984).

SUMMARY

Women and minority officers have been working in police agencies for over 140 years. However, it is only during the past thirty years or so that women and minority members have been permitted to function as police officers. This chapter has examined a number of historical problems both women and other minorities have been forced to contend with in their efforts to gain acceptance by police organizations and the communities they serve.

This chapter begins with an examination of women in policing and traces their historical roots as nurturing matrons to present-day concerns about becoming defeminized. In addition, this chapter discusses a number of changes in civil rights laws throughout the 1960s and 1970s, which provided access to police positions for many previously excluded minorities. As part of this consideration, this chapter discusses the nature of institutionalized discrimination and its effect on women and minority police officers.

Finally, this chapter reviews several pertinent elements regarding police organizations, minorities, and community relations. As the chapter outlines, the police are fundamentally guardians of society's value and legal system. But, when police departments and the minority communities they serve become adversaries, strain results for the entire society.

Although impressive steps have been made for both women and minority police officers, it will take a considerable amount of time and effort if equality is to be realized. For example, women and minority police officers are being actively recruited. Yet, despite increases within the lower ranks, there remains a disparity in the number of women and minority officers who hold command positions.

In short, while definitely improved, the problems that women and minority police officers have endured in the past are not over today.

REVIEW QUESTIONS

1. What are some of the major arguments commonly used to suggest women should not enter careers in law enforcement? How accurate are these arguments?

2. What were the original purposes women were recruited for police agencies? In what ways have these traditional roles and attitudes changed?

3. What were some of the important effects of Title VII of the 1964 Civil Rights Act? What additional benefits arose under the amended act of 1972?

4. What might be some of the problems associated with defeminization of women in law enforcement?

5. What is meant by "institutionalized discrimination," and how has it played a role in regard to women and minorities in law enforcement?

REFERENCES

Alex, Nicholas. *Black in Blue: A Study of the Negro Policeman.* New York: Appleton-Century-Crofts, 1969.

Batz, Bob. "She's Laying Down the Law in Dayton's Busy 5th District." *Dayton Daily News* (November 24, 1985):12.

Bell, Daniel. "Policewomen: Myths and Reality." *Journal of Police Science and Administration* 10(1982):112–20.

Berg, Bruce L., and Kimberly Joyce Budnick. "Defeminization of Women in Law Enforcement: A New Twist in the Traditional Police Personality." *Journal of Police Science and Administration* 14(1986):314–19.

Berg, Bruce L., and Kimberly Joyce Budnick. "Defeminization of Women in Law Enforcement: Examining the Role of Women in Policing." In Daniel B. Kennedy and Robert J. Homant, eds. *Police and Law Enforcement* Vol. 5. New York: AMS, 1987.

Bittner, Egon. *The Function of Police in Modern Society.* Cambridge, Mass.: Oelegeschlager, Gunn, and Hain, 1980.

Block, Peter, and Deborah Anderson. *Policewomen on Patrol: Final Report.* Washington, D.C.: Police Foundation, 1974.

Braun Rachel. "Equal Opportunity and the Law in the United States." In Gunter Schmid and Renate Weitzel, eds. *Sex Discrimination and Equal Opportunity: Labor Market and Employment Policy.* New York: St. Martin, 1984.

Bryant, L., D. Dunkerley, and G. Kelland. "One of the Boys?" *Policing* 1, (1985):236–44.

Carter, David L. "Hispanic Perception of Police Performance: An Empirical Assessment." *Journal of Criminal Justice* 13(1985):487–500.

Charles, Michael T. "Women in Policing: The Physical Aspects." *Journal of Police Science and Administration* 10(1982):194–205.

Chesler, M. "Contemporary Sociological Theories of Racism." In P. Katz, ed. *Towards The Elimination of Racism.* New York: Pergamon, 1976.

David, James. "Perspectives of Policewomen in Texas and Oklahoma." *Journal of Police Science and Administration* 12(1984):395–403.

Eshleman, J. Ross, and Barbara G. Cashion. 1983. *Sociology: An Introduction.* Boston, Mass.: Little, Brown and Company, 1983.

Feinman, Clarice. *Women in the Criminal Justice System.* New York: Praeger, 1986.

Ford, Beverly. "Woman in Top Police Job for First Time." *Boston Herald* (March 30, 1986):3.

Greenberger, Marcia. "The Effectiveness of Federal Law Prohibiting Sex Discrimination in Employment in the United States." In Ronnie Ratner, ed. *Equal Employment Policy for Women.* Philadelphia: Temple, 1980.

Gross, Sally. "Socialization into Law Enforcement: The Female Police Recruit." Final Report for the Southeast Institute of Criminal Justice, Miami, Fl., 1981.

Gross, Sally. "Women Becoming Cops: Development Issues and Solutions." Report for the South East Florida Institute of Criminal Justice, Miami Fl., 1983.

Gross, Sally. Comments offered during discussion at the Annual Meeting of the Academy of Criminal Justice Sciences. Orlando, Florida, (March 1986).

Hallinan, Joseph T. "IPD Promotes First Women to Captain." *Indianapolis Star* (October 17, 1985):1.

Hamilton, Mary E. *The Policewoman Her Service and Ideas.* New York: Arno Press and the New York Times, 1971 [1924].

Harriman, A. *Women/Men/Management.* New York: Praeger, 1985.

Harris, Richard N. *The Police Academy: An Inside View.* New York: Wiley, 1973.

Hartman, Heidi. "Capitalism Patriarchy, and Job Segregation by Sex." In Nona Glazer and Helen Youngelson Waehrer, eds. *Women in a Man-Made World* 2d ed. Chicago, Ill.: Rand McNally, 1977.

Hartman, Heidi. "The Family as the Locus of Gender, Class, and Political Struggle: The Example of Housework." *Signs* 6(1981):366–94.

Heffner, P. "The Impact of Policewomen on Patrol: Contributions of Sex-Role Stereotypes to Behavior in an Astereotypic Setting." Unpublished doctoral dissertation, Department of Psychology, Wayne State University, Detroit, 1976.

Heffnernan, William, and Timothy Stroup. *Police Ethics: Hard Choices in Law Enforcement.* New York: John Jay, 1985.

Henneberger, Milinda. "Two Women Become Dallas Police Captains." *Dallas Morning Star* (July 4, 1985):1.

Higgins, Lois, L. "Historical Background of Policewomen's Service." *Journal of Criminal Law and Criminology* 41(1951):822–35.

Hochstedler, Ellen. "Impediments to Hiring Minorities in Public Police Agencies." *Journal of Police Science and Administration* 12(1984):227–40.

Hochstedler, Ellen, Robert M. Regoli, and Eric D. Poole. "Changing the Guard in American Cities: A Current Empirical Assessment of Integration in Twenty Municipal Police Departments." *Criminal Justice Review* 9(1984):8–14.

Hochstedler, Ellen, and John A. Conley. "Explaining Under-representation of Black Officers in City Police Agencies." *Journal of Criminal Justice* 14(1986):319–28.

Homant, Robert J. "The Impact of Policewomen on Community Attitudes Toward Police." *Journal of Police Science and Administration* 10(1983):194–205.

Homant, Robert J., and Daniel B. Kennedy. "Police Perceptions of Spouse Abuse: A Comparison of Male and Female Officers." *Journal of Criminal Justice* 13(1985):29–47.

Jacobs, James, and Jay Cohen. "The Impact of Racial Integration on the Police." *Journal of Police Science and Administration* 6(1978):182–86.

Jaggar, Alison M., and Paula Rothenberg, eds. *Feminist Frameworks* 2d ed. New York: McGraw-Hill, 1984.

Joyner, I. "People and Police." In H.J. Bryce, ed. *Black Crime: A Police View.* Washington, D.C.: Joint Center for Political Studies, 1977.

Kandel, T. *What Women Earn.* New York: Simon and Schuster, 1981.

Kennedy, Daniel B., and Robert J. Homant. "Nontraditional Role Assumption and the Personality of the Policewomen." *Journal of Police Science and Administration* 9(1981):346–55.

Kuykendall, Jack L., and David E. Burns. "The Black Police Officer: An Historical Perspective." In Abraham S. Blumberg and Elaine

Niederhoffer, eds. *The Ambivalent Force.* New York: Holt Rinehart and Winston, 1985. Originally published in *Journal of Contemporary Criminal Justice* 1(1980):4–12.

Leinen, Stephen. *Black Police, White Society.* New York: New York University, 1984.

Locke, H. "Racial Attitudes and Institutional Racism: Display Issues." *Social Development Issues* 4(1980):7–20.

Martin, Susan E. "*Police*woman and Police*woman*: Occupational Role Dilemmas and Choices of Female Officers." *Journal of Police Science and Administration* 7(1979):314–23.

Martin, Susan E. *Breaking and Entering: Policewomen on Patrol.* Berkeley, Calif.: University of California Press, 1980.

Martin, Susan E. "Female Officers on the Move?: A Status Report on Women in Policing." In Roger G. Dunham and Geoffrey P. Alpert, eds. *Critical Issues in Policing: Contemporary Readings.* Prospect Heights, Ill.: Waveland, 1989.

Mastrofski, Stephen. "The Prospects of Change in Police Patrol: A Decade in Review." *American Journal of Police* 9(1990):1–81.

Milton, Catherine. *Women in Policing.* Washington D.C.: The Police Foundation, 1972.

Morash, Merry, and Jack R. Green. "Evaluating Women on Patrol: A Critique of Contemporary Wisdom." *Evaluation Review* 10(1986):230–55.

New York Times. "The Police Exam That Flunked." The News of the Week in Review. (November 24, 1985).

New York Times. "Miami Police Scandal Raising Questions on Minority Recruits." (January 9, 1986):9.

Nieva, V., and B. Gutek. *Women and Work: A Psychological Perspective.* New York: Praeger, 1981.

Parsons, Talcott, and Robert Bales. *Family, Socialization and Interaction Process.* New York: Free Press, 1955.

Potts, Lee W. *Responsible Police Administration: Issues and Approaches.* University, Alabama: University of Alabama Press, 1983.

Radelet, Louis A. *The Police and the Community,* 4th ed. New York: Macmillan, 1987.

Schaefer, Richard T., and Robert P. Lamm. *Sociology* 3d ed. New York: McGraw-Hill, 1989.

Sherman, Lawrence J. "Evaluation of Police on Patrol in a Suburban Police Department." *Journal of Police Science and Administration* 3(1975):434–38.

Shpritzer, Felicia. "A Case for the Promotion of Police Women in the City of New York." *Journal of Criminal Law, Criminology, and Police Science* 50(1959):415–19.

Siegel, Larry J. *Criminology*. 2d ed. St. Paul, Minn.: West, 1986.

Sullivan, Peggy S. "Minority Officers: Current Issues." In Roger G. Dunham and Geoffrey P. Alpert, eds. *Critical Issues in Policing: Contemporary Readings*. Prospect Heights, Ill.: Waveland, 1989.

Talney, R. "Women in Law Enforcement: An Expanded Role." *Police* 14(1969):49–51.

Townsey, Dianne Roi. "Black Women in American Policing: An Advancement Display." *Journal of Criminal Justice* 10(1982):455–68.

Uniform Crime Reports. Federal Bureau of Investigations. Washington, D.C.: Government Printing Office, 1985.

Van Wormer, Katherine. "Are Males Suited to Police Patrol Work?" *Police Studies* 3(1981):41–44.

Walker, Samuel. *Popular Justice*. New York: Oxford , 1980.

Walker, Samuel. *The Police in America: An Introduction*. New York: McGraw-Hill, 1983.

Walker, Samuel. "Racial Minority and Female Employment in Policing: The Implications of 'Glacial' Change." *Crime and Delinquency* 31(1985):555–72.

Wexler, Judice Gaffin, and Vicki Quinn. "Considerations in the Training and Development of Women Sergeants." *Journal of Police Science and Administration* 13(1985):98–105.

Whitaker, Gordon P., and Charles David Phillips, eds. *Evaluating Performance of Criminal Justice Agencies*. Beverly Hills, Calif.: Sage, 1983.

"Who Is Guarding the Guardians? A Report on Police Practices for the U.S. Commission on Civil Rights." Washington , D.C.: Government Printing Office, 1981.

CHAPTER 10

THE POLICE SUBCULTURE

Understanding of police officers is hindered by stereotypes and character-izations made popular by the print and electronic media. Part of this image involves the idea of a police subculture to which police officers are assumed to be blindly devoted. One aspect of the police subculture that fascinates writers of fiction and television writers alike is the esprit de corps *among police officers. This loyalty is usually portrayed as one officer lying for another or in some other manner covering up for another officer. Another element in the stereotypic police image is that of an authoritarian, militaristic brute. But who and what are police really like? Chapter Ten attempts to examine these issues and provide some insight into what kinds of people become police officers. Additionally, Chapter Ten provides an examination of police culture, esprit de corps, and the role of police academy training in affecting recruits and the so-called police personality.*

INTRODUCTION: TWO MYTHS ABOUT POLICE BEHAVIOR

Until recently sociologists and criminologists were blinded with a type of myopia when it came to police. This myopia involved taking for granted that they knew what the police as a social institution really is and who becomes police officers. This myopia prevented many researchers from raising questions about the institution and who actually enters police work. In turn, this led to two prevalent myths about police behavior. For some, police were idealized as altruistic personalities who minis-tered the law exactly and without discretion, bias, or prejudice. For others, the myth was that police officers were authoritarian person-alities who administered the law however they wanted to, swaggering through life enforcing laws against whomever they chose whenever they saw fit. This meant that police officers enforced laws against residents according to their racial, social, and even sexual prejudices.

Unlike either of these extremes, police are neither free to enforce laws in an arbitrary or whimsical fashion, nor are they expected to rigidly enforce all laws at all times. Police officers are influenced by a wide variety of social forces, as are other members of society and social institutions. A variety of mechanisms for social control moderates the actions of police officers. Some of these control mechanism are informal and identical to those that each of us learn during our lifetimes through the process of socialization. Other control mechanisms are formal and rely upon written laws, codes, and policies.

This chapter explores the police not only as a social institution, but as a social group operating in our society. Theoretical explanations for why police may behave in certain ways, possess certain kinds of personalities, or perform their duties in specific ways are explored. The central purpose of this chapter is not to identify exactly what the police as a social institution is, but rather to consider who police officers might be.

THE NEED FOR GROUP SUPPORT

Chapter One of this book suggested that all social groups seek some form of individual and group security. The major emphasis in that chapter was physical security (protection from physical harm) and material security (protection of one's property). But social groups also require a less tangible type of security, namely, emotional security. To assure emotional support, empathic understanding, like values and beliefs, and shared ways of seeing and doing things, the police have evolved what is commonly referred to as a **police subculture.**

The formal concept of a police subculture was originally advanced in a work by William A. Westley entitled *Violence and the Police* (1970). This book resulted from Westley's study twenty years earlier of the police in Gary, Indiana. In a manner similar to Studs Terkel's 1974 examination of the "Royal Blue" construction workers and their social norms and occupational pride, Westley examined police from the perspective of an occupational subculture. As Westley (1970, 11) expresses it, his goal was to "isolate and identify the major social norms governing police conduct and to describe the way in which they influence police action in specific situations."

In his research, Westley identified police as grouping together into what he described as a distinct subculture. Westley, and later other researchers, stressed the importance of a distinct police subculture in shaping the views, values, attitudes, and behaviors of police officers.

Westley, in fact, indicates the attitudes the police subculture supports or encourages are perpetuated in policing. Conversely, those elements the police subcultures do not endorse are short-lived. For example, if the police subculture accepts or condones gift-taking by police officers, new recruits will learn to approve of this behavior and see it as normal. Westley's argument further suggests that police view the public as the enemy. This, Westley explains, results from police officers never meeting civilians on particularly good terms. Most meetings are with civilians who would prefer no contact with the police. Westley describes these sorts of meetings as representing "an unpleasant job, a threat, the bad ones, unpleasant and whining, self-concerned, uncooperative, and unjust" (1970, 49). What results is a kind of us-versus-them attitude among many police officers.

Because of the perceived public hostility, Westley argues that police officers begin to rely heavily—or exclusively—upon other officers for their social support. Hence, a kind of self-imposed social isolation envelops police. It is this symbolically circumscribed social support and friendship network that Westley terms the police subculture.

Michael Brown (1981) has similarly talked about a police subculture. Brown, however, specifies three core values that, he maintains, ground officers to the police subculture: honor, loyalty, and individualism. *Honor* is the officers' claim to honor work well done and services rendered to the community. Since part of an officer's expectation is to provide service, police officers do not expect to be honored by either their departments or the public. This makes it all the more important that the officers honor one another. *Loyalty* is required in police subculture. It is expected to be instantaneous and unflinching and, according to Brown, loyalty is the most important characteristic a rookie officer can display to veteran officers. Among the illustrations Brown offers is the bond that develops between partners.

Loyalty and honor are directed toward others. In contrast to this, Brown suggests that the more self-centered value of *individualism* also grounds officers to police culture. Individualism is characterized by officers receiving reward from involvement in police work, the thrill of a chase, or making a good arrest.

Somewhat more recently Elizabeth Reuss-Ianni (1984) characterized the police culture as divided between two systems or codes, formal and informal. Reuss-Ianni maintains that the formal code is represented by the law, rules, regulations, policies, and procedures of the agency. The informal code, however, fills in the cracks and becomes the actual way officers go about their work. This informal code is passed from experienced officers to less experienced officers through various social activities.

To better understand what Westley, Brown, and Reuss-Ianni actually mean by police culture, it is necessary first to understand the more general concepts of *culture* and *subculture*.

Culture

Virtually all introductory sociology textbooks have a chapter on culture. Each will offer a slightly different definition for what this term represents. But, at some level, all of these variations amount to the same thing. Specifically, culture refers to a society's total way of doing things. It includes all human-made objects, knowledge, beliefs and values, customs, laws, technologies, and virtually all other products of human endeavor. Additionally, all definitions of culture convey the notion of generational inheritance. In short, one generation teaches the next generation the group's cultural elements. Sharing a similar culture is what allows us to define various different societies. Typically, one thinks of a society as a group of people residing within an identifiable territory and sharing a common culture (Schaefer and Lamm 1989).

Subculture

Within the confines of the overall, or dominant, culture of a society, one finds various smaller subgroupings. Members of these subgroupings, while sharing in many of the dominant culture's values, norms, and other social ideals and patterns, differ distinctly in some manner. Each of us belongs to various subgroups that powerfully influence our beliefs and behaviors: social clubs, friendship cliques and groups, families, school classes, and so forth. But these social organizations fail by themselves to adequately represent the nature of a subculture.

Subcultures frequently develop an *argot* or specialized language that both distinguishes them from the dominant culture's as well as establishes fairly clear lines between in-group members or subgroup members and out-group members or non-subgroup members. These groupings are sometimes identified by sociologists as a distinction between insiders and outsiders (See Becker 1963). *Cop speak* offers an example of a distinctive argot used by insiders, the police. When the police are searching for a child rapist, they may speak about hunting a *skinner* or a *short-eyes*. The New York City's transit police use the term *lushworker* to describe people who rob drunks and sleeping passengers on the subway trains (Theroux 1982, 74). But more important than a distinct argot is the *weltanschauung* or ideological world view that permeates the subculture. Stated differently, members tend to share deeply certain ways of looking at people and situations, ways of behaving, and values.

In many ways, subcultures may be understood to represent small versions of fully operating cultures present within the dominant culture of a society. As such they are distinguishable from mere friendship groups and social clubs. Unquestionably, police officers are part of the larger American culture and share a sense of commonality with others who participate in certain American customs, beliefs, and ways. But, as Geoffrey P. Alpert and Roger G. Dunham (1988, 80) suggest:

> *In many ways, the police develop traditions and survival skills that are unique to their vocational group because of their duties and responsibilities. These distinct differences in culture qualify them as members of a subculture, a group that shares a great deal of the dominant culture, but that is set off from the general society because of its unique aspects.*

Often police officers are not even aware of the significant influence membership in this subculture holds over them. Yet, it is common for police officers to seek the companionship of other officers rather than civilians to avoid social activities that might draw them into civilian social circles, to avoid mention of their occupation unless directly asked, and to generally foster an attitude of *them* (civilians) and *us* (police officers).

In its most extreme form, this them-and-us concept views civilians as the enemy. As mentioned previously, most of the civilian contact that police have during the course of their work day is with people who really do not want contact with the police. Ironically, when police come in contact with other figures in the justice system—lawyers, social workers, political figures—interactions also may be strained. Even these workers in the justice system tend to view the police in a negative manner, as corrupt in some way. In turn, the police are leery of all civilians—even those who are involved in the justice system—unless they are members of the in-group, the police subculture.

Entrance into the police subculture does not automatically occur when one puts on a police uniform. Entrance is gained slowly through a learning process that allows the individual to gain both knowledge and internalize values appropriate to the group. In short, entrance into police culture requires one to adopt a police weltanschauung. Sociologists call this learning process socialization.

Socialization into police culture is a process by which recruits acquire the various values, attitudes, and acceptable behaviors in policing. It is similar to other forms of "occupational socializations" (Klofas, Stojkovic and Kalinich 1990). In addition to the increased social support among peers that arises from membership in the police culture, behavior in the police organization remains remarkably stable. This is true in spite of personnel or policy changes.

Stuart Scheingold (1984) suggests that three features of police work tend to encourage initiation in the police culture. First, in the past the traditional police officers came from the working class or the lower middle class. Hence, they shared similar backgrounds, values, and ways of looking at the world. Even in today's police departments and in the face of higher educational requirements, police recruits primarily come to the job sharing middle class views and values. Second, Scheingold indicates that police share a particularly stressful working experience. This, in turn, tends to create solidarity between officers. Third, Scheingold (1984, 98) states that "the police live and work together within a largely closed social system that tends to cut them off from the outside and their ideas." Young recruits realize, often in the academy, that their social networks change the moment they become police officers.

By this juncture, it should be clear that the nature of a police subculture and the perception of them-versus-us creates a dilemma for the police. On the one hand, police must emotionally detach or distance themselves at least partially from their neighbors and other civilians in order to operate effectively. Certainly, it would be difficult to enforce laws against people who were close friends with any consistency. It is similar to the generally held taboo against surgeons operating on their own family members. Such situations create extreme anxiety and reduce effectiveness.

On the other hand, when the police distance themselves from civilians and their non-police neighbors, they are perceived as secretive, divisive, and tainted in some manner. The notion that policing is in some manner a tainted occupation is a view held by many civilians. This perception assumes that police are, in general, just slightly better than the criminals they arrest. When a police officer is indicted in a crime, many civilians hold this instance up as a prime example of police law-breaking. Some commentators suggest that the police often perceive a more extreme antagonism on the part of residents than what really exists (Alpert and Dunham 1988). Yet, the contempt for the police because they are thought to be just a little dirty or because they had the discretion not to write that ticket but did, is a fairly common attitude among civilians. A new recruit learns quickly that, even if the public does not appreciate the work undertaken by police, other police officers do.

The remainder of this chapter will examine various aspects of the police subculture, including entrance during police training, its effects on cynicism and authoritarianism, and the police personality. Stated generally, the remainder of this chapter examines various nuances of the *culture of policing*.

THE POLICE ACADEMY

Sir Robert Peel aptly suggested in the nineteenth century that the selection of good candidates for police training is the first step in assuring a high quality police force. The next step, of course, becomes the training itself. It seems unreasonable to expect a high caliber of law enforcement protection from a poorly trained or untrained police force, irrespective of the motivation or dedication of the officers (Holden 1986). Yet, in 1965, the International Association of Chiefs of Police (IACP) learned that the vast majority (85 percent) of police agencies in the United States did not offer any formal training to new officers. According to Jack Kuykendall and Peter Usinger (1975), in many jurisdictions new officers were issued guns, badges, and rule books, but no formal training.

Today, this phenomenon has virtually reversed. What has not radically changed, however, is the variety of formal training programs that exist across the nation. In some jurisdictions, the police academy is a double struc-

Police recruits practice crowd and riot control tactics

ture. Recruits must first attend a standard minimum training program. In Florida, for example, this minimum period is 320 hours of classroom instruction. After completing this initial training, the recruit is certified to serve as a police officer in the state of Florida. The second component of academy training involves any training required by the recruit's hiring agency. For example, in the state's capital of Tallahassee, the police department requires an additional 40 hours of classroom training, the sheriff's department an additional 20 hours.

The minimum training to gain certification for policing ranges from a low of 120 hours in Missouri to a high of 954 hours in Hawaii. Table 10.1 shows how, what, and the number of hours police recruits are trained is substantially different from state to state. Differences also exist within states among various agencies.

Inside the Academy

The content and duration of training does differ in various locations and agencies. Yet, all police academies share in the process of shaping new recruits' views on policing and civilian life, crime and order, and their principle goals and functions as police officers.

The police academy is perhaps the first formal socialization process a recruit comes in contact with within the law enforcement organization. Some police training programs are intentionally designed to break down the recruit, in order to build him or her up as a police officer. This technique is sometimes referred to as **stress reaction training** in police academies. Sociologically, this concept derives from two related stages of an indoctrination process intended to socialize group members into various total institutions. *Total institutions* are defined as settings or organizations in which members are isolated in real or symbolic terms from the rest of society. Members of total institutions are subject to the control and authority of the administrative staff. Examples of total institutions typi-

cally include prisons, mental hospitals, religious cults, the military, and paramilitary agencies such as the police.

The two stages in this indoctrination process are **desocialization** and **resocialization** (See Goffman 1961). During desocialization, the organization or training program attempts to strip away the self-image and outsider perspectives of the recruit. These perspectives, values, and beliefs, of course, are the result of previous socialization in the larger society. Resocialization, then, becomes the replacement of these old ways of thinking and believing with values, outlooks, and self-images supportive of the organization.

In the police academy, desocialization can be most clearly observed during the first few days. Recruits are frequently reminded of their outsider status through numerous degradation rituals. These may include being required to have military haircuts (crew-cuts or very short-cropped hair), maintaining high-gloss shines on their shoes or boots, wearing uniforms clearly distinguishable from those of real police officers, having orders and frequently derogatory names barked at them by instructors, or following near-ritualized routines.

For example, in one northeastern police academy, it is common for recruits to halt, come to attention, and state, "Sir, By your leave, Sir!" whenever they walk by an academy instructor (Berg 1989). Failure to recite these lines immediately might earn the errant recruit 25 push-ups on the spot.

In a similar paramilitary fashion, recruits spring from their seats to attention whenever an academy instructor enters their classroom. As in the military, at least one of the recruits shouts, "Attention on deck!" Recruits are usually ordered to line up silently, are shouted at by instructors, and run through morning exercises, creating a program that in general tends to resemble mini-boot-camp. Minor infractions are dealt with by the Gig-Demerit system, a penalty system borrowed directly from the U.S. armed forces and further contributing to the military parallel.

TABLE 10.1   Minimum Training Hours Required for Entry-Level Policing
Type of Competency, Area, and State, as of 1985

STATE	TOTAL NUMBER OF HOURS REQUIRED	HUMAN RELATIONS	FORCE & WEAPONRY	COMMUNI-CATIONS	LEGAL TRAINING	PATROL & CRIMINAL INVESTI-GATION	CRIMINAL JUSTICE SYSTEMS	ADMIN-ISTRATION
Hawaii	954	17	153	65	133	444	29	113
Rhode Island	661	42	65	0	48	480	0	26
Vermont	553	4	80	30	74	330	3	32
Maine	504	27	62	17	73	277	21	27
West Virginia	495	14	98	20	120	195	36	12
Pennsylvania	480	76	88	10	94	196	16	0
Maryland	471	0	0	0	73	366	0	32
Massachusetts	460	35	132	28	90	167	8	0
Utah	450	19	73	27	49	247	15	20
Connecticut	443	23	48	8	64	284	11	5
Indiana	440	21	73	4	83	192	32	35
Michigan	440	9	105	8	48	244	0	26
Washington	440	34	152	24	85	145	0	0
New Hampshire	426	20	75	8	60	205	8	50
New Mexico	421	30	69.5	18	56	238.5	9	0
Arizona	400	24	110	16	78	135	12	25
California	400	15	80	15	60	185	10	35
Iowa	400	33	75	12	44	175	13	48
Kentucky	400	6.5	84.5	3.5	75.5	182.5	6	41.5
South Carolina	382	18	77	12	72	178	2	23
Texas	381	14	48	18	68	233	0	0
North Carolina	369	28	64	20	72	170	0	15
Delaware	362	12	64	17	87	174	6	2
Montana	346	22	77.5	14	19.5	183.5	15	14.5
Nebraska	341	36	58	10	62	158	2	15
Colorado	334	19	55	22	79	141	18	0
Florida	320	24	39	18	54	158	9	18
Kansas	320	34	42	20	45	170	1	8
Mississippi	320	8	70	20	50	153	7	12
Wyoming	320	10	71	14	53	119	33	20
North Dakota	313	10	23	20	84	139	16	21
Idaho	310	0	47	9	51	169	16	18
New Jersey	310	26	40	13	49	116	17	49
Arkansas	304	14	60	6	19	190	0	15
New York	285	9	38	7	44	169	10	8
Alabama	280	14	49	8	48	138	3	20
Ohio	280	16	42	10	76	111	20	5
Oregon	280	14	64	12	62	104	8	16
Alaska	276	1	20	7	74	139	13	22
Georgia	240	18	45	5	47	110	2	13
Louisiana	240	16	57	8	36	78	5	40
Tennessee	240	2	50	7	31	136	8	6
Wisconsin	240	18	30	9	16	121	10	36
Nevada	200	8	28	11	46	96	2	9
South Dakota	200	17	32	8	22	109	6	6
Missouri	120	3	23	10	28	55	1	0

Note: Data obtained through a mail survey of law enforcement training directors. Oklahoma, Illinois, Virginia, and Minnesota were omitted from the study due to incomplete data on curriculum content.

Source: U.S. Department of Justice, *Sourcebook of Criminal Justice Statistics—1986.* Washington, D.C.: U.S. Government Printing Office, 1986:16

As time in the academy progresses, these desocialization rituals tend to lessen. In their place, various resocialization rituals appear. For example, awards are given to recruits who master various police skills. A top-gun award, for instance, may be given to the recruit who achieves the highest score during the firearms training. Or, an academic award may be given to the recruit who achieves the highest overall gradepoint average from classroom course work. However, throughout the academy experience there is the subtle understanding among recruits that they will still have to prove themselves out on the streets.

Recently, the academy training of police officers in the Commonwealth of Massachusetts came under scrutiny. On September 19, 1988 fifteen of fifty-one police recruits attending the Agawam, Massachusetts police academy were hospitalized for dehydration. Another recruit's dehydrated condition was complicated by liver failure. This recruit was flown to Pittsburgh where he received a liver transplant, but tragically died several weeks later. Allegations that police academy trainers had systematically brutalized and tortured recruits in the name of police training quickly surfaced in the Boston papers. Within a few weeks, what happened at Agawam had become national news (See Kindleberger 1988, Wadler 1988). Central to these news reports were allegations of excessive exercise–induced illness and an induced stress program referred to as "Modified Stress-Reaction-Training."

Several official investigations of police training in Massachusetts were initiated throughout September and early October. By December, all of the ranking officials associated with the Massachusetts Criminal Justice Training Council—the agency responsible for administering police training across the state—were fired and replaced. In May 1989, Governor Michael Dukakis of Massachusetts released the results of the various investigations in the "Report of the Governor's Panel to Review Police Training Programs."

Among the findings was the failure of the high-stress environment created in the first days to perform any necessary or intended functions. The panel also stated that the "surrogate stress environment" that academy directors were told to create throughout training was dysfunctional ("Governor's Report" 1989, 46ff). Academy instructors received no training or certification in creating their surrogate stress environments. Instead, each academy staff relied on a kind of apprenticeship system composed of observing previous first-day activities ("Governor's Report" 1989, Berg 1989; 1990a).

Among the tasks assigned to the new members of the Criminal Justice Training Council was implementing the recommendations of the governor's panel. Among these were changes in the initial screening of recruits, as well as physical training activities in the academy. Finally, the panel recommended that a standardized core curriculum be developed and that each core area be taught by a trained and certified instructor.

In general, the national trend in police training is moving away from the boot-camp mentality and toward a more college-like model. Emphasis in the classroom on cultural factors, communications skills, and problem solving rapidly have been replacing less functional resocialization tasks such as punishment push-ups.

The Classroom Experience

In the classroom, recruits are instructed in penal code statutes necessary for their work, certain constitutional restrictions and privileges, motor vehicle laws, standardized procedures and protocols, the use of firearms, emergency first aid–first responder, communications skills (oral and written), and the use of an assortment of police equipment—radios, batons, cuffs, gas masks. The necessity for standardized training should not be underemphasized. It is enormously important that the police use objective procedures, forms, and records. As suggested in Chapter Eight, the use of established procedures assures more systematic standards for behavior, creates a measure of consistency in officers' responsibilities, and allows administrators to plan and coordinate agency activities more systematically.

Throughout the academy experience, recruits are influenced by the values and beliefs of their peers and their instructors. Frequently, these attitudes and beliefs move recruits in the direction of perceiving non-police officers as **them**. For example, it was common during one recent academy class for instructors to use war stories to illustrate their classroom lectures (Berg 1990b). Typically, these were brief vignettes that described the personal actions of the instructor in some routine police situation. But, in virtually every case, civilians were described as stupid, difficult, assholes, or in some manner unresponsive to police authority. For example, on the fifth day of the academy class, one female instructor uttered five negative examples, using war stories to illustrate proper police–civilian communications, in less than ten minutes. One of these examples was:

> . . . When I was working the airport, I couldn't believe the stupid calls I'd get working the desk. I'd be sitting there at 4:30 in the morning, and the phone would ring. Some guy would ask, "Is the airport open?" I'm here aren't I? [grimaces, shakes her head, and throws her hands up in exasperation] "I have a plane to catch at 8 a.m., is the airport going to be open then?" asks the caller. "So," I say, "Well, I can't tell you, it's only 4:30 a.m. I don't know what things will be like in three-and-a-half hours. If it snows at a rate of two inches an hour, I don't think so!" Stupid questions!

Earlier in her lecture, the instructor had half-jokingly stated that the single law missing in the traffic regulations was the one for being stupid. "Being stupid," again illustrated by war stories, included parking in marked "no parking" zones and, when asked to move

the car, having the civilian respond by moving it six inches forward. Or, when stopping a minor in possession of a can of beer and warning the youth to "lose the beer while I check something in the cruiser," having the kid argue about not wanting to empty the can onto the street. In sum, civilians are always depicted as slow to understand, stupid, uncooperative, and a portion of the job that officers simply have to learn to put up with.

In many academy training programs, the recruits move out of the classroom and into the field toward the end of their program. As they do, the romanticized and idealized role of the police officer that many possessed upon entrance into the academy gives way to a more realistic one.

Typically, all occupations in America indoctrinate new recruits into their way of thinking and doing things. These occupationally specific ways of thinking are usually based upon the various activities with which participants are routinely involved. Doctors, for example, tend to look for organic or medical cures to various problems they confront and may attempt to restore harmony in situations of conflict. Lawyers may seek remedies to problems or question participants in a situation in search of the truth. Automobile mechanics may consider a problem by examining how it got started, how various things fit together, how one participant stalls the situation or another participant's comments combust into an argument. In other words, these occupational views carry over into each member's every day life.

Importantly, this notion of ways of thinking and behaving extends far beyond the mere semantics presented here. For police, perhaps even more than for other occupations, such a weltanschauung eventually permeates the officer's belief and value orientations. Walking beats with experienced training officers exposes recruits to this other type of socialization process. They begin to see the world they have signed on to protect and work in, and they begin to hear and learn about the police world view from their training officer. In many cases, this training period conveys a cynical image of the world and the justice system.

Cynicism and Authoritarianism

In his classic book, *Behind the Shield: The Police in Urban Society* (1969), Arthur Niederhoffer, himself a former police officer, argued that cynicism and authoritarianism were inevitable aspects of the police personality. The police are, after all, confronted daily with the worst sorts of violence and inhumanity. As a consequence, it seems understandable that their view of the world might be slightly distorted. As a matter of definition, cynicism may be seen as a negative or distrustful attitude about things. Cynical people are often thought to view the actions of others as motivated by self-interest. Authoritarians can be understood as persons who adhere to a general philosophy of blind submission to authority.

In his research, Niederhoffer claimed that it was possible to distinguish between two focuses of cynicism among police officers: general cynicism directed toward the public and a specific cynicism targeted at the police system itself. Regarding the first form of cynicism, Niederhoffer felt that it was experienced by all ranks and types of officers. But the second, more specific form of cynicism, according to Niederhoffer, although fairly common among patrol officers, was not felt by what he termed the professional police officers. These were individuals who, following in the orientation of August Vollmer (See Chapter Four), looked forward to a transformed police system that they could eventually administer.

Niederhoffer attributed the origins of police cynicism to anomic situations the officers encountered in their work. *Anomie* was a concept coined by the sociologist Emile Durkheim (1951 [1897]). Durkheim introduced the term to describe a loss of direction felt in situations in which an individual's behavior becomes ineffective. The definition of anomie is sometimes given simply as normlessness. In other words, anomie is not knowing the rules governing a certain situation and consequently not being able to behave effectively.

Relating this notion to the police, Niederhoffer maintained that the acquisition of a cynical attitude by police officers occurred as a result of failures and frustrations from the job. For some, this led to job dissatisfaction and alienation—isolation and increased feelings of separateness from the community. For others, these cynical feelings were believed to motivate renewed commitment to the job.

It has been suggested that police officers are socialized into a culture of policing. In some cases, this socialization process begins when they enter the police academy. Niederhoffer, for example, maintained that while most police officers were authoritarians, it was the police system that had transformed them. He was quite adamant that officers do not enter policing with this particular trait.

In other cases, it is suggested that some form of police socialization occurs much earlier and may, in fact, be attributed as the motivating factor for the individual's joining the police. There has been extensive research directed at the question of whether people enter the police possessing certain characteristics or personality types (Alpert and Dunham 1988). If this latter argument is accurate, then applicants for police work may share certain traits long before they enter policing as a career.

Research on authoritarianism and cynicism has led to a questioning of the methodological accuracy of Niederhoffer's findings. Regoli (1976), for example, argued that Niederhoffer had tapped into what were really five different types of cynicism, not a single type with two focuses. According to Regoli, these were cynicism directed toward the public, police dedication to duty, police solidarity, organizational functions, and training and education. Thus, Regoli suggests that cynicism must be viewed as multidimensional. As such, cynicism may be interpreted as more than simply a single attitude.

Wilt and Bannon (1976) also identified several problems with the earlier Niederhoffer study. In their work on Detroit police recruits, Wilt and Bannon found a substantially lower rate of cynicism than Niederhoffer (1969) had in his sample of police officers in New York City. They felt that several of Niederhoffer's questions reflected realism (how the world actually is) rather than cynicism. Wilt and Bannon concluded that the rise in cynicism they found among recruits during the first few weeks of training may have been a result of the cynicism projected by more experienced and jaded officers instructing at the academy.

Later studies conclude that cynicism among police officers may be related to work alienation and job dissatisfaction, and that these factors are themselves related to an officer's level of education, duration of service, social class, ethnicity, gender, and the size of the department (Regoli, Poole, and Hewitt 1979; Lester 1980; Berg, True, and Gertz 1984; O'Connell, Holzman, and Armandi 1986).

Niederhoffer's notion that occupational tasks contribute to the transformation of police officers' attitudes, whether uni-dimensionally or multi-dimensionally, do appear, as Wilt and Bannon suggest, to be amplified or begun at the police academy. Yet, it remains questionable whether various attitudes such as authoritarianism or cynicism result from the kinds of people electing to become police officers (predispositions to these attitudes) or from the socialization process of becoming a police officer (Burbeck and Furnham 1985, Broderick 1987).

Acquiring a Police Personality

Throughout the 1970s two main explanations for how police acquire a police personality competed for acceptance among researchers: the predisposition and the socialization models. The predisposition model maintains that certain personality traits of individuals who become police officers are significantly different from those persons who choose other careers. The idea that persons with certain specific personality traits (such as a need to control situations, cynical views of the world, etc.) seek law enforcement careers, where such traits are encouraged, is often associated with this general theory (Rokeach et al. 1971).

The other, and slightly more persuasive, model argues that the attitudinal and value differences identified between police and civilians results from a transformation or resocialization of the individual into a police orientation. Usually, this theoretical perspective considers both the structural elements of police work and the process by which recruits are identified and selected for the job of police officer.

Richard Bennett and Theodore Greenstein (1975) were among researchers seeking to test explanations that favored predisposed police personalities. According to Bennett and Greenstein, police personalities, or for that matter any personality, can be seen basically as a value orientation. In other words, a person's personality traits are related to his or her beliefs and value system.

In their research, Bennett and Greenstein use a value survey developed by Milton Rokeach (1973). Essentially, this survey offers subjects a listing of terminal and instrumental values. Bennett and Greenstein's study subjects were students attending a state university. Each subject was asked to prioritize values in order of importance as guiding principles in life.

Terminal values used in the survey tended to be more expressive in their orientation and referred to a concern for maintaining harmony and internal emotional stability with one's self or within one's family. Instrumental values referred to tasks, focused on distinct goals, and included reference to a concern over external relationships of one's family and other social institutions. Examples of several terminal values include happiness, equality, and pleasure. Examples of instrumental values include a comfortable life, a sense of accomplishment, and social recognition.

Subjects in the Bennett and Greenstein research were subdivided into three groups: police officers, police-science majors, and non-police-science majors. Intuitively, one might assume, as Bennett and Greenstein did themselves, that police officers and police-science majors would have value orientations that closely resemble one another. However, the research showed this to be false. Instead, Bennett and Greenstein found that police-science majors and non-police-science majors had virtually identical values systems. Furthermore, they found that both non-police subgroups held values markedly different from the values demonstrated in the police officers' surveys. From these surprising findings, Bennett and Greenstein (1975, 444) concluded:

> If the predispositional, personality hypothesis were correct, we would have expected the converse: that the value systems of the police science majors would be significantly different from the non-police science majors while similar to the experienced officers' [reflecting the presence of a personality predisposition].

Arising from these various contributing factors is the question of whether police recruits are in some manner different or unique in comparison with the general public. Unfortunately, few studies have compared police profiles to those of other occupational groups. One recent exception to this trend is research undertaken by Bruce Carpenter and Susan Raza (1987). In their study, Carpenter and Raza examine various characteristics of police applicants and compare them with those of security guards, nuclear submariners, and air force trainees. In the end, using the Minnesota Multiphasic Personality Inventory (MMPI) and the Mayo Clinic adult norms scale, Carpenter and Raza found little meaningful difference between any of these groups. In summarizing their findings, Carpenter and Raza (1987, 16) state:

> The job demands and job status of police officers, security guards, nuclear submariners, and air force trainees appear to differ enough for us to expect meaningful differences in the personality characteristics of applicants to the different professions. We found a number of statistically significant differences, but few differences large enough to be considered very important.

In sum, the question of how (or when) one acquires a police personality remains filled with controversy. Certainly, arguments can be aired both for and against the predisposition model. However, currently available research does not support the idea that persons entering policing possess personality characteristics that are disproportionately different from persons entering other careers.

Formulating the Police Working Personality Concept

The idea of a police personality first began to gain public awareness in the late 1960s. The 1960s were a turbulent period for the police and the country. Anti-war protests were a regular occurrence, as were racially motivated neighborhood fights and riots. In the face of a series of political assassinations and attempts and general civil unrest across the country, police officers frequently found themselves assailed as brutal, mindless storm troopers. With these social situations as backdrop, it is easy to understand criticisms of the police as secretive, violent, cynical, and authoritarian. The concept of a police personality associated with these negative characteristics, then, fast gained in popularity as a stereotype. The perpetuation and reinforcement of this stereotype among civilians was frequently accentuated by media representations and factual accounts of violent police and civilian encounters.

Jerome Skolnick (1966) is sometimes credited with developing the concept of a working personality in his book *Justice Without Trial*. Skolnick's book examines police attitudes and discretion and suggests that police develop a working personality as a consequence of their working environment. Working personalities, then, are not the result of pre-existing personality traits. It was Skolnick's contention that two principal elements in policing—danger and authority—lead to the development of a police personality. According to Skolnick (1966, 42), "Danger typically yields self-defense conduct." Officers quickly learn to be continually concerned for their own safety.

Skolnick believes that the potential dangers from police work (both real and perceived) lead officers to grow uneasy with civilians, making these officers more suspicious of people in general. Being hyper-suspicious, these officers tended to isolate themselves from civilians. Instead, police officers were described as seeking the social support of other officers. Skolnick (1966, 42–70) indicated that in order to deal with danger, the officers develop a "perceptual shorthand to identify certain kinds of people" who pose a greater threat to safety than others. This perceptual shorthand amounts to a mental listing of various visual clues and signals, with special emphasis on a person's physical appearance.

Regarding the use of authority by police, Skolnick looks to their authority to restrain residents and, thereby, effectively deny them liberty. Since many individuals, when denied their liberty (placed under arrest), resist or challenge the officer's prerogative, the officer's perception of danger is reinforced. Skolnick also implies that the police learn to use their authority as a defensive mechanism. Indeed, arrest or the threat of arrest, physical force or the threat of physical force, and even the potential for deadly force provide an officer with a powerful means for effective control over people and situations.

Studies by David Bayley and Harold Mendelson (1969) and Joel Lefkowitz (1975) began to dispute the supposed police personality stereotype held by the general popula-

tion. In a study of the Denver police, Bayley and Mendelson (1969, 15) found that "on all personality scales the data show that policemen are absolutely average people." According to Bayley and Mendelson, police recruits may even be more idealistic when they first enter the academy than members of the general population.

Reviewing the research conducted up to that point, Joel Lefkowitz (1975) commented that most of the literature suggested mere opinions that police officers were more authoritarian than other occupational categories and not empirical evidence. He concluded that while police personalities do differ in systematic ways from civilians', these differences were effectively neutral. In other words, while the police may be more conservative in their attitudes and behaviors, they are not necessarily pathological in their authoritative approach. More recently, Elizabeth Burbeck's and Adrian Furnham's (1985) review of the literature on attitudes of the police has pointed toward a kind of police weltanschauung distinguishable from that of the general population. For example, police officers were found to place considerable emphasis on concrete or terminal values, such as the family, mature love, and work accomplishments. Conversely, officers tended to have lesser concern over non-tangible, abstract values such as equality.

Whether the police personality is acquired before entering the academy, as a result of the academy training, or once the officer enters the field remains unclear. Similarly, there are questions about whether classroom instruction at the academy and field experience as officers are equally useful. To be sure, a fair amount of an officer's training is accomplished in the classroom. But, an enormous amount of how an officer will use book knowledge can only be accomplished through experience gained in the streets, while on the job (Rubenstein 1973; Van Maanen 1975; Brown 1981; Bennett 1984). As already suggested, the harsh realities of the kinds of people and problems officers must contend with may create anomic situations for the officers. In response, these officers may invoke various defensive mechanisms. The defensive mechanisms, then, may de-emphasize what some have called the softer, more abstract affective values and require increased emphasis on more concrete ones (Burbeck and Furnham 1985; Alpert and Dunham 1988).

Similarly, these defensive mechanisms may move officers into positions of social isolation from their neighbors and, in some cases, even from family members. What results is an extraordinary type of group unity among officers collectively. This mutual support and solidarity among the police provides the social cement that binds the police subculture. The confidence, shared feelings of threat and isolation, and support offered to one another enable officers to endure the hostility, conflicts, and disapproval confronted daily. Some researchers have argued that loyalty is among the most important elements associated with the police subculture.

Michael Brown (1981), for example, writes in *Working the Street*:

> As one patrolman expressed the matter, "I'm for the guys in blue! Any-body criticizes a fellow copper that's like criticizing somebody in my family; we have to stick together." The police culture demands of a patrol unstinting loyalty to his fellow officers, and he receives, in return, protection and honor: a place to assuage real and imagined wrongs inflicted by a (presumably) hostile public; safety from aggressive administrators and supervisors; and the emotional support required to perform a difficult task. The most important question asked by a patrolman about a rookie is whether or not he displays the loyalty demanded by the police subculture.

In addition to offering emotional support, increasing self-esteem, and self-confidence, the solidarity among officers has roots in officer survival needs. Bittner (1980) has detailed these survival concerns in his elaboration on the esprit de corps associated with the institution of policing.

Esprit De Corps

Egon Bittner's book, *The Functions of Police in Modern Society*, outlines the notion and nature of police esprit de corps. Briefly, Bittner describes a version of the traditional military "code of honor and secrecy." According to Bittner (1980, 63):

> The esprit de corps has some basis in the realities of police work and is, in its own way, purposeful. Policing is a dangerous occupation and the availability of unquestioned support and loyalty is not something officers could readily do without. In the heat of action it is not possible to arrange, from case to case, for the supply of support, nor can the supply of such support be made dependent on whether the cooperating agents agree about abstract principles. The governing consideration must be that as long as "one of us" is in peril, right or wrong, he deserves help.

To a large measure, however, and as several commentators on policing have observed, this "fraternal spirit" is a double-edged sword. While it is certainly a comfort in the lives of officers, it may also produce serious ethical problems. For example, what on the surface may appear a uniform buddy system may actually have an infinite variety of collusive arrangements.

At some level officers may be bound together entirely as a single group. At another level, however, there may be smaller bunchings of solidarity that pit one group of officers against another. The corruption and secrecy uncovered by the Knapp Commission, which will be discussed in Chapter Twelve, encompassed an entire city's police organization. Officers lied for one another to conceal graft, vice, and racketeering, both from the public and superior officers. Many of the superiors were themselves involved in rampant corruption. A more recent example may be seen in the "Exam-Scam" of the Boston Police (1978–87). In this instance, police officials and a number of officers were alleged to know about police promotion exams being stolen for as long as six years before any action was taken (Doherty 1987). These officers and officials may well have remained mum because of the spirit of "one for all and all for one"—at all costs.

Although the police may not be, as many perceive, one big happy family, officers are required to work with and depend upon one another (Bittner 1980). As a result, even in situations where one officer may be disapproving of another's actions, it may be difficult to do anything about it actively. The 1973 film *Serpico* illustrates the problems faced when honest officers turn in dishonest ones. Although a slightly fictionalized account, the film chronicles how Frank Serpico, a real New York City police officer, blew the whistle on a number of extremely dishonest officers at the height of the Knapp Commission hearings. More important for our current discussion, the film shows how, after doing so, other officers were unwilling to be his partner. In fact, the opening scene of the film, which is then presented in flash-backs, shows Frank Serpico and other vice officers attempting to enter an apartment where drugs are being sold. At a critical moment, when Serpico has wedged himself between the partially opened door to the apartment and the door jamb, his fellow officers fail to assist him. He is shot in the face at point-blank range. Although Serpico did survive the shooting, he suffered partial paralysis and, shortly after his recovery, quietly resigned from the police department.

It should be obvious that police work requires absolute trust in one's colleagues. The veil of silence that sometimes envelops a segment of a police department, then, may reflect this need for mutual dependency. While this cloak of secrecy may not originate as a malevolent situation, certainly it may easily become one. But, it must be remembered that when such a situation arises, it likely is a fairly small number of police officers who have undermined the trustworthiness of the police institution. This area of police corruption will be more comprehensively consid-

ered in Chapter Twelve. For now, it is important to note that despite the opposite appearance, the culture of policing is not intended to indoctrinate people into breaking the law or covering up law violations of other officers.

THE OCCUPATIONAL ROLE OF THE POLICE OFFICER

We have previously discussed the idea that when one hears "police work," one conjures images of police cars with lights flashing and sirens wailing as they race to the scene of a crime. Some may envision an officer crouched in a defense combat position with gun trained on some highly dangerous criminal. Still others may envision the trench coat and note pad of some Columbo-like or Kojak-like detective. To be sure, when civilians think about police officers, who they are, and what they do, this vision is clouded by media representations of the police as supercops.

As part of this imagery, civilians tend to think about the police as one-dimensional creatures whose days and nights are filled with a never-ending stream of excitement, danger, and intrigue. There is a tendency, therefore, to think of police as preoccupied exclusively with crime and crime fighting. But police start out their lives as civilians. They are subject to the same social problems, prejudices, costs of living, conflicts with parents and friends, and general life decisions as others in society.

Unfortunately, the line separating the real life of police officers from their media-created counterparts has grown increasingly blurred. Many of the stereotypes that the public holds for police are based on the belief that most of an officer's work time is spent dealing with criminals and enforcing laws. These stereotypes seldom depict accurately the actual nature of the occupational role of the police officer.

The term *role* has been used by social scientists in a variety of ways, depending in great measure upon the focus of their research

(Zurcher 1983). It typically refers to various behavior patterns and attitudes expected of individuals who occupy specific social categories. In a general sense, these social categories include formal status positions in the social structure of society, as well as informal, more temporary statuses. In the case of the former, one might think of mothers, fathers, teachers, and police officers as examples. In the case of the latter, one might consider being a member of the audience at a rock concert, a patron of a record store, or a player on a sand-lot softball team.

In addition to these more regular status categories, there are labels used to categorize people in society that reflect either cultural or subcultural values. For example, Van Maanen (1974, 1985, 147) suggests that many police officers view their occupational world as comprised of three categories of people: suspicious persons, people the police have reason to believe may have committed a crime, assholes, people who fail to accept or understand the police officer's definition of a situation, and know-nothings, people who fit neither of the other two categories but who are not police and, therefore, do not know what the police are really about.

In examining these various role categorizations, some social scientists concentrate upon roles as static elements of an already established social structure of society. From this vantage, roles are considered with regard to how they influence the behavior of people. Others depict roles in a more fluid and flexible manner. In these cases, roles are seen as arising in social settings and are viewed with regard to how individuals influence, alter, or maintain certain behavioral expectations (Zurcher 1983).

Throughout this section, police roles have been alluded to and will be further discussed as behavioral expectations for an officer (Heiss 1981, 95). The *should* concept derives from several sources, including expectations generally held for recognized formal or fixed role categories, with less formal and emergent

roles, and with the officer's self-concept. Role labels and behavioral expectations are learned through the process of socialization.

It is safe to suggest that some people grow up feeling favorably toward the police, while others feel antagonistic. These attitudes may reflect the kind of orientation each person has received during early home life. Many among us have heard small children who, when asked what they want to do when they grow up, consistently say, "I want to be a police officer." Others never mention policing as a choice. Whether the first kind of child really does become a police officer may be significant.

The sociological literature is replete with research demonstrating that the occupational socialization process begins before an individual becomes a member of this occupation. Brim and Wheeler (1966) and Merton and Rossi (1968) argue that applicants for a given occupational role begin to anticipate the demands and expectations of their future occupation. Typically, the urge to choose a given occupation as a career is related to one's *reference group(s)*.

Children frequently play out the roles of police and bad guys. Adult attitudes toward police may be significantly influenced by childhood socialization.

In some cases, this may be a real group, represented by family members, friends, or associates who are members of or who may be knowledgeable about some occupation. In some other cases this may represent an imagined or idealized reference group—provided by television, newspaper accounts, the movies, or one's imagination. In any case, this period in the career decision process, unconscious as it may be, has been labeled by Richard Bennett (1984) *anticipatory socialization.*

According to Bennett (1984), anticipatory socialization is the first stage in a three-stage process of becoming a police officer. The second stage, called *formal socialization,* refers to the recruit's exposure to more experienced police officers in the academy and while a probationary officer. The third stage of continuing socialization involves reinforcement of belief and values while working in the field. As a trainee, Bennett (1984) hypothesizes, the police officer grows increasingly similar to more experienced officers in terms of cognitive ways of seeing things. In other words, novice police officers begin to acquire what this chapter has repeatedly referred to as a police weltanschauung. The third and continuing stage of socialization into policing involves learning appropriate ways of thinking and acting in order to function successfully in the everyday work world of police officers. The actual rate of speed that this socialization process requires, according to Bennett, varies according to certain background characteristics such as socioeconomic status, race, and education. Bennett (1984, 50) summarizes his argument as follows:

> The model explaining recruit and probationary officer occupational socialization is a three stage process involving individual change manifested through affiliation with and influenced by occupational reference groups. In addition, the nature and content of the influence as well as the individual's need to affiliate are determined by structural factors that coalesce during work-related encounters. Finally, individual characteristics will either enhance or retard the process.

Recent research suggests that police recruits who are eventually selected from applicant pools frequently share certain characteristics and come from similar social backgrounds (Wilbanks 1987; Broderick 1987; Alpert and Dunham 1988). If these findings are correct, and Bennett's socialization explanation is also accurate, one can anticipate a fairly speedy transition from civilian value orientations to police value orientations. It may well be that such a transition simply is not detectable by the various personality screening surveys used by many researchers. As a result, some measures may detect a certain orientation at one time in the career of a recruit or officer, but fail to identify a change in that view. It is possible, then, to attribute inconsistencies in research results concerning reasons and explanations for why people become police officers, and the kinds of people who do so, on the basis of survey devices that simply do not match the situation (Lester 1980; Bennett 1984; Aylward 1985; Carpenter and Raza 1987).

A less controversial situation concerning the culture of police than predisposed or socialized personalities, is the concept of **styles of policing.**

Police Officer Styles

Earlier discussions in this chapter regarding the culture of policing, police personalities, and roles laid the foundation for understanding various styles of policing. Stated differently, in order to comprehend why and how styles of policing differ among officers and to some extent among police agencies, it was first necessary to recognize some of the possible origins of and strains on the police officer's value system and perceptions.

For definitional purposes, style of policing refers to a kind of working attitude. This working attitude, like its collateral concept, the working personality, is used by officers to manage and interpret various aspects of their law enforcement lives. For instance, some police officers may view their jobs simply as petty bureaucratic positions in civil service. As such, the officer may see his or her principal role as a paper pusher with a gun. Other officers may see themselves as sentinels whose mission it is to protect society from the ravages of vile criminals. The diversity in policing styles is based upon a number of influences, ranging from personality variables to police institutional goals and regulations. Michael Brown (1981, 223) defines the concept of styles of policing as follows:

> A patrolman's operational style is based on his response to . . . the difficulties and dilemmas he encounters in attempting to control crime . . . [and] the ways in which he accommodates himself to the pressures and demands of the police bureaucracy.

Like others, Brown further suggests that the officer's style of policing is related to how aggressively and how selectively the officer chooses to operate in the streets. *Aggressiveness* includes the idea of proactively attempting to initiate crime control measures and criminal apprehension. It also includes the notion of how forcefully the officer will respond to challenges to authority. *Selectivity* refers chiefly to the officer's use of discretion. Discretion, in turn, refers both to initiating and pursuing crime detection prevention activities and the intensity of these pursuits.

Carl Klockars (1985) suggests that such aggressiveness and selectivity has led some officers to a social dilemma he describes as the "Dirty Harry Problem." Klockars explains that the Dirty Harry problem derives its name from the popular 1971 Warner Brothers film character, Police Inspector Harry (Dirty Harry) Callahan. Briefly, the Dirty Harry problem involves the question of "when and to what extent does the morally good end warrant or justify an ethically, politically, or legally dangerous means to its achievement?" (Klockars 1985, 429). In other words, is the forceful or marginally legal use of police powers characteristic of the Harry Callahan character ever really justifiable? Klockars (1985, 437) concludes that it is never justifiable to

employ a "dirty" style of policing even "to achieve some unquestionably good and morally compelling end."

As police officers develop their particular styles of policing, each must weigh the consequence of his or her decisions. On one side are the social injustices that confront officers every day. Along with these are realities about civil liabilities, the judicial system, the bail system, and constitutional restrictions on lawful searches and seizures that often appear to work in the favor of wrongdoers.

Against these pessimistic concerns the officer must weigh moral responsibility, maintenance of the law of the land in order to preserve liberty, and a conscious attempt not to violate department policy. As the officer weighs these various elements, the officer is confronted with the enormous temptation to use a Dirty Harry approach. To do so, of course, removes the thin blue line that symbolically stands between social order and disorder (Skolnick and Bayley 1986).

William G. Doerner (1985), a university professor who became a police officer, describes how rookies search for a style of policing. Doerner (1985, 396) writes:

> I maintain that the work group molds the officer's personality. I call it street survival. Rookies find themselves under tremendous pressure and tend to gravitate from one end of the pendulum to the other in their search to find a comfortable style of policing. Every rookie knows his or her reputation needs to be established before being fully accepted as a fellow officer. Hence, rookies tend to be impetuous, aggressive, and very rough around the edges. They need to learn when and how to bullshit in the street, how to finesse the person they are confronting, and how to read the interactional cues and body language that dictate appropriate courses of action and impending danger.

Against the preceding ideas and concepts, it should be easier to understand how styles of policing are formed. It should also soon become clear, if it is not already, that an officer's style of policing affects both the officer's immediate community and the society at large.

Policing Styles

A number of studies have tried to identify and classify various police styles in formal role categories. These classification schemes, sometimes called *typologies*, attempt to generate categories that represent particular approaches to policing. The purpose of such classification schemes has been to provide political leaders, the public, and police administrators with information on the perceptions and priorities of police officers. This information, in turn, has been used to rearrange departmental policies in order to encourage certain styles and discourage others. This has proven particularly beneficial in police–community relations conflicts.

Until recently, the literature on policing styles has identified four primary categories: crime fighter, social agent, law enforcer, and watchman. Each is considered below.

The Crime Fighter. Officers who fall into this category see their role primarily as serious crime investigators. In terms of priorities, this type of officer sees crimes against persons as the most serious and property crimes much less so. Mundane misdemeanors are viewed as trivial and better suited for social service agencies than the police. From this perspective, police personnel time and financial allocations should be directed predominately toward interception of serious criminals.

Crime fighters are almost exclusively interested in dealing with actual crime, rather than paper work or social service calls. Although they are often first on the scene of a serious assault, murder, or burglary, they may ignore radio calls in their area concerning traffic accidents or other minor incidents. In many ways, these crime fighters fit the public's image of the supercops of fiction. They are no-nonsense, old-style crime fighters, who frequently use more force than may be required to maintain order in a street situation (Brown 1981, Doerner 1985).

The Social Agent. As a virtual opposite of the crime fighter stands the social agent type of officer. A major function of police officers involves answering a variety of social service calls. Supporters of the social agent style of policing argue that police officers should recognize this reality. Accordingly, supports recommend spending more time and effort on activities that simply need to be done and less effort on imagining that the singular role of policing is crime fighting.

The social agent may even point out that historically, policing included health, sanitation, and fire protection. Hence, social agents conceive the notion of community security in a broad, generalized context that includes crime prevention and criminal apprehension as mere elements among others.

The Law Enforcer. In a manner similar to the crime fighter, law enforcers have a tendency to emphasize investigation, interception of crimes, and apprehension of criminals. In contrast to the crime fighter, however, law enforcers do not make a distinction between serious and trivial crimes. Like other types of police officers, law enforcers see being involved in real police work, such as investigating serious or major crimes, as desirable and rewarding. But, law enforcers also see the necessity of enforcing *all* statues and ordinances—no matter how minor. The law is the law! Law enforcers are reminiscent of the fictional Officer Joe Friday character made famous by the popular 1960s television series "Dragnet." They work by the book, letter of the law, and "Just the facts, ma'am," as Officer Friday was so often heard to say.

The Watchman. While both the crime fighter and the law enforcer stress enforcement of the law, watchman-style policing emphasizes order maintenance. If this means enforcing the laws, so be it. On the other hand, if maintaining public order means ignoring minor infractions or brushing off requests for social service assistance, then watchmen will do this as well. The priority among watchmen is preservation of the social and political order of society. James Q. Wilson (1968) is frequently credited with coining this description. According to Wilson (1968, 141):

> The police are watchman-like not simply in emphasizing order over law enforcement but also in judging the seriousness of infractions less by what the law says about them than by their immediate and personal consequences. . . . In all cases, circumstances of person and condition are taken seriously into account.

Modern Policing Styles

More recently, however, John Broderick (1987) has developed a modern typology of policing styles that may be more suitable for modern police practices. Broderick's typology incorporates both types of officers and styles of policing. Unlike earlier typological classification systems, Broderick's does not reify his proposed categories. Instead, Broderick cautions that his is an analytic schema in which some characteristics found in one category may be found in others as well. Broderick further asserts that not all police officers may be neatly cast into one or another of his proposed categories, giving the impression that his may not be an exhaustive set of categories.

Broderick's typology, however, draws together characteristics commonly associated with police personalities and suggests how these variables tend to overlap with styles of policing. In doing so, "he (the police officer) provides a useful and convenient way of examining a very complex area of human behavior" (Broderick 1987, 4). Broderick's classification system includes enforcers, idealists, realists, and optimists. Each is detailed below.

Enforcers. Enforcers are similar to the crime fighter and emphasize clearing the streets of criminals. Although they place a high value on maintaining social order within the community, they place a low value on individual rights, due process, and empathic understanding of civilians.

Idealists. In contrast to enforcers, idealists sincerely believe in the law. They view procedure, departmental policy, statutory law, and due process as potential solutions to criminal activity in society. Idealists look at constitutional rights afforded all citizens, even criminals, as necessary to preserve social order. Idealists also see education as an important and may seek college degrees—sometimes in fields other than law enforcement. Hence, officers fitting this category may report lower levels of commitment to policing than those in other categories.

Realists. Unlike enforcers and idealists, realists place little emphasis on either preservation of individual rights or maintenance of the social order. Officers falling into this category tend to be cynical and dissatisfied with the failure of the criminal justice system. Often, these officers become alienated from their colleagues, administrators, and the communities they police. They may withdraw into themselves and avoid making any difficult decisions.

Optimists. Broderick's final category, the optimist, perceives his or her role as a police officer as really making a difference. These officers see their mission as one that assists people, and it brings them intrinsic reward. In many ways, optimists are reminiscent of the social agents described earlier. Although fighting crime is seen as a necessary part of the job, the primary function of policing is seen as providing service to the public.

Other researchers have recently identified characteristics similar to those suggested by

Broderick (Hatting et al. 1983, Walsh 1986). A central theme through all attempts to typologize policing is that police officers are not a homogeneous group. Although police officers share many characteristics, interests, and ideals, each officer responds to the demands of the job in a distinct manner. How officers begin to react in police situations eventually settles into what Doerner (1985) called "a comfortable style of policing."

SUMMARY

In the preceding discussion of the culture of policing, it has been suggested that research has uncovered certain variables commonly associated with police officers. These variables, or more accurately traits, have been long believed to represent certain stereotypical expectations about how a police officer is likely to think and act. These stereotypic role expectations have given rise to the concept of a police personality.

The research and understandings about police personalities, however, remain somewhat inconclusive. Of particular controversy is the question of whether police recruits are somehow selected because they display predispositions favorable to acquiring a police personality or acquire a police personality through socialization after joining the force, irrespective of predisposition.

The existence of a police subculture has been suggested to represent the collective result of a group's need to create a socially supportive and secure network. This subculture provides officers with assistance in coping with alienation, stress, and difficulties emerging from performance of their role as law enforcers. In other words, the police subculture provides coping and defensive mechanisms for officers.

The existence of and socialization into the culture of policing is not unlike other occupational subcultures. A portion of the socialization process is designed to instruct neophyte officers about specialized ways of speaking (argot) that insiders use. Another portion of the process acknowledges certain ways of doing things. Finally, and perhaps the most important aspect of this indoctrination into the occupational subculture of policing, is a transferring of their particular way of seeing the world, a weltanschauungen.

The preceding chapter has also examined the extension of a general police personality concept and considered the officers' working personalities and policing styles. In this regard, it has been suggested that a number of typologies have been generated by research. Although each varies slightly with its categorical labeling, all tend to share a basic premise. This premise concerns the diversity among police officers in terms of how they operate in their daily policing activities. In short, in spite of many common characteristics and interests, police react differently from one another even in similar situations.

REVIEW QUESTIONS _____

1. What is meant by the concept of a police weltanschauung?

2. Why might "war stories" told by police academy instructors to their recruits pose a potentially problematic situation for these recruits?

3. What is the central purpose of the police esprit de corps?

4. How do police officers acquire their policing styles? Do these various styles of policing serve any real purpose?

5. Would police officers be able to function in their role as keepers of the peace if there were no police subculture?

REFERENCES

Alpert, Geoffrey, and Roger G. Dunham. *Policing Urban America.* Prospect Heights, Ill.: Waveland Press, 1988.

Aylward, Jack. "Psychological Testing and Police Selection." *Journal of Police Science and Administration* 13 (1985): 201–10.

Bayley, David H., and Harold Mendelsohn. *Minorities and the Police.* New York: Free Press, 1969.

Becker, Howard S. *The Outsiders: Studies in the Sociology of Deviance.* New York: Free Press, 1963.

Bennett, Richard R., "Becoming Blue: A Longitudinal Study of Police Recruit Occupational Socialization. *Journal of Police Science and Administration* 12 (1984): 47–58.

Bennett, Richard R., and Theodore Greenstein. "The Police Personality: A Test of the Predispositional Model." *Journal of Police Science and Administration* 3 (1975): 439–45.

Berg, Bruce L., Marc Gertz, and Edmond True. "Police, Riots, and Alienation." *Police Science and Administration* 12, (1984): 186–90.

Berg, Bruce L. "First Day: Stress Reaction Training As A Police Screening-Out Strategy." Paper presented at the annual meeting of the American Society of Criminology, Reno, Nevada, November 1989.

Berg, Bruce L., "First Day At The Police Academy: Stress Reaction Training As A Screening-Out Technique." *Journal of Contemporary Criminal Justice* 6, (1990a): 89–105.

Berg, Bruce L. "A Typology of Municipal Police Academy Instructors," *American Journal of Police* 9, (1990b): 79–100.

Bittner, Egon. *The Function of Police in Modern Society.* Cambridge, Mass.: Oelegeschlager, Gunn and Haire, 1980.

Brim, Orville G., and Stanton Wheeler. *Socialization After Childhood.* New York: John Wiley, 1966.

Broderick, John. *Police in a Time of Change,* 2d ed. Prospect Heights, Ill.: Waveland, 1987.

Brown, Michael K. *Working the Streets: Police Discretion and the Dilemmas of Reform.* New York: Russell Sage Foundation, 1981.

Burbeck, Elizabeth, and Adrian Furnham. "Police Officer Selection: A Critical Review of the Literature." *Journal of Police Science and Administration.* 13, (1985): 58–69.

Carpenter, Bruce N., and Susan M. Raza. "Personality Characteristics of Police Applicants: Comparisons Across Subgroups and With Other Populations. *Journal of Police Science and Administration* 15, (1987): 10–17.

Doerner, William G. "I'm Not The Man I Used to Be: Reflections on the Transition from Professor to Cop." In Abraham S. Blumberg and Elaine Niederhoffer, eds. *The Ambivalent Force* 3rd ed. New York: Holt, Rinehart and Winston, 1985: 394–99.

Doherty, William F. "Class Action Suit Accuses Bellotti of Failure to Halt Police Exam Thefts." *The Boston Globe.* December 8, 1987: 1,30.

Durkheim, Emile [1897]. *Suicide.* Translated by John A. Spaulding and George Simpson. New York: Free Press, 1951.

Goffman, Erving. *Asylums: Essays on the Social Situation of Mental Patients and Other Inmates.* Garden City, New York: Anchor, 1961.

Hatting, Steven H., Alan Engel and Philip Russo. "Shades of Blue: Toward an Alternative Typology of Police." *Journal of Police Science and Administration* 3 (1983): 319–26.

Heiss, Jerold. "Social Roles." In M. Rosenberg and R.H. Turner eds. *Social Psychology: Sociological Perspectives.* New York: Basic, 1981.

Holden Richard. *Modern Police Management.* Englewood Cliffs, N.J.: Prentice Hall, 1986.

Kindleberger, Richard. "Three Probes Announced into Cadet Illnesses." *The Boston Globe.* September 28, 1988: 1,63.

Klockars, Carl B. *The Idea of Police.* Beverly Hills, Calif.: Sage, 1985.

Klofas, John, Stan Stojkovic, and David Kalinich. *Criminal Justice Organizations, Administration, and Management.* Pacific Grove, Calif.: Brooks/Cole, 1990.

Kuykendall, Jack and Peter Usinger. *Community Police Administration.* Chicago: Nelson-Hall, 1975.

Lefkowitz, Joel "Psychological Attributes of Policemen: A Review of Research and Opinions." *Journal of Social Issues.* 31, (1975): 3–26.

Lester, David "Are Police Officers Cynical?" *Criminal Justice Review* 2 (1980): 51–56.

Merton, Robert K., and Alice Kitt Rossi. "Contributions to the Theory of Reference Group Behavior." In Herbert H. Hyman and Eleanor Singer, eds. *Readings in Reference Group Theory and Research.* New York: Free Press, 1968:26–68.

Niederhoffer, Arthur. *Behind the Shield: The Police in Urban Society.* Garden City, N.Y.: Anchor, 1969.

O'Connell, Brian J., Herbert Holzman, and Barry R. Armandi. "Police Cynicism and Modes of Adaptation." *Journal of Police Science and Administration* 14, (1986): 307–313.

Regoli, Robert M. "An Empirical Assessment of Niederhoffer's Police Cynicism Scale." *Journal of Criminal Justice* 4 (1976) :231–41.

Regoli, Robert M., Eric M. Poole, and John D. Hewitt. "Exploring the Empirical Relationship Between Police Cynicism and Work Alienation." *Journal of Police Science and Administration* 7 (1979): 336–39.

Report of the Governor's Panel to Review Police Training Programs. Mass.: Office of the Governor, May 1989.

Reuss-Ianni, Elizabeth. *Two Cultures of Policing.* New Brunswick, N.J.: Transaction, 1984.

Rokeach, Milton, Martin G. Miller, John A. Snyder. "The Value Gap Between the Police and the Policed." *Journal of Social Issues* 27 (1971): 155–71.

Rokeach, Milton. *The Nature of Human Values.* New York: Free Press, 1973.

Rubenstein, Johnathan. *City Police.* New York: Farrar, Strauss and Giroux, 1973.

Schaefer, Richard T., and Robert Lamm. *Sociology* 3d ed. New York: McGraw-Hill, 1989.

Scheingold, Stuart A. *The Politics of Law and Order: Street Crime and Public Policy.* New York: Longman, 1984.

Skolnick, Jerome H. *Justice Without Trial.* New York: Wiley, 1966.

Skolnick, Jerome H., and David H. Bayley. *The New Blue Line: Police Innovation in Six American Communities.* New York: Free Press, 1986.

Terkel, Studs. *Working.* New York: Random House, 1974.

Theroux, Paul "Subway Odyssey." *New York Times Magazine.* (January 31, 1982): 20–23, 71, 74–76.

Van Maanen, John. "Working the Streets: A Developmental View of Police Behavior." In H. Jacobs, ed. *Reality and Reform: The Criminal Justice System.* Beverly Hills, Calif.: Sage, 1974.

Van Maanen, John. "Police Socialization: A Longitudinal Examination of Job Attitudes in an Urban Police Department." *Administrative Science Quarterly* 20 (1975): 207–229.

Van Maanen, John. "The Asshole." In Abraham S. Blumberg and Elaine Niederhoffer, eds. *The Ambivalent Force.* New York: Holt, Rinehart and Winston, 1985: 146–58.

Wadler, Joyce. "Inhuman Error," *People Magazine.* October 17, 1988: 52–56.

Walsh, William F. "Patrol Officer Arrest Rates: A Study of the Social Organization of Police Work." *Justice Quarterly* 3, (1986): 271–90.

Westley, William A. *Violence and the Police.* Cambridge, Mass.: MIT Press, 1970.

Willbanks, William. *The Myth of a Racist Criminal Justice System.* Monterey, Calif.: Brooks/Cole, 1987.

Wilson, James Q. *Varieties of Police Behavior: The Management of Law and Order in Eight Communities.* Cambridge, Mass.: Harvard, 1968.

Wilt, Marie G., and James D. Bannon. "Cynicism or Realism: A Critique of Niederhoffer's Research into Police Attitudes." *Journal of Police Science and Administration* 4 (1976): 38–45.

Zurcher, Louis A. *Social Roles.* Beverly Hills, Calif.: Sage, 1983.

_____ CHAPTER 11 _____

POLICE DISCRETION

*The matter of autonomy among police officers merits special attention
and is usually characterized as police discretion. Like other members of
the criminal justice work force, the exercise of discretion by police officers
is often subject to public scrutiny. It is during instances of police authority, police power, and police corruption as detailed in Chapters Six and
Twelve that police discretion is put to the test.*

*As Chapter Six indicated, police officers are granted a considerable
amount of latitude during the course of the routine police activities. They
are, however, subject to certain legal limitations. In other words, police
officers are not permitted to exercise their authority by whim or caprice.
Police officers are held accountable for their behavior, not only individually but as a group. As suggested in Chapter Twelve, when a single
officer blemishes the institution of policing through a corrupt act, the
general image of police officers is tarnished as well.*

*Ideally, police officers are expected to enforce the law equally for all.
The notion of "fair access to law enforcement protection," described in
Chapter Twelve, represents this ideal. Unfortunately, implementation of
such an ideal is not as simple as one might think. If it were, there would
likely be considerably less concern about how police officers make discretionary choices. The law simply does not cover every situation that a
police officer encounters in the field. In some circumstances, even where
the law may be clear, it might be more prudent for the officer to ignore
strict interpretation—for example, if an arrest might ignite a riot, or a
verbal warning about speeding seems to suffice, or when dispersing
adolescents hanging out on a corner seems more reasonable than arresting them for loitering.*

Chapter Eleven examines this discretionary nature of policing. The purpose of this examination is several fold: First, to outline several of the major areas where discretion often outweighs strict letter-of-the-law interpretations; second, to consider the question or, more precisely, the myth of full enforcement of laws. Technically speaking, the police are expected to enforce all laws and to arrest everyone they see committing law violations. Implementation of such a task, as Chapter Eleven will detail, is simply untenable.

Finally, Chapter Eleven will consider discretionary situations surrounding the use of deadly force. Related to this concern will be a discussion of recent changes in "fleeing felon" rules following the case of Tennessee v. Garner (1985). The purpose of this discussion is to examine the need to control police discretion through policy and written departmental guidelines.

INTRODUCTION: DISCRETION AND DECISION-MAKING

Of the wide assortment of problems that confront law enforcement officers daily, discretion is surely among the most complex. Police officer discretion may or may at least appear to deteriorate into discrimination, violence, unfair access to protection, or other abuses of official authority. Research remains inconclusive about the extent to which extra-legal variables such as race, gender, ethnicity, age, and demeanor affect officer discretion. Yet, there is little question that these factors do influence an officer's thinking. It would be difficult to argue that personal judgments are not inculcated by one's life experiences, personal hang-ups, and prejudices. Often, however, it is very difficult to accurately draw a line between discretion and discrimination.

Discretion in law enforcement, and for that matter throughout the entire criminal justice system, is not a new phenomenon. Yet, serious examination of officer decision-making, with an eye on curbing the wide latitude that police discretion allows, did not arise until the late 1960s and early 1970s. As part of a larger social movement directed toward reducing arbitrariness and discretion practiced by many American social institutions, a movement to infuse rules in the police decision process arose (Hanewicz 1985).

Some police sources suggest that various judicial attempts to minimize or regulate discretionary decision-making by police may have actually hand-cuffed police. In these instances the inference is that police require a greater, not lesser, degree of discretionary powers. It would be difficult to dispute Howard Cohen's (1986,27) claim that "the use of discretion is not an option for police officers; it is a necessary, unavoidable part of the job."

With few exceptions, all police activities require some degree of discretion and decision-making. These decisions may involve simply selecting what the officer sees as the best course of action in a mundane situation. Or, these decisions may require the officer to decide whether to shoot and perhaps kill a suspected criminal.

This chapter will examine the problems with discretion in policing. Included are considerations of the range of choices and their social implications. The chapter will review various strategies designed to reduce or regulate police exercise of authority. Along with this discussion will be a consideration of the police officer as policy maker. The chapter will also discuss the use of force, including deadly force.

Discretionary Situations

In the recent past, social scientists have become increasingly interested in the discretionary nature of decision-making by police officers. Douglas Smith (1987) points out that throughout the past two decades, studies repeatedly indicate that law alone is an ineffective predictor of police behavior where decisions about arrest are concerned (See Banton 1964; Black 1970; Lundman 1974; Smith and Visher 1981; Berk and Loseke 1981). In one early study of American policing, Michael Banton (1964) remarked that the most striking thing about police officers was their frequent choice *not* to arrest a suspect. This observation by Banton has resulted in others pursuing examinations of the rather routine aspects of police work, which in turn has increased scholarly knowledge about the complexities of the police role and decision process.

Various past studies provide the basis for a useful typology of situations in which police discretion typically arises. These situations include traffic citations, juvenile arrests, police shooting incidents, and daily police policies.

Traffic Citations.   Among the most obvious situations in which police discretion arises, and perhaps the least distasteful for most people, is during the issuance of a traffic ticket. In one study, John Gardiner (1969) found that Dallas police officers wrote as many as twenty

times the number of traffic tickets as police in Boston—although the cities had approximately the same population size (Walker 1983). Similarly, Richard Lundman found discrepancies in the issuance of traffic citations and the making of traffic stops. In his investigation Lundman (1980) found that only 47 percent of 293 violators were issued citations.

Referring to production pressures and ticket quotas, Jerome H. Skolnick (1966, 1986) describes how police may lie in ambush near tricky intersections in order to assure capture of their quotas of traffic violators. But, once they have met their quotas, they would not necessarily continue this practice.

Juvenile Arrests.   Studies repeatedly demonstrate that police use a wide degree of discretion in dealing with juveniles. Nathan Goldman (1963) examined the arrest records of over 1,000 juveniles from four communities in Pennsylvania. He found that arrests per thousand ranged from a low of 12.4 to a high of 49.7. He concluded that the majority (64 percent) of police–juvenile contacts never reached the courts, but were handled informally. In another study, conducted by Irving Piliavin and Scott Briar (1964), 30 officers in a juvenile unit in a large industrialized city were observed. Piliavin and Briar found that factors such as a juvenile's prior record played an important role in whether an officer would make an arrest.

Some studies have indicated that the seriousness of a crime affects the decision-making processes. Donald Black and Albert Reiss (1970) reported that arrests of juveniles committing felonies tended to be twice as high as the number of arrests of juveniles for serious misdemeanors. Richard Lundman, Richard Sykes, and J.P. Clark (1978) replicated the Black and Reiss (1976) study and concluded that the probability of arrest increased with the legal seriousness of the juveniles' alleged offenses. More recently, Bruce L. Berg (1986) observed that in jurisdictions in which juvenile alternative-to-incarcerations programs did not exist, many cases would be informally handled by the police.

There is also evidence that the race and gender of the offending youth are factors that influence an officer's decision about whether to arrest (See Sullivan and Siegel 1972; Cox and Conrad 1987; Pope 1984). In spite of an increase in females committing crime, male juveniles continue to be taken into police custody more frequently. For example, the Port Authority Police of New York and New Jersey reported 2,515 contacts with youth for the calendar year 1985. Only 97 youths were taken into custody: 34 females and 63 males (Port Authority 1986). Although systematic research on the impact of gender on decision-making is limited, there seems to be some police bias in favor of girls who commit serious offenses and against them when the offense is trivial or is not a crime traditionally associated with females (Cavan and Ferdinand 1981).

Police Shootings.   Police shootings engender heated debates and will be discussed in greater detail later. For now it should be sufficient to point out that according to Catherine H. Milton and her associates (1977, 30), in 1977 the shooting of civilians ranged from a low of 4.2 shootings per 1,000 officers in Portland, Oregon, to a high of 25 shootings per 1,000 officers in Birmingham, Alabama.

Some studies suggest that a factor involved in an officer's decision to shoot is race. Jay Albanese (1988, 125) reports that a survey of five major studies on police shootings reveals discrimination. The studies which include eleven different cities, suggest that blacks tend to be shot by police two to four times more often than whites. For example, in a Philadelphia study by Robin (1963) where 22 percent of the population was black, 88 percent of the shooting victims also were black. In a study of shootings in Chicago by Harding and Fahey (1973) where the black population was 33 percent, the black shooting victims accounted for 75 percent. In Milton et al. (1977) seven cities were investigated with an aver-

age black population of 39 percent. The average percentage of black shooting victims was 79 percent. In New York City (Fyfe 1978) where the black population was 20 percent, the percentage of black shooting victims was 60 percent. In Los Angeles, Meyer's (1980) found a black population of 18 percent and a black shooting victim percentage of 50 percent.

In a recent review of the literature on police shootings, James Fyfe (1988, 189) reported that "regardless of the care employed in restricting officers' shooting, every study that has examined this issue found that blacks are represented disproportionately among those at the wrong end of police guns." Most population studies suggest a national black population of approximately 13 percent. In his effort to outline some of this research Fyfe (1988) cites a study by Takagi (1974). Takagi (1974, 29) found that among 2,441 males reported by the National Center for Health Statistics to have been killed by American police officers from 1960 to 1968, 1,188 (48 percent) were black. In a slightly more recent study, Harring, et al. (1977) reported that death rates for blacks at the hands of police officers nationwide were as much as ten times those of whites.

In partial contradiction to allegations of discrimination in police shootings, Arnold Binder and Peter Scharf (1982) suggest that comparisons of black victims with the proportion of blacks arrested for violent crimes might be a more reliable indicator of discrimination in police shootings (Albanese 1988, 126). In fact, Binder and Scharf (1982, 19) found that when "one compares victimization rates with arrest rates, one comes up with remarkably close numbers." In further support of this notion, several ancillary findings in recent studies suggest that blacks appear to possess guns when involved in police shootings more often than do whites (Fyfe 1978; Meyer 1980).

Binder and Scharf also point out that it may be a mistake to equate black shooting victims with blacks in the general city populations, as most studies do. Binder and Scharf assert that police seldom shoot certain kinds of people—college professors, doctors, merchants and so forth—whether they are white or black. Hence, it is not race per se that may make one more prone to being shot; it is exposure to certain types of situations that increases one's likelihood of being shot. If one is involved in law violating, one is more likely to be exposed to situations in which a shooting is possible than if one does not break the law.

These recent findings and observations account for some of the disparities that exist in the proportion of blacks (as compared to whites) injured or killed in police shootings. As Fyfe (1988, 191) comments, "Researchers have found close association between racial distributions of police shooting subjects and measures of the risk of being shot at, such as arrests for murder, robbery, aggravated assault, weapons offenses, and burglary. . . arrests for FBI Crime Index offenses. . . and arrests for violent Crime Index offenses." It remains questionable, however, how accurate arrest proportions are as an indicator of discrimination in police shootings. Certainly, arrests may be tainted by discriminatory decision-making practices that result in greater numbers of blacks than whites being arrested.

Nonetheless, recent studies that examine whether both arrest and deadly force statistics result from discriminatory police practices suggest they do not (See Fyfe 1981, Blumberg 1981). Mark Blumberg found that regardless of race, approximately seven in ten of those individuals shot by Atlanta police and half of those shot by Kansas City police from 1971 to 1978 had attacked officers with weapons. Blumberg also found that regardless of the intensity of officer response shooting victims (assessed on the basis of the number of officers who shot and the number of shots fired) or the results of shootings (measured by the ratio of non-fatal to fatal wounds) varied by subjects' race.

One interpretation of the various contradictions observable in recent studies on police shootings is a kind of measurement imprecision: the failure of many researchers to consider the setting in which the police shooting occurred. Certainly, some settings, like some neighborhoods, are seen by police officers as more safe than others. Realistically, an officer operating in an area perceived as dangerous may be more likely to misinterpret a furtive movement than in a neighborhood perceived as safe. If this interpretation is correct, then at least some of the explanation for why police shooting rates reflect disproportionate numbers of blacks may rest on the location of these shootings, rather than the race of the individuals shot.

Policies for Routine Police Functions. The area of policies for routine functions refers to prioritizing investigation, arrest, and use-of-force policies as routine control and order-maintenance issues. One of the principal problems associated with even mundane police activities is the general absence of statutory or legislative guidelines (LaFave 1965; Walker 1983; Goldstein 1985). Even when they do exist, as Wayne LaFave found, the language may be vague or conduct criminalized (defined as illegal) broadly to avoid loopholes. As a result, police must make decisions about various alternative forms of action that fall within their purview, but may not be outlined by department policy.

In his attempt to study law enforcement policies, Kenneth Culp Davis (1975) surveyed twenty-one district police stations in Chicago and asked if a person would be arrested for drinking in a public park. Officers at three of the district stations replied they would arrest the person, four answered they would probably make an arrest, and eleven said they would not arrest the person or would probably not do so.

In some instances, even when standard guidelines are adopted, controversy persists. Consider, for example the issuance of a *Miranda* warning. Violations of the *Miranda* rule may result from when the warning is given, the order of the elements included in the warning, or even the age and maturity of the suspect receiving the warning.

To a large extent, even when official policies do exist, officers must rely upon their training, resourcefulness, and often their imagination to get through a tour of duty. Unfortunately, this leads to inconsistencies in policy application as officers operate in situations with a variety of circumstances.

To Arrest or Not to Arrest?

As suggested above, the police must make many decisions daily. Among these concerns, of course, is whether to make an arrest. This problem actually is fairly complex. For example, even when statutes provide that an arrest *may* be made, and with the exception of certain felonies, it is typically at the discretion of the officer. There also are decisions on which charges should be made.

For example, consider an officer called by a complainant at 2 A.M. because a neighbor has been playing loud music and seems to be drunk. The officer additionally observes the neighbor urinating in his front yard. As the officer approaches the neighbor, he raises his fist in the air, shouts some obscenity, and then rushes back into his house, slamming the door.

Should the officer make a summary arrest for disorderly conduct? In most jurisdictions, disorderly conduct is an arrestable statutory crime. If an arrest is to be made, is the charge of disorderly conduct sufficient or should additional charges of resisting be included, since the man ran into his house? What about public lewdness or public indecency owing to the act of urinating on the lawn? Or, perhaps, the officer should simply find out what's happening and counsel the man to lower the music and to stop urinating on his lawn.

It is rather common for officers not to make arrests—even as in the example above, where there are certainly sufficient reasons to do so. In some situations, the demeanor of the offender may sway an officer one way or another. In other situations, the way in which the officer was summoned may play a role. In other words, an officer might respond in one way if dispatched by a superior and in quite a different manner if summoned by a resident running up to the cruiser. In other situations, the seriousness or nature of the crime may affect the decision of whether to arrest. Another factor that can affect an officer's decision about an arrest concerns previous encounters. If the officer has repeatedly been called about an individual or the individual is known to be a local troublemaker, this, too, may affect the decision.

A less frequently discussed issue involves an officer's decision to make an arrest, or a search, knowing full well that there is insufficient probable cause or no appropriate warrants. Nonetheless, there are circumstances, gray areas as they are sometimes referred to, in which an officer will chance a motion to suppress evidence in order to find a cache of drugs or weapons. What leads the officer to this decision is a desire to rid the streets of what the officer expects to find—even if it means losing the case, not filing a case, or not even filing a report. In some instances the officer may feel justified to violate the law in order to preserve the peace.

For instance, an officer is called to a family dispute and during the course of calming things down spies a shotgun hanging on the wall. Upon closer inspection, the officer finds that it is loaded and unlocked. Should the officer, after calming the parties down, leave the gun in the house? Even assuming that its owner has the correct papers or necessary license, the officer might remove the weapon and instruct the owner to retrieve it from the station in the morning. Technically, the officer has no legal power to remove private property from the home. The decision to do so, however, may follow from the level of hostility the officer encountered upon arrival. Many people might be shocked at the idea that a police officer would technically break the law to maintain the peace. Ironically, many of these same people would be appalled if the

Box 11.1 _____

Massachusetts v. *Sheppard*: A Decision to Search

On May 5, 1979, Boston police officers found the body of a woman who was about twenty-nine years old. It was the tenth black woman found slain in a bizarre string of killings in the Roxbury section of Boston. The ninth victim was identified as Sandra Boulware. She had been beaten, bound with wire, and left in a vacant lot located fewer than 150 feet from the rear of the Roxbury YMCA. The grass around her had been set on fire in an apparent attempt to conceal her body (Bradlee 1979).

Detective Emmett McNamara told reporters that the police had spoken with Boulware's boyfriend, Osborne (Jimmy) Sheppard. Sheppard was released shortly after questioning, after providing the police with an alibi for his activities during the day and evening of the slaying. However, upon further investigation the police learned that Sheppard had lied.

The police became convinced that Sheppard was the prime suspect. They wanted to search his home to determine whether any evidence connected to the case might be concealed there. Fearing that Sheppard might destroy evidence if he were given sufficient time, the police planned to obtain a search warrant immediately. The police also were working under the pressure of a increasingly frightened Roxbury population who wanted the individuals responsible for the string of deaths arrested quickly.

Unfortunately, the investigating officer could not find the correct form for applying for a search warrant. What he did find was a form for a search warrant in drug cases. The officer scratched out the phrase "controlled substances" on the form to adapt it. On a separate sheet of paper the officer specified the location of the residence to be searched and the places within the residence (the basement and second floor). The officer also indicated that the evidence being sought included wire and blood samples. Next, the officer took his amended application for a search warrant to the magistrate. The magistrate read the form and the attached sheet. Although he saw the place where the officer had scratched out the words "controlled substances," he missed another instance of this phrase. The warrant was issued, the premises searched, and evidence was found. The evidence included blood samples that matched the blood of

the slain woman and wire matching that which had bound her hands and feet.

Sheppard was arrested and charged with the death of his girlfriend. In court, he was convicted on the weight of the evidence collected in his home. After his conviction and sentence to life in prison, his attorney motioned for a new trial. The attorney's grounds were that the search warrant was not proper and thus its execution invalid. Invoking the exclusionary rule (See Chapter Seven), Sheppard's attorney indicated that any evidence obtained under this faulty document was inadmissible.

The attorney maintained that in addition to failing to correctly indicate the charges, the warrant was on an improper form and was incorrectly stapled. The Supreme Judicial Court of Massachusetts agreed with the defense counsel and ordered a new trial.

The case was appealed to the U.S. Supreme Court. On the last day of its 1983–84 session, the High Court reversed the Massachusetts Supreme Court decision and reinstated Sheppard's conviction in a 6–3 decision. For the first time since the exclusionary rule had been adopted in 1914, the Supreme Court had ruled admissible evidence obtained under a technically faulty warrant. In the majority statement, Justice Byron R. White wrote:

> The marginal or non-existent benefits produced by suppressing evidence obtained in objectively reasonable reliance on a subsequently invalidated search warrant cannot justify the substantial cost of exclusion . . . Even assuming the rule effectively deters some police misconduct and provides incentives for the law enforcement profession as a whole to conduct itself in accord with the Fourth Amendment, it cannot be expected, and should not be applied, to deter objectively reasonable law enforcement activity.

In effect, the High Court had set forth a new application of the exclusionary rule. This new application has been called the good faith exception to the exclusionary rule. By virtue of this decision and a related one in *U.S.* v. *Leon* (1984), if the police can convince the court that evidence was seized in good faith reliance on the existence of valid judicial authority, the evidence will be admissible in court proceedings. This is true even if the authority for the seizure is subsequently found to be invalid. In other words, the objective intentions and procedures of the officer(s) and magistrate involved are measured, rather than the technical correctness of the document (the search warrant).

However, not everyone in the justice system agrees with this notion. In their dissenting opinion, Justices Brennan, John Paul Stevens and Byron White suggest that the ruling in the *Sheppard* case trampled the rights of the individual and successfully "strangulated the exclusionary rule." "Victory over the Fourth Amendment is complete," they wrote.

What effect the good faith doctrine will have on future cases, and the impact of this decision on the exclusionary rule in general remains to be seen.

---

officer left the gun and one of the parties killed the other.

Another example can be seen in the case of *Massachusetts v. Sheppard* (1984), where an officer's decision nearly brought about the acquittal of a convicted murderer. The facts of this case are detailed in Box 11.1. In brief, the investigating officer decided to adapt and substitute a form used to obtain warrants in drug cases because a proper form for his homicide case was not available. After Sheppard had been convicted, his case was appealed to the Massachusetts Supreme Court. The court agreed with the defense attorney's argument that evidence had been obtained under a faulty search warrant. However, the U.S. Supreme Court, on an appeal brought by the Commonwealth of Massachusetts, ruled that the evidence was admissible (*Massachusetts v. Sheppard* [1984]; See also *U.S. v. Leon* [1984]).

The necessity for police officers to exercise discretion without benefit of viable guidelines places tremendous pressure on them. Michael Gottfredson and Don Gottfredson (1980, 87) have observed:

> *The police really suffer the worst of all worlds: They must exercise broad discretion behind a facade of performing in a ministerial fashion; and they are expected to realize a high level of equality and justice in their discretionary determinations though they have not been provided with the means most commonly relied upon in government to achieve these ends [guidelines].*

The exercise of discretion is not the problem; it is the abuse of discretion that is. The abuse of discretion might be reduced by the adoption of rigid guidelines. But guidelines can never be sufficiently inclusive to stipulate all the elements and facts that might arise in various situations. In fact, the more complicated the guidelines, the less flexible they are likely to be under different circumstances. The types of activities that law enforcement officers confront daily are enormously varied and complex. The police must respond to each new situation with confidence, authority, and discretion.

On the other hand, completely uncontrolled discretion can lead to officers enforcing the law according to their personal standards and values. Such sidewalk justice creates a completely untenable situation of highly selective justice. As mentioned throughout Chapter Seven, among the basic tenets of American law enforcement is the notion of full access to law enforcement protection for all people. In addition to access to law enforcement protection, Americans are constitutionally guaranteed that when two people violate the same law, they will receive equal treatment under the law. Yet, as already suggested, police do not always respond to similar sets of circumstances in identical ways.

The situation of limited enforcement, or more accurately selective enforcement of laws is difficult for many police officials to acknowledge. The admission that some people who break the law go free, while others are made to pay the full price levied by the justice system, tends to fly in the face of the equal legal protection concept. Nonetheless, the rhetoric of full enforcement of all laws, or the myth of full enforcement, as Wayne LaFave (1965) and Samuel Walker (1983) describe it, persists.

In his attempt to explain the manifest effects of adherence to a myth of full enforcement, LaFave (1965, 391) states:

> *Continued adherence to the myth of full enforcement of the law results in the police exercising wide discretion without acknowledging that it occurs and without attempting to explain and re-evaluate systematically the criteria by which the discretion is exercised.*

One reason for the perpetuation of this myth involves the legal truth that police officers are not authorized to ignore or not enforce the law. In fact, in most states, the failure of an officer to enforce the law is at least a dereliction of duty and may be a criminal offense.

Another reason for the myth's persistence is the failure of the public to comprehend that real police work is not like television. In the face of this public sentiment, police administrators and police organizations vigorously guard against intrusions by civilians. In other words, unlike the public's perception, law enforcement is not the singular function of the police nor accomplished by bumbling detectives who can only solve crimes with the assistance of civilian novelists or private investigators. But, until these frames of reference are corrected, police administrators will continue to be reluctant to discuss openly departmental polices or procedures.

Samuel Walker (1983) points to a third factor connected with the persistence of a myth of full enforcement, the image of police authority. The police rely heavily upon their ability to imply or express the threat of an arrest in order to maintain control over many situations. To admit openly that certain laws are not usually enforced or may be frequently ignored could undermine their image of authority and might create problems in main-

taining order. For instance, across the state highways of the United States, a fairly consistent unspoken enforcement policy is an approximate ten-mile-per-hour leeway above the posted limit of 55 miles an hour. This is less true in states where the limit has been raised to 65 miles an hour. Naturally one travels at speeds in excess of the posted limit at one's own risk as it is a statutory violation. But, violation of this particular statute is not one especially likely to result in a citation. It is largely in light of this understanding that many states have resisted the temptation to increase their speed limits to 65 miles an hour, although granted the prerogative in 1987. The fear, of course, is that a ten-mile grace will be expected by drivers even at this higher speed limit. However, speeds in excess of 70 and 75 miles an hour are not likely to be viewed as acceptable by most law enforcement agencies.

Factors Affecting the Myth of Full Enforcement

For many experts on policing, the resistance among law enforcement agencies to debunking the myth of full enforcement is seen as a serious impediment to professional growth in policing (Davis 1975, Goldstein 1977, Walker 1983). Increasingly, law enforcement officers have been called upon to offer greater conformity in their application of criminal law during an arrest (More 1985). Also, police agencies during the 1980s developed numerous departmental policies for routine police activities. These may include how and when to call in a K-9 team; how to secure a crime scene; use of force policies; courtroom demeanor policies; *Miranda* warning polices; stop-and-frisk policies; social service referral policies; and juvenile rights policies. Each of these policies moves in the direction of an **accountability system,** but one that does not rigidly remove certain elements of discretion.

In most instances, police officers retain the right to determine whether to arrest, whether to stop and question suspicious persons, and a host of other discretions. In many agencies police discretion is affected by factors related to the criminal justice system as a whole. These may include limitations on financial or personnel resources, time lags in court processing, seriousness of the offense and likelihood of conviction, and related concerns.

Owing to serious limits on time, money, and officers, law enforcement agencies simply cannot effectively enforce all law violations all of the time. As a result, most agencies develop informal priority systems. In effect, the agency's administrators and supervisors are making discretionary decisions about which offenses and law violations will warrant enforcement and which will not.

Another factor related to the imposition of discretionary decision-making among police involves situational factors. Douglas Smith (1987) examined discretion among police officers responding to situations in which there was violence. Smith found a number of extra-legal variables did influence police decision-making. Smith states that social factors, such as race and gender of the parties involved and their demeanor, significantly influence whether police choose to handle the problems by mediation or arrest.

Police officers frequently describe an acquired ability to assess an individual and determine if he or she is a suspicious person. In some instances, this may mean the individual fits the officer's image or stereotype of a drug user, pimp, hustler, or simply a person of low moral character. The obvious problem with this, of course, is that it may go far beyond acceptable discretion, to arbitrariness. An example of this arose in the case of Edward Lawson (See Box 11.2).

Edward Lawson, a fairly tall, muscular black man, had been repeatedly stopped by California police officers for no more reason than he looked "suspicious." His appearance, although perhaps out of the norm for the areas he walked (upper-class white neighborhoods) would not seem to justify either his fifteen stops or five arrests. Nor would it

justify his being handled roughly by the police each time he was stopped and detained. Assessments of Lawson, chiefly because he was out of place in the view of the officers, erroneously identified him as a person who needed to be stopped. The case of Edward Lawson rather clearly illustrates the tension between police claims of a need for discretionary stops and the rights of residents.

A third factor that plays heavily in discretionary decision-making by police is the individual characteristics of officers. Police, like all members of society, have been socialized into accepting or rejecting various values, attitudes, and beliefs. Some officers may feel more strongly about one issue than others, but all police officers have fairly strong opinions on some issue that may seriously affect their decision-making. Albert Reiss (1971, 134) argues that officers often act on the basis of their personal "moral belief." In some instances, this may mean the officer views the "suspect as guilty, and an arrest is therefore just." On other occasions, officers may believe that an individual is innocent—regardless of evidence to the contrary—and the arrest is unjustified.

It would be naive to think that some police officers do not allow racial, sexual, social class, demeanor, or other extra-legal elements to affect their decisions of whether to arrest an individual. Among the more controversial questions regarding discretion is whether racial bias may disproportionately influence arrest decisions. Most recent studies are unable to conclude that racially biased decisions predominate. Rather, studies repeatedly conclude that police officers are more likely to consider the nature of the offense and the demeanor of the suspect than they are to consider race (Terry 1967, Reiss 1971, Black 1980).

Discrimination by police officers typically refers to undue decision-making influences from age, gender, race, or ethnicity. In the real world of policing, many officers must actively fight against stereotyping certain categories of people. Because of experience in

Box 11.2 _____

Suspicious People or Suspicious Police? The Case of Edward Lawson

It has been argued that among the more serious problems with police discretion is that it encourages police to abuse their legitimate authority. "Terry stops" (referring to *Terry* v. *Ohio*, 1968), in which an officer stops and frisks a person who has demonstrated suspicious actions or behaviors, have been fairly well regulated with departmental policies and through court cases. However, simple stops of suspicious persons to question them or obtain identification have until recently been less restrained. Often, an individual who in some manner "stands out" is subjected to a stop and questioning by police. But, such unwarranted stops appear to exceed the limits of police authority and discretion. This conclusion is supported by the U.S. Supreme Court decision in the case of *Kolender et al.* v. *Lawson* (1983).

THE CIRCUMSTANCES AND FACTS OF THE CASE

Edward Lawson was a resident of California who, for over 30 years, enjoyed walking. Lawson walked everywhere and often did so at late hours of the night. Although perhaps eccentric, this desire to walk and to do so at odd hours is perfectly legal. But, the thirty-six-year-old Lawson had an appearance that made many police officers suspicious of his behavior. Lawson was a tall, muscular black man, with the long braids known as dreadlocks. In Jamaica, Lawson's appearance would be fairly commonplace. In fact, in San Francisco, where he later moved, his appearance is indistinguishable from others who dress in extraordinary styles of clothing or wear their hair in styles that more conservative types might call strange. But, in San Diego, where Lawson resided during the 1970s, his appearance, coupled with his walking at odd hours, made him a prime target for frequent suspicious-person stops (Press and Sandza 1982).

Between March 1975 and January 1977, Lawson was stopped and questioned by police officers approximately fifteen times. When stopped, police referred to a California statute that prohibited loitering or wandering "upon the streets or from place to place without apparent reason or business, and who refuses to identify himself and to account for his presence when requested by any peace officer to do so, if the surrounding circumstances are such as to indicate to a reasonable man that the public safety demands such identification" (California Penal Code, Section 647e). Violation of this statute was a misdemeanor.

In all, Lawson was arrested five times, convicted once, and served several weeks in jail. In every instance of a stop or arrest, the officers involved were white. The *Lawson* case demonstrated a need to take a serious look at the issue of identification and whether police have a constitutional right to arrest persons for strolling the streets and because they refuse to identify themselves.

Lawson did appeal his conviction to the U.S. Supreme Court, which reversed it on the grounds that the statute under which Lawson had been convicted was simply too vague. The problem with the statute, then, was not that police had initially stopped a suspicious person. Rather, the Court found: "Although the initial detention is justified, the state fails to establish standards by which the officer may determine whether the suspect has complied with the subsequent identification requirements." The High Court's concern was that this statute provided police officers with discretion for "virtually unrestrained power to arrest and charge a person with a violation" and, consequently, "furnishes a convenient tool for harsh and discriminatory enforcement by local prosecuting officials against particular groups deemed to merit their displeasure" (*Kolender et al.* v. *Lawson*, 1983).

_____

the field, education, and training, or simple prejudice, police officers are more likely to stop and question a young black male than, for example, a middle-aged white man who may seem to be acting suspiciously.

The literal point at which good policing ends and discrimination begins is difficult or impossible to identify in every case. For example, during one of Edward Larson's stops, he was pulled from a coffee shop by an officer who was seeking a one-legged white man (Press and Sandza 1982).

Excessive Force

Police officers in America are given the authority to use reasonable force in a variety of situations. Lawmakers and the courts do not expect police officers to operate in life-threatening situations without defending themselves, but neither will they permit officers to use unnecessary or unreasonable force. Excessive force can be defined as the use of force that exceeds that which is necessary under a given circumstance to bring a situation under control or effect an arrest.

Clemens Bartollas (1988, 176) outlines three categories of excessive force, or police brutality:

1. Situations in which emotions of both the police and the participants are high, such as riots or mass demonstrations. Tempers flare on both sides, and the police often are difficult to control. Direct orders by supervisors are often disregarded at these times, and police discipline collapses.

2. Situations in which a police group or organization systematically and in regular patterns inflicts excessive force, or brutality on citizens. This is most common in areas where there is racial hostility between the police and citizens.

3. Situations in which the police, during their day-to-day activities, use force beyond that which is necessary to control the situation, or make an arrest. Most police officers admit that at some time in their career they lost control of a situation and used excessive force or more force than was necessary, either to control a situation or make an arrest.

David L. Carter (1985, 322–23) has similarly developed a tripartite definition for excessive force. Carter's typology offers a broadly encompassing reference to physical abuse–excessive force, verbal–psychological abuse, and legal abuse–violations of civil rights.

Physical abuse–excessive force This category of abuse is described as involving the use of more (physical) force than is required of an officer to fulfill his or her duty in a given situation.

Verbal–psychological abuse Verbal–psychological abuse arises when an officer verbally assaults, ridicules, or in other ways demeans or harasses an individual.

Legal abuse–violations of civil rights The legal abuse or violation of civil rights may arise in conjunction with other categories of excessive force or alone. It amounts to any violation of the constitutional rights.

Decision Making and Police Liability

Civil litigation against police officers also has had a major effect on law enforcement decision-making policies. Lawsuits can result from an assortment of reasons. These may include dereliction of duty, misprision of duty, unlawful detention, or failure to follow appropriate departmental policies. Certainly, lawsuits against police can be seen as appropriate and necessary means of censuring errant officers and remedying with monetary awards for damages. But lawsuits against police officers can additionally be viewed as a nuisance and an ineffective means for a person to vent frustrations of society for which he or she has no other, more appropriate channel. Whether or not police administrators like the situation, the possibility of a lawsuit has provided an additional control over police discretion and decision-making.

Among one of the more interesting and likely unanticipated effects of the threat of civil liability is the inability to decide to release an individual. Traditionally, police have maintained an attitude that once an individual has been formally arrested, it requires a magistrate or clerk of the court to release the individual from arrest. Typically, this may result when probable cause for the arrest disappears. That may be the case when the complainant drops charges, the breathalyzer registers below illegal levels, or numerous other circumstances. According to law, at the moment that probable cause is lost, the arrestee must be released. Failure to release or attempts to coerce the individual to sign waivers of liability, as have become popular among many agencies, are unlawful.

Keeping the individual incarcerated for an additional thirty minutes or an hour constitutes unlawful detention. Attempting to get a waiver signed, but leaving the individual in a cell, or explaining they can leave but only after signing the forms, constitutes coercion and likely abuse of authority. Technically, even the period of time between a request for a magistrate's order to release after the evaporation of probable cause and the actual releasing of the individual constitutes unlawful detention.

During the past several years, many police departments have found themselves facing expensive and completely unnecessary civil litigation over their inability to decide to release an arrested person. In many departments, officers are carefully warned that failure to adhere to agency guidelines and procedures may result in civil liability. More important, if the officer has flagrantly disregarded policy, he or she may be held personally liable. This could mean having to pay settlements and legal fees out of pocket, as well as responding to criminal charges if appropriate.

Non-deadly Force

Speaking generally, most people do not strenuously object to police officers arresting persons suspected of committing crimes. Even persons being placed under arrest often resist only slightly, and then frequently only with verbal demands to know why they are being arrested, or by insisting that the officer has made a mistake. In some instances, of course, people being placed under arrest do resist with force. Throughout the late 1970s and 1980s, police agencies and training academies began to generate various policies and procedures regarding use of force during arrest.

In addition to circumstances arising during an arrest, most guidelines specify that the use of force may be lawfully employed when conducting searches and seizures, to prevent escapes of persons in custody, in self-defense and the defense of others (i.e., to protect oneself or others from bodily injury or death), to prevent the commission of an offense, and to prevent suicide or self-infliction of injury.

The amount of force used by an officer is usually described in agency procedures as limited to that which is no greater than necessary and reasonable in a given situation. This is sometimes delineated in guidelines as variable depending upon certain aspects of the situation, such as the nature of the offense, the behavior and response of the subject against whom force is to be used, the presences and actions of third parties, physical odds against the officer (substantial differences in size or weight), and the feasibility or availability of alternative actions. It is generally understood that an officer acting alone may be required to resort to a much greater degree of force than might be necessary if another officer were present.

Progressive Stages of Permissible Force

Often, policy guidelines for non-deadly force describe a four-stage scale of escalating intensity. Figure 11.1 illustrates the four general stages usually detailed.

The first stage is customarily the **verbal command stage,** and involves officers identifying themselves (when not in uniform) and informing suspects they are under arrest. This stage may include verbal orders related to a frisk and handcuffing, but cannot move beyond use of words unless a subject is physically uncooperative and offers resistance or attempts to escape custody.

The second stage arises in the event that the suspect offers simple physical resistance and may be termed the **physical strength or skill stage.** Police officers are trained in defensive restraint and take-down procedures. Although physical force is required during

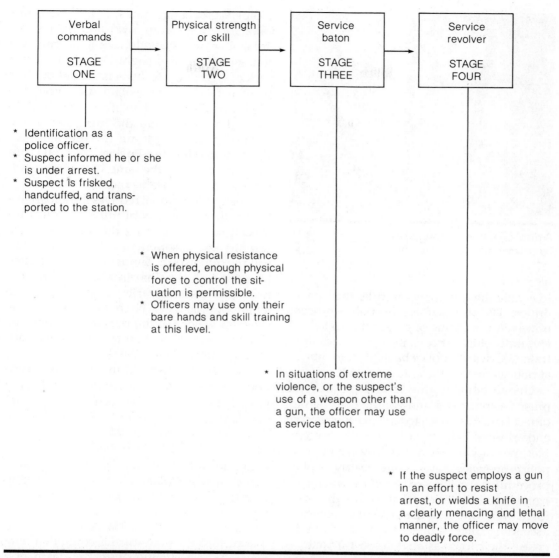

FIGURE 11.1   Escalating Levels of Permissible Force by Police Officers

this second stage, it is restricted to the officer's training and skill with bare hands.

The third, or **service baton stage** represents the need for an officer to employ a fairly high level of physical force. If the suspect further escalates the level of resistance by using a weapon other than a gun, the officer may use a service baton. Again, police officers are trained in the use of their service ba-

tons—both defensively to fend off an attack and offensively to take down a violent suspect. In the event that a suspect being placed under arrest resorts to resistance with a gun, the process is elevated to the level of deadly force, when the officer may draw a service revolver and fire.

Law enforcement officers obviously will be required at times to resort to physical force

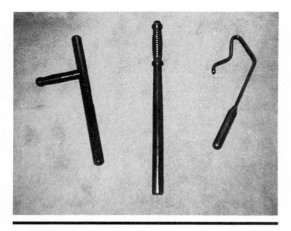

A display of three different kinds of batons used by police officers for different activities.

to enable them to carry out fully their police duties. The use of force by police officers, however, is an issue of great concern to society, individual officers, and police administrators. Cries of "police brutality" are hurled at police whether they are accurate or not.

Unquestionably, the lawful use of force must be controlled and confined so that an officer is neither subjected to unnecessary civil and criminal liability or inhibited from complete performance of duties. Toward this end, police agencies have created fairly explicit procedures for officers to follow when confronted with situations that require the use of force. In addition to the general sequence of ascending force, officers are expected to decrease their force as a situation warrants. A situation that may require the officer to use a service baton one minute may require only verbal commands a few minutes later. In fact, as Geoffrey Alpert (1985) has suggested, often an officer's best weapon is verbal.

The Stun Gun: Benefit or Hazard?

Among the several new weapons in the arsenal of non-deadly, defensive equipment used by police officers is the stun gun. By 1985 over 400 police departments in every state

except Alaska had purchased Taser stun guns (an acronym for Tom Swift and his Electric Rifle). Explained briefly, the stun gun is a rectangular device, slightly smaller than a pack of cigarettes. At one end, there are two small metal posts that extend just beyond the edge of the device. When pressed against the body of a subject and the trigger engaged, this pocket-size apparatus delivers a 50,000-volt charge (Hull and Frisbie 1987). The stun gun is powered by the same kind of nine-volt battery used in portable radios.

When an individual receives the jolt of electricity, there is a loss of muscle control for several seconds. During this period of discomfort and disorientation, the officer can subdue the suspect. The actual length of time an individual remains disoriented and out of muscular control varies according to the length of time that a charge is rendered, the size and weight of the person receiving the charge, and the location the charge was administered (See Felter 1985).

The use of the stun gun, which was cautiously viewed as a wonder device by many people, has come to be seen as a potential problem. For example, in 1985, the *New York Times* reported that five New York City police officers had been indicted for using a stun gun to torture an alleged drug dealer, Mark Davidson (Raab 1985). A sheriff's lieutenant in San Antonio, Texas received two years' probation for repeatedly zapping a handcuffed suspect in 1984. And in the summer of 1985 the Los Angeles county coroner began an investigation into the death of a drug user who had also been tortured by police officers using Tasers.

Naturally, it is not the fault of the device that several unscrupulous people used it in an inappropriate manner. However, the ease with which a charge can be delivered and the resulting potential harm must be considered. An even more frightening prospect is the potential harm that stun guns might cause in the hands of private citizens or from such criminals as burglars. Because of these dangers, a number of states have banned stun guns or restricted them to the police.

Another question arises when one considers the actual effectiveness and safety of the stun gun. One recent report examined whether the stun gun was equally effective when used on a variety of materials (Lesce and Smith 1985). Although the report indicates that a charge can effectively penetrate most common forms of clothing, it is ineffective on body armor. Tests on animals suggest that thick-coated dogs are unaffected by a jolt from the device. One may assume that a charge rendered through a heavy, lined coat would also be less effective on a human.

Stun gun manufacturers maintain that the device is safe and causes no permanent damage to the subject. However, there has been little objective testing of these devices by uninterested parties. Even the manufacturers warn that when the device is misused, such as discharging a jolt to a subject's face or head, the individual may be injured (Hull and Frisbie 1987). The jolt also could endanger a person prone to cardiac arrest. On a more superficial level, the probes on the device may cause scratches on the subject's skin, while the charge frequently produces small spark or burn marks. These marks usually heal leaving no scar.

Among police agencies, considerable debate remains over the use and effectiveness of the device. Although several agencies have successfully used the device, others suggest they create too great a liability risk. It is doubtful that the stun gun will soon replace the service baton or service weapon as standard police issue. Nonetheless, when properly trained in its use, police officers may be able use this device to defuse situations that fall somewhere between the need for their baton and the need to use deadly force.

Deadly Force

The foremost element in the decision to use deadly force is whether the officer has suffi-

cient cause to believe that the suspect poses a real and probable threat of serious physical harm, either to the officer or others. Similarly, it is not constitutionally unreasonable to use all necessary measures, including deadly force, to prevent escape of dangerous suspects. In other words, if a subject has threatened the officer with a weapon, or there exists probable cause to believe that the subject has committed a crime involving the infliction of physical harm or has placed someone in fear of physical harm through threats, deadly force is permissible to prevent an escape. In the absence of these factors, however, police officers may not use deadly force to effect arrests or prevent escapes.

As mentioned with regard to the use of force generally, one important factor that offers a kind of controlling or tempering effect on the use by police of deadly force is litigation against police officers. Less regularly considered, however, is the administrative and personal ramifications that accompany an officer-involved shooting.

Whenever an officer discharges a weapon in a deadly force situation, in most jurisdictions the event is administratively reviewed.

Pictured are a nine-millimeter pistol (upper right-hand corner) and a .357 Magnum revolver (lower left-hand corner); many police agencies have replaced the traditional police revolver with nine-millimeter pistols as standard issue.

As part of this shooting review, the officer may be subject to criminal and civil jeopardy. Individually, the officer may be held in violation of state laws, as well as federal ones for civil rights violations. The department for which the officer works also may be subject to civil liabilities.

In addition to these various legal and civil problems, police officers involved in shooting situations may carry away a serious emotional problem. An assortment of stressful situations may impair the health of police officers. The psychic effects of being involved in a shooting situation, whether the suspect is injured or killed, is quite dramatic. In the event of a death, however, the officer must reconcile the taking of another human being's life. Too, the officer must deal with the reality that his or her own life had been in peril—an enormously discomforting thought.

To be sure, the use of deadly force by police officers is extremely controversial and complex. There are three primary focuses for consideration of police officers' use of deadly force. These include the fleeing felon rule, firearms training, and predictability about those who are likely to resort to the use of deadly force.

The authority for police officers to use deadly force derives from English common law. Under this legal tradition, an arresting officer was permitted to use deadly force to prevent the escape of a fleeing felon. Officers were not, however, permitted to use deadly force to prevent escapes by fleeing misdemeanants. The justification for such permissible lethal force was that most felonies during the late fourteenth and fifteenth centuries (See Chapter Two) were punishable by death.

Fleeing Felons

As English common law was the central basis for both the early and modern American legal system, it is not surprising to find that the **fleeing felon rule** found its way into the laws. The number of crimes classified as felonies has risen significantly since fifteenth century England. Interestingly, as the felony crimes increased in number on the American legal books, the imposition of the death penalty for felony crimes decreased. By the late nineteenth century, the historical justification for the fleeing felon rule had all but disappeared (Albanese 1988).

Most state laws continue to permit police officers to use any force—including deadly force—necessary and reasonable to arrest an individual suspected of a felony. The latitude once provided by the fleeing felon rule, however, has been drawn into serious question during the past several years. Scrutiny of policies surrounding shooting fleeing felons has risen as the result of two primary factors: first, the enormous amount of criticism and bad publicity departments receive every time an officer fires a weapon at a felony suspect claiming, "I thought I saw a weapon!" only to recover none; second, a recent U.S. Supreme Court decision concurring with critics of the fleeing felon rule. The ruling may well result in all jurisdictions being required to alter their laws. In many jurisdictions, even in the face of statutes that permit officers to shoot fleeing felons, departmental policies prohibit this action. At the time that the *Garner* case was heard, 19 states had fleeing felon statutes, 4 other states had no statutes, but apparently followed the "fleeing felon rule"; and 22 other states used some variation of the violent fleeing felon rule. All these states reconsidered their laws on fleeing felons following the *Tennessee* v. *Garner* (1985) ruling (Kaune and Tischler 1989).

An important underlying question regarding the use of deadly force in instances of fleeing felons is whether this action is constitutionally permissible. Until recently, when cases involving police use of deadly force reached the courts, it was an unacceptable defense that the fleeing felon rule violated the rights of the suspected felon. But, in 1985, after the U.S. Supreme Court heard and ruled in the case of *Tennessee* v. *Garner*, state laws

Box 11.3

Fleeing Felons: The Case of *Tennessee* v. *Garner* (1985)

It began on October 3, 1974 at about 10:45 p.m. Two Memphis police officers, Elton Hymon and Leslie Wright, received a radio call to investigate a prowler. When the officers arrived, they found a woman standing on her porch who told them that she had heard someone breaking into the house next door. As Wright radioed the dispatcher to indicate their disposition, Hymon moved to the rear of the house where the prowler(s) had been heard. Suddenly, a door slammed, and Hymon saw someone run across the back yard and toward a six-foot chain-link fence. Hymon shined his flashlight in the direction of the runner and observed what he believed to be a seventeen or eighteen year-old youth. Scanning with his light he could see no sign of a weapon in the hands of the youth, who appeared to be 5'5" or 5'7".

In fact, the youth was Edward Garner, a 15-year-old, 5'4" eighth grader who weighed approximately 100 pounds. As Garner crouched at the bottom of the fence, Hymon identified himself as a police officer and ordered him to halt. Garner ignored the order and began to climb the fence. Believing that Garner was the prowler and that he would clear the fence and evade capture, Hymon fired his service revolver. The shot struck Garner in the back of the head, and he was taken by ambulance to a local hospital. Garner died from his wound while still on the operating table.

At trial, Hymon justified his use of deadly force by indicating that he had been convinced that Garner would evade pursuit and, under Tennessee law, he was permitted to use his weapon in such circumstances. The statute reads: "[I]f after notice of the intention to arrest the defendant, he either flees or forcibly resists, the officer may use all the necessary means to effect the arrest" (Tennessee Code, Section 40–7–108, 1982). The U.S. Supreme Court (*Tennessee* v. *Garner,* 1985) ruled:

> The use of deadly force to prevent the escape of all felony suspects, whatever the circumstances, is constitutionally unreasonable. It is not better that all felony suspects die than that they escape? Where the suspect poses no immediate threat to the officer and no threat to others, the harm resulting from failing to apprehend him does not justify the use of deadly force to do so. It is no doubt unfortunate when a suspect who is in sight escapes, but the fact that the police arrive a little late or are a little slower afoot does not always justify killing the suspect. A police officer may not seize an unarmed, nondangerous suspect by shooting him dead.

As a result of the *Garner* case, many departments voluntarily altered their general shooting policies. States that had fleeing felon laws were forced to strike them. Yet, the High Court did not unanimously agree on its findings. The vote was 6–3. It is likely that this lack of unanimity is reflective of a wider social attitude of the public's regarding the shooting of fleeing felons by police officers.

---

and agency polices on use of deadly force were drastically changed (See Box 11.3). The High Court ruled that the shooting of an individual who posed no immediate threat to the safety of others was a violation of the Fourth Amendment ban against unreasonable seizure.

The position taken by the High Court in *Garner* has been strongly criticized by some law enforcement officials who feel that it leaves the police officer in the precarious position of deciding whether the suspect is dangerous. Like any other decision related to police work, decisions about the use of deadly force are inescapable. But, unlike the decision to write a citation or not to arrest some juvenile shoplifter, use of deadly force is an irreversible decision.

Firearms Training

In most jurisdictions, departmental policies on use of force are separate from guidelines on use of deadly force. Many police agencies have long adopted a defense-of-life shooting policy or some guideline geared to empower an officer for self-protection or the protection of others from imminent threat of serious bodily harm or death. But, as suggested in the four-stage model of ascending force, the use of an officer's service revolver (deadly force) is permissible only in circumstances in which it cannot be avoided.

As part of this policy orientation, police academy training in firearms has moved in the direction of restrained use of weapons. Although not all circumstances can be outlined in a classroom, many academies have gone to the increased use of role-playing and scenario discussions in order to get officers practiced in selecting alternatives to deadly force. Unfortunately, the game-like circumstances of these activities cannot duplicate the rapid breathing and pounding heart from an adrenal surge as an officer is actually confronted with the decision to use, or not to use, deadly force on the street.

In the past, academy training in firearms was geared toward preparing recruits to qualify with their weapons. What this literally means is the ability safely to load and discharge a prescribed number of rounds and strike a graded target with sufficient accuracy to reach a required score within a limited time frame.

While most police academy programs spend as much as 40 or 48 hours on the shooting range in firearms training, the majority of this time is spent practicing or attempting to qualify. This type of training acquaints the recruit with firearms safety, proper procedures for cleaning weapons, correct and appropriate non-hostile firing postures, and at least a minimum degree of accuracy when shooting.

Although some academies limit the bulk of their firearms training to stationary targets, others employ pop-ups or movable ones. The training in these cases is usually centered around the concept of shoot–don't shoot.

The characters on the pop-ups and targets depict good guys and bad guys. When a tar-

A Massachusetts State Police firearms training officer demonstrates a "shooting from the hip" firing style.

Police recruits practice on an outdoor firing range.

get appears, the officer must rapidly assess whether to fire. The shoot–don't shoot style of training has grown in popularity. As technology improved, the cardboard and wooden pop-up targets were replaced by interactive television laser systems and interactive video disc systems like the Firearms Training Systems (FATS). Although far more sophisticated, the basic technology of these computerized laser systems is similar to children's toys such as "Captain Power."

In the case of FATS, a standard Smith and Wesson model 66, .357 Magnum revolver has been adapted with a laser-emitting device and is supplied with a simulator. The basic forty scenarios in the system's package have been developed by the Federal Law Enforcement Training Center.

The interactive television programs allow an officer to watch a complex set of circumstances in deciding whether or not to shoot, rather than responding to a two-dimensional drawing as it pops up. In many ways, these interactive programs do not offer a simple shoot–don't shoot situation. Instead, the officer views a scene in which a series of decisions must be made, simulating at least partially the kinds of decisions officers must make on the street (See Scharf and Binder 1983, Geller 1985).

The interactive program also shoots back, complete with a loud gun blasts and appropriate responses from onlookers. Because they are computer linked, interactive programs also can assess whether a shooter has fired a weapon too soon or too late. In complete systems such as FATS, the computer can both display on the screen and provide a computer print-out of the officer's reaction time, the officer's accuracy by number of hits and misses, whether the officer fired before or after the suspect. These last factors may actually set this style of firearms training above others.

Although obviously not duplicative of real life, the realization by a recruit that he or she has fired upon a good guy or hesitated too long before firing, causing the bad guy to kill a hostage, can be quite sobering. Considerable benefit can be derived if classroom discussions follow these practice shoots, and recruits learn when they should shoot and when they should avoid shooting entirely.

The interactive television and video disc systems have grown in popularity because of their flexibility and relative cost-effectiveness. Because they are fairly compact and can be adapted to any regular television, these systems can be used in the classroom itself. These devices also provide recruits with practice in firing at moving targets. Recently, many police agencies have lost civil law suits for wrongful deaths when the courts learned the officers had no training in moving targets.

In addition to classroom instruction, role-playing, and interactive television systems, many academies conduct simulated training exercises. In some instances, this may involve the use of an actual residence, a warehouse, or school building during off hours. In other situations, police training facilities have built streets complete with storefronts, two-story buildings, alleys, and other common buildings. Combined with more traditional firearms training and target-shooting, these more

Police recruits are trained in night firing strategies. Notice how the flashlight is held up and away from the recruit's body. The intention here is to avoid allowing the light to provide a target too near the officer's body.

interactive and decision-based strategies may represent what William Geller (1985) has referred to as the new frontier in police shooting.

Predicting Misuse of Deadly Force

If social scientists were able to devise some means to predict accurately the profile of a trigger-happy or excessively violent police officer, this discussion would be unnecessary. Unfortunately, just as it has yet to be determined with any accuracy which felons will be recidivists, no study exists that convincingly offers a profile or composite of officers who are most likely to misuse their weapons or to be brutal (Geller 1985, Blumberg 1985).

There are, however, several worthwhile relationships suggested in the current literature. For example, Van Wormer (1981) suggests that female police officers are less likely to use their guns than male officers. In fact, as Robert Homant and Daniel Kennedy (1985) point out, female officers are better than male officers at verbally reducing volatile and potentially dangerous domestic fight situations. Second, younger officers, perhaps owing to less street experience, are more likely than older, more experienced officers to resort to their service revolvers. Third, and as suggested by James Fyfe (1980, 1981) and William Geller (1985), the rate of violence in a community and the rate of assaults upon police officers appears to be related to occurrences of police shootings.

But, even these suggested relationships must be viewed through cautious eyes. Female officers have only recently been permitted full patrol duties. As a consequence, their recorded presence and activities in high-crime, high-risk situations is dwarfed by comparison with those experienced by male officers. It will be some time before any meaningful longitudinal patterns can be accurately addressed. Regarding the second relationship, age and police experience may have less to do with the situation than military experi-

ence prior to becoming a police officer. Until the mid-1970s most police officers possessed prior military training. This included previous self-defense and firearms experience. It is conceivable, then, that the additional tactical training that some older officers received in the military contributes to their being less likely to resort to deadly force. At least for the present, the most credible relationship appears to come from the suggestion that shootings are more likely to occur in geographic areas in which crime rates and assaults on police officers are highest.

SUMMARY

This chapter examined the basic issue of police discretion, including its limitations and the need for its control. In addition, this chapter explored the tension between the need for selective enforcement of certain laws, while simultaneously assuring full constitutional protection to all people. The chapter further suggested that police work is a complex matrix of situations that often present an officer with a unique set of circumstances. As a result, police officers cannot rigidly enforce the law.

But, there is a serious need to assure that police officers do not exceed their discretionary limits. Uncontrolled discretion may lead to reckless and arbitrary whim or to the implementation of discriminatory or excessively brutal practices. In an effort to control the exercise of discretion by police officers, many agencies have created formal guidelines and procedural policies. These guidelines are often lengthy and extensive, but permit sufficient latitude and/or options so that police officers may flexibly apply them in varied situations.

As the chapter indicates, the use of force and particularly deadly force operates in the face of a number of competing factors. These factors include the rights of the police to protect themselves, their duty to protect the lives of third parties, and the legislated responsibility to suppress community violence, reduce crime, and provide security and access to law enforcement for all through use of reasonable and necessary force. All of these obligations must be balanced against the assurance of constitutionally guaranteed rights of the suspect. These rights include individual liberty, equal protection under the law, and most important, the constitutional right of everyone to be presumed innocent until proven otherwise in a court of law.

The chapter also considered various controlling and tempering elements, such as guidelines and departmental procedures. In addition to the department policies, another source of control of police discretion discussed was civil litigation. The mere threat of civil litigation against police officers is proving a significant motivating factor for officers carefully to adhere to their departmental guidelines. Beyond these legal and constitutional factors, the chapter considered the social factors and effects using deadly force may have for police officers themselves.

Finally, this chapter detailed the use of both non-deadly and deadly force. Regarding the former, the chapter explored a model of ascending force and its implications for police officers. With respect to deadly force, the chapter first discussed the constitutionality of the fleeing felon rules. Finally, the chapter considered the nature of firearms training and the ability of agencies to predict brutal or trigger-happy officers.

REVIEW QUESTIONS _____

1. Why might it be said that police discretion can be a double edged sword?
2. When Samuel Walker referred to the "myth of full enforcement," what did he mean? What are some of the factors that affect this myth?
3. At what point has an officer gone beyond "reasonable force" to "excessive force"? What, then, is "permissible force"?
4. What is the current policy in most states regarding shooting fleeing felons? How has the *Garner* case affected this policy during the past several years?
5. How effectively can police administrators identify and predict which officers are likely to use excessive or deadly force?

REFERENCES _____

Albanese, Jay S. *The Police Officer's Dilemma: Balancing Peace, Order, and Individual Rights.* Buffalo, N.Y.: Great Ideas, 1988.

Alpert, Geoffrey P. *The American System of Criminal Justice.* Beverly Hills, Calif.: Sage, 1985.

Banton, Michael. *The Policeman in the Community.* New York: Basic Books, 1964.

Bartollas, Clemens, and Loras A. Jaeger. *American Criminal Justice.* New York: Macmillan, 1988.

Berg, Bruce L. "Arbitrary Arbitration: Diverting Juveniles into the Justice System." *Juvenile and Family Court Journal* 37, (1986): 31–42.

Berk, Sarah F., and D. Loseke. "Handling Family Violence: Situational Determinants of Police Arrest in Domestic Disturbances." *Law and Society Review* 15 (1981): 314–44.

Binder, Arnold, and Peter Scharf. "Deadly Force in Law Enforcement." *Crime and Delinquency* 28 (1982): 1–23.

Black, Donald J. "The Production of Crime Rates." *American Sociological Review* 35 (1970): 733–48.

Black, Donald J. *The Manners and Customs of the Police.* New York: Academic, 1980.

Black, Donald J., and Albert J. Reiss, Jr. "Police Control of Juveniles." *American Sociological Review* 35 (1970): 63–77.

Blumberg, Mark. "Race and Police Shooting: An Analysis in Two Cities." In James F. Fyfe, ed.

Contemporary Issues in Law Enforcement. Beverly Hills, Calif.: Sage, 1981.

Blumberg, Mark. "Research on Police Use of Deadly Force." In Abraham Blumberg and Elaine Niederhoffer, eds. *The Ambivalent Force,* 3d ed. New York: Holt, Rinehart and Winston, 1985.

Bradlee, Ben Jr. "Suspect Charged in 10th Murder," *The Boston Globe.* (May 7, 1979): 1, 14.

Carter, David L. "Police Brutality: A Model for Definition, Perspective and Control." In Abraham Blumberg and Elaine Niederhoffer, eds. *The Ambivalent Force,* 3d ed. New York: Holt, Rinehart and Winston, 1985.

Cavan, Ruth, and T. Ferdinand. *Juvenile Delinquency.* New York: Harper and Row, 1981.

Cohen, Howard. "Exploiting Police Authority." *Criminal Justice Ethics* 5, (1986): 23–30.

Cox, Steven M., and John J. Conrad. *Juvenile Justice: A Guide to Practice and Theory,* 2d ed. Dubuque, Iowa: Brown, 1987.

Davis, Kenneth Culp. *Police Discretion.* St. Paul, Minn.: West, 1975.

Felter, Brian A. "The Nova XR-5000 Stun Gun, Hi-Tech Alternative Control Device," *Police Marksman* (January-February, 1985): 35–40.

Fyfe, James J. "Shots Fired: An Examination of New York City Police Firearms Discharges." Unpublished Ph.D. dissertation, State University of New York at Albany. Albany, N.Y., 1978.

Fyfe, James J. "Geographic Correlates of Police Shootings: A Microanalysis." *Journal of Research in Crime and Delinquency* 17 (1980): 101–113.

Fyfe, James J. "Observations on Police Deadly Force." *Crime and Delinquency* 18 (1981): 376–89.

Fyfe, James J. "Police Use of Deadly Force: Research and Reform," *Justice Quarterly* 5, (1988): 165–206.

Gardiner, John A. *Traffic and the Police: Variations in Law Enforcement Policy.* Cambridge, Mass.: Harvard University Press, 1969.

Geller, William. "Officer Restraint in the Use of Deadly Force: The Next Frontier in Police Shooting Research," *Journal of Police Science and Administration* 13 (1985): 153–57.

Goldman, Nathan. *The Differential Selection of Juvenile Offenders for Court Appearance.* New York: National Council on Crime and Delinquency, 1963.

Goldstein, Herman. "Police Policy Formulation: A Proposal for Improving Police Performance." In Harry W. More Jr. ed. *Critical Issues in Law Enforcement.* Cincinnati, Ohio: Anderson, 1985.

Hanewicz, Wayne B. "Discretion and Order." In Fredrick A. Elliston and Michael Feldberg, eds. *Morale Issues in Police Work.* Totowa, N.J.: Rowman and Allanheld, 1985.

Harding, Richard W., and Richard P. Fahey. "Killings by Chicago Police, 1969–70: An Empirical Study." *Southern California Law Review* (March 1973): 284–315.

Harring, S., T. Platt, R. Speiglman, and P. Takagi. "The Management of Police Killings." *Crime and Social Justice* 8 (1977): 34–43.

Homant, Robert J., and Daniel B. Kennedy. "Police Perceptions of Spouse Abuse: A Comparison of Male and Female Officers." *Journal of Criminal Justice* 13 (1985): 29–47.

Hull, Grafton H. Jr., and Joseph C. Frisbie. "The Stun Gun Debate: More Help than Hazard?" *The Police Chief* 54 (1987): 46–51.

Kaune, Michael M., and Chloe A. Tischler. "Liabilities in Police Use of Deadly Force." *American Journal of Police* 8, (1989): 89–106.

LaFave, Wayne R. *Arrest: The Decision to Take a Suspect into Custody.* Boston, Mass.: Little Brown, 1965.

Lesce, Tony, and Robert Smith. "Electronic Zappers for Police: A Product Survey." *Police Marksman* (July-August 1985): 18–25.

Lundman, Richard J. "Routine Police Arrest Practices," *Social Problems* 22 (1974): 127–41.

Lundman, Richard J., Richard Sykes, and J.P. Clark. "Police Control of Juveniles: A Replication." *Journal of Research in Crime and Delinquency* 15 (1978): 74–91.

Lundman, Richard J. *Police Behavior: A Sociological Perspective.* New York: Oxford, 1980.

Meyer, Marshal W. "Police Shootings of Minorities: The Case of Los Angeles. *Annals of the American Academy of Political and Social Science* (November 1980): 98–110.

Milton, Catherine H., J.W. Hallack, J. Larder, and G.L. Abrecht. *Police Use of Deadly Force.* Washington, D.C.: Police Foundation, 1977.

More, Harry W. Jr., ed. *Critical Issues in Law Enforcement.* Cincinnati, Ohio: Anderson, 1985.

Piliavan, Irving, and Scott Briar. "Police Encounters with Juveniles." *American Journal of Sociology* 70 (1964): 206–14.

Pope, C.E. "Blacks and Juvenile Crime." In Dan George-Abeyie, ed. *Criminal Justice Systems and Blacks.* New York: Chandler, 1984.

Port Authority of New York and New Jersey. *Annual Report.* New York: Youth Services Unit, 1986.

Press, Aric, and Richard Sandza. "The California Walkman," *Newsweek* (July 19, 1982): 58.

Reiss, Albert J. *The Police and the Public.* New Haven, Conn.: Yale, 1971.

Raab, Selwyn. "Two More Officers Charged in Inquiry into Torture at a Queens Precinct." *New York Times* (April 25, 1985): A1.

Robin, Gerald D. "Justifiable Homicide by Police Officers." *Journal of Criminal Law, Criminology, and Police Science* (June 1963): 225–31.

Scharf, Peter, and Arnold Binder. *The Badge and the Bullet: Police Use of Deadly Force.* New York: Praeger, 1983.

Skolnick, Jerome H. *Justice Without Trial.* New York: Wiley, 1966.

Skolnick, Jerome H. "Deception By Police." In Thomas Barker and David L. Carter, eds. *Police Deviance.* Cincinnati, Ohio: Pilgrimage, 1986.

Smith, Douglas A. "Police Response to Interpersonal Violence: Defining the Parameters of Legal Control." *Social Forces.* 65, (1987): 767–82.

Smith, Douglas A. "Street-Level Justice: Situational Determinants of Police Arrest Decisions." *Social Problems.* Vol. 29, 1981: 167–177.

Smith, Douglas A., and Christy Vishner. "Street-Level Justice: Situational Determinants of Police Arrest Decisions." *Social Problems* 29 (1981) 167–71.

Sullivan, D.C., and Larry J. Siegel. "How Police Use Information to Make Decisions." *Crime and Delinquency* 18 (1972): 253–62.

Takagi, P. "A Garrison State in a 'Democratic' Society." *Crime and Social Justice* 15 (1974): 34–43.

Terry, Robert. "Discrimination in the Police Handling of Juvenile Offenders by Social Control Agencies," *Journal of Crime and Delinquency* 14 (1967): 218.

Van Wormer, Katherine. "Are Males Suited to Police Patrol Work?" *Police Studies* 3, (1981): 41–44.

Walker, Samuel. "Employment of Black and Hispanic Police Officers: Trends in Fifty Largest Cities." *Review of Applied Urban Research* 11, (1983): 33–40.

CASES CITED

Kolender et al., v. Lawson, 461 U.S. 352, 360, 361 (1983).

Massachusetts v. Sheppard, 104 S.Ct., 3424 (1984).

Tennessee v. Garner, 105 S.Ct., 1694 (1985).

U.S. v. Leon, 104 S.Ct., 3405 (1984).

CHAPTER 12

POLICE DEVIANCE AND CORRUPTION

What others think about us has considerable influence upon our behavior and attitudes. As a result, our self-images and our public images tend to be complementary phenomena. In other words, how we see ourselves and how others view us are related. Sociologically, it can be said that people act according to their understandings of the expectations of others. As individuals or members of some group, each of us plays various roles according to our understanding of public image expectations for these roles.

For police officers, the public image is always subject to assault by accusations of police misconduct and corruption. Quite apart from whatever the facts may be in a given department or surrounding a specific event, public impressions of the nature and extent of unprofessional, deviant, or corrupt behavior have a serious impact on police organizations. Negative impressions of a police officer, even when unsupported by fact or evidence, can be an important symbolic barometer of the community faith and trust in the police department.

The notion of policing as a tainted occupation, where all officers are more or less corrupt, is an extremely difficult public image for officers to deal with. The fact that there has been considerable amounts of documented police deviance and corruption throughout the history of American policing contributes to the difficulty.

This chapter examines the nature of police deviance as distinguished from police corruption. As mentioned in the first chapter of this textbook, deviant behavior by the average person is not always viewed as intolerable or criminal. The question then becomes whether similar acts of deviance by police officers is within the limits of social tolerance. This chapter will also consider distinctions between certain theoretical models of police corruption, such as "rotten pocket" and "rotten barrel" theories.

Finally, Chapter Twelve will consider various ways that police deviance and corruption can be controlled by organizational–administrative means.

INTRODUCTION: THE LINE BETWEEN DEVIANCE AND CORRUPTION

The issue of police misbehavior is an important one to address. Also important is whether all police misbehavior should be placed at the same point on an imaginary continuum of deviance. The issue of police misbehavior discussed in this chapter should not cloud the fact that *most police officers are honest and possess a high level of moral integrity.*

During the past decade it has become relatively commonplace to see newspaper headlines chronicle police officers' law breaking. In 1980 several police officers—including a police captain—broke into a bank during a three day weekend and robbed safe-deposit boxes in Medford, Massachusetts (Clemente and Stevens 1987). In 1987, seven Boston officers were alleged to be involved in shakedown, bribery and racketeering activities throughout greater Boston (see Cullen 1987; Doherty and Connolly 1987). Earlier that year, fifty officers were investigated on charges that included shake-downs of restaurant owners for license violations. Later that year, it was revealed that a scheme to sell police promotion examinations had been operating for perhaps as long as fifteen years throughout Massachusetts.

In other areas of the country, scandals and police crimes were also reported in the news media. During the early 1980s in Miami, scarcely a week went by without some report of police indiscretion. Throughout 1983, the headlines reported on Luis Alvarez, an officer accused but later acquitted of shooting Nevell Johnson. Johnson, an unarmed black man, was shot at an electronic game arcade as Alvarez attempted to take him into custody (Stuart 1983). Newspapers also reported on Dade County, Miami police officers involved in cocaine smuggling, theft, and murder (See Peterson 1986; United Press International 1987; Associated Press 1987).

Newspapers reported on a four-year FBI investigation into police corruption in Philadelphia capped by the arrest in 1986 of Eugene Sullivan for alleged RICO violations. Sullivan, considered by many Philadelphians the next candidate for police commissioner, was the 29th officer convicted during this FBI probe (See *Washington Post* 1986).

Beyond the newspaper accounts, each of us has likely heard of some type of police indiscretion. It may have been a story from a friend that claimed that a police officer had stopped an attractive motorist in order to obtain her telephone number. Or it may have involved a police officer accepting money in exchange for not issuing a speeding ticket. It may even have been the allegation that a police officer suggested that in exchange for a sexual favor he or she would not write a citation. Perhaps it was the observation that a police officer left a restaurant without paying the check. Certainly, these situations happen and perhaps more often than many police administrators would care to acknowledge. The question is, are these situations all examples of corruption? Can there be gradations to corruption, that is, certain amounts that can be tolerated? Or is corruption absolute and clear-cut in every instance? Answers to these questions should become apparent as this chapter examines systemic and occupational factors that make deviance and corruption seem endemic to police work. This chapter also will consider ways of controlling the problem of police ethical and legal violations.

What Constitutes Corruption?

In police work, like many other occupations and professions, it is difficult to make hard and fast statements about accepting or distinguishing between friendly gifts, gratuities for services, bribes for favors, and general corruptions and misuse of one's official position.

For example, with the drop in the numbers of students applying to law school, many schools have taken to subtly soliciting student referrals. Special informational conferences are held where pre-law school advisers are brought to some law schools from all around the country with all expenses paid. These pre-law advisers are wined and dined, put up at the best hotels, and given tours of the schools' facilities. Naturally, the intention here is to impress these advisers, but certainly not to bribe them—right?

The apparel industry is notorious for its wooing of out-of-town buyers. These buyers are frequently treated to expensive meals and hotels and, in some instances, even provided with prostitutes. Many buyers accept these gratuities and do not view them as bribes because they claim not to be swayed by them. The buyers' argument is that unless they can make a profit from a line of clothes, they aren't going to buy it regardless of the gifts and good times provided by the seller. These dividends are merely seen as the "perks" of the job, not bribes.

When you leave the mailman a card with $5 stuffed into it for Christmas, this is not a bribe or gratuity, just a Christmas present. It's just like the bottle of top-shelf liquor you probably buy your boss.

It is likely that most police officers at some time have been offered some sort of gratuity. Similarly, it is very likely that many have taken one. Gratuities to police officers typically are quite small. Perhaps the delicatessen prepares sandwiches at half-price for uniformed police officers or the local grocery tosses the beat cop a couple of steaks on his birthday or a turkey on Thanksgiving; the dry cleaner may give a reduced rate for cleaning police uniforms, the gas station may repair private cars owned by police officers for cost, and the local doughnut shop may offer police officers free coffee.

Although these gratuities are rather petty in value, most police agencies are likely to discourage their officers from accepting them. Some agencies may even regard the acceptance of even petty items as a serious breech of their ethical policy and procedures and sanction the offending officer. In some ways, one might even suggest that the acceptance of even petty gratuities runs counter to the "Law Enforcement Code of Ethics," (shown in Box 12.1). For many people, police officials and civilians alike, accepting even a free cup of coffee is viewed as potentially lessening the fair access to law enforcement protection to which all people are entitled.

Stated differently, the retailer presenting the gift is buying additional police protection. The usual cliche is to suggest that while the officer sits sipping free coffee in the restaurant, this restaurant owner is receiving increased police protection. Without debating this point, there may be other, less arguable illustrations of partial treatment by police and increased access to protection. Consider, for example, a row of stores damaged by a storm and being looted. Whether consciously or unconsciously, it is likely that a store owned by someone who has offered even petty gratuities will receive slightly better attention than one owned by a patron who has offered the officer nothing.

Some police administrators, however, see nothing wrong with officers getting items "for

Box 12.1

The Law Enforcement Code of Ethics

As a law enforcement officer, my fundamental duty is to serve mankind; to safeguard lives and property; to protect the innocent against deception, the weak against oppression or intimidation, and the peaceful against violence or disorder; and to respect the constitutional rights of all men [and women] to liberty, equality and justice.

I will keep my private life unsullied as an example to all; maintain courageous calm in the face of danger, scorn, or ridicule; develop self-restraint; and be constantly mindful of the welfare of others. Honest in thought and deed in both my personal and official life, I will be exemplary in obeying the laws of the land and the regulations of my department. Whatever I see or hear of a confidential nature or that is confided to me in my official capacity will be kept ever secret unless revelation is necessary in the performance of my duty.

I will never act officiously or permit personal feelings, prejudice, animosities, or friendships to influence my decisions. With no compromise for crime and with relentless prosecution of criminals, I will enforce the law courteously and appropriately without fear or favor, malice or ill-will, never employing unnecessary force or violence and never accepting gratuities.

I recognize the badge of my office as a symbol of public faith, and I accept it as a public trust to be held so long as I am true to the ethics of the police service. I will constantly strive to achieve these objectives and ideals, dedicating myself before God to my chosen profession . . . law enforcement.

---

cost." In other words, reduced-rate items and services are seen as distinguishable from freebies. In these instances, the discounts and even an occasional cup of coffee are viewed as a courtesy to the officer by an appreciative person. The implication here, of course, is that police deviance or corruption has not occurred unless it involves cash or the outright gift of products (a free television, a pair of shoes, or a washing machine).

The perhaps not-so-obvious problem with this is how such transactions are viewed by the public. In Chapter Nine, the notion of the police as a tainted occupation was mentioned. Briefly, this involves a pervasive attitude among residents that the police are all dishonest, it's simply a matter of degree. Consequently, when officers are seen receiving reduced rates for products or services—essentially just for doing their duty—many people are affronted. The operative assumption is that when an officer is willing to take a half-priced dinner, he or she is also likely to take a bribe. Perhaps this officer is also likely to steal drugs from the property room to sell

on the street. Although it may seem a big jump from a cheap meal to becoming a drug dealer, it is a small step in the minds of many people. Patrick Murphy (Elliston and Feldberg 1985, 267), former commissioner of the New York city police, has said that for police officers, "except for your paycheck, there's no such thing as a clean buck."

There has been a great deal of interest in police corruption. In addition to journalistic accounts and successful movies, such as Paramount Pictures' 1973 film "Serpico," and Warners' (1982) movie "Prince of the City," several corrupt officers have described their activities in fairly well-read stories and books (Schecter and Philips 1973, Barrett 1973, Clemente and Stevens 1987). Throughout the 1970s, the public witnessed a number of large-scale investigations into criminal behavior by police officers and police organizations in New York, Philadelphia, Chicago, and Indianapolis ("The Knapp Commission Report" 1973, Pennsylvania Crime Commission 1974, Beigel 1974). During the 1980s, the media again drew attention to police improprieties as it identified police corruption from drug smuggling and protection to murder (Golden 1987, Phillips 1987).

It is indisputable that corruption exists in some police departments. From their moment of formulation during the nineteenth century, police departments in various cities have been riddled with scandals and corruption: abuses of power, sales of promotions, elaborate systematic schemes of protection and racketeering. Although the vast majority of police officers in America could not be classified as corrupt, the few who are grossly crooked bring dishonor and disgrace to the entire occupation.

Police corruption may be viewed as a number of different activities. Some observers find acceptance of gratuities and corruption as synonymous, while others see these as distinguishable. Howard Cohen and Michael Feldberg (1983, 31) attempt to clarify this ambiguity and define police gratuities:

> Any goods or services which are given to law enforcement officers because *they are law enforcement officers, which are not part of their regular remuneration.* [Emphasis added]

For some observers, the ambiguity inherent in defining police gratuities owes to two complicating factors. These factors include the intent of the person offering the gratuity and the effect of the gratuity on the behavior of the officer. In other words, if a gift, service, or discount is given freely with no intent to prejudice or gain greater access to police services, and the offering results in no actual behavioral change in the officer's performance of his or her lawful duty, then these gratuities would seem harmless. From this vantage, such gratuities would not appear to represent police corruption.

Extending this notion of gratuities, one begins to see that corruption in some manner involves misuse of one's official authority. This broad canopy of corruption includes both misuse that may result in personal gains to an errant officer, as well as unnecessarily using

force, making unreasonable searches, or moral turpitude (immoral activities).

To better understand the various forms police corruption may take, a number of social scientists have developed categorical schemes. For example, in 1972, the Knapp Commission investigated what may be the most widely publicized investigation of police corruption of this century (See Box 12.2).

In its report, the commission categorized dishonest officers in two principal categories: "meat eaters" and "grass eaters." Meat eaters were described as those officers who aggressively misuse their police powers for personal gain. Grass eaters, on the other hand, simply accepted the payoffs that the happenstances of police work threw their way. The Knapp Commission concluded that while meat eaters received huge sums of money as payoffs and filled the newspaper headlines, they represented the tip of the iceberg. The much larger body of the iceberg, which remained under water, was the grass eaters. As the Knapp Commission report suggested, the great numbers of grass eaters tended to create an image of corruption as respectable.

Other categorical schemes of police corruption have been suggested. Michael Johnson (1982, 75) suggests that police corruption may be divided into four major categories: internal corruption, selected enforcement–non-enforcement, active criminality, and bribery and extortion.

According to Johnson, *internal corruption* occurs among police officers and involves bending or breaking agency rules and regulations as well as criminal law violations. An example of this sort of corruption might be the theft and sale of police promotional exams in the Boston Police Department (See Stewart 1987).

Selective enforcement or non-enforcement involves misuse of police authority and discretion. For example, if an officer chose to let a speeder go with a verbal warning, it would be a legitimate use of discretion. But, if the officer allowed the speeder to go because

Box 12.2 _____

A Brief History of the Knapp Commission's Activities

It was on August 3, 1972 that then-Mayor John V. Lindsay of New York was given a 34-page preliminary report drafted by Whitman Knapp. Knapp chaired the "Commission to Investigate Alleged Police Corruption" in New York City. The report had taken a full two years to compile and offered a summary from a detailed examination of police corruption run rampant throughout the New York City police department. This report would eventually result in numerous firings and indictments of police officers throughout all five boroughs of New York City.

The probe into police misconduct had begun on April 23, 1970 when Lindsay appointed a five-member committee that came to be known as the "Rankin Committee." This panel consisted of J. Lee Rankin, the city corporation counsel; Police Commissioner Howard R. Leary; Investigation Commissioner Robert K. Ruskin; New York County District Attorney Frank S. Hogan; and Bronx District Attorney Burton B. Roberts. These men were given the responsibility of examining the general procedures used by New York City for investigating cases of police corruption (Burnham 1970; Dempsey 1972).

The Rankin Committee was charged with three principal responsibilities: 1) consideration of the procedures employed by the police department to investigate allegations of police corruption; 2) to offer recommendations for improvements in these general procedures; and 3) to investigate the specific charges of corruption and other allegations of police misconduct that grew out of the announcement of the committee's formation.

By May 11, 1970 the Rankin Committee had received 375 complaints of police misconduct. Among these were 316 that specifically spoke to alleged police corruption. The committee report indicated the following breakdown for these complaints:

Eleven percent of the complaints alleged a payment of money or other item of value to a policeman who could be identified with a fair degree of certainty; in thirty percent of similar complaints the officers could not be identified; in seven percent of the complaints an identified officer was charged with failure to take necessary police action; in forty-eight percent of the total number of complaints an unidentified officer was charged with failure to take action. [Rankin Committee Report, 1970]

The Rankin Committee's final report to Lindsay asked that an independent investigative body be appointed to replace it and that this body be charged with the responsibility of a full investigation into police corruption in the city. Within one week's time, Lindsay appointed a "Committee to Investigate Allegations of Police Corruptions," also known as the Knapp Commission. The members of the Knapp Commission included Whitman Knapp, a New York attorney who had previously served as head of the Indictment and Frauds Bureau of the New York County District Attorney's Office; Cyrus W. Vance, secretary of defense during President Lyndon Johnson's administration; Joseph Monserrat, president of the Board of Education; Franklin Thomas, a former deputy police commissioner for legal matters; and Arnold Bauman, a former assistant U.S. attorney for the Southern District of New York (Dempsey 1972). Arnold Bauman later resigned and was replaced by John E. Sprizzo, a former assistant U.S. Attorney and professor of law at Fordham University.

Once established, the Knapp Commission drew its authority to make an investigation from the executive order of the mayor. This order provided both subpoena powers for the commission (to assure that witnesses would come in to speak with the commission) and funds for an operating budget.

FINDINGS OF THE KNAPP COMMISSION

The Knapp Commission (1972, 1) reported:

We found corruption to be widespread. It took various forms depending upon the activity involved, appearing at its most sophisticated among plainclothesmen assigned to enforcing gambling laws. In the five plainclothes divisions where our investigations were concentrated we found a strikingly standardized pattern of corruption. Plainclothesmen, participating in what is known in police parlance as a "pad," col-

(continued)

BOX 12.2   continued

lected regular bi-weekly or monthly payments amounting to as much as $3,500 from each of the gambling establishments in the area under their jurisdiction, and divided the take in equal shares. The monthly share per man (called the "nut") ranged from $300 and $400 in midtown Manhattan to $1,500 in Harlem. When supervisors were involved they received a share and a half. A newly assigned plainclothesman was not entitled to his share for about two months, while he was checked out for reliability, but the earnings lost by the delay were made up to him in the form of two months' severance pay when he left the division.

The Knapp Commission also reported corruption among the remaining divisions, which they had not investigated in depth. The commission report also suggested that several other forms of corruption existed. These included a slightly less organized payment system among narcotics officers called "scores," where officers sometimes received huge amounts of cash; shakedowns of individuals by the general investigative detectives; payments by officers to other officers in order to secure better assignments or to speed paperwork; and uniformed officers, particularly those assigned to patrol cars, found to be participating in gambling

pads—although much smaller ones than the plainclothesmen's.

The Commission included the police officers' sense that the public had become preoccupied only with "police corruption" and had lost sight of the fact that corruption existed in other agencies as well. The officers viewed this as unfair and believed that it tended to intensify their general feelings of alienation and hostility toward their jobs, not just in New York City, but everywhere. Interestingly, this attitude is similar to how members of delinquent subcultures are traditionally described as justifying (or rationalizing) their law violations (Cohen 1955; Sykes and Matza 1957; Matza 1964).

The Knapp Commission has also been given credit for having denounced the "rotten apple" theory of police corruption. In this theory, individual officers are viewed as corrupt—as rotten apples that must be removed from "an otherwise clean barrel." Thus, the identification of individual corrupt officers, according to the theory, does nothing to remedy a more complex or extensive problem. The commission examined and rejected this theoretical explanation. They concluded that a much greater good would be accomplished by thoroughly examining the barrel, as well as the apples.

---

money had been clipped to the driver's license—money the officer took—it would represent corruption.

Active criminality, as implied, represents actual participation in illegal behavior. For example, *The Cops Are Robbers* by Gerald Clemente and Kevin Stevens (1987) details how Clemente and other police officers routinely burglarized retail stores they had been expected to protect. In fact, police burglary rings have long troubled both large and small cities across the nation (Simpson 1977, Stoddard 1983).

Bribery and extortion are goal-directed activities designed to obtain financial gains for police officers through misuse or abuse of their authority. Although similar in nature,

one may distinguish between bribery and extortion according to who initiates the transaction. A bribe typically is initiated by a civilian. In extortion, the bribe is initiated by the officer.

Jay Albanese (1988) defined three basic forms of police corruption: non-feasance, misfeasance, and malfeasance. Each of these is detailed below.

Non-feasance.   Non-feasance may be understood as an omission of duty or an officer's failure to perform his or her lawful duty. For example, when an officer stops a motorist who was exceeding the speed limit, but chooses not to ticket because the driver shows remorse, it is technically non-feasance.

Misfeasance. A misfeasance may be classified as the failure of an officer to perform his or her lawful duty in an appropriate manner. For example, a misfeasance is committed if an officer on patrol peeps through windows hoping to see people undressing or undressed, under the guise of patrolling the neighborhood.

Malfeasance. An officer has committed a malfeasance if he or she commits an act that simply could not be performed as part of lawful duty. For example, an officer answers a burglary call at a retail store. Arriving after the burglar has fled, the officer nonetheless enters the store and goes shopping. That is, the officer takes items from the store and allows the retailer to think the burglar stole these items.

It is fairly clear to see that all cases of malfeasance can be classified as corruption. Yet, many instances of non-feasance and misfeasance may not represent corruption. Some non-feasance and misfeasance may represent deviance, stretches in the social limits of tolerance. But this, in itself, may not represent corruption. In many police departments, a choice is made to establish enforcement priorities. In essence, these enforcement priorities set patterns of police activities in which petty offenses are either ignored entirely or given only superficial attention. In such instances, it is the organizational policy, rather than an individual officer or group of officers, that is responsible for the non-feasance or misfeasance.

An Unintentional Effect of Enforcement Priorities

The idea behind enforcement priorities is not intentional non-feasance. Rather, it is to ensure that the more serious crimes, and crimes for which suspects are most likely to be apprehended if action is taken immediately, receive the greatest priority by investigators.

Thus, in an ideal sense violent crimes, homicides, and major robberies should receive greater attention than incidents of shop-lifting or car theft. Yet, in some large cities, the police may have unintentionally forfeited some of their law enforcement franchise in the name of enforcement priorities.

For instance, it may be suggested that, at least to a some extent, the New York City Transit Police Department has given up some of its monopoly on law enforcement by implicitly accepting the Guardian Angels. The Guardian Angels are composed primarily of teenagers and young adults who patrol high crime areas in more than sixty cities across the United States (Lab 1988). This citizen's patrol frequently concentrates its energies in the poorer sections of a city and on its mass transportation. The membership of some chapters of the Guardian Angels is exclusively composed of college students. In these instances, the patrol typically is limited to their college campus.

Although the Guardian Angels are viewed by many as inherently good and necessary for the safety of passengers on New York subways, they have nonetheless taken over certain one-time law enforcement functions. Originally, the police saw what the Guardian Angels did as fulfilling unessential activities. These included providing a kind of extra patrol to make a visible presence. This, in turn, was viewed as potentially discouraging would-be graffiti artists and apprehending turn-stile jumpers. But, since they are present, Guardian Angels additionally have been involved in apprehending muggers, purse-snatchers, and even rapists. The overall effect is that even these serious crimes are trivialized in the organizational policy of the New York City Transit Police. Theoretically, the police have not intentionally committed any non-feasance by relinquishing their franchise on law enforcement. Again, their intention is to offer greater attention to more serious crimes (major robberies, homicide, drug distribution, racketeering, and rape).

There is a similar possibility that some misfeasance is unintentionally created though simple officer error or from a lack of understanding of a particular law. For example, if an officer believes that a suspect who *has not* been advised of his constitutional rights has been Mirandized, and in casual conversation learns about additional crimes or evidence of other crimes, this information may become useless. The officer did not intentionally or willfully violate the suspect's rights or potentially destroy elements of the state's case. Rather, the officer simply goofed.

What remains for us, at this juncture, is the suggestion of a working definition of police corruption. It must be sufficiently broad to capture the vast diversity of inherently corrupt activities, but adequately narrow to avoid inclusion of minor acts of deviance. Turning once again to Albanese (1988, 113) a useful definition for corruption can be identified:

> *Illegal acts or omissions by a law enforcement officer in the line of duty who, by virtue of his official position, receives or intends to receive, only gain for himself or others.*

It is important to note two central focuses in this definition—that the illegal behavior or omissions must occur while on duty and that these activities are undertaken with the intent to receive a reward. In other words, part of the definition is that these activities are profit-motivated—whether this profit is cash, merchandise, or political favor. Taken together, these components of Albanese's definition suggest that police corruption is inherently the misuse of police authority for personal advantage or gain.

Although Albanese's definition is generally workable, it does possess at least two serious limitations. By stressing the idea that the illegal behavior must occur while on duty, a wide variety of behaviors is eliminated. Consider, for instance, an officer who, while on duty, gains information about when a wealthy local resident will be away on vacation. While off-duty, the officer could use this informa-

tion and burglarize the home of this wealthy local resident. While still within the general spirit of Albanese's definition, it certainly does not really comply with the specifics of an illegal behavior while on duty.

A second limitation rests on the fact that Albanese's definition directs attention to the individual and away from the department or the institution of policing. Later in this chapter this will be shown to be somewhat imprecise.

Several researchers have offered additional insights to and explanations for police corruption. For the most part, these may be divided into one or the other of three kinds: explanations that focus upon individual officers, explanations that center on departmental or organizational problems, and explanations that identify contributory problems from outside the department.

Corruption of Individual Officers

Individual explanations of police corruption see the locus of initial illegal behavior as originating among particular police officers. Supporters of this perspective argue that if a few rotten apples were eliminated from police agencies, corruption would vanish. When one thinks about this sort of officer, one imagines someone of low moral character who is unable to resist the temptation of fast but dirty money or illegal deals and negotiations. Another image related to this officer is one that misuses authority for personal gain, rationalizing that since the job pays so poorly and he or she works so hard, the officer deserves certain perks. In contrast to the officer of low moral character, this second type more aggressively seeks opportunities to receive financial gains or favors in return for omissions of duty (e.g., not making an arrest, not issuing a ticket, not reporting a license violation, etc.).

The explanation of a few rotten apples spoiling the barrel was fairly popular during the 1960s (Peterson 1960, Goldstein 1977). Today, however, few law enforcement researchers fully embrace this explanation of police corruption. As Samuel Walker (1983, 180) says:

> By focusing on the individual it explains corruption in terms of the moral failure of a few officers. According to this view, corruption spreads because the rotten apple spoils the rest of the barrel . . .
>
> Despite its popularity, the rotten apple theory is rejected by most experts. First, it fails to explain the pervasiveness and persistence of police corruption— otherwise one would have to assume that there are an enormous number of "bad" people recruited into police work. On the contrary, studies of police recruitment indicate that persons attracted to policing are relatively idealistic . . .
>
> Second, the rotten-apple theory fails to explain the differences between departments and differences within a particular department over time . . .

Walker also suggests that if one accepts the rotten-apple theory, one must additionally accept the notion that at least some police departments have attracted a disproportionately high number of rotten apples—and have done so for a very long time.

Writing shortly after the Knapp Commission (1973) had concluded its investigation, former New York City Police Commissioner Patrick Murphy (1973, 72) stated:

> The "rotten-apple" theory won't work any longer. Corrupt police officers are not natural born criminals, nor wicked men, constitutionally different from their honest colleagues. The task of corruption control is to examine the barrel, not just the apples—the organization, not just the individuals in it, because corrupt police are made, not born.

Two things should be evident about individual explanations of police corruption. First, they insufficiently account for changes in idealistic recruits who become corrupt shortly after becoming police officers. Secondly, individual explanations do not specify why certain departments have historically and consistently had greater amounts of corruption than other departments.

Patrick Murphy's comment suggests a second and slightly more popular type of explanation: corruption viewed as originating in the structure of the police organization.

Corruption of Departments

Departmental explanations of police corruption look at the small groups of officers who typically band together within police departments. These police cliques may serve positive ends. But, in some instances, these cliques may foster sentiments antagonistic to their jobs, the community they serve, or even the justice system. This mutual support of one another's negative and antagonistic feelings may lead to corruption. Lawrence Sherman (1974) has described this situation as a *rotten pocket*. Sherman further suggests that rotten-pocket departments may be subdivided into those with pervasive, unorganized corruption and those with pervasive, organized corruption. In the first case, a majority of police in a given department are corrupt, but have little contact and make few cooperative efforts in their illegal personal gains. Gerald Clemente (Clemente and Stevens 1987) describes this sort of department in *The Cops Are Robbers* (See Box 12.3).

In the second case, the department may be seen as filled almost entirely with officers actively involved in systematic and organized corruption. Departments with organized corruption are places where bribes, payoffs, and shake-downs are routinized to the extent that they become mundane aspects of daily police activity. Robert Daley's 1978 book, *The Prince of the City*, illustrates this sort of organized corruption. The book details the story of Frank Leuci, a New York City detective, whose testimony against officers involved in crime made him an outsider in his department.

Richard Lundman (1980, 140–141) outlines five principal elements that distinguish individual police deviance from organized corruption. First, for police behavior to be seen as departmentally or organizationally corrupt, "it must operate in a manner contrary to

Box 12.3 _____

How Cops Go Bad: Gerald Clemente's Tarnished Badge

One may certainly question how cops, who entered the field of law enforcement with altruism and good intentions, became involved in the largest bank robbery in American history. In his book, *The Cops Are Robbers* (Clemente and Stevens 1987) one-time police Captain Gerald Clemente describes his evolution from law enforcer to law breaker. His criminal career culminated in the 1980 Memorial Day weekend bank robbery of the Depositors Trust in Medford, Massachusetts. The estimated haul in this robbery was approximately $25 million dollars in cash and jewels. The following section from the book describes Clemente's first night as a police officer in 1959 and his introduction to the world of police corruption.

Few people like to talk about police going bad. Few people like to admit that corruption exists. But it does. And I'm not talking about isolated incidents or occasional lapses. I'm talking about wholesale, deep-seated, extensive corruption, the kind that wraps a young man in its grasp and caresses him into believing that if he wants to get on in the world there just isn't any other way to go. I'm talking about the kind of corruption that fools a public servant into thinking he is not responsible to any authority, the kind that takes three cops like Jerry Clemente and Tommy Doherty and Joe Bangs, each completely different from the other, and makes them accomplices by appealing to the single, overriding characteristic they share—greed.

For the first four years following my discharge from the service, I worked a variety of jobs, including a stint with my dad's [rug] company. I used the GI Bill to finance a course in locksmithing—a subject that became an obsession with me and turned out to be very valuable to my criminal exploits in later years. Then, in 1959, I reached the first big turning point in my professional life—I took the civil service exam for entry into the Medford Police Department. I did well (I've always done well on exams), and I was accepted onto the force. On May 17, 1959, I reported for my first night of work, clean-shaven and innocent. I was excited because I was finally in a job where I could work hard and get on. I had faith in my own ability—and in the system.

My faith in the system was compromised immediately. I arrived at the station punctually, my uniform neatly pressed, my shoes spit-and-polish shiny, my badge, gun and club fresh in my possession. I had butterflies in my stomach. I was eager to make a good impression and gain acceptance from the veterans on the force. I'd heard that camaraderie was important in Medford, that the cops didn't like loners.

I was introduced to a few guys. The cops were aloof but friendly. I started to settle down. The sergeant assigned me to a cruiser and got me together with my first partner, Jackie Mullins, known on the force as Crusher. Crusher was a big, genial Irishman with a thick mustache and a wide smile. He talked to me with real warmth and treated me paternally. He'd show me the ropes, he said. He'd take care of me. I began to feel comfortable.

He took me out to the cruiser, telling me what to expect, educating me on procedure. The night was clear and warm and full of promise. I was a cop. I was learning my trade. But before the night was through I was to learn a lot more than I had bargained for.

About two in the morning we were cruising along Medford Avenue, looking crosswise down empty, moonlit streets and listening to the occasional crackle of the scanner. Crusher pointed out spots where he had broken up a fight or collared a burglar, but nothing much seemed to be happening that night.

"Action is the exception, kid, not the rule. Better get used to nights like this."

But just as he finished speaking, we spotted a shadowy figure sprinting across the avenue and down an adjoining street, carrying what looked like a large lawn chair in his arms. Crusher flipped on the flashers and hit the accelerator. We turned the corner and eased up beside the guy. I tensed, my hand near the butt of my revolver I had not even fired in practice yet. My first piece of action.

But when I looked at this guy I saw that he was another Medford cop, in full uniform. I relaxed, a bit disappointed. Crusher and I got out of the car.

"Hey, Jack," the guy said.

"Dick, how ya doin'?"

Dick leaned the chair against the idling cruiser and pointed vaguely up the street.

"Good, Jack, good. Just caught a couple of guys breaking into Zayres."

He gestured at the lawn chair.

"Dropped this and took off before I could get a good look at them."

Crusher nodded, stroking his mustache. Over-eager rookie that I was, I decided to get my two cents in.

"Well, let's bring the chair back."

Dick and Crusher shot each other knowing glances. Crusher picked up the chair and handed it to Dick.

"Get back in the car, kid," he growled at me.

Confused, I looked back and forth between them. He wasn't kidding. I returned to the front seat while Crusher and Dick spoke quietly. Dick left with the chair and Jackie wheeled the cruiser around, heading in the opposite direction. After a silent couple of blocks, he spoke:

"Lesson number one, Jerry: you see another cop with a chair, television, whatever, you keep your mouth shut. You say your hellos and you move on your way. Whatever he's doing is his business.

He paused and held up two fingers.

"Lesson number two: don't play high and mighty. You want to be part of the club, you act like people in the club. You don't want to, hey, that's up to you—but don't expect people to trust you."

He kept talking. As I listened I learned the real meaning of camaraderie in Medford. There would be no acceptance without compliance. Stealing made you one of the guys, part of the club. If you didn't participate, you weren't trusted; it was as simple as that. The others had to have something on you so that they knew you wouldn't talk if you saw them transgress. And everybody, or almost everybody, transgressed. If you were dispatched to the scene of a break-in, you lifted a couple of items and stored them in the trunk of your cruiser while waiting for the owner to show up. And it was easy enough to justify: the crooks got away, the owner got his insurance money, and the cop got a new radio or wrench set, or garden hose. Everybody was happy. I may have been shocked to discover this activity, but for a young man used to seeing favors traded in business and politics, it was an easy step to take.

But I soon discovered that the corruption cut a lot deeper. If a cop wanted something badly he wouldn't necessarily wait for a break-in—he often became the burglar himself. Night shift then became a boon instead of a pain.

norms or rules maintained by legal institutions outside of the police department."

Second, to distinguish between individual deviance and organized police corruption, the "deviant act must be supported by internal operating norms which conflict with the police organization's formal goals and rules . . ."

Third, in order to maintain the subterranean norms of illegal behavior, a socialization process "supportive of police misconduct" must exist to indoctrinate recruits.

Fourth, a general condition of mutual and "peer support of the misbehavior of colleagues" must be present throughout the department.

Finally, for police misconduct to be organizationally corrupt, "it must be supported by the dominant administrative coalition of the police organization." The idea of a deviant police subculture and negative results from its related, secret esprit de corps are certainly implied in Lundman's elements.

It is certain that some conditions that arise within departments will make organized corruption more or less conducive. In other words, there may be an interrelationship of certain groups of officers as rotten-pockets and certain organizational structures or agency administrators and policies that lead to organized corruption. The third possible explanation of police corruption mentioned previously is the effects of external factors.

External Factors That Explain Corruption

The external factors explanation of police corruption draws heavily from sociological theory. From this perspective, police corruption is seen as the latent effect of society's attempt to execute certain unenforceable or socially controversial laws (Barker 1986). These may include behaviors that are violations of statutes or ordinances, but that all parties have engaged in voluntarily, such as gambling, prostitution, and drug use—the so-called victimless crimes. These crimes are difficult to enforce, both because there are few complaints and because pervasive attitudes permissive of these activities tend to exist throughout society.

While external factor explanations contribute to some species of police corruption, such as bribes and payoffs, these are rather limited in their applicability. For example, this theory fails to explain why an officer might be willing to fix a traffic ticket for a local politician or why an officer who desires a new color television might turn to burglary to obtain it.

The Occupational Opportunity Explanation

A more promising explanation of police corruption arises when one considers law enforcement from an occupational perspective. Police deviance and corruptions, then, become forms of occupational deviance. All occupations present their members with various opportunities to use, or more accurately misuse, their positions or authority for personal gain. Stockbrokers may use insider information to make themselves wealthy. Members of the supermarket night stock crew may make themselves expensive steak diners while working. Department store salespersons may place sale tags on full-price merchandise for friends, relatives, or themselves. University professors may trade grades for cash or sexual favors from students. Automobile factory workers may take tools home in their lunch pails. Occupational opportunity and human greed frequently combine to produce deviant situations.

With regard to police officers, most are placed in circumstances that present them with opportunities for misconduct at some time or another. Even in the smallest of exurbs (beyond the suburbs), patrol officers may base an arrest decision on some extra-legal criteria, accept money for letting a speeder go unticketed, or use physical force to effect an attitude adjustment with a smart-mouthed teenage suspect.

Given the enormous amount of work-based deviance/corruption apparent in various occupations and professions, why is there special concern about police deviance? One explanation, of course, is that the occupational setting of police officers, and the accompanying opportunity structure, offers a far greater range of choices and corrupting circumstances. Also, compared with other occupations, the public has far less compassion for transgressions committed by police officers (Coleman 1985). After all, no other occupation has been officially granted the authority to preserve liberty, even to the extent of taking another person's life.

Additionally, policing provides access to numerous occasions to engage in occupationally deviant activities that do not provide a material or financial gain. For example, police officers are required to testify in court as part of their law enforcement duties. In spite of having taken an oath to tell the truth, some officers may bend this truth or lie in order to improve the likelihood of a conviction (Ericson 1981, Barker 1986).

Some acts of perjury, such as lying under oath, suggest commonly understood types of corruption, such as having taken a bribe. Some acts of perjury, however, do not. Occasionally, an act of police perjury simply reflects an overzealous officer's attempt to get a conviction at any cost. It well may be that the defendant is a known felon, who whether guilty or not of the current crime, is seen by the officer as guilty of some crime. In this case, the end of obtaining the conviction—even to the extent of perjury—may outweigh the means of obtaining it in the mind of the officer. But no matter how noble the intentions, this sort of perjury remains a misuse of one's authority. It is police deviance in the truest tradition of Dirty Harry—yet it is characteristically different from police corruption.

Researching police deviance and misconduct in Canada, Richard Ericson (1982) has similarly identified a trend among officers to ignore or violate certain laws in order to conform to some greater police standard. This general attitude suggests that officers morally justify getting around the law or departmental policy, if it increases the likelihood of obtaining a conviction for a suspect they believe to be guilty. Ericson indicates that the sole concern of the police then becomes taking precautions to avoid being discovered in their rule-bending activity.

Jerome Skolnick (1986, 125) offers the following explanation for why police officers may lie or perjure themselves:

The policeman lies because lying becomes a routine way of managing legal impediments—whether to protect fellow officers or to compensate for what he views as limitations the courts have placed on his capacity to deal with criminals. He lies because he is skeptical of a system that suppresses truth in the interest of the criminal. Moreover, the law permits the policeman to lie at the investigative stage, when he is not entirely convinced that the suspect is a criminal, but forbids lying about procedures at the testimonial stage, when the policeman is certain of the guilt of the accused.

There is another problem related to the opportunity for police officers to perform misconduct. This other inducement is the huge economic base many organized criminal operations possess today. For many criminals a large cash payoff to the police is simply a business expense. With the increased impor-

tation of cocaine in tons rather than in pounds, millions of dollars are at risk when police seize a shipment. A ten-thousand dollar payoff to a police officer, then, is chicken-feed. As a result, police officers sometimes find themselves offered bribes that amount to as much or more than they earn in an entire year. Often, merely for not being somewhere at a certain time (an omission of duty), an officer can receive a large sum of money.

For example, imagine that an officer who usually patrols a warehouse areas between 8:00 and 8:30 P.M. is asked not to make patrol until 9:00 P.M. For this delay, the officer will receive $50,000. Now imagine that this officer chooses to comply. During that half-hour delay of the patrol, someone drives the cab of an 18 wheel rig into the warehouse area. Next, person or persons unknown hook this cab to a trailer fully loaded with cases of cigarettes—perhaps a million-dollar shipment—and drives off. The next day, the officer receives an envelope with $50,000 in small bills. Through omission of duty, this officer has both facilitated and committed a crime.

The high degree of discretion characteristic of policing and the independent and largely unsupervised patrols of officers further increase the possibilities for corruption. In addition, discretionary decisions, such as whether to make an arrest, are essentially invisible to the general public. In short, most police activities are unseen by the average person. Unless one is witness or victim to a crime, one seldom gets to see real police work. When a resident does happen to see police in action, such as officers leaving the scene of a burglary, it is virtually impossible to know whether legitimate police activities or misconduct have occurred. This ambiguity additionally increases the conduciveness for police deviance and corruption.

The various factors inherent in policing as an occupation provide an opportunity that can facilitate police misconduct and corruption. It is extremely important to emphasize that the vast majority of law enforcement officers, like the majority of other occupational members, do not take advantage of their positions and authority. The majority of police officers remain law-abiding bearers of the trust society has bestowed upon them.

In fact, when alleged wrongdoing is identified, police officers frequently rush to the defense of the organization, even at the expense of the accused officer(s). Although civilians under law are innocent until proven guilty, the police are more often treated (particularly by other police officers) as guilty until proven innocent. This general trend has resulted in a somewhat unusual attitude within police organizations. Since the officers in a given department rally to condemn the suspected party in the group, the agency itself is presented as exempt from any responsibility for the misconduct (Goldstein 1986).

An illustration of this occurred recently in Boston. On February 2, 1988, Boston Police Commissioner Francis M. Roache fired a rookie police officer six days after the officer had brandished a gun and pointed it at the head of a cab driver during a dispute. The entire incident was inadvertently captured on video tape by a nearby shopping mall's surveillance camera. During the press conference Commissioner Roache called specifically to announce this firing, he said, "There is no way this type of activity will be tolerated in this department" (Ribadeneira 1988, 16).

In a subsequent newspaper article (Stewart 1988), it was reported that Boston Police Department officials had twice tried to nix the offending officer's police appointment. Their reason was her arrest in 1980 on two counts of assault and battery with a dangerous weapon—her foot. The charge was a felony and a conviction would have automatically disqualified her from appointment as a police officer in Massachusetts. However, the charges were reduced to two counts of assault and battery, misdemeanors. The appointment went through because the department did not have sufficient cause to reject the recruit.

The question, of course, becomes: Is the organization really exempt from responsibility simply because it has fired this officer and filed charges against her for yet another assault and battery? Although largely a rhetorical question, it does certainly offer a direction for police agencies to move in. Specifically, supervisors and administrators need to become responsible for their personnel. These commanders also need to be certain that departmental policy and procedure have been clearly articulated and understood by subordinate officers. The attitude of some administrators who, after the fact, claim, "I knew that so-and-so was a time bomb, waiting to go off" is insufficient. No action on the part of an administrator is action. The consequences of the bomb, should it go off, are indeed the legal and civil responsibility of both the offending officer and the agency.

Controlling Police Corruption

The question that should arise about now is, "If the occupation of policing virtually facilitates corruption, how is it to be controlled?" Several possible solutions have addressed this inquiry. First, a fairly strong argument can be made for the beneficial effect of an organizationally supported internal affairs division. Another approach, and one initiated by Patrick Murphy while he was still New York City's police commissioner, is the accountability system. In some ways this system is reminiscent of the mutual responsibility characteristic of the old English tithing system (see Chapter Two). In this modern system, supervisors at every level were held accountable for the illegal behaviors of the officers under their supervision. Just as tithings could be made to pay for damages created by their errant members, commanders could be made to resign, or might be demoted, if officers under their command were found guilty of crimes. Unfortunately, close monitoring of a commander's department not only reduced the likelihood of corruption, but also lowered officer morale. The suspicion and mistrust that this type of close scrutiny fosters also increases police cynicism and dissatisfaction with the job among officers. These same elements of cynicism and job dissatisfaction are repeatedly identified in research as justifications or rationalizations for police misconduct.

In the United States, interest in controlling or monitoring police conduct first began to gain impetus in the 1950s. As part of a national judicial trend that addressed the question of due process, the U.S. Supreme Court grew more critical of cases involving poor police practices. Throughout the 1960s, and with the rulings set forth in such cases as *Mapp* v. *Ohio* (1961), *Miranda* v. *Arizona* (1966), and *Terry* v. *Ohio* (1968) the tone for the judicial review of police conduct was set.

Also during the 1960s, the police found themselves facing urban rioting and massive political protests. Protesters and disgruntled residents, many of whom had been injured at the hands of police who were attempting to control public disturbances, added their voices to a growing demand for more effective mechanisms to express complaints about police conduct (Goldstein 1985). What evolved was a fairly widespread movement calling for the establishment of **civilian review boards.**

The civilian review board process involves the creation of a group of civilian advisers to review allegations of police misconduct. Although this style of police monitoring is fairly popular with critics of the police, it is usually met with resistance among police officers themselves (Epstein 1982, Walker 1983).

Typically, review boards are composed of members intended to represent a cross-section of the community and operate independently of the police agency. Frequently these members are appointed by mayors and consequently are sometimes criticized as unrepresentative of the community (U.S. Commission on Civil Rights 1982). Interestingly, many police officials similarly protest

such political appointments, fearing that politicians might be attempting to gain a foothold on the department's activities. Among the problems associated with civilian review boards is what has been called "Epstein's law of increasing hostility" (Epstein 1982, 58), which states:

> The public complains and accuses. The police deny and defend. Mutual suspicion and hostility grow, making a future complaint more likely.

In a similar tone, Richard Bennett and Robert S. Corrigan (1982, 111) have stated:

> The deterioration of police–citizen relations has had a major impact on the administration of justice. Mutual suspicion, hostility, distrust and fear have resulted in minimal citizen cooperation and, consequently, an increase in police use of aggressive enforcement procedures.

Among the traditional explanations for the hostility of police toward civilian review boards, one finds the attitude that as outsiders, civilians do not understand police work. As a result, these "liberal reformers" (a police stereotype for most civilians) are believed to be soft on crime and criminals. Evaluations and policy changes that result from civilian boards, therefore, are viewed by police officers as potentially compromising to real police operations.

Finally, and as suggested with regard to accountability systems, civilian review boards frequently reduce overall police morale within a department. This results chiefly because police view civilians as outsiders incapable of understanding police values and behaviors.

Another approach to controlling police misconduct is through increased training and education. As suggested in Chapter Ten, much of a police officer's formal socialization occurs at the police academy and during the first few months on the street. Thomas Barker (1983) has suggested that many police recruits enter the academy already believing that some amount of corruption is present in every police department. These recruits, then, need to be carefully instructed not only in the laws they are expected to enforce, but the laws and ethics they themselves are expected to follow.

Many academies already offer brief courses in police ethics. Unfortunately, these frequently amount to little more than a single two- or three-hour lecture squeezed somewhere among the twelve to sixteen weeks of academy training.

As a result, the press is full of instances of young, often rookie officers, misusing their authority, using excessive force, or becoming entwined in some organized misconduct of more senior officers (Murphy 1985; Quittner 1988; Reynolds 1988; Richard 1988; Merrill 1988). Although police organizations have certainly come a long way from the corruption-riddled agencies of the 1960s, in many ways they have taken only a few short steps.

SUMMARY

This chapter began with the premise that not all gratuities taken by police officers necessarily constitute corruption. In developing this argument the chapter asserts that one consideration involves whether the gift or service interferes with fair access to law enforcement protection all people are entitled to. Another serious problem associated with gratuities is how the public perceives them. Speaking generally, there tends to be an attitude among many people that accepting even that free cup of coffee may symbolically represent potential, if not actual, police corruption.

The chapter also draws attention to the notions of intent and effect with regard to gratuities and police officer behavior. When a gift or service is given without the intent to gain greater access to police protection or gain partial treatment in any manner, and when this gift does not result in a change in the officer's behavior, there seems little objective harm.

In an effort to distinguish various sorts of police deviance (e.g., rule bending) from police corruption (law violations), the chapter examines a number of categorical schemes. Included among these were explanations that were directed toward individually corrupt officers (sometimes referred to as rotten apples). Explanations directed toward the department and cliques of corrupt officers were identified in text as rotten-pockets arguments. Finally, explanations that considered various factors external of the police department and individual officers were discussed. These external explanations included certain difficult-to-enforce crimes and social attitudes.

The chapter concluded with an examination of police corruption as a variety of occupational deviance. Included in this discussion were several recommendations for controlling police corruption.

REVIEW QUESTIONS _____

1. What are some of the problems with a rigid definition of police corruption?

2. What are some of the elements that distinguish "rotten pocket" and "rotten apple" explanations of police corruption?

3. How can the occupational structure of policing contribute to or at least facilitate police deviance?

4. In what ways can "accountability systems" control police corruption?

5. What are some of the strengths and weaknesses of civilian review boards?

REFERENCES

Albanese, Jay S. *The Police Officer's Dilemma: Balancing Peace, Order and Individual Rights.* Buffalo, N.Y.: Great Ideas, 1988.

Associated Press. "Corruption Figure Disappears in Miami; Second Hospitalized," *The Washington Post* (November 19, 1987):22.

Barker, Thomas. "Peer Group Support for Police Occupational Deviance." In Thomas Barker and David L. Carter, eds. *Police Deviance.* Cincinnati, Ohio: Pilgrimage, 1986.

Barrett, J.K. "Inside the Mob's Smut Racket." *Reader's Digest* (November 1973):128–33.

Beigel, Herbert. "The Investigation and Prosecution of Police Corruption." The Journal of Criminal Law and Criminology 65, (1974):135–56.

Bennett, Richard R., and Robert S. Corrigan. "Police Occupational Solidarity: Probing a Determinant in the Deterioration of Police Citizen Relations." Journal of Criminal Justice 8, (1982):111–22.

Burnham, David. "Graft Paid to Police Said to Run into Millions," *The New York Times* (April 25, 1970):1,18.

Clemente, Gerald, and Kevin Stevens. *The Cops Are Robbers.* Boston: Quinlan Press, 1987.

Cohen, Albert. *Delinquent Boys.* New York: Free Press, 1955.

Cohen, Howard, and Michael Feldberg. *Ethics for Law Enforcement Officers.* Boston: National Association of State Directors of Law Enforcement Training, 1983.

Coleman, James. *The Criminal Elite.* New York: St. Martin's, 1985.

Cullen, Kevin. "Police Probers Indict 7," *The Boston Globe* (November 11, 1987):1,23.

Daley, Robert. *Prince of the City: The True Story of a Cop Who Knew Too Much.* Boston: Houghton-Mifflin, 1978.

Daley, Robert. *Prince of the City.* Videotape produced by Burtt Harris; New York: Warner Home Video. Screenplay, Jay Presson Allen and Sidney Lumet, 1982.

Dempsey, Lawrence. "The Knapp Commission and You." *The Police Chief* (November 1972):20–29.

Doherty, William F. "Boston Police Officer Faces Cocaine Trafficing Charges." *The Boston Globe* (January 7, 1987):A7.

Doherty, William F., and Richard J. Connolly. "Boston Detectives Allegedly Took Bribes," *The Boston Globe* (November 11, 1987):1,20.

Epstein, David G. "The Complaint: Advisory Reflections to the Law Enforcement Agency Head." *The Police Chief* (May 1982):58–61.

Ericson, Richard V. "Rules for Police Deviance." In Clifford D. Shearing, ed. *Organizational Police Deviance.* Toronto: Butterworths, 1981.

Feldberg, Michael. "Gratuities, Corruption and the Democratic Ethos of Policing. In Fredrick A. Elliston and Michael Feldberg, eds. Moral Issues in Police Work. Newark, N.J.: Rowman and Allanheld, 1985.

Golden, Daniel. "Can Police Corruption Be Stopped?" *The Boston Globe.* (November 15, 1987):A25.

Goldstein, Herman. *Policing a Free Society.* Cambridge, Mass.: Lippincott, 1977.

Goldstein, Herman. "Controlling Police Deviance." In Thomas Barker and David L. Carter, eds. *Police Deviance.* Cincinnati, Ohio: Pilgrimage, 1986.

Johnson, Michael. *Political Corruption and Public Policy in America.* Monterey, Calif.: Brooks/Cole, 1982.

Klockars, Carl B. *The Idea of Police.* Beverly Hills, Calif.: Sage, 1985.

Knapp Commission Report, The. *The Knapp Commission Report on Police Corruption.* New York: Braziller, 1973.

Lab Steven P. *Crime Prevention.* Cincinnati, Ohio: Anderson, 1988.

Lundman, Richard J. "Police Patrol Work: A Comparative Perspective." In Richard Lundman, ed. *Police Behavior: A Sociological Perspective.* New York: Oxford, 1980.

Matza, David. *Delinquency and Drift.* New York: Wiley, 1964.

Merrill, Jack Jr. "The Brutal Truth: Suburban Police Walk a Fine Line Between Proper and Excessive Force," *Newswest* (February 3, 1988):6,7.

Murphy, Patrick. "Police Corruption," *The Police Chief* (December 1973):36–72.

Pennsylvania Crime Commission. "Report on Police Corruption and the Quality of Law Enforcement in Philadelphia." St. Davids, PA: Pennsylvania Crime Commission, 1974.

Peterson, Bill. "Miami Virtue, or Vice?" *The Washington Post.* (January 12, 1986):6,A11.

Peterson, Virgil. "The Chicago Police Scandals." *Atlantic* (October 1960):58–64.

Phillips, Frank. "Bribery Allegations Reported in Lowell." *The Boston Globe* (October 16, 1987):1,24.

Quittner, Joshua. "Ex-Cop Found Guilty." *Newsday* (January 21, 1988):1,36.

Rankin Committee Report. "Report on Police Complaints Made to Rankin Committee April 24, 1970–May 11, 1970," dated May 13, 1970.

Reynolds, Pamela. "Black Man's Death Jolts Texas Town into Addressing Its Race Relations." *The Boston Globe* (January 19, 1988):1,9.

Ribadeneira, Diego. "Officer Seen on Tape Is Fired." *The Boston Globe* (February 2, 1988):14.

Richard, Ray. "City Officer's Duties Limited After Quarrel." *The Boston Globe* (January 23, 1988):24.

Schecter, L., and W. Phillips. *On the Pad.* New York: Putnam, 1973.

Sherman, Lawrence. *Police Corruption.* Garden City, N.Y.: Doubleday/Anchor Books, 1974.

Simpson, Anthony. *The Literature of Police Corruption* Vol. 1. New York: John Jay, 1987.

Skolnick, Jerome H. "Deception by Police." In Thomas Barker and David L. Carter, eds. *Police Deviance.* Cincinnati, Ohio: Pilgrimage, 1986.

Stewart, Richard. "Boston's Voided Police Tests: Perception a Costly Reality." *The Boston Globe* (November 23, 1987):1.

Stewart, Richard. "Police Request to Bypass Fired Officer Was Denied by State." *The Boston Globe* (February 6, 1988):1.

Stoddard, Ellwyn. "Blue-Coat Crime." In Carl Klockars, ed. *Thinking About Police.* New York: McGraw Hill, 1983.

Stuart, Reginald. "Officer Indicted in Miami Shooting," *The New York Times* (February 18, 1983):A18.

Sykes, Gersham, and David Matza. "Techniques of Neutralization: A Theory of Delinquency." *American Sociological Review* 22(1957):644–70.

United Press International. "Suspension of 30 More Officers Predicted in Miami Police Scandal." *The Washington Post* (November 23, 1987):A5.

Walker, Samuel. *The Police in America: An Introduction.* New York: McGraw Hill, 1983.

Washington Post. "Former Officer in Philadelphia Receives 13-Year Sentence," (March 4, 1986): A20.

"Who Is Guarding the Guardians? A Report on Police Practices for the U.S. Commission on Civil Rights." Washington, D.C.: Government Printing Office, 1981.

HAZARDS OF POLICING: DANGER, STRESS, AND AIDS

Police work places officers in a number of circumstances with unusual and unique hazards. There is, of course, the potential danger of being injured or killed while carrying out the day-to-day activities commonly associated with police work. In addition, when compared against other occupations, police work offers a significant amount of work-related stress. The stress results from, among other things, the officers' ability to decide whether to use deadly force in certain circumstances. This job-related stress creates additional social and physical complications for many police officers (e.g., divorce, alcohol–drug abuse, heart disease, ulcers, and even suicide). Throughout the past twenty years, law enforcement administrators have grown increasingly aware of and concerned about job stress and other hazards related to police work.

In Chapter Thirteen, the real and perceived dangers of police work are examined. The purpose here is to show that stress results whether the danger is actual (real dangers to health and life) or imagined (as part of police mythology). In addition, the relationship between day-to-day police work and stress are considered. In this case, the discussion centers on both the impact of stress on the officer and on his or her family.

Finally, this chapter considers a recent hazard to police officers: exposure to AIDS. This section of the chapter raises some serious concerns of police officers when dealing with AIDS-infected populations. It also considers in a somewhat futuristic manner the complications likely to arise as police officers contract this disease.

INTRODUCTION: DANGERS IN THE
POLICE ENVIRONMENT

Among the many elements that exist in the police officer's occupational environment, danger has long been identified in research as among the most important determinants of police attitudes and behavior (See Niederhoffer 1969; Goldstein 1977; Bennett and Greenstein 1975; Bennett 1984; Albanese 1988). As suggested in Chapter Ten, long before a recruit ever seriously considers a career in law enforcement, he or she is being subtly conditioned about danger by various factors in society. The media, such as television, motion pictures, novels, stories, magazines, newspapers, and so forth, each paint a romanticized, adventure-filled picture of police work. For most, *dangerous* quickly becomes synonymous with *adventurous*.

When youthful recruits do eventually enter the police academy, they are subject to the police socialization process. Speaking generally, recruits enter the academy believing they are already fully informed about danger. Based upon their civilian socialization process, they associate police work with danger and adventure.

Recruits are issued their guns, nightsticks, and handcuffs, and are trained in the academy to use these tools—both offensively and defensively. These too may initially be viewed as very clear symbols of the dangers of police work. Occupationally speaking, however, these are simply tools of the trade. They are not, in fact, significantly different from the medical instruments (hypodermics, stethoscopes, tongue depressors, etc.) used regularly by medical students as they become doctors.

It is undeniable that police work encompasses a number of tasks and functions that effect a set of potential risks to safety not present in other occupations. In fact, there appear to be an unusual amount of stress and related health problems associated with police work. This stress is also commonly seen as related to other social problems that plague police officers, such as divorce, alcoholism, drug abuse, and even suicide. Some police officers are injured or killed in the line of duty.

Both the law enforcement community and the general public take the killing of a police officer very seriously. For instance, even before many states had begun reinstating the death penalty for the crime of homicide during the early 1980s, most already carried a capital sentence on their statutes for the killing of a police officer.

Traditionally, newspapers and television newscasts spend several days discussing the circumstances surrounding the killing of a police officer. Large numbers of police and police officials often attend the funerals of a fallen comrade—even when they may not have known the slain officer personally. For example, in January 1988, a Dallas, Texas police officer was killed by a deranged homeless person. The street person wrestled the officer's gun away from him and then shot him three times. Over 1,000 police officers and city officials attended a memorial service in the officer's honor.

In February 1988, a Boston, Massachusetts officer was killed as he attempted to break down the door to a drug dealer's apartment. Shots were fired through the door as Detective Sherman C. Griffiths struck it with a sledgehammer. He was critically wounded in the head and died eleven hours later (Lewis 1988). Over 700 officers and police officials attended his funeral.

One week after the Boston shooting, another officer was gunned down, this time in New York City. At 3:30 A.M. on February 26, 1988 Officer Edward Byrne was shot three times in the head—execution style—as he sat in his patrol car. Officer Byrne had been assigned to a fixed patrol outside the home of a state's witness in a large-scale crack case. The witness had received death threats, and his home had been fire-bombed two weeks before Byrne's shooting (Fried 1988).

The occurrence of police killings certainly draws considerable public attention and is a genuine problem. But the publicity tends to mask a problem at least as serious: stress from officers' perception of danger. What is interesting about this perception of danger, and its concomitant stress, is the fact that while the threat of danger is very high in police work as an occupation, the reality of danger is relatively low, perhaps owing to precautions taken as a result of the threat. In other words, compared to the number of officers actually working in the field, the number who are seriously injured or killed is relatively small. As Table 13.1 illustrates, in 1985 a total of 78 officers were killed during incident-

TABLE 13.1 Law Enforcement Officers Killed During 1985 (By circumstances at scene and type of assignment)

CIRCUMSTANCES AT SCENE	TOTAL	2-OFFICER VEHICLE	1-OFFICER VEHICLE SOLO/ASSIST		FOOT PATROL SOLO/ASSIST		DETECTIVE SPECIAL ASSIGN. SOLO/ASSIST		OFF-DUTY
Total	78	10	33	11	0	0	5	7	12
Disturbance calls (general disturbances)	6	0	4	0	0	0	1	1	0
Domestic disturbances (family quarrels)	7	1	4	2	0	0	0	0	0
Burglaries in progress or pursuing burglary suspects	4	1	1	2	0	0	0	0	0
Robberies in progress or pursuing robbery suspects	12	1	5	1	0	0	0	0	5
Attempting other arrests	7	2	0	1	0	0	0	3	1
Civil disorders (mass disobedience, riots)	0	0	0	0	0	0	0	0	0
Handling, transporting, custody of prisoners	4	1	2	0	0	0	1	0	0
Investigating suspicious persons or circumstances	9	0	4	2	0	0	0	1	2
Ambush (entrapment and premeditation)	6	0	3	0	0	0	0	1	2
Ambush (unprovoked attack)	2	0	1	0	0	0	1	0	0
Mentally deranged	0	0	0	0	0	0	0	0	0
Traffic pursuits and stops	16	2	8	3	0	0	1	0	2
Drug-related matters	6	2	1	0	0	0	1	2	0

Source: *Sourcebook of Criminal Justice Statistics—1986*. Table 3.100, page 273. U.S. Department of Justice, Bureau of Justice Statistics. Washington, D.C.: U.S. Government Printing Office.

related actions nationally. When one stops to consider that there were just under one half million sworn officers nationally (470,678), the number of officers killed begins to pale. In full, fewer than two out of every 10,000 law enforcement officers were actually killed in the line of duty during 1985.

In fact, the killing of a police officer is a relatively rare occurrence (compared to the number officers in the field). As Table 13.2

TABLE 13.2   Law Enforcement Officers Killed Between 1976 and 1985 (By circumstances at scene and type of assignment)

CIRCUMSTANCES AT SCENE	TOTAL	2-OFFICER VEHICLE	1-OFFICER VEHICLE SOLO/ASSIST		FOOT PATROL SOLO/ASSIST		DETECTIVE SPECIAL ASSIGN. SOLO/ASSIST		OFF-DUTY
Total	921	148	300	149	10	4	53	144	113
Disturbance calls (general disturbances)	105	24	25	27	2	0	1	11	15
Domestic disturbances (family quarrels)	49	10	16	17	0	0	0	4	2
Burglaries in progress or pursuing burglary suspects	55	15	22	9	1	0	4	1	3
Robberies in progress or pursuing robbery suspects	144	16	35	18	0	2	9	13	51
Attempting other arrests	132	19	33	26	2	1	7	37	7
Civil disorders (mass disobedience, riots)	1	0	0	0	0	0	0	1	0
Handling, transporting, custody of prisoners	36	7	7	3	0	0	10	8	1
Investigating suspicious persons or circumstances	104	15	48	14	3	0	4	11	9
Ambush (entrapment and premeditation)	57	8	16	8	0	0	5	7	13
Ambush (unprovoked attacks)	33	3	13	1	2	0	6	2	6
Mentally deranged	18	2	4	7	0	0	1	3	1
Traffic pursuits and stops	128	26	79	16	0	0	2	1	4
Drug-related matters	59	3	2	3	0	1	4	45	1

Source: *Sourcebook of Criminal Justice Statistics—1986*. Table 3.99, page 272. U.S. Department of Justice, Bureau of Justice Statistics. Washington, D.C.: U.S. Government Printing Office.

illustrates, during the ten-year period of 1976 to 1985, a total of 921 officers were killed in the line of duty. This approximates an average rate of 92 officers killed each year, a figure slightly higher than most years.

Another element related to the dangers associated with police work is injury in the line of duty. As Table 13.3 suggests, during the seven-year period of 1979 to 1985, an average of 59,138 police officers nationally were injured. Another glance at Table 13.3 and some quick calculations reveal that the vast majority of these injuries were from the combined categories of personal weapons and other dangerous weapons. Typically, personal weapons include feet, elbows, fists, and teeth (bite wounds). Similarly, other dangerous weapons represent items such as lamps, keys, and pens used as weapons against an officer. While injuries certainly can and are sustained, most do not result in long-term disabilities.

In a recent study, David H. Bayley and James Garofalo (1989, 6) report that "the unambiguous fact is that patrol officers rarely face violence in encounters with the public." Bayley and Garofalo (1989) found that officers faced physical danger only occasionally, and then the violence frequently was not directed against them.

This discussion is not intended to diminish the very real potential dangers in police work. As Bayley and Garofalo warn, precautions are necessary since even a single act of violence may have catastrophic results for the officer. However, this discussion is intended to keep consideration of potential risks to police officers in perspective. Furthermore, the tables presented in this chapter merely

TABLE 13.3 Assaults on Law Enforcement Officers and Percent Receiving Personal Injury (By type of weapon used)

	1979 TOTAL	1979 PERCENT RECEIVING PERSONAL INJURY	1980 TOTAL	%	1981 TOTAL	%	1982 TOTAL	%	1983 TOTAL	%	1984 TOTAL	%	1985 TOTAL	%
Total Victims:	59,031	37	57,847	34	57,116	36	55,775	31	62,324	33	60,153	33	61,724	34
Types of weapons used:														
Firearms	3,237	21	3,295	23	3,330	18	2,642	16	3,067	22	2,654	20	2,793	21
Knife or cutting instrument	1,720	34	1,653	34	1,733	34	1,452	27	1,829	31	1,662	30	1,715	27
Other dangerous weapons	5,543	41	5,415	38	4,800	41	4,879	39	5,527	40	5,148	42	5,263	41
Personal weapons	48,531	38	47,484	38	47,253	36	46,802	31	51,901	33	50,689	34	51,953	34

Source: *Sourcebook of Criminal Justice Statistics—1986*. Table 3.104, page 275. U.S. Department of Justice, Bureau of Justice Statistics. Washington, D.C.: U.S. Government Printing Office

focus on "physical" assaults on officers. To date, little empirical research has calculated the emotional impact on police officers from being placed regularly in situations where one could be killed or injured. In other words, placed in what James Fyfe (1989) terms "potentially violent situations or PVs." Little emphasis has been placed on the emotional toll paid by officers when colleagues in their department or city have been permanently disfigured, disabled, or killed.

In many ways, and as this chapter will suggest, it is not the reality of a gunman shooting an officer during the course of a robbery that is the most serious threat to the life or health of this officer. Rather, it is the stress created from knowing that such a situation could occur (Cullen et al. 1983).

Police Work and Stress

The problem of stress as related to police work has received considerable attention throughout the past fifteen years. As Samuel Walker (1983, 277) suggests, much of the early writing on the subject was alarmist and frequently exaggerated. Estimates of suicides, divorces, and alcohol–drug dependency among police officers were often disproportionate to reality. As one might expect, the strongest supporters of such alarmist mythology are often police officers themselves. Ironically, the fear or concern created by such a police folk belief is itself likely to increase police officer stress.

A somewhat more even-handed approach to stress and police work begins with the recognition that stressful situations occur among all occupations. As a result, the cardiovascular diseases, hypertension, ulcers, depression, stress-induced diabetes, alcoholism–drug abuse, and assorted other somatic afflictions, are not unique to law enforcement officers.

Elements generally thought to contribute to occupational stress or stressors include the loss of a sense of efficacy, reduced participation in decision-making processes, disillusion-

ment with organizational goals, inequities in hiring, firing, and promotional structures, and task overloads. In addition to these general stressors, police work has several job-specific stressors. Ironically, the most devastating stressor is actually a paradoxical combination of long, tedious periods of inactivity, coupled with brief, unpredictable periods of severe and lethal danger.

Although trouble and volatile situations may arise only four or five times during an eight-hour shift, if that frequently, police are trained to be ever aware of potential threats to safety (See Whitaker 1982; Bayley 1986; Bayley and Garofalo 1989). The innocent-looking drunk sleeping in the alley could just as easily be a look-out for a burglar already inside a building. The three youths casually standing under a street lamp smoking cigarettes may actually be waiting for a woman to pass so they can grab her handbag. Police are repeatedly taught that nothing is necessarily as it seems. This sort of near-paranoid concern with even mundane things certainly can create emotional stress.

Too, patrol activities can lead to various health problems, such as poor eating and sleeping patterns, and leg or back problems. Related to these various stressors, of course, are assorted family conflicts, arguments with spouses, divorce, heavy drinking and/or alcoholism, and a potential host of medical afflictions (Schwartz and Schwartz 1975).

Discussions of police stress usually identify sets of stressors in similar ways. For example, quoting William Kroes (1976), Leonard Territo and Harold J. Vetter (1981) have grouped stressors into four categories: organizational practices; criminal justice system practices and characteristics; public practices and characteristics; and police work itself.

Clinton Terry III (1985, 400) has similarly identified four types of police stressors (See also Blackmore 1978, 1985; Stratton 1978; Wallace 1978). The four categories include external stressors; internal stressors; task-related stressors; and individual stressors.

External Stressors. External stressors, according to Terry (1985), include frustrations from seeing many arrests end up in dismissal in the courts, or seeing lenient treatment of felons who are convicted. External stressors may involve disdain for local media coverage of police or crime-related incidents, resentment of civilian committees and governmental bodies that may be empowered to intervene in, or affect performance of law enforcement functions.

Internal Stressors. Internal stressors represent a wide array of institutional problems. These may include flaws in training, nonfunctional procedures, insufficient or inadequate equipment, short pay and long hours, and a generally vague and unsatisfying system of rewards and recognition for good police work. Other internal stressors may be related to various forms of political favoritism or nepotism at the hands of supervisors, which limit or delay advancement. Internal stressors also may result from a kind of self-fulfilling prophecy in which officers define police work as stressful and identify instances that justify this definition.

Task-Related Stressors. Task-related stressors can be identified as those elements that stem from the performance of police duties. These may include shift rotations, boredom, repeated exposure to violent or brutal crimes, and the long-term fear for personal safety.

Individual Stressors. In contrast to the other three stressors, individual stressors are chiefly idiosyncratic, that is, they originate within the individual officer. These stressors may include feelings of self-doubt, marital problems, difficulties arising from being a member of a minority group, difficulties arising from an inability to get along with other people, and various physical and mental health problems.

One important point that should be made is that none of these stressors must be real in

order to have an effect on the officer. For instance, if an officer believes that a supervisor is racist, this situation will be stress-provoking even if it is entirely untrue. If an officer is confronted by a man who draws what the officer believes to be a real hand gun, the fear that runs through the officer is very real. If the officer later learns that the gun in question is a toy, it will likely make little difference. The emotional trauma the incident aroused will have already had some effect on the officer.

This phenomenon is similar to the concept of self-fulfilling prophecy and derives from a theory credited to W.I. Thomas (Thomas and Swaine 1928). According to Thomas, situations that are defined as real by humans, become real in their consequences. In other words, if an officer believes that the felon's hand in a pocket holds a gun, the officer will respond to that situation. The objective reality that the felon's hand clutches a toy or a roll of pennies is of no importance. The officer's emotional and somatic effects from the felon's simulation of a gun will be identical to those the officer would experience if confronted with a real gun.

Organizational Benefits from Eustress

Eustress is a term coined by Hans Selye (1975) meaning "good stress." Organizationally induced eustress is often seen as a positive management approach in policing (Leonard and More 1987). The use of eustress assumes that an individual can and will take a positive view of certain life events. Thus, one's attitude can determine whether an experience is perceived as pleasant or unpleasant. By adopting a positive attitude, one can convert unpleasant stress into productive and pleasant eustress. The result, then, becomes a more gratifying and satisfying work environment.

Some stress from police work can be identified as very harmful to officers. Some other stress can be viewed as both helpful and necessary for the officers' healthy survival in police work. According to Hans Selye, the total absence of stress can be lethal. In fact, Selye (1975, 83) suggests that stress should be viewed as the "spice of life."

Police managers may use stress to deal with employees' response to the organizational structure of the department. In these cases, managers attempt to create a work environment based upon an awareness of how officers view their department. Both the overall attitudes and the morale of officers are taken into consideration. Department policies, in turn, are developed in an effort to maintain a high level of job satisfaction. In order to accomplish this, the organization accommodates individual officers with regard to their levels of stress endurance and ability to adapt to stressful situations that occur in police work.

The overall emphasis of this orientation is that the organization is to use stress that exists in the work place in a positive way. The rationale is that occupational stress can and should contribute to individual health, productivity, and physical well-being.

Stress and the Officer's Family

When an individual signs on as a law enforcement officer, he or she has accepted more than merely a job or career. As Leonard Territo and Harold Vetter (1981) suggest, policing is a way of life for both the police officer and his or her family. Francis T. Cullen and his associates (1985) have suggested that police stress falls along two discernible dimensions, one involving the family and the other involving the job.

Most occupations expect employees to work during some specified period of hours and then to stop working and go home to a private life. For example, a taxi cab driver can switch the duty light off, climb out of the cab, and go home as a private person. A police officer cannot as easily turn off the job.

First, law enforcement officers are never really off-duty. Rather, they are off the clock.

A private person can ignore a felony they observe in progress or merely call the police. Under similar circumstances, an off-duty officer could be charged with dereliction of duty if he or she makes no attempt to intercede. When a neighbor hears a prowler at 3:00 A.M., who gets called—the officer neighbor next door and two minutes away, or the police department?

Second, law enforcement officers find it difficult to leave their feelings about the job at the precinct. As a result, they frequently bring their frustrations, disappointments, fears, and dissatisfactions home to their families. Conversely, and like any other kind of worker, law enforcement officers may bring anger, hostility, or family problems to the job. Many of us have been stopped by a police officer for a traffic infraction. During those moments of waiting for the officer to walk from the cruiser to the window, certainly many people are whispering, "I hope the cop didn't have a fight at home this morning!"

It is only recently that police administrators have begun to recognize that discord in an officer's family life can contribute to serious disruptions in the officer's effectiveness. Also, it is only during the past few years that police agencies have acknowledged that police work stress is carried home to the family. Many of the perceived threats to safety experienced by police officers are perceived by their spouses and children. In many cases these stressors adversely affect the health of family members as seriously as they affect officers themselves. With this in mind, some agencies, such as the Kansas City, Missouri, police department have established programs that involve spouses in an effort to reduce stress (Saper 1980).

Stress, Coping, and Alcoholism

To be sure, police stress is much more than an abstract concept. Stress can lead to a host of somatic and psychological problems. For some, the use of alcohol may serve as a form of self-medication for stress. Violanti, Marshall, and Howe (1985) imply that police officers may drink in order to unconsciously relieve symptoms of stress—as a kind of coping strategy.

In fact, early police stress programs were directed almost exclusively at officers with alcohol problems. Among the earliest programs was one founded by Monsignor Joseph Dunne, a chaplain with the New York City police department. Between 1958 and 1966, Dunne fought the red tape and cynical attitudes of the police bureaucracy in order to establish an alcoholism program.

A large portion of Dunne's problems stemmed from the social attitude that problem drinking was an individual's own problem and reflected a character flaw. Institutionally, the department handled drinking on the job or intoxication while on duty as a disciplinary problem. Violators were subject to suspensions, being docked thirty days' salary, and put on a year's probation. Because of the severity of these penalties and the stigma of having an alcohol problem, many supervisors resisted reporting their personnel when minor drinking incidents arose. In 1966, under a new and more forward-thinking administration, Dunne successfully organized an alcohol counseling program.

Throughout the late 1960s, a number of police agencies began to take serious action to reduce the effects of police problem drinking. In New York, Philadelphia, and Chicago police departments established in-house counseling programs to work with alcoholic officers. As psychologists began working with these officers, they soon realized that alcoholism was not the problem, but merely a symptom. The problem was police stress.

More extensive counseling programs began to emerge, first on the West Coast in Los Angeles, under the directorship of Doctors Martin Reiser and William Kroes (Blackmore 1978). But, by the mid-1970s, most large city police departments had developed some type of counseling service for their officers. In some

cases this meant simply arranging with a local psychologist or social worker to offer crisis intervention when needed. In some other cases, counseling services involved full-blown programs of stress management.

In 1974, the Boston police stress program emerged, first as an alcohol counseling service, but eventually as a full-scale peer-counseling program. Today, the Boston program operates from a house in Mattapan, a poor, high-crime, residential community on the outskirts of the city. The center is located away from both local police stations and police headquarters. The service is organized around a peer-counseling model, in which officers share their problems with one another. Peer counseling draws its therapeutic strength from experiential guidance and empathy. Because officers are speaking with other officers for the most part, the potential stigma of having gone to a therapist is not present. The program also offers a complete referral service for problems that peer counselors cannot handle.

Other agencies have innovated a variety of styles and types of counseling programs. Some, like those in the Detroit Police Department, operate as part of the agency's medical section and either provide officers with counseling or offer referrals to local counselors. Unfortunately, in many instances officers continue to resist seeking psychological services on their own. As a result, supervisors are still placed in a position of having to identify and direct officers to these services.

When officers are suspected of having a drinking problem, some agencies, such as the Denver Police Department, use closed-circuit television systems to record the officers and encourage them to join an in-house program (Territo and Vetter 1981). From this in-house program, many of the officers with more serious drinking problems are persuaded to enter a clinical treatment program at a local hospital.

Loo (1984) has suggested that, traditionally, police agencies have sought psychological services in a reactionary manner. Counseling services were implemented only in crisis situations or to resolve immediate problems, such as an officer's drug problem, low morale, and community complaints against police officers. Frequently, outside psychologists brought into these situations met with resistance and suspicion from the officers. The peer-counseling programs, which Boston and many other agencies have used, have enjoyed a fair amount of success as intervention strategies (Graf 1985). Klyver (1983), reporting on the Los Angeles Police Department's peer-counseling program, emphasizes the point that many officers with stress-related problems are unlikely to seek professional help. Yet, these same officers, argues Klyver, find it acceptable and comforting to discuss personal problems with colleagues or peer counselors.

Role Conflicts and Stress

Among the many contributory factors to stress among police officers are role conflicts. A role, as used here, is defined as the expression of a set of patterned behavioral expectations associated with a given social position or status (father, mother, teacher, police officer, and so forth). Ralph Linton (1937) distinguished between status and roles by saying that individuals *occupy* a status, but they *perform* a role. Roles are interactional because they define social behavior between people. However, roles are also relational because they define expectations of behavior between certain statuses. For example, one ideally defines the role associated with the status of parent in terms of behaviors or responsibilities associated with child-rearing. In turn, one ideally defines the roles associated with such statuses as sons and daughters in terms of relational behaviors directed toward a parent.

Thus, roles are paired, and expected patterns of behaviors occur between these pairs (teachers and students, employer and em-

ployee, lawyer and client, etc.). Since most individuals occupy many statuses or what is called a *status set,* they express a variety of roles. In fact, individuals often perform many roles while occupying a single status. This is because individuals perform variations in role behavior depending upon their relationship with the other person's role. Merton (1968) has defined these multiple roles attached to a single status as a *role set.*

Although several roles may be linked to a single status, they may not always be in accord. When this occurs, an individual can feel pulled in several directions at once. Role conflict, then, is defined as this clash between roles corresponding to a single status. Ritzer's and Walczak's (1986) explanation for role overload similarly describes conflicting role expectations and resulting strain. In these instances, an individual is confronted with a role set filled with conflicting role expectations and finds it impossible to satisfy all of them.

For example, a police officer might be assigned to a midnight-to-eight shift throughout the month of December. Traditionally, this officer may have spent Christmas Eve with the family at the home of his or her parents. Additionally, the officer is assigned to work with an unmarried, inexperienced rookie who asked to work Christmas Eve for the street experience.

In this hypothetical case the officer experiences conflict in the attempt to be a parent, spouse, dutiful child, breadwinner, and field training officer. Each of these is a status that demands focused time and energy. Under the circumstances, however, it will be impossible to simultaneously perform each role fully. Because the officer will not be able to fully perform all these roles, a degree of role strain will result, hence stress.

Stress that results from role conflicts may be reduced in several ways. For example, one might emphasize one facet of one's roles while withdrawing from those that cause conflict. In the hypothetical officer's case, this might mean withdrawing from family responsibilities or perhaps changing occupation. Another way some individuals manage role conflicts is through what Merton (1968) refers to as *insulation strategies*. In this case, an officer might compartmentalize his or her life. Essentially, this involves limiting certain statuses and role behaviors to certain settings or during only specific times of the day.

For example, many people are capable of changing their complete persona as quickly as switching on or off the lights. How they speak and act at home may be very different from how they speak and behave in their work environment. If a family member enters the work setting for a visit, the persona may return to the at-home version.

Of course, another way to eliminate stress caused by role conflict is to obliterate it with alcohol, drugs, or ultimately through suicide.

Police Stress and Suicide

Arthur Niederhoffer (1969) described the unusually high incidence of suicide among police officers over twenty years ago. Niederhoffer (1969, 101) states:

> *After the necessary adjustments are calculated, the suicide rate for males in the general New York City population is about 15 per 100,000. The average police [suicide] rate of 22.7 is almost exactly fifty per cent more than this.*

Suicide, as related to police stress, is not a simple matter. Although less common among youthful officers, it does occur. Typically, the suicide of a young officer can be associated with some serious family crisis that is complicated by the everyday stress of police work.

Among older law enforcement officers, suicide is more likely to be associated with alcoholism or drug abuse, severe physical illness, being connected to some illegal activity, or approaching retirement.

Although little empirical evidence has been amassed about the connection between retirement and suicide among police officers, some researchers have suggested such a relationship exists (See Territo and Vetter 1981). It is, for example, fairly widely known that persons from many occupations frequently become depressed shortly after retirement. This depression may lead to a lack of interest in physical appearance and well-being, increased drinking, and ultimately to suicide.

There are a number of possible reasons for the appearance that a disproportionately high number of police commit suicide. First, police are trained in the use of and have ready access to firearms. When crisis situations occur or stress overpowers an officer, the access to a gun would make suicide easy.

Second, the psychological effect of constant exposure to frequent and extreme brutality, murder, and mayhem may cause some officers to become overwhelmed.

Third, long, erratic shift hours and unsatisfying working conditions may contribute to role conflicts and strain on social and family relations. This, in turn, may isolate an officer who, in a time of crisis, feels further overloaded, isolated, and lost or alone.

Fourth, the media and the public are often vocal in their criticisms and accusations of police wrong-doings, leading many good officers to feelings of self-deprivation and alienation.

Finally, police officers often experience a feeling of "what's it all for?" in the face of contradictory judicial decisions, changes in statutes, and what they perceive as eroding social values (Territo and Vetter 1981).

Terry (1981) suggests that, like divorce rates, figures on police suicides may be slightly misleading. While Niederhoffer (1969) and several others have indicated disproportionately high rates of suicide among police officers, some researchers have suggested a downward trend (Lewis 1973, Reiser 1973). Certainly, some of this ambiguity can be explained by the fact that regionally, suicide rates in New York, San Francisco, and Chicago (three principal study cities) had gone down between study periods (Heiman 1975).

Reductions among police officer rates, therefore, may be relative.

Another partial explanation for ambiguities about police suicide rates may rest on the nature of suicide itself. Traditionally, suicide is viewed by society as a cowardly inability to face up to one's problems. In an occupation such as policing, which boasts discipline, self-control, and bravery, the admission that many officers commit suicide may be difficult to handle. As a result, most police departments do not formally keep records of the number of officers from their agency who take their own lives.

Regardless of the various ambiguities, considerable evidence does suggest that police as an occupational group suffer from higher suicide rates than many other occupational groups.

AIDS: A NEW STRESSOR

The research on police work stress regularly divides two main types of stress endemic to policing: acute or situational stress and chronic stress (See Ellison and Genz 1978; Violanti, Marshal, and Howe 1985). The first type of stress includes stressors of a short-term nature or those that are circumstance/situationally based. These may include exposure to some traumatic or grotesque homicide scene, child victimization, or exposure to some sudden physically dangerous situation. The second type of stress, chronic stress, includes stressors of a long-term nature. These are typically police function based, or the frustrations that result from various role conflicts, police life-styles, and agency processes.

The preceding discussion in this chapter has examined these two categories of stress in general terms. At this point, the discussion shifts to consideration of a specific and increasingly serious chronic stressor: police officer encounters with individuals with AIDS.

During the past several years, AIDS (acquired immune deficiency syndrome) has be-

come both an increasingly serious public health concern and an emotionally charged stressor for persons working in the justice and health fields. A fair amount of the stress associated with AIDS stems from fear and misinformation about contamination and transmission of the disease.

AIDS affects law enforcement personnel in several important ways. First, many of the suspects and offenders police regularly encounter in their work are people who fit the profiles of **high risk** for AIDS (prostitutes, intravenous drug abusers). Consequently, street level law enforcement and corrections officers are concerned that they, too, may fall into an increased risk category for AIDS contamination. Second, in their effort to alert Americans to the seriousness of AIDS as a public health concern, the U.S. surgeon general, various state departments of health, the Red Cross, and the mass media have inadvertently terrorized many law enforcement and health care workers. Recent research on AIDS transmission has shown that the risk of contamination from casual contacts such as saliva or biting, is virtually impossible. But many law enforcement officers, convinced by the earlier scare campaigns, continue to perceive themselves as being in extreme risk for contamination.

Third, law enforcement officers could serve as a vital educational conduit through which accurate information about AIDS could flow to high-risk groups they encounter—intravenous drug abusers, prostitutes, and homosexuals. But first, the fears and misinformation under which many law enforcement officers currently labor must be cleared up (Hammett 1987a).

Finally, police are potentially affected by AIDS if an officer contracts the disease and continues working as a police officer. The fear of contamination already is very high among many police officers. The added pressure of perceived risks from working with someone with AIDS amplifies concern. To combat this potential problem, departmental policy and community relations problems must identify ways of educating officers and the community.

Ironically, and as will be discussed in greater detail later, police officers and health care workers are as or perhaps more likely to contract hepatitis-B than they are AIDS. Hepatitis-B is a highly contagious infection transmitted by blood which results in liver damage, and, frequently, in death. In fact, most of the law enforcement procedures concerning AIDS and handling persons believed to be AIDS contaminated, are derived from protocols from the U.S. Department of Health and Human Service, and the U.S. Centers for Disease Control for hepatitis-B.

A natural question is "Exactly what is the nature of AIDS and what are the implications for law enforcement personnel?" Let us begin with the obvious first concern, defining what AIDS is.

AIDS Defined

AIDS is a disease characterized by an increasing deficiency in the natural immune system of an individual, leaving the person highly susceptible to a wide range of opportunistic infections and other diseases (Hammett 1987a). Persons with AIDS become vulnerable to various health crises and illnesses that are normally not life-threatening to people with healthy immune systems.

AIDS is caused by a virus called **Human Immunodeficiency Virus,** or more commonly, HIV. AIDS infects and destroys white blood cells, which are normally used by the body to fend off infections and illness. Infection with the virus HIV does not immediately lead to AIDS. Many persons infected with the virus remain in perfectly good health for years without developing symptoms. It is not known whether all will actually develop AIDS. Others may grow more susceptible to infection and illness by varying degrees. These complications and illnesses are sometimes referred to as **AIDS-related complex** (ARC).

Although drug experiments and research are ongoing, and the disease is preventable, at this writing AIDS, once active, is almost always fatal (Koop 1987; Hammett 1987b). During the past several years the number of cases reported to the Centers for Disease Control (CDC) has increased, but at a much slower rate than during the first few years of the epidemic (1981–1983). During these early years the number of identified cases doubled every six months. By the summer of 1987, the doubling took fourteen months. Approximately 41,730 AIDS cases had been reported in the United States by September 1987 (*Medical and Health Annual* 1988). The estimated number of Americans infected with HIV by 1987 was 1.5 million, and researchers believe that the number of AIDS cases may reach as many as 270,000 by 1991. To date, there has been no evidence of prolonged remission of AIDS, and most patients have died within two or three years after diagnosis of their disease.

Transmission of AIDS

Although highly lethal if contracted, the AIDS virus is actually quite difficult to transmit outside of the body. The virus can be destroyed and disinfected by heat, many common household cleansers, bleaches, and by washing with soap and hot water.

In a manner remarkably similar to the transmission of hepatitis-B, the AIDS virus is primarily transmitted through exposure to contaminated blood, semen, and vaginal secretions. The indisputable means of transmission are through unprotected sexual intercourse and sharing of hypodermic needles among intravenous drug users. Until recently, women in the U.S. who were not IV drug abusers were not believed to be at much risk for HIV infection (in sharp contrast with several underdeveloped nations). However, today, it is clear that they are very much involved in the overall picture of AIDS, and potentially in transmission to their children

(*Medical and Health Annual* 1989). In 1987 the CDC estimated that 113,250 American women were infected, representing more than 7 percent of CDC estimated cases of infection. Although there have been no studies, much debate continues over the question of whether the risk of transmission is greater from males to females or vice versa.

In addition to changes in attitudes about women and AIDS, CDC's view about infant risk of AIDS has recently altered. In 1988, 884 cases of AIDS in children under five had been reported to the CDC (*Medical and Health Annual* 1989). The majority of these babies (78 percent) were infected by their mothers who were IV drug abusers or women who had sexual relations with infected men—many of whom were themselves drug abusers. According to the *Medical and Health Annual* (1989) these infected children tend to be concentrated among minority groups and certain geographic areas; 89 percent were born to blacks or Hispanics, and 70 percent of the infected babies were born in New York City, Newark, New Jersey, and Miami, Florida.

Finally, although in enormously decreased numbers since the mid-1980s, transmissions from contaminated blood used in transfusions during operations continue to occur.

The AIDS virus simply cannot be transmitted through casual contacts, such as sharing kitchen utensils, kissing, having saliva spat upon the skin—even skin with cuts or abrasions—shaking hands, urine splashes, or other forms of nonsexual contacts (Hammett 1987b; Berg and Berg 1988; Lifson 1988; Blumberg 1990). There have been no documented cases of police officers, paramedics, correctional officers, or firefighters becoming infected during the course of their normal duties.

In fact, with the exception of a very small number of health care workers who attribute their contracting of AIDS to having been accidentally pricked with contaminated needles or other exposures to blood, there are no reports of AIDS transmissions from occupational activities (Ross and Krieger 1989). Even

among these instances, there has been some controversy over whether some of these health care workers may not also have fit known high-risk groups (intravenous drug users, homosexuals, or sexually active with partners carrying the AIDS virus).

In spite of increasing numbers of identified cases of AIDS, the early breakdown of groups at highest risk to contract HIV has remained exceedingly stable. According to the U.S. Centers for Disease Control, as of March 1987, homosexual and bisexual males remained the largest category of persons at risk and account for 66 percent of all identified cases. Intravenous drug abusers composed the next largest risk category, accounting for 17 percent. Another 8 percent were represented by persons who are both intravenous drug abusers and homosexual or bisexual males. Heterosexuals whose partners fell into one or another of the preceding categories comprised 4 percent of known cases. Hemophiliacs and transfusion recipients who contracted HIV represented 1 percent and 2 percent of the cases, respectively. The remaining 4 percent represented cases of incomplete information about risk due to death or refusal to identify with a particular category.

Most research continues to show that heterosexual transmission of HIV infection is still considerably less common than among other higher risk groups in the U.S. and Europe (*Medical and Health Annual* 1989; 1990). Women, children, and heterosexual transmissions, however, do represent a substantial portion of the evolving global AIDS problem, especially in underdeveloped nations.

Law Enforcement Implications

AIDS has rapidly become a central concern in the law enforcement community. In one recent study of 35 police agencies, 33 reported that officers had voiced serious concerns about AIDS and their duties as officers (Hammett 1987b). This same study indicates that patrol officers from 94 percent of the departments surveyed reported anxiety about their potential exposure to AIDS.

Most police academies nationally now offer training designed to educate new police officers in AIDS safety. In some academy curricula, this may arise as part of the First Responder/First Aid training. In other acad-emies, this may arise as a separate and specific course or series of lectures (Berg 1990). Many department in-service programs for officer survival have also augmented the training to include AIDS safety. A variety of AIDS-related concerns to law enforcement personnel and some appropriate educational elements are shown in Table 13.4.

TABLE 13.4   AIDS-Related Law Enforcement Concerns and Answers

QUESTIONS OR CONCERNS:	ANSWERS:
Are human bites likely to result in transmission of HIV?	Usually, the person doing the biting receives the victim's blood, and not the reverse. Since saliva is a poor medium for the HIV virus to be transmitted, it would seem most unlikely that a bite alone will result in infection. The wound should be made to bleed and then washed thoroughly.
Can spitting transmit the disease?	Viral transmission from saliva alone has received no support in the research literature. It is virtually an impossibility.
Do urine or feces contain the HIV virus of infected people?	Although HIV virus has been identified in the urine of infected persons, the concentrations have been so small that transmission from this medium is usually judged impossible. There has been no documentation of HIV virus being found in feces.
Will cutting oneself with a contaminated tool, or puncturing oneself with a contaminated needle necessarily lead to HIV infection?	Although even a single puncture could result in transmission, the majority of "needle studies" show risk of infection is very low. Receipt of repeated punctures or cuts from sharp objects contaminated by the HIV virus, however, may lead to infection with the virus.
Can one become infected during CPR or when performing other first-responder activities?	Although there are only minimal risks that one will become contaminated by performing CPR, masks and airways are strongly urged. During other first-responder activities, officers should be careful to avoid blood-to-blood contacts, and should keep open wounds covered. Rubber gloves are also strongly recommended.
Are transmissions possible from casual contacts such as kissing, sharing food utensils, hand-shakes and the like?	There have been no documented cases of AIDS transmission as a result of solely casual contacts.
Is it possible to become contaminated by touching dried blood?	There have been no instances in which contamination has been traced to exposure to dried blood (such as during crime scene investigations). The very process of drying appears to inactivate the virus. Nonetheless, caution dictates wearing protective gloves and masks if the potential contact with even dried blood is great.

Stress from Perceptions of AIDS

There are essentially three areas where the threat of AIDS transmission operates as a stressor for law enforcement officers. These anxiety producing situations include street apprehensions, the lock-up, and during first responder calls.

Street Apprehensions.   Whenever an officer finds it necessary to make a formal arrest, there is the possibility of resistance or assaultive behavior on the part of the offender. As indicated in the preceding section, many of the injuries sustained by police officers each year occurring in connection with such apprehensions are from personal weapons—including teeth. The fact that it is extremely unlikely that for an officer to become contaminated from a simple bite wound from an AIDS-infected person is of little comfort to most officers (Berg 1990).

In fact, it has been suggested by some researchers that for such a bite wound to have serious potential for contamination, the assailant would need to have a mouthful of contaminated blood and bite with sufficient ferocity to assure some of the contaminated blood gained entry into the officer's bloodstream. Although the HIV virus has been clinically isolated in saliva and tears, it is in such low concentrations as to render them ineffective as transmissions media (Berg 1990; Blumberg 1990).

Police Lock-ups.   Another area of concern for many law enforcement officers involves police lock-ups and holding cell facilities. In addition to fears about bites and other assaults, officers tend to be anxious about an AIDS-infected person's threats or attempts to intimidate other prisoners. Also, there are concerns about contamination from being intentionally splashed with urine or spat upon by AIDS-infected prisoners. As with saliva, urine, while carrying very low concentrations of the HIV virus, is an unlikely transmission me-

dium. No documented cases of AIDS have been linked to contaminated urine being splashed on someone.

First Responder Calls.   First responder calls, or the giving of immediate and temporary first aid to a victim, are fairly common for police officers. In some jurisdictions, local police agencies also house primary paramedic response teams or operate emergency ambulance services. Among the most stress producing elements associated with fear of AIDS transmission involves cardio-pulmonary-resuscitation (CPR).

Even before the threat of AIDS contamination, performing CPR on people was somewhat problematic for many law enforcement officers. For example, it is not uncommon for persons to vomit as they regain consciousness following CPR. In some situations, the vomit may contain blood as well as stomach contents. Because of this, a variety of air-ways, and mouth-masks with filters and one-way valves are used. These one-way valves permit the officer to blow air in, but will not permit fluids from being expelled into the mouth of the officer—theoretically. Unfortunately, many officers remain dubious about the effectiveness of these masks even after repeated demonstrations.

Another element of anxiety related to first responder activities concerns the treatment of bleeding and bandaging of wounds. Here, the anxiety involves a fear of having contaminated blood come in contact with either one's skin or clothing. There are frequent instances when officers do come in contact with persons injured in an automobile accident, hunting accident, or during the course of some crime. Because of frequency, the potential for coming into contact with contaminated blood might be fairly high.

Since people with AIDS should not be expected to wear a large scarlet "A" around their necks, it is impossible to know when an injured and bleeding victim carries the AIDS virus. Like many health care facilities, police agencies have begun to adopt treatment protocols that assume that persons are AIDS-infected. Often this includes the use of rubber gloves and masks or air-ways when treating all persons. It may mean sterilizing areas on the ground where blood has spilled with bleach.

Handling People with AIDS: Agency Procedures

In 1986, police agencies began to respond to the fears and anxieties arising among law enforcement officers by issuing AIDS related training bulletins and protocols (The Minneapolis Police Department 1986; Skokie Police Department 1987; Baltimore County Police Department 1987). Typically, these notices were drawn from the agency's general communicable/infectious disease policies and guidelines and often borrowed heavily from procedures outlined for hepatitis-B.

Law enforcement officers, however, remain somewhat reluctant to provide hands-on service to known AIDS-infected persons. At this time there is no evidence of any police officer falling victim to AIDS strictly from performing police duties. Yet, the perception of risk about contracting AIDS is fast becoming among the most serious stressors facing law enforcement officers.

Ironically, while law enforcement is perceived by many potential police officers as fraught with risk and danger, AIDS seems somehow more ominous then many other threats officers must face. The moment an individual becomes a law enforcement officer, he or she assumes a certain amount of this risk. Few officers are injured and killed in the line of duty. Certainly, individuals who enter law enforcement as an occupation have weighed these risks. The anxiety about AIDS that many officers feel today, then, must be weighed along with other kinds of risks. To be sure, the fear of contamination does not free officers from their obligation to perform police duties.

It would be wrong for law enforcement agencies to foster an alarmist approach to the problems associated with AIDS. Perceptions of risk that officers maintain can certainly contribute to interference in their police functions. It would be equally ineffective, however, for agencies to foster too complacent an attitude or approach. The development and application of specific guidelines for officers to follow has been one appropriate step. Another important element, however, will be the educating of officers about real as compared to imagined risks.

Police Officers with AIDS

One of the questions often left unasked in discussions on AIDS and the police is, "What should be done about police officers who contract the disease?" Mark Blumberg (1989) suggests that historically, police agencies have not hired openly homosexual persons for police positions. Overt bans on homosexual applicants are both discriminatory and illegal in some states. In the past, institutional discrimination because an applicant was believed to be gay systematically prevented many homosexuals from entering policing. Even when departments did not openly or institutionally ban homosexuals, various elements in the recruitment and training of recruits may have been used as a means of screening out homosexual individuals (Blumberg 1989). Some agencies, however, actively seek homosexual recruits. San Francisco, for example, because of its large gay population, periodically recruits officers from the gay community (Shilts 1980, 32–33). Active recruitment of gay officers, however, occurs in very few police departments. As a result, it is unlikely that many practicing homosexuals would seek employment as police officers or manage to secure positions if they did. Although based upon conjecture, it seems likely that there are fewer secret or closet homosexuals employed as police officers than in other occupations (Blumberg 1989). As a result, the potential for members of this high-risk AIDS group, practicing homosexuals entering policing, is not very large.

The other possible high-risk group that might enter policing is intravenous drug users. Refusal to hire drug abusers would not create any legal problems for police agencies. It has become a common practice in many police departments to refuse employment to applicants who have ever used heroin, cocaine, and even marijuana. These refusals may even occur when the drug use was experimental and happened many years before applying to the department. Although this latter category of one-time, but discontinued, drug-user applicant has caused considerable policy debate among police administrators, no challenges of this position have yet occurred in the courts.

What we observe, then, is that police departments generally are employing very few persons who fall into the current high-risk for AIDS categories. In the face of this, it is understandable that police departments have not previously devoted a great deal of attention to the issue of police officers with AIDS. However, given that this disease is expected to continue on its general growth pattern over the next several years, infected police officers are potentially inevitable. Therefore, department policies concerning police officers infected with AIDS must begin to surface.

There are chiefly two major issues police administrators and communities need to address regarding their response to officers with AIDS. First, what threat does the infected officer actually present to colleagues or the community (Blumberg 1989)? Second, how are community residents likely to respond to an infected officer, should they learn of his or her illness? Because of the futuristic nature of this problem, we are forced to speculate on possible resolutions to these concerns.

Since it has been established that AIDS cannot be spread through casual contacts that officers typically have with one another, police administrators must work to educate co-workers of the infected officer in order to reduce their fears. In this regard, police organizations are really no different from other work places where AIDS infected personnel have been identified during the past several years. Through carefully planned training programs, many organizations have succeeded in reducing the fears of their employees.

Speculating on how the community might respond to the infected officer's presence is a bit more difficult. As previously mentioned, most daily work routines of police officers with coworkers will not extend beyond casual contacts with one another. This is not always the case with citizen-police situations. Police officers called to the scene of a traffic or industrial accident may have to assist people with serious gashes or open wounds. There is, therefore, a remote possibility that an infected officer could, under certain circumstances, contaminate the wounded person. Again, although possible, there as yet have been no recorded transmissions of the AIDS virus by contaminated persons administering first aid to someone. Nonetheless, educational programs sponsored by the police are likely the best method of allaying community residents' fears.

AIDS and the Law

In addition to considering general procedures for working with or handling offenders who may be AIDS victims, law enforcement officers must be mindful of the law as it relates to AIDS. The bulk of law related to AIDS derives from those statutes that relate to discrimination in work places and assembly in public places, while some also concerns privacy and confidentiality (Luxenberg and Guild 1989).

Most jurisdictions have made it illegal to be fired from one's job strictly because of AIDS. Typically, statutes provide that so long as an individual is able to perform the tasks for which he or she had originally been hired, the person is entitled to continue working. It also is unlawful in most jurisdictions to refuse retail services to an individual on the basis of their being believed to be infected with the AIDS virus.

Perhaps a more curious trend evolving in the law, however, involves the attempt to criminalize activities by persons known to have AIDS. For example, there have been several attempts to charge AIDS-infected prostitutes with attempted homicide when they engage in sexual acts without warning their clients. Similarly, there has been at least one instance where a California man who knew he had AIDS tried to sell his blood to a blood bank. He was arrested and charged with attempted murder although the charges were later dropped. Persons with AIDS who intentionally infect others have also been charged with assault (Associated Press 1987). One of the more publicized cases involved James Vernell Moore, who was convicted of assault in 1987. The facts of the Moore case are as follows: Moore was a federal prisoner being held in Rochester, Minnesota. Recently he had learned he was positive for HIV. Although he was fully aware of the deadliness of his disease and how HIV could be transmitted, he bit two correctional officers during a scuffle (*U.S.* v. *Moore,* 1987). Moore was found guilty of assault and on appeal, Moore's conviction was upheld (Luxenberg, Guild, and Dubner 1990).

On July 27, 1988 a military court found Private Adrian Morris Jr. guilty of two AIDS-related court-marital charges. Morris was convicted on charges of discrediting the Army and of sodomy with a former soldier. Morris had tested positive for the AIDS virus and subsequently failed to use condoms during sex. He was accused of threatening the health of his sexual partners by the military court (Doherty 1988). What impact the Morris case and the Moore case will have on future cases, and to what extent the law will criminalize such activities, will remain for the courts to determine. The real issue for society, however, is what role the government should play in producing criminal sanctions in the area of AIDS.

SUMMARY

This chapter began by introducing the notion of police work as a potentially hazardous occupation. The chapter points out that the actual dangers, while certainly real, may not be nearly as detrimental to the health of officers as their perceptions of these dangers. In other words, the idea of certain dangers produces among officers a powerful emotional effect called stress. In turn, stress may contribute to law enforcement officers' developing a variety of somatic and psychological afflictions.

Stress was described as creating problems in both the everyday life of many police officers, as well as during the performance of their police duties. In order to combat these stress-related problems, many agencies have begun to develop counseling programs. The chapter details how, in some agencies, these programs operate as integral parts of the medical unit. But, in some other agencies, the counseling programs are independent of organizational constraints and operate more as peer counseling programs.

Among the various coping strategies to which many officers have turned, alcoholism has long provided one means to adapt to stress. In fact, it was chiefly in an effort to treat officers with drinking problems that many of the early counseling programs began.

As if the traditional stressors of danger, boredom, shift work and the like were not sufficient, a new and potentially lethal stressor has recently arisen—AIDS. This chapter discusses the current knowledge about AIDS and its transmission and describes several important implications AIDS cases hold for law enforcement personnel. These implications include perceived risks associated with street apprehensions, police lock-ups, and first responder calls. The chapter concludes by suggesting the need to balance police officers' dysfunctional-alarmist panic about AIDS with comprehensive educational information about actual risks of contamination. These education programs, as the chapter indicates, are necessary both in the communities and police agencies.

REVIEW QUESTIONS

1. Why does the average person believe that police officers are killed in great numbers each year?

2. What are some of the elements many experts believe now contribute to occupational stress among police officers?

3. How might stressors associated with the family be distinguished from those that arise during police work itself?

4. What are some of the ways police officers cope with their stressful work? Are some stress-management strategies better than others?

5. How has AIDS contributed to creating a new stressor that adversely affects police officers?

REFERENCES

Albanese, Jay. *The Police Officer's Dilemma: Balancing Peace, Order and Individual Rights.* Buffalo, N.Y.: Great Ideas, 1988.

Associated Press. "AIDS Patient Who Bit, Guilty of Lethal Assault." *Kansas City Times* (June 25, 1987: A2).

Baltimore County Police Department, "Communicable Disease Policy Guidelines and Procedure." Towson, MD.: Department *Training Manual of Procedures,* 1987.

Bayley, David H. "The Tactical Choices of Police Patrol Officers." *Journal of Criminal Justice* 14 (1986): 329–348.

Bayley, David H., and James Garofalo. "The Management of Violence by Police Patrol Officers." *Criminology* 27, (1989): 1–26.

Bennett, Richard R. "Becoming Blue: A Longitudinal Study of Police Recruit Occupational Socialization." *Police Science and Administration* 12, (1984): 47–58.

Bennett, Richard R., and Theodore Greenstein. The Police Personality: A Test of the Predispositional Model. *Journal of Police Science and Administration* 3 (1975): 439–445.

Berg, Bruce L. "Police Officer Stress and AIDS." Paper presented at the American Academy of Criminal Justice Sciences. Denver, Colo., March 1990.

Berg, Bruce L., and Jill Berg. "AIDS in Prison: The Social Construction of a Reality." *International*

Journal of Offender Therapy and Comparative Criminology 32 (1988): 17–28.

Blackmore, John. "Are Police Allowed to Have Problems of Their Own?" *Police Magazine* 1 (1978): 47–55.

Blackmore, John. "Police Stress." In W. Clinton Terry III., ed. *Policing Society.* New York: Wiley, 1985: 393–99.

Blumberg, Mark. "The AIDS Epidemic and The Police." In Roger G. Dunham, and Geoffrey P. Alpert, eds. *Critical Issues in Policing.* Prospect Heights, Ill.: Waveland, 1989.

Blumberg, Mark. *AIDS: The Impact on the Criminal Justice System.* Columbus, Ohio: Merrill, 1990.

Cullen, Francis T., Bruce G. Link, Lawrence F. Travis III, and Terrence Lemming. "Paradox in Policing: A Note on Perceptions of Danger." *Journal of Police Science and Administration* 11 (1983): 457–462.

Cullen, Francis T., Terrence Lemming, Bruce G. Link, and John Wozniak. "The Impact of Social Supports on Police Stress." *Criminology* 23 (1985): 503–22.

Cullen, Kevin. "A Roll of the Dice Every Time." *The Boston Globe* (February 21, 1988): 1, 23.

Doherty, Tim. "Soldier Convicted," *USA Today.* (July 28, 1988: 3A).

Ellison, K.W., and J.S. Genz. "Police Officers as Burned-Out Samaritans." *FBI Law Enforcement Bulletin* 47 (1978):1–7.

Fried, Joseph P. "Officer Guarding Drug Witness Is Slain." *The New York Times.* (February 27, 1988): 1,34.

Fyfe James. "Police/Citizen Violence Reduction Project." *FBI Law Enforcement Bulletin* (May 1989): 19–23.

Goldstein, Herman. *Policing a Free Society.* Ballinger, Cambridge, Mass.: 1977.

Graf, Francis A. "The Relationship Between Social Support and Occupational Stress Among Police Officers." *Journal of Police Science and Administration* 14 (1985): 178–86.

Hammett, Theodore M. *AIDS and the Law Enforcement Officer: Concerns and Policy Responses.* U.S. Department of Justice, National Institute of Justice. Washington, D.C.: GPO, 1987a.

Hammett, Theodore M. *AIDS and the Law Enforcement Officer.* U.S. Department of Justice, National Institute of Justice, NIJ Reports No. 206. Washington, D.C.: GPO, 1987b.

Heiman, M.F. "Police Suicide." *Journal of Police Science and Administration* 3 (1975): 267–273.

Klyver, N. "Peer Counseling for Police Personnel: A Dynamic Program in the Los Angeles Police Department. *Police Chief* 50 (1983): 66–68.

Koop, C. Everett. *The Surgeon General's Report on Acquired Immune Deficiency Syndrome.* U.S. Department of Health and Human Services, Washington, D.C.: GPO, 1987.

Kroes, William H. *Society's Victim, The Policeman: An Analysis Job Stress in Policing.* Springfield, Ill.: Thomas, 1976.

Kroes, William H., Bruce Margolis, and Joseph J. Hurrell Jr., "Job Stress in Policemen." *Journal of Police Science and Administration* 2 (1974): 145–55.

Leonard, V.A., and Harry W. More. *Police Organization and Management.* Mineola, N.Y.: Foundation, 1987.

Lewis, Diane. "Police Arrest 2nd Suspect in Officer's Death." *The Boston Globe* (Sat. Feb. 20, 1988): 1,22.

Lewis, R. "Toward an Understanding of Police Anomie." *Journal of Police Science and Administration* 1 (1973): 484–90.

Lifson, Alan R. "Do Alternative Modes For Transmission of Human Immunodeficiency Virus Exist? A Review." *Journal of the American Medical Association* 259 (1988): 1353–6.

Linton, Ralph. *The Study of Man.* New York: Appleton-Century, 1937.

Loo, R., 1984 "Occupational Stress in the Law Enforcement Profession." Canada's Mental Health 10–13. Cited by Francis A. Graf in "The Relationship Between Social Support and Occupational Stress Among Police Officers." *Journal of Police Science and Administration* 14 (1985): 178–86.

Luxenberg, Joan, and Thomas E. Guild. "Health, Privacy and AIDS." Paper presented at the annual meeting of the American Society of Criminology, Reno, Nev., November 1989.

Luxenberg, Joan, Thomas E. Guild, and Robin A. Duber. "Criminal Liabilities in the Transmission of AIDS." Paper presented at the annual meeting of the Academy of Criminal Justice Sciences, Denver, Colo., March 1990.

Medical and Health Annual "AIDS," Chicago: Encyclopedia Britannica, 1988.

Medical and Health Annual "AIDS: The Pattern Is Changing," Chicago: Encyclopedia Britannica, 1989: 52–61.

Medical and Health Annual "AIDS," Chicago: Encyclopedia Britannica, 1990.

Merton, Robert K. *Social Theory and Social Structure.* New York: Free Press, 1968.

Minneapolis Police Department. "Infectious Diseases: What is AIDS?" *Training Journal Minneapolis Police Department.* No. 9. Minneapolis: Minn.: Minneapolis Police Department Training Unit, 1986.

Niederhoffer, Arthur. *Behind the Shield: The Police in Urban Society.* New York: Doubleday, 1969.

Reiser, Martin. *Practical Psychology for Police Officers.* Springfield, Ill.: Thomas, 1973.

Ritzer, George, and David Walczak. *Working: Conflict and Change,* 3d ed. Englewood Cliffs, N.J.: Prentice Hall, 1986.

Ross, Susan O., and John N. Krieger. "The Latest Studies on Occupational Exposure to HIV." *American Journal of Nursing* (November 1989): 1424–25.

Saper, Marshall. "Police Wives: The Hidden Pressure." *The Police Chief* 47 (1980): 28–29.

Schwartz, Jeffrey A., and Cynthia B. Schwartz. "The Personal Problems of the Police Officer: A Plea for Action," in William H. Kroes, and Joseph J. Hurrell, eds. *Job Stress and the Police Officer: Identifying Stress Reduction Techniques.* Washington, D.C.: GPO, 1975: 135–36.

Selye, Hans. *Stress Without Distress.* New York: Lippincott, 1975.

Shilts, Randy. "Police Come to Terms with the Gay Community." *Police Magazine* (January 1980: 28–36).

Skokie Police Department. "Acquired Immune Deficiency Syndrome." *Training Bulletin* No. 87–27. Skokie, Ill.: 1987.

Stratton, John B. "Police Stress, Part I: An Overview." *The Police Chief* 45 (1978): 58–62.

Territo, Leonard, and Harold J. Vetter. "Stress and Police Personnel." *Journal of Police Science and Administration* 9 (1981): 195–207.

Terry, W. Clinton III. *Policing Society.* New York: Wiley, 1985.

Thomas, William I., and Dorothy Swaine. *The Child in America.* New York: Knopf, 1928.

Violanti, John M., James R. Marshall, and Barbara Howe. "Stress, Coping, and Alcohol Use: The Police Connection." *Journal of Police Science and Administration* 13 (1985): 106–10.

Walker, Samuel. "Employment of Black and Hispanic Police Officers: Trends in Fifty Largest Cities." *Review of Applied Urban Research* 11 (1983).

Wallace, L. "Stress and Its Impact on the Law Enforcement Officer." *Campus Law Enforcement Journal* 8 (1978): 36–40.

Whitaker, Gordon P. "What Is Patrol Work?" *Police Studies* 4 (1982): 13–22.

CASE CITATION

U.S. v. *Moore*, 669 F. Supp. 289 (D. Minn., 1987), 846 F. 2d. 1163 (8th Cir. 1988).

CHAPTER 14

PROFESSIONALISM AND ACCREDITATION

In many contemporary police circles, "police professionalism" is a common topic. One hears it discussed at professional academic meetings, reads about it in both police trade and scholarly journals, and hears police administrators debating its merits or limitations. The underlying assumption in all these situations is that everyone enjoys the same meaning of the concept of police professionalism. There is the further assumption that full-fledged police professionalism represents better salaries, greater social status, and is highly desirable.

Chapter Fourteen begins with consideration of what we mean by a profession and how one might be classified a professional. The purpose is to examine whether police officers are truly professionals and whether such a status is as desirable as generally assumed.

To consider police professionalism and the professionalization of policing, Chapter Fourteen additionally examines the role played by police unions. Nearly three-fourths of all contemporary U.S. police officers are members of some type of police union. During the past decade or so, police unions have grown into powerful economic and political institutions that influence not only salary and related fringe benefits, but affect law enforcement policy in many ways. As Chapter Fourteen will discuss, the emergence of police unions may well be among the most significant developments in policing in the last seventy years.

Chapter Fourteen also considers a fairly new development in police professionalism, police agency accreditation. Although it has been less than ten years since the police agency accreditation movement began to take shape, over one hundred agencies have become accredited and nearly double that are in the process. Chapter Fourteen examines both the benefits and possible limitations of police agency accreditation.

Finally, Chapter Fourteen explores the growing tendency among police agencies to secure private contractors to fulfill one-time police functions.

INTRODUCTION: PROFESSIONAL POLICE OFFICERS OR POLICE PROFESSIONALS?

During the twentieth century, policing as a social institution has undergone many organizational reforms. Often when one thinks of these changes, one simultaneously thinks of administrative efforts to make the police more professional. One might even suggest that many of the police reforms of the recent past occurred because of intentional efforts to achieve police professionalism.

The next natural question is, exactly what is police professionalism? In fact, the nature of what police professionalism actually constitutes has been heatedly debated for decades. Many textbooks, including this one, credit O.W. Wilson and August Vollmer as having spurred modern American policing in the direction of professionalism. But an answer to the question—what does police professionalism represent?—is not always offered. This chapter will examine what is generally held by police researchers as a definition for police professionalism, as well as a number of related areas and factors. Among these related areas will be discussions of police unions, accreditation of police agencies, and the privatization of law enforcement services.

The Profession versus the Professional

To understand the movement toward police professionalism, one must begin with a distinction between the concept of a profession in the traditional sense and a professional in the vernacular sense. When one hears the term *profession* several specific occupations come to mind: doctors, lawyers, professors, and the clergy. These occupations have been long recognized as professions. Yet in everyday language we often speak about a much wider variety of jobs as professional. One regularly hears basketball players and other athletes called *professionals*. Similarly, it is common to call a professional plumber to install your boiler, and a professional electrician to hook up the furnace. The term professional, then, has come to represent two distinct categories of occupation. First, and as the term is used most often in common language, professionals are persons with specialized skills or training. Because these individuals possess specialized skills, they receive salaries for their expertise. In short, professionals are the opposite of amateurs.

The second usage of the term professional directs attention to the more traditional connotation of the word. In this second case, the term refers to a specialized, white collar occupation that requires considerable formal education, membership or entrance standards, a body of theoretical knowledge, adherence to a system of socially regulated rules or a code of ethics, and the ability to self-regulate and sanction members (Goode 1960, Ritzer 1972).

Beyond the traditional professions, several other occupations have emerged as new professions. These include such occupational categories as architects, social workers, teachers (elementary and secondary), and bankers and accountants. These new professions closely approximate the characteristics generally associated with the traditional professions. But, because high social status and prestige are commonly associated with the term profession, many occupations during the past several decades have sought to capture the title of professional. Police are a prime occupation that has diligently worked to this end. In spite of the effort, however, law enforcement has achieved little more than what might be called shadow-box professionalism.

Shadow-box Professionalism

The concept of shadow-box professionalism refers to the idea that some occupations attempt to professionalize by imitating attributes of more traditional professions. But rather than successfully replicating various necessary characteristics, shadows or near-replication occur. In some respects, there may be a surface resemblance to a profession, but one that does not consistently hold up under the light of scrutiny. The light removes the casting of shadows. In the case of policing, attempts to effect professionalization have met with both resistance and serious complications from within and without the law enforcement institution.

In the 1930s the International Association of Chiefs of Police (IACP) established a committee for the professionalization of police. This committee put forth the notion that a profession should consist of five elements:

1. An organized body of knowledge, constantly augmented and redefined, with special techniques based thereon.

2. Facilities for formal training in this body of knowledge and procedure.

3. Recognized qualifications for membership in, and identification with, the profession.

4. An organization which includes a substantial number of the members qualified to practice the profession and to exercise an influence on the maintenance of professional standards.

5. A code of ethics which, in general, defines the relations of the members of the profession to the public and to other practitioners within

the group and normally recognizes an obligation to render services on other than exclusively economic considerations. [Mannle and Hirschel 1988, 300]

Although the theoretical end of this plan may be quite noble and altruistic, the implementation is not. Typically, when the topic of police professionalism is discussed—even among police officers—financial compensation is a prime factor. The principal impetus to professionalize law enforcement has long been entangled with the attempt to increase the financial compensation for police work.

As a result, IACP's establishing of a code of ethics for police officers in 1957 tended to "window-dress" the general attempt to professionalize policing. Similarly, the establishment of uniform minimum standards for entrance did not actually begin to occur until sometime after 1964 and has not been fully accomplished yet. There also is little if any police theory that originates from the police professional exclusively. Rather, most police theory borrows from or identifies itself outright as originating from other fields and disciplines (psychology, sociology, and other cognate disciplines).

The question of whether policing is or should be considered a profession in the traditional sense, then, has been complicated by these and other factors. Among these other factors is the reality that policing involves both training and education and that these are not synonymous terms. In the case of training, police must acquire certain technical skills, such as how to direct traffic, how safely and accurately to use firearms, how safely and defensively to drive in high-speed pursuit situations, how to access information from a computer system, how to administer immediate first aid, and so forth.

In the second case, law enforcement officers must learn various cultural characteristics and theories about cultural value conflicts that may arise in the communities they police, how to use language and cogently write technical reports, how to think inductively, how to communicate effectively and supportively, how to assess certain criminal patterns leading to theories of criminal motivation or cause, and so forth.

Along some dimensions, law enforcement might merit elevation to the status of a traditional profession. For example, were one to separate municipal police from certain federal agencies, such as the Federal Bureau of Investigation, one might make the argument for the FBI as a near-profession. Similarly, one might separate line officers from administrative officers and suggest that the administrators may resemble a professional group. However, in both of these illustrations, the weight of professionalism rests heavily on non-police qualification, rather than on police qualifications. The FBI agents are near-professionals by virtue of their simultaneous membership in more traditional professional groups, such as lawyers, or new professional groups, such as accountants. Administrators are closer to a professional group by virtue of the new professional classifications of upper management administrators in general. In most respects, municipal law enforcement tends to be more trade-like than profession-like. As a consequence, many of the attributes of policing shadow, rather than duplicate, the usual requisites for a traditional profession. Although some people continue to argue that policing is evolving into a profession, the point may be moot.

It is without question that police officers are considered by most people to be professionals as compared to amateurs. This public attitude carries with it the impression that police officers are highly trained and skilled at their jobs. The social status of law enforcement personnel is never likely to achieve the same social plane as that of physicians, lawyers, or clergy. In short, policing may never exceed the level of a shadow-box profession.

Ritzer and Walczak (1986) similarly described policing and suggest at best it is a semi-profession. According to Ritzer and Walczak, professionalism is based more on a political (power) basis than it is on other issues. Police officers possess only a limited ability to control their clientele or to predict what situations they will find. This ability to plan systematically the activities of one's clientele is characteristic of more traditional professionals. For instance, when one arranges an appointment with a physician, one usually is given a date, time, and location for this meeting. The kinds of people police *are* capable of controlling typically possess little political efficacy. These kinds of people have been described by some researchers as the *underclass*. Ritzer and Walczak concluded that police can most accurately be characterized as free semi-skilled workers.

Yet, there seems to be a benefit from accepting policing as at least a shadow-box profession. Certainly, during the past twenty years, policing as an occupation has evolved into a better educated, more effective, and efficient work force. Characteristic of this evolutionary change is the growing emphasis in police academies on decision-making and problem-solving skills, rather than on offensive and defensive tactics. A serious emphasis also has been placed on formal education. Many jurisdictions now require patrol officers to possess a minimum of an associate's degree or two years of college as a basic requirement for hiring. For example, the municipal police department in Tallahassee, Florida requires a baccalaureate degree of all its entry-level officers. In Massachusetts, several attempts have been made to pass legislation that would financially reward officers entering a department with college credits or degrees and increasing current officers' salaries as the college credits accumulate.

A recent national study conducted by the Police Executive Research Forum (PERF) identified what police executives would like to see colleges and universities doing for current and potential police officers. Contrary to what some people might expect, the majority of police executives do not want colleges and universities to teach police skills. Instead, they want these academic settings to provide graduates with a balanced understanding of police officers' roles and responsibilities, democratic values, tolerance, and integrity (Sapp, Carter, and Stephens 1989, 1). The consensus is that a broad-based liberal arts curriculum should be part of every criminal justice program at U.S. colleges and universities.

Also, it was through the advances in professionalizing policing that nepotism and favoritism slowly yielded to civil service regulations for hiring and promoting officers. As the following section will detail, the ability of unions to take a foothold in policing also reflects an attempt to modernize and professionalize law enforcement.

Police Unions

Many authors have indicated the apparent relationship of police reform, police modernization, and attempts to professionalize policing (Niederhoffer 1969; Folgeson 1985; Walker 1983; Terry 1985; Skolnick and Bayley 1986). Each of these activities has made deliberate efforts to advance police practice and performance. As Terry (1985, 154) suggests, "The unionization of police forces has been difficult and traumatic." The basic arguments in favor of unions are labor, not professional ones. These have focused upon improved working conditions, equipment, and better wages. As a result, as efforts to advance police unions progressed, they inadvertently impeded efforts to gain recognition as a traditional profession. In order to negotiate status, positions, and wage levels, traditional professions typically have relied upon their associations, not unions and bargaining units.

Even excluding the issue of professions, there are several arguments that have been levied against police unions. First, it has been argued that police lose their right to strike

when they accept positions as public service employees. The explanation here, of course, is that there is enormous potential for harm to the public from the sudden suspension of policing services. Since threats of strike are the principal clout of a union, an immediate conflict emerges. A second argument concerns the ensuing problems that may arise between contractual negotiations between the union and administration, and the legal responsibilities of the police. For example, the union may prefer officers to work in safer environments, but setting such contractual limitations may simply be unenforceable, or prevent fair access to law enforcement protection. For example, if the union determined that some high-crime neighborhood was too unsafe for the officers to patrol, the union might negotiate to exclude this area in its contract with the city. If such a contract were negotiated, persons residing in these high-crime areas would not receive police protection.

A third argument sees placing unions in a negotiating position between police officers and police administrators as potentially undermining the authority of the administrators. If the union determines the agency policy, it, not the administrators are in charge.

In spite of the detractions, police officers across the country have organized into various fraternal orders, police benevolent associations, and out-right unions. Regardless of what one chooses to call them, these organizations are primarily collective bargaining agents for their membership— the principal activity of any union. Although threats of police strikes are administratively discouraged and are absolutely illegal, they are not always avoided. Under the guise of blue flu, by-the-book slow-downs, or, as recently occurred in a small Vermont town, a department-wide resignation, walk-outs and sick-outs among police do occur.

Historically, police strikes have occurred since as early as 1889, when the police of Ithaca, New York (five officers) walked off their jobs because their pay had been reduced from $12 to $9 per week (*"Police Labor Relations"* 1973, More 1985). In 1918 450 officers of the Cincinnati, Ohio police department walked off their jobs to protest the firings of four officers. The four had been fired for attempting to organize the officers and hold a meeting in order to discuss a salary raise. Finally, perhaps the most famous police strike is the Boston Police Strike of 1919, regarded as the first fully organized labor strike by police officers.

As with earlier police labor actions, the Boston police were challenging extremely low salaries, poor work conditions, long work weeks, and unresponsive administrators. Officers first formed the Boston Social Club, which was chartered by the American Federation of Labor (AFL). In itself, this action was a direct violation of the city's police policy and nineteen of the union leaders were summarily discharged. On September 19, 1919, in angry response to these firings, 1,117 officers from a full complement of 1,544 went on strike. So outraged by their action was Massachusetts Governor Calvin Coolidge, he fired and replaced all of the striking officers (Burpo 1971).

Although the firing of these 1,117 officers was quite tragic, a kind of silver lining to the dark cloud did surface. The Boston community had seen first-hand that the social and real property damage costs from a police strike were extremely high. As a result, the officers who replaced the strikers were hired at a salary level $300 a year higher than their predecessors. Also, a benefit package was established that included a pension plan and city-supplied uniforms (Burpo 1971). Finally, the Boston strike stood as a tangible illustration of the effects of a police strike for other cities and their police agencies and discouraged similar strikes.

Before World War II most police officers were fairly well off for poorly educated and unskilled laborers. Robert Folgeson (1985, 169) quotes a Washington patrolman who told a congressional committee that police officers were not "fit for anything except police duty or some kind of laboring work." The public attitude was that police officers received a sufficient salary, particularly since most supplemented it with various payoffs. The officers' complaints of "long hours and short pay" were regarded by most people as no different from those of other laborers working in factories, loading trucks, or doing similar manual work (Folgelson 1985).

During and particularly following World War II, the general complacency of officers and the attitude of the public began to change. As the war came to an end, many veterans began to enter policing. With these men came their middle class values, better educational levels, and greater demands for non-political promotions, improved salaries, and working conditions. Throughout the 1940s and early 1950s police salaries and benefits barely kept up with inflation and were often much lower than factory workers'. In the mid-1950s, salaries began to improve and in many parts of the nation began to rise faster than the costs of living. But many officers across the country still found it necessary to moon-light in supplementary jobs as painters, salesmen, and so forth (Folgeson 1985).

Officers' dissatisfaction with their working conditions led many to leave policing for private industry or federal agencies. This dissatisfaction turned into outrage and alienation during the late 1950s and throughout the 1960s. It was during this period that the American Civil Liberties Union (ACLU) began to call for the creation of civilian review boards to hear what seemed to be a growing number of complaints against police officers. Too, the 1960s saw what seemed like a record number of U.S. Supreme Court decisions that protected the constitutional rights of accused criminals.

In addition, the 1960s were marked by riots and civil unrest that made the nation's social problems—including poverty, racism, and sexism—impossible to ignore. One of the central themes of the 1964 presidential campaigns was law and order. This issue continued as a main theme throughout most of the remaining years of the 1960s, and resulted in President Lyndon Johnson's creating the President's Commission on Law Enforcement and the Administration of Justice. The commission carefully examined the role of the police in American society, as well as the standards and requirements of police officers in cities across the nation, allegations of corruption and brutality, and the public's responses to law enforcement officers.

Police officers nationwide grew discontent and frustrated with their role and the public's attitude toward them. In response to the enormous anger and accompanying feelings of helplessness in the face of these social changes, police unions swept the nation's large city departments—with the exception of those in the South. The unionization of the 1960s created an enormous reform movement within policing agencies. As this reform movement grew in momentum, another federal agency, the Law Enforcement Assistance Agency (later to be changed to "Administration"), or LEAA as it is more commonly referred to, was created (See Box 14.1). The central purpose of the LEAA was to aid in the solution of problems uncovered during the examination undertaken by the President's Commission on Law Enforcement. As part of the agency's work it established the Law Enforcement Assistance Program (LEAP), which provided grants of money for various police agency projects and programs. Also, LEAA worked for increased educational requirements among officers—and increased benefits for officers who achieved them. As a consequence, many of the nation's departments began to reward officers with increased salaries for returning to college and obtaining degrees.

But, the existence of LEAA was controversial almost from its inception. Detractors saw it as symbolic of the Nixon administration's law and order platform, which itself was viewed as a means of arming police with the means to suppress legitimate grievances (Feeley and Sarat 1980). Supporters defended the expenditures and policies behind these as necessary for reestablishing order and the role of police in society. In 1980, after its federal funding had been removed, the LEAA began to fall out of existence.

POLICE AGENCY ACCREDITATION

One example of a project that began with a LEAA grant is the Commission on Accreditation for Law Enforcement Agencies, Inc., (CALEA). The LEAA initially funded what it believed to be an innovative idea conceived by IACP (Raub and Van Zandt 1986). This initial funding amounted to just over $5 million, which derived from the Department of Justice through LEAA (Cotter 1983). The fund was to be distributed over several years ending in 1983, when it was expected that CALEA would be able to support itself through self-generated revenue as a non-profit organization (Diegelman 1983, Cotter 1983).

The original CALEA commission was composed of 21 members appointed by the executive boards of IACP (the International Association of Chiefs of Police), NOBLE (the National Organization of Black Law Enforcement Executives), NSA (the National Sheriffs Association), and PERF (the Police Executive Research Forum). This original commission included 11 individuals with practical law enforcement experience, and 10 citizens representing a fairly wide gamut of educational, business, and political interests (Cotter 1983, Raub and Van Zandt 1986). Members of this commission were to serve three-year terms.

The concept of accreditation has a long and rich history, although it is fairly new in the area of criminal justice and law enforcement. Accreditation developed in the United States when the New York state regents were established in 1787. The purpose of these regents was to monitor and certify that all colleges operating in New York state met certain

Box 14.1 _____

The Rise and Fall of LEAA

The growing need for police services during the turbulent 1960s and 1970s resulted in a large number of federally created investigations and commissions. In 1965 President Lyndon Johnson appointed the President's Commission on Law Enforcement and Administration of Justice. During that same year, Congress established the Office of Law Enforcement Assistance and Justice. Between 1967 and 1973 seven major national commissions were created to deal with the issues of crime control and the rising crime in America. Of considerable concern during this period was the civil unrest, riots, and violence in American streets. These activities had become commonly associated with antiwar and political demonstrations, and with what seemed to be a disproportionate number of political assassinations (See Finckenauer 1978).

Among the items identified as a problem by these investigations and commissions was the fragmented structure of law enforcement in America. Historically, policing has always been linked to local governments. As a result, police agencies, law enforcement practices, and procedures have traditionally reflected these fragmentations and regional nuances. However, crime is not subject to quite the same limitations. The fragmented structure and truncated nature of law enforcement efforts in America made systematic coordination on a larger than local scale quite difficult.

Chiefly in response to these conditions, Congress responded by establishing the Law Enforcement Assistance Administration (LEAA) in 1968. The agency was established under the auspices of the U.S. Department of Justice, under Title I of the Omnibus Crime Control and Safe Streets Act (Public Law 90–351, 90th Congress, June 19, 1968). LEAA was given a mandate to fund various research projects and programs to improve crime control and modernize the criminal justice system. Since law enforcement agencies were viewed as the primary crime deterrent tools in America, police agencies received a sizable piece of LEAA's multibillion dollar pie. Between 1968 and 1977 LEAA disbursed over $6 billion to various crime control programs and research projects. The majority of these recipients (61 percent) were police agencies.

Unfortunately, little planning or careful consideration was given to many of the funded projects.

A virtual funding frenzy occurred, and many departments obtained LEAA funds only to squander it on exotic or bizarre riot-control equipment (most of which arrived on the heels of the riot era).

Allegations began to surface concerning questionable projects and disproportionate levels of funds being allocated to police agencies. Critics quickly levied charges that while wild police projects were being funded, other segments of the criminal justice system were being ignored. By the late 1970s, a fairly strong movement to abolish LEAA had emerged. Plans were made for other federal agencies to take over some of LEAA's evaluation tasks, and LEAA was phased out of operation by 1982. Although LEAA did indeed fund some strange projects, it also provided an important and necessary federal–state–local link. Furthermore, LEAA did fund some very worthwhile criminal justice programs. For example, in Massachusetts funding permitted the experimental closing of juvenile institutions and their replacement with community-based facilities. Also, a number of prototype probation counseling, public defender, and police training programs were financed with LEAA seed money.

The abolishment of LEAA did not mark the elimination of all funding conduits for crime control and law enforcement improvement programs (such as LEAA's Law Enforcement Educational Program). Efforts to coordinate crime control on a larger than local scale were slowed, but not ignored. In 1980, Congress passed into law the Justice System Improvement Act. This act established the Office of Justice Assistance, Research, and Statistics (OJARS), which included the National Institute of Justice (NIJ), and the Bureau of Justice Statistics (BJS). The intention of the OJARS was to provide a funding source for criminal justice research and programming—but in a more limited way than had LEAA.

Particularly in the face of an increasing national drug problem in the United States, one can expect to see further growth in funding sources for criminal control. It even has been speculated that during the early 1990s, another attempt will be made to federally assist local law enforcement agencies, perhaps in the shape of a body one might call LLEA (Local Law Enforcement Agency).

basic standards. The New York State Legislature required that the regents make site-visits to each college and annually review the work of every college. From these visits and reviews, the regents were required to issue a written report to the legislature.

From these early educational roots, accreditation spread to other settings, such as hospitals and mental institutions, in order to assure comparable training for student doctors without interfering with the quality of patient care. During the 1950s, accreditation spread to other disciplines and professions and, in 1974, accreditation entered the criminal justice arena when the Commission on Accreditation for Corrections (CAC) was founded. The question that arises, of course, is what is *accreditation*? Stated in basic terms, accreditation is the formal recognition that an agency or institution conforms to some specific body of regulations and standards. In the section that follows, the accreditation of law enforcement agencies is discussed.

Throughout the nation, police agencies have become voluntarily involved in seeking accreditation for their departments. James Cotter (1983, 19), CALEA's first executive director, explains the accreditation of police agencies as follows:

> *Accreditation is a process by which agencies bring themselves into compliance with a body of established standards; it is also a status awarded to agencies that meet or exceed all requirements of the standard.*

The process of which Cotter speaks can be generally seen as constituting the initial attempts on the part of agencies to obtain accreditation. The status, on the other hand, involves being awarded the title of an accredited agency. Although few disagree about the improvements likely to occur during the process stage (improved equipment, entrance standards, training protocols, etc.), considerable controversy rages over the alleged benefits of obtaining the status of accredited. Also, now that over 90 agencies have obtained accreditation, another consideration must be faced by CALEA: reaccreditation. Since agencies are permitted to retain their accreditation status for only five years, a kind of second level must be developed. In this second process an agency must prepare itself to be visited again and maintain its minimum standards level.

Suggested Benefits of Accreditation

Proponents of accreditation believe that the standardization of police agencies across the nation demonstrates commitment to excellence and furthers the cause of professionalizing policing. Among its manifest goals, accreditation seeks to establish a minimum standard of performance for all police agencies at a level that until recently only a few departments had reached. A number of benefits are suggested by the Commission on Accreditation (See Box 14.2). For example, the commission suggests that a more detailed knowledge of an agency's policies and procedures among line officers will lead to better service and fewer indefensible liability suits. Written and objective criteria for promotions and administrative actions should result in improved job satisfaction. Improvements in police–community relations are expected, owing to neighborhood residents gaining confidence in the competence and professionalism of their local police officers. Other basic assumptions are that accredited police agencies will be more likely than unaccredited ones to provide both law enforcement and social services that exceed the minimum law enforcement mandates (Dearborn 1985, Smith 1987).

Detractions of Accreditation

Detractors of accreditation offer five major criticisms. First, they claim that standardizing all departments in the nation may be viewed as a first step in creating a national police force (Bartollas and Jaeger 1988, 158).

Box 14.2 _____

Benefits of Accreditation

The CALEA Commission claims ten principal benefits accrue to police agencies that complete the accreditation process. These benefits include:

1. Nationwide recognition of professional excellence;
2. Increased community understanding and support;
3. An elevation of employee confidence, and increased esprit de corps;
4. Improvement in confidence levels among state and local governmental officials;
5. "State-of-the-art" guidelines for evaluation and reform when necessary;
6. Clearly articulated and written proactive management systems, policies, and procedures;
7. Decreases or containment of insurance premiums;
8. Deterrence of liability litigation and increases in gaining out-of-court settlements;
9. Improved communications and coordination with neighboring agencies and other segments of the criminal justice community;
10. Increased access to information about modern law enforcement and training practices.

Adapted from Kenneth Medeiros, "Accreditation for Small Police Departments," *The Police Chief* 52(1985):40–41; and Kenneth Medeiros, "Accreditation as a Shield Against Liability and as a Protection for the Line Officer," presented during the Fifth Annual Conference on the Civil Liabilities of Law Enforcement Officials, Needham, Mass., 1988.

The fear of a national police force has long been a concern of the American people. Second, some critics view the broad and general minimum standards required by the commission as set too low. Often, these standards appear elastic to a point of non-existence since an agency may petition not to comply with various mandates if these standard requirements go beyond local laws, policy, or budgetary constraints. As a result, an agency that gains accreditation may actually remain riddled with inadequate protocols, incompetent officers, and substandard equipment.

A third and similar criticism is a nearly chauvinistic attitude concerning who should determine an agency's standards. Many police executives resent the implication that their rules and policies are not as good or better than those set by the commission (McAllister 1987). These executives suggest that in order to remain sufficiently flexible and generally applicable, many of the commission's standards require only the barest essentials for compliance. As a result, some police chiefs

feel they would be taking steps backward rather than forward by seeking accreditation.

A fourth criticism leveled against accreditation is that it may impede already progressive and modern departments from further progression. If local politicians see that the agency is able to achieve accreditation at its current level of training and performance, they may be reluctant to allocate funds to update equipment and technology, personnel needs, or advanced training.

Finally, and particularly in the northeastern regions of the country where police unions have grown enormously influential, line officers view accreditation with skepticism. Their general view is that accreditation benefits administrators by providing a shield against departmental liabilities, media attacks, objective-appearing mechanisms for sanctioning patrol officers, and similar management-benefits. But little benefit is seen for the line officers themselves.

In fact, many line officers view the increased educational expectations, additional training, and advanced technology and equipment demands as quite threatening. In these instances, officers may turn to their unions to protect them from what they perceive as liabilities and risks to the security of their jobs. Interestingly, a minority of agencies located in northeastern states have sought and obtained accreditation. The majority of agencies that have successfully completed the accreditation process are located in southern and midwestern states. Unions were less successful in gaining strong footholds in the South than they were in the North.

Perhaps the real question that remains is whether the status of accredited agency is actually as valuable as the process of its achievement. The history of police reform has witnessed resistance from within and without the justice system with virtually every change. Certainly, one element that may account for some of this resistance has been the concern and fear held by members over the perceived effects of a given change. If a particular alteration is viewed as beneficial and requires little or no effort on the part of officers, one can usually expect little internal resistance. These sorts of reforms may include such things as salary increases, new patrol cruisers, reimbursements for voluntary educational course work, or pension packages.

Yet, if the change is perceived as threatening one's position in the organization, one's ability to gain rank and raises, and involves learning new procedures or acquiring certifications and/or additional amounts of education, resistance is likely. For example, many police officers acknowledge the usefulness of canine teams when conducting building searches, body searches, bomb and drug sweeps, or tracking felons through rough terrain. Yet, serious resistance could be expected if many of these same favorably inclined officers were told they were joining canine teams. Such a change would require their attending a specialized training program, learning how to be a dog handler, working and caring for their dogs, and assorted financial expenses.

In some ways, the prospect of going through an accreditation process may be perceived by line officers as similar to being told they are joining canine teams. Put simply, they view it as a lot of time, effort, and risk in order to obtain little tangible personal gain. In fact, for some officers, the prospect of their agency undergoing accreditation is seen as one in which potential for loss may be far greater than for gain.

For instance, in order to obtain better work schedules, notice of promotion schedules, and even better positions on promotion lists, it is often who you know. The existence of even subtle old-boy power networks is sometimes uncovered during the process of accreditation. Once identified, these old-boy structures can be eliminated through objective, written policies on promotion and salary increases. As a consequence, department power-brokers may find themselves dethroned. Additionally, because accreditation tends to require increases in accountability, the process of obtaining accreditation may reveal pockets of corruption that had gone previously unnoticed or ignored.

What may be missed by many detractors of police agency accreditation is that once the accreditation status has been achieved, this is not truly an end in itself. This status is better viewed as a kind of holding category in a continuous process of reaccreditation. Viewed in this manner, the question of accreditation's worth as a status may be moot. The value of accreditation clearly rests upon the process of achieving it initially and maintaining it once obtained.

It may yet remain for the Commission on Accreditation to convince northeastern line officers—and their unions—that they, too, can benefit from the process of accreditation. To be sure, efforts to upgrade law enforcement training and performance standards on a national basis seem to offer benefits that far outweigh even the most strongly voiced criticism. As Police Chief John E. Granfield of Fairfax County, Virginia was quoted as saying, "Accreditation is to a police department what the Underwriters Laboratory tag is to an electric appliance" (McAllister 1987).

SUMMARY

This chapter began with an overview of professionalism and police reform during the twentieth century. Policing was examined in the light of traditional occupations, as contrasted to more vernacular understandings of the notion of professional. It was argued that while attempts have been made to professionalize policing, what has resulted amounts to little more than a reflection, or a shadow-box image, of law enforcement as a profession.

The effects of and from police unions were detailed. In this regard, unions were suggested to represent the labor, rather than the traditional professional image many law enforcement administrators sought.

The contemporary issue of police agency accreditation was also considered. Following a brief historical account of the origins of police accreditation, the chapter considered several potential benefits from undergoing the accreditation process. It was suggested that even when agencies fail to complete their accreditation process, they might benefit. In these cases, benefits were described in terms of increases in officers' educational and training levels.

REVIEW QUESTIONS

1. How might one distinguish between traditional professions (medicine, the clergy, etc.) and professionals?
2. What is meant by the statement, "Police possess a shadow-box professionalism"?
3. What role have police unions played in reforming policing? How effective have union innovations been?
4. What were the activities of the now defunct Law Enforcement Assistance Agency (LEAA)? How does the Law Enforcement Assistance Program (LEAP) relate to LEAA?
5. What are some of the benefits associated with the process of acquiring police agency accreditation? What are some of the drawbacks?

REFERENCES

Bartollas, Clemens, and Loras Jaeger. *American Criminal Justice.* New York: Macmillan, 1988.

Burpo, John H. *The Police Labor Movement.* Springfield, Ill.: Thomas 1971.

Commission on Accreditation for Law Enforcement Agencies, Inc., *Accreditation Program Book.* Fairfax, Va.: CALEA (June, 1985).

Cotter, James V. "Accreditation Programs for Law Enforcement Agencies." *The Police Chief* 50(March 1983):65–68.

Dearborn, David. "Police Department Aiming for National Accreditation." *The Glastonbury Citizen* (May 2, 1985:6).

Diegelman, Robert F. "Accreditation for Law Enforcement," *The Police Chief* 50(February 1983):1819.

Feeley, Malcolm M., and Auston D. Sarat. *The Policy Dilemma: Federal Crime Policy and Enforcement 1968–1978.* Minneapolis: University of Minnesota Press, 1980.

Finckenauer, James O. "Crime as a National Political Issue: 1964–1970, from Law and Order to Domestic Tranquility." *Crime and Delinquency* 24(1978): 13–27.

Fogelson, Robert. "Unionism Comes to Policing." In W. Clinton Terry III, ed. *Policing Society.* New York: Wiley, 1985.

Goode, William J. "Encroachment, Charlatanism, and the Emerging Profession: Psychology, Sociology and Medicine." *American Sociological Review* 25(December 1960): 902–14.

Mannle, Henry W., and J. David Hirschel. *Fundamentals of Criminology* 2d ed. Englewood Cliffs, N.J.: Prentice Hall, 1988.

McAllister, Bill. "Spurred by Dramatic Rise in Lawsuits, Police Agencies Warm to Accreditation." *The Washington Post*, (March 17, 1987):A7.

Moore, Mark H., and Robert Trojanowicz. "Corporate Strategies for Policing." *Perspectives on Policing. Washington, D.C.: U.S. Department of Justice*, 1988.

More, Harry W. Jr., ed. *Critical Issues in Law Enforcement.* Cincinnati, Ohio: Anderson, 1985.

Niederhoffer, Arthur. *Behind the Shield: The Police in Urban Society.* New York: Anchor, 1969.

"Police Labor Relations." *IACP Public Safety Labor Reporter* (1973). Cited in Harry W. Moore Jr., ed. *Critical Issues in Law Enforcement.* Cincinnati, Ohio: Anderson, 1985, 144.

Raub, Richard A., and Jack Van Zandt. *Illinois Department of State Police. First Accreditation of a State–Wide Law Enforcement Agency: Accreditation of the Illinois Department of State Police.* Illinois, 1986.

Regoli, Robert M., John P. Crank, and Robert G. Culbertson. "The Consequences of Professionalism Among Police Chiefs." *Justice Quarterly* 6(1989):47–67.

Ritzer, George. *Man and His Work: Conflict and Change.* New York: Appleton–Century–Crofts, 1972.

Ritzer, George, and David Walczak. *Working: Conflict and Change* 3d ed. New Jersey: Prentice Hall, 1986.

Sapp, Allen, David Carter, and Darrel Stephens. "Police Chiefs: CJ Curricula Inconsistent with Contemporary Police Needs." *ACJS Today* 7(1989):1.

Skolnick, Jerome H., and David H. Bayley. *The New Blue Line: Police Innovation in Six American Cities.* New York: Free Press, 1986.

Smith, Robert. "Accreditation: Impact on Police Departments." *The Police Chief* 54(March 1987):37–38.

Terry, W. Clinton III. *Policing Society.* New York: Wiley, 1985.

Walker, Samuel. *The Police in America.* New York: McGraw-Hill, 1983.

CRIMINALISTICS AND THE POLICE

Criminalistics, or the scientific investigation of crime, has markedly grown during recent years. In part the growth has been prompted by scientific breakthroughs since World War II and in part by the infusion of federal support for scientific and computerized law enforcement projects. As Chapter Fifteen outlines, much of criminalistics centers on the collection, preservation, and transfer of objects and information as evidence in a criminal investigation.

    This chapter focuses on the nature of evidence and the concept of admissibility or inadmissibility of evidence. As Chapter Fifteen will describe, evidence can be multifaceted. Some evidence may be rendered by someone who has just witnessed a crime, while other evidence must be interpreted through various scientific, investigative techniques. Some evidence is large and obvious, like a gun or a broken pane of glass. Other pieces of evidence, or "microtraces," are too small to see adequately with the human eye alone. Yet, all may contribute to explaining how a crime was committed or identifying a suspect.

Because criminal investigation technology has grown more sophisticated, police and prosecutors have grown more dependent upon persons with special technical knowledge. These forensic experts, as they are known, are necessary both during the investigation of crimes and in courtrooms to explain their findings to jurors. As Chapter Fifteen will detail, some forensic experts have earned legitimate credentials and expertise and are able to make necessary interpretations of technologically sophisticated elements of evidence. Unfortunately, there are also many charlatans, who pretend to have specialized training and/or credentials they do not possess. Chapter Fifteen examines these forensic experts and their potential usefulness in criminal investigations.

This chapter also examines the growing tendency of police agencies to use computers in their crime investigations. Even when a small agency is unable to afford its own computer resources, computer access is becoming more available through pooling or state agencies sharing their resources.

INTRODUCTION: FORENSIC SCIENCE AND SCIENTIFIC INVESTIGATIONS

Criminalistics, or what may be more broadly referred to as forensic science, can be defined as the scientific investigation of crime. Stated simply, forensic science involves the use of various natural sciences (chemistry, physics, biology), photography, and computers to solve crimes and identify criminals. Patrol officers typically do not conduct forensic examinations at crime scenes. When forensic examinations are required, a team of specialists is called to the scene. Nonetheless, police officers can be profoundly affected by the work of forensic science.

In some crimes, forensic science plays a major role in establishing that a particular implement was used in the commission of a crime. In other cases, various items identified by forensic technicians may lead police to the individual who committed a crime. In still other cases, forensic science never enters the picture. Unlike many television shows would have you think, not every lawyer has a forensic scientist on the payroll. For that matter,

most lawyers are not amateur criminalists. Similarly, the police seldom locate a clear set of fingerprints carelessly left on the telephone or murder weapon. Police also are not likely to rush in with a forensic team every time a home or business is burglarized.

Unfortunately, television shows have created a great number of misconceptions and misunderstandings about what police forensic labs can accomplish. Although some of the technologies depicted on television can certainly be used by forensic laboratories in some large metropolitan cities, most of the sophisticated techniques are beyond the budgetary reach of the average town or municipal department. Although the technology may exist, the costs of certain services mean they are used for only major crimes and not more mundane ones.

This chapter will discuss the general area of forensic science and its role in law enforcement. The chapter will begin with a brief description of the origins of forensic labs in the

United States. Next, this chapter will consider the nature of evidence and how it is collected. Following this, the chapter will examine some of the major evidence-gathering strategies used during crime-scene investigations.

The Origin of American Forensic Laboratories

The United States entered the field of forensic laboratory investigations in approximately 1929. It was during this year that Chicago witnessed one of the most vile and bloody gangland, execution-style murders recorded, commonly referred to as the St. Valentine's Day Massacre. Seven Chicago hoodlums and their associates were lined up against a brick wall and sprayed for several minutes with rounds fired from machine guns, shot guns, and .45-caliber automatic pistols (Wilson 1975).

Several witnesses reported that they had seen men carrying weapons escape from the scene in what appeared to be police cruisers and that they were wearing some sort of uniform. The community leaders of Chicago were appalled. In their attempt to restore faith in local law enforcement, civic leaders established a special coroner's jury to investigate the circumstances of the crime and allegations of the witnesses.

Among those appointed to this special coroner's jury was Bert A. Massey, a local businessman and financier. With Massey's financial backing, Col. Calvin Goddard, an independent forensic consultant, was brought into the case. Goddard maintained a small crime laboratory in New York City and by 1929, when he was summoned to Chicago, had already established himself as an expert in firearms (Wilson 1975).

In cooperation with the special coroner's jury, Goddard recounted an extremely complete description of the slaying of those seven individuals on St. Valentine's Day, based on his examination of the physical evidence collected at the scene. His evaluation was published in the first issue of the *American Journal of Police Science* (Goddard 1930) [This Journal was later published as a section in the prestigious *Journal of Criminal Law and Criminology*, which subsequently split into two separate journals].

The law enforcement community and Massey, were so impressed with the accomplishments of Goddard that they urged him to move permanently to Chicago. As inducement, Massey offered to assist financially in establishing a modern crime laboratory. Goddard agreed and, with the $125,000 donated by Massey, established his forensic laboratory at the Northwestern University Law School.

Goddard hired a full-time staff and special consultants from across the United States who had already established respected careers in law enforcement and various aspects of forensic science. Some of the more noteworthy among them included Leonarde Keeler, credited as one of the early pioneers in polygraphy; Col. Seth Wiard, a firearms expert of considerable reputation; Albert Osborn of New York, often regarded as the father of handwriting analysis identification; and August Vollmer of Berkeley, California, regarded in 1930 as the leading expert in law enforcement administration, methods, and systems.

Northwestern remains today a leading American university in the field of criminalistics. Officers from across the nation are trained in accident-scene reconstruction and traffic control, as well as other forensic areas.

During their nearly sixty years of existence, American crime labs have been controlled by various individual state and local police agencies. These labs resisted guidance or control from the federal government. In time, these labs became extremely individualistic, reflecting the interests and priorities of local police officials and the often limited scientific qualifications of the personnel who staffed them. The criteria used by each lab to hire personnel, examine evidence, and validate findings were unique to each laboratory. At least in part, this explains the lack of consistency among crime labs across the nation in terms of capabilities, quality controls, and expertise of personnel.

Evidence

In every criminal court case, two opposing sides present arguments in an attempt to demonstrate the guilt or innocence of the defendant. The state, through its agent the prosecuting attorney, will attempt to demonstrate "beyond a reasonable doubt" that the defendant committed all elements of the charges levied against him or her. In turn, the defense will endeavor to refute these charges and cast at least some reasonable doubt as to the guilt of the client (the defendant).

The material the prosecuting attorney will use to demonstrate the state's argument, and that the defense attorney will attempt to discredit, is derived from **evidence**. Evidence, for the most part, arises as one of two major types, **direct** or **indirect evidence.**

Direct Evidence. Direct evidence typically is viewed as *proof in itself* of the guilt or innocence of the defendant. In terms of implementation, this means some type of eyewitness testimony concerning the crime at hand. For example, assume that two men, Mr. Jones and Mr. Smith, are in a bar arguing. Jones draws a gun from his belt and fires it at Smith in the presence of the bartender. Jones drops his gun and flees the bar. Any official statement given by this bartender concerning what he saw will be direct evidence against Jones.

But what if the bartender had gone to the storeroom while the two men were fighting, heard a shot, and returned to find Smith on the ground bleeding and Jones gone? The bartender certainly could offer direct evidence concerning the argument between the two men, which he witnessed, and could even place Jones in the bar just prior to the shooting. But the bartender could not provide direct evidence that Jones shot Smith.

Obviously, prosecutors cannot rely upon only eyewitness testimony. Fortunately, various kinds of indirect pieces of physical evidence can also be used to build a case against the defendant. For example, in our illustration of the barroom shooting, it may be possible to identify Jones' fingerprints on the gun. This piece of physical evidence, in addition to the bartender's description of the events leading up to his hearing the shot fired, may be sufficient to convince a jury that Jones is guilty of shooting Smith.

Indirect Evidence. Stated simply, physical evidence refers to indirect or circumstantial pieces of information. In other words, it is evidence that in itself cannot demonstrate the guilt or innocence of the defendant. Nonetheless, physical evidence does provide the pieces of the puzzle that, once put together, form a picture complete enough to show a defendant's guilt or innocence. The old adage that "you can't get a conviction with a case built entirely on circumstantial evidence" is untrue. In fact, a good many felons sitting in prison can attest to the invalidity of that saying.

In many crimes, unlike the illustration of Jones shooting Smith, all that the police have is a victim and a crime scene. If it is a major crime, such as homicide or robbery of a large sum of money, a forensic team will be called in to examine the crime scene. The identification of various pieces of physical evidence, in fact, is viewed by many law enforcement agents as more reliable than an eyewitness who can always lie, make mistakes, or have a change of minds. But physical objects, imprints, and traces of various substances cannot by themselves lie.

Naturally, the reason that physical objects cannot lie is they cannot speak. In order to hear what physical evidence has to say about a crime, law enforcement agencies and the courts must rely upon experts. These forensic experts or criminalists, as they are sometimes called, are charged with the responsibility of explaining what various pieces of physical evidence mean. Forensic experts, in an ideal sense, are persons with specialized training and experience in a number of different scientific and academic areas. Using their various expertise, these experts decipher otherwise silent pieces of evidence for police officers and/or courtroom judges and juries.

Although police officers have a wide variety of specialized skills, most police officers are not adequately trained to serve as forensic experts. As a result, police officers often must rely upon forensic experts to assist in determining how some piece of evidence connects a suspect to a crime. Forensic experts are also used in court to demonstrate the guilt or innocence of a defendant based upon various pieces of evidence.

Truth and the Forensic Scientist: The Delicate Balance

One would assume that considerable care must be taken with regard to who is awarded forensic-expert status. Regrettably, as Richard Saferstein (1988) points out, all too frequently unqualified persons represent themselves as forensic experts of one sort or another. This is particularly unfortunate since many forensic experts actually do possess considerable knowledge and expertise. Their examination and explanation of some piece of evidence might mean the difference between finding an innocent defendant guilty or not guilty. The shadow of doubt about the legitimacy of some experts, therefore, should not be seen as invalidating the enormous good provided by the majority of forensic experts.

With this caveat in mind, the following section will consider several facets of illegitimate forensic experts. Saferstein outlines two major categories of falsely qualified forensic experts—what he calls "mountebanks." These two categories include the *academites* and the *careerists*.

Academites. The academites are individuals who have (or claim) to have various academic credentials. In some cases their degrees may not exist at all, while in other situations their academic titles and accumulation of association memberships may simply not be applicable to their claimed expertise. Or, their credentials may derive from unaccredited institutions (mail-order diploma mills).

Saferstein (1988, 7–8) details the exploits of several academites, including Milton V. Kline. In the case of Kline, his credentials as a Ph.D. in clinical psychology from Pennsylvania State University were completely bogus. Yet, Kline had a fairly successful career as a court-room forensic expert in hypnosis. His several celebrated cases include his testimony at the 1979 pre-trial hearing of Theodore (Ted) Bundy who was accused of killing a 12-year-old Lake City, Florida girl, Kimberly Leach. Kline had been hired by Bundy to refute the testimony offered by a state's witness under hypnosis. Ironically, Kline questioned the level of training that the state's expert on hypnosis had obtained.

In 1980, newspapers in New York City reported that Kline had been hired by attorneys defending Mark David Chapman, the man who shot ex-Beatle John Lennon. Kline was to assist in the development of Chapman's insanity defense (Saferstein, 1988). It was the the alertness of the state's prosecutor in this case that proved to be Kline's downfall. As the prosecutor read over Kline's alleged credentials, he noticed one particularly interesting item. Kline had listed that he was a "visiting teaching faculty of forensic hypnosis at the FBI Academy in Quantico, West Virginia." However, the FBI's Academy is not located in West Virginia, but rather in Virginia. Kline's error aroused the prosecutor's suspicions. With a little more digging, the prosecutor learned that all of Kline's alleged credentials appeared to be fabricated (Saferstein, 1988). In October of 1981, Kline pleaded guilty to an indictment in New York City concerning his falsified qualifications. In

March 1982, Kline was indicted and later found guilty in Florida of perjury during the Ted Bundy trial.

Careerists. The careerists, according to Saferstein (1988), are alleged forensic experts who augment their experiential and training qualifications by fiction and fraud. These may include false claims of training and certification at accredited laboratories, such as the FBI's. Or, a careerist might fabricate an affiliation with some agency or laboratory. In some instances, careerists possess legitimate academic credentials, but not those appropriate to their expert testimony, such as a Ph.D. in political science, with no formal training in firearms, offering expert testimony in a ballistics case.

Saferstein (1988, 7) points to R.A. Steindler as "the granddaddy among careerists, [who] incautiously put himself in the forefront of scientific creativity in the twentieth century." Steindler, among other accomplishments, claimed to have assisted in the development of penicillin, the Pap smear, and even the atomic bomb (See Box 15.1).

Courtroom Evidence

During the courtroom proceedings in a criminal case, various objects and items germane to the case and point at issue are admitted as pieces of evidence. Technically speaking, these objects and items are nothing more than objects until their admission in court as evidentiary elements. In common parlance, various items and information that will eventually be introduced in court are simply referred to as evidence, even preceding their admission.

For the most part, evidence can be seen as two principal types. First, there is direct and circumstantial evidence. Yet, there is a second category of evidence, sometimes neglected in law enforcement textbooks and chapters on criminalistics. This second type of evidence is commonly called **hearsay evidence.**

Hearsay Evidence

Hearsay can be understood to be verbal or written information offered by a third party to a situation. As example, let us return to our hypothetical barroom shooting involving Jones and Smith. Let us assume that the bartender went home after the shooting and fully informed his wife about the event he witnessed. During the night, perhaps because of the day's stress, the bartender suffered a heart attack and died. Although the bartender's wife, in fact, may be in possession of all the pertinent facts of the shooting, she cannot offer direct (testimonial) evidence. Any comment she makes regarding the shooting incident derives from her conversation with her husband. She is third party to the shooting.

However, law enforcement officers are keenly aware of the potential usefulness of a third party or hearsay witness. Often, an eyewitness will relate certain points of information to a third party that were omitted accidentally or intentionally when speaking with the police. In some cases, this may involve the location of some piece of physical evidence, such as a missing weapon or booty from a robbery. In other cases, the inadvertent statement might lead to another eyewitness.

In any event, while hearsay evidence is technically inadmissible in courtroom proceedings, it is sometimes used in court. In some instances the ploy is to get certain comments on the official court transcript. The purpose here may be to influence the jury. However, hearsay is frequently more useful for police officers investigating a case, since it can potentially lead to witnesses and evidence.

Exceptions to the Hearsay Exclusion

The rules of evidence as pertain to hearsay provide trial judges considerable latitude in dealing with hearsay evidence. Hearsay as described in the preceding section derives from the fairly rigid rules established in com-

Box 15.1 _____

The Unmasking of a Charlatan Expert

R.A. Steindler had been brought in as a firearms expert in the case of William Hanna. Hanna was accused of having shot Richard Wells in North Chicago on September 11, 1981. Hanna had been observed approaching the car in which Wells had been found shot dead. Hanna was also observed in possession of two hand guns (a .25-caliber automatic and a .38-caliber derringer). These indirect pieces of evidence were never disputed by defense counsel. The shape of the head wound on Richard Wells was consistent with that of contact wounds, where the pistol has made contact with the victim (stellate or star-shaped). The circumstantial evidence certainly pointed to William Hanna.

Hanna's defense was that a third person had fired at Wells from afar as Hanna was preparing to enter Wells' car. The central disagreement, then, was over whether Hanna's .38-caliber derringer was the weapon that fired the fatal shot and whether the shape and nature of the wound could be attributed to a contact wound (as opposed to a shot fired from some distance).

R.A. Steindler had been brought into the case by Hanna's defense attorney. Unfortunately for Steindler, the prosecuting attorney had done extensive homework on his credentials. Under *voir dire* of Steindler's qualifications, the prosecutor determined that Steindler had repeatedly lied about his professional experience and educational credentials. Also, Steindler had enhanced his publication record to make it appear that he had written articles and textbooks on firearms, when he had not. In the end, Steindler was discredited as an expert witness.

The question of how to punish unmasked char-

latans is not easily answered. Although criminal perjury charges may be used, conviction may be slow or impossible to obtain. Perjury is a difficult charge to prove. First, it must be demonstrated that the information conveyed under oath is untrue. Next, it must be shown that these falsehoods are material to the "point at issue" in the trial. In other words, if the trial concerns an expert's ability to identify ballistic characteristics and it is learned that he has lied about which undergraduate college had bestowed his baccalaureate degree (in order to enhance his overall image), this may not be material.

If, on the other hand, this expert has lied about alleged training and/or certifications or expertise in firearms, this would be germane and material to the "point at issue"—regardless of other, perhaps legitimate academic credentials. In addition to these elements, a successful prosecution for perjury typically requires the testimony of competent persons in the appropriate field, who can and are willing to attest to the lack of credentials the expert alleges exist (Saferstein, 1988).

In the face of these difficulties, time lags, and negative publicity for legitimate experts, many prosecutors seek alternative remedies. The obvious option would seem to be some sort of plea bargain. Yet, given the brazen attitudes and outrageous credentials put forth by many of these charlatans, one suspects that they must be informed about the perjury laws they flagrantly disregard. It seems likely that most successful charlatans are also aware of the difficulty a prosecutor will have in making a perjury charge stick.

Adapted from material offered in Saferstein, Richard, ed. *Forensic Science Handbook Vol. 2.* Englewood Cliffs, N.J.: Prentice Hall, 1988.

_____

mon law. However, there are times when evidence that technically qualifies as hearsay is nonetheless reliable and useful information. Because of this, the law has provided a number of exceptions to the exclusion of some type of hearsay evidence. Three of the more interesting exceptions include **previously re-**

corded testimony, dying declaration, and **admissions of guilt.**

Previously Recorded Testimony. Technically, the recorded (eyewitness) testimony of a witness offered at one trial proceeding is hearsay in a subsequent trial. In other words, the transcript of this previous statement constitutes a statement made out of the current courtroom, but intended to prove the truth of some assertion.

For instance, imagine that an armed robber has gone to trial and been found guilty. On appeal, the felon is granted a second trial. However, during the time between the first and second trials, the eighty-year-old eyewitness has suffered a stroke and died. In substitution for this actual witness, the court reporter from the first trial is called to read the witness's previously recorded statements. Under the previously recorded testimony exception to the hearsay rule, this evidence is admissible.

The rationale behind allowing this type of hearsay evidence is simple. First, the previously recorded testimony was given by the witness while under oath. Second, the transcript is a certified and accurate copy of this previously offered testimony. Third, the witness who uttered the testimony was available for direct and cross-examination when he or she originally offered the statement during the first trial. Finally, during a subsequent trial it is permissible to introduce into evidence the witness's examination from a previous trial in its entirety.

Dying Declarations. The exception to the hearsay exclusion for "dying declarations" was originally limited to homicide cases in which a party names the killer or describes the specific details of a homicide, including but not limited to admission of guilt. Under federal rules of evidence, dying declarations exceptions have been extended to civil cases as well (Waltz 1983).

The rationale behind permitting dying declarations was an assumption of intrinsic trustworthiness of such statements. As such, it was viewed as unnecessary to require cross-examination. The justification for such an assumption was built upon the belief that someone who knew they were dying and about to meet the maker would be truthful. Naturally, the validity of both the assump-

tion and the dying declaration itself are open to debate. To be sure, an individual might lie in order to gain revenge on some party. One also might question how reliable one's memory and sensibilities are moments prior to death. Finally, there is no assurance that the dying individual is religious or even believes in God—the central basis for justifying the truthfulness of the declaration.

Admissions of Guilt. The exception to the hearsay exclusion that permits admissions of guilt is an important point. It is permitted both in criminal and civil litigation and is frequently employed. In civil cases, this type of hearsay often involves the defendant's admission of negligent conduct during or immediately after the cause of action. For example, in an automobile accident, one driver might apologize to another, explaining that he or she had looked away from the road for only a moment to answer a spouse's question.

In a criminal case, admissions may be made to co-conspirators during casual conversations. For instance, following a gang fight, one youth brags to another that he was so fast while stabbing with his knife that no blood was left on it. He then describes in detail how he stabbed some particular youth to death. Later, at trial, the confederate may make a deal to testify against his partner in exchange for a reduced sentence or immunity from prosecution. In court, the confederate may testify to what the other youth has told him about the knifing.

One might be struck by the unusual circumstance of considering someone's own words as hearsay. Technically speaking, however, an accused's admission or confusion is classified as hearsay because it was offered outside of court.

Admissible and Inadmissible Evidence

In order for information, objects, or substances to be admissible as evidence, they must meet five basic requirements. First, they must have been obtained legally. Prior to *Mapp* v. *Ohio*

(1961) (See Chapter Seven, "The Exclusionary Rule"), materials obtained illegally by federal agents could be used during state trials. Today, evidence—regardless of how convincing or incriminating—will be disallowed if it has been obtained illegally.

Second, any material introduced in court must be germane to the point at issue (Dunning 1985). In other words, it must be of some value in either proving or disproving guilt of the defendant.

Third, the contribution made by admission of some material as evidence must be important. In short, admission of some material as evidence must strengthen or demonstrate either the prosecution or the defense's argument.

Fourth, material introduced in court as evidence must be competent. Competence, in regard to physical evidence, includes demonstrating several important elements. Among them is the documentation of an appropriate **chain of custody** for the material intended as evidence. When crime scenes are examined, various pieces of objects, substances, castings, imprints, and the like are collected. Between the time that these are collected at the crime scene or taken from the suspect, all pieces of potential evidence must be carefully tracked and written records maintained. These written records indicate who, when, and for what purpose the material leaves the custody of one individual and goes to another. If the chain of custody is broken at some point, the material in question may lose all value as evidence in court, since the question of tampering can be raised.

Another critical factor concerning admissible evidence is its correct identification and tagging. For example, it would be important that the gun submitted in evidence of the Jones/Smith shooting was indeed the gun taken from the floor of the bar. If it were merely a similar gun, but not the one from the bar, it simply would not be evidence in the case. Too, evidence must be in essentially the same condition as it was when originally obtained and identified. Naturally, certain al-

lowance is made in order to obtain samples of certain substances for testing and identification. But, for the most part, materials are carefully handled with instruments rather than hands and packaged in bags or containers with appropriate identification tags in order to preserve their competence and integrity as evidence.

COLLECTING PHYSICAL EVIDENCE

Physical evidence may initially offer a certain amount of use merely because of its position or location at the crime scene. As a consequence, crime scenes are frequently photographed exactly as they are found in order to preserve in time the juxtaposition of all potential material objects at the scene.

Television shows might suggest that when some street cop stumbles upon a crime scene and sees a gun on the ground, the officer will pick it up and place it carefully in a pocket. But in reality, that just isn't how things happen. The first order of business, as detailed in Chapter Six, will be to call in a supervisor and secure the scene. The importance of securing the scene cannot be overemphasized.

The chain of custody is among the several critical issues relevant to whether some item will be permitted as evidence. One argument against admission of items could be the inefficient or incorrect preservation of the crime scene as soon as it was identified as one. The dropping of a cigarette butt by some passerby could be problematic if it were, for example, the same brand as a suspect usually smoked. Or, conversely, the moving, trampling, or in other ways damaging or obscuring of potentially useful bits of physical evidence by bystanders could ruin an investigation.

During later tests of substances in the laboratory, an error in procedure can be fairly easily corrected. One simply needs only to repeat the test. But in the field, at a crime scene, once physical evidence is damaged, it may become useless.

In most cases, shortly after crime scene investigators have left, the control of the area is returned to the owner or occupant of the property. It is unusual for forensic teams to make successive sojourns to the crime scene over a period of days. When on occasion this is necessary, the scene—as with any other piece of potential evidence—must follow a chain of custody, which includes an officer being posted to assure preservation of the items located there.

Coarse Identification of Items

After the crime scene has been secured and photographed a coarse and general examination of the scene may be undertaken. During this stage of the crime scene investigation, forensic technicians seek items that are clearly apparent to the naked eye. These may include indications of pry-bar marks or other tool marks by windows that have been forced open, paint chipped by prying or other implements, grossly apparent damage to locks or door jambs, various small objects (buttons, jewelry, papers, pens, etc.) strewn about the room. Striation and impressions are made by a variety of tools and, in many cases, it is possible to match physical traces of these marks with the tools that made them. Striations are parallel scratch marks etched into the surface of a material that is softer than the implement that made them. Similarly, impressions are indentations made on the surface of some material that is softer than the tool or device that created it.

Most tools, when manufactured, inadvertently are fabricated with some type of imperfection. It may be a small burr at the edge or a slight chip or nick in a corner. When the tool causes a scratch or gouge impression in some soft material such as wood, aluminum, or linoleum tile, it leaves a trace of this imperfection. Frequently, these imperfections can be used under magnification to match a particular tool to a specific scratch or gouge mark.

During this stage of the crime scene investigation, officers and technicians will seek implements that appear to have been involved in the crime. For example, in the event of a homicide by gun shot, the logical weapon—a gun—will be sought. In the case of what may be a self-induced death from a drug overdose, a search for the pill container will be undertaken, and so forth.

Television often makes it appear that the forensic team rushes in, and in a matter of minutes finds conclusive and clear-cut evidence that identifies and incriminates the offender beyond reasonable doubt. Unfortunately, things move much slower and are frequently far less dramatic and conclusive in the real world of forensic science.

Fingerprints

Usually, as part of the initial coarse examination of the crime scene, likely locations for fingerprints are "dusted." Dusting involves the spreading of a fluffy dust with a fine brush over a smooth, hard surface where an intruder's finger or palm may have made contact. What develops from this dusting, if a print is present, is called a **latent print.** Latent prints literally develop from particles of the dust adhering to residual oils and surface dirt left by the skin of the individual who touched the surface being dusted.

Fingerprints are composed of lines, arches, and ridges unique to every individual. All portions of the body that are subjected to fairly continuous and vigorous use, are subject to the development of these **friction ridges,** as they are sometimes called (Kirk 1974). These body surfaces include the fingers, palms of the hand, toes, and soles of the feet. These ridges tend to be more or less parallel to each other and are unique in each individual. Even when one intentionally attempts to damage these friction ridges, in order to alter or obliterate the conformation of these ridges, they have a tendency to repair themselves to their original configuration.

Records of fingerprints derive from a fairly wide assortment of origins. For example, each time a person applies for a position with any governmental agency, the person is finger-printed and sometimes photographed. In many states, applications for gun, liquor, and driver's licenses require the applicant to provide a least a thumbprint.

In the late 1970s, the Educational Testing Service, the people who are responsible nationally for administering the Law School Aptitude Test (LSAT), among other entrance examinations, began taking thumbprints of all applicants prior to each LSAT.

In the early 1980s, in partial response to a massive rise in the value of silver, coin dealers, jewelers, and old-silver buyers began to require thumbprints of anyone selling more than $100-worth of silver or gold. The purpose here was to maintain a record of the seller in the event it was later discovered that the silver sold had been stolen.

Of course, the obvious place where law enforcement agencies obtain records of an individual's fingerprints is during the booking of a suspect in some offence. At that time copies of all ten fingerprints of the suspect are imprinted on a file card called a **ten-print card.** (See Box 15.2). Some agencies have additionally begun to take prints of a suspect's palm. These prints have, until recent years, been stored in various indexed files and, when used, required a hand search and an extremely time-consuming, thorough comparison when a latent print was found at a crime scene. As will be discussed later, the advances in computer technology have also moved in the direction of latent fingerprint identification.

In addition to maintaining a set of ten-print cards in each local law enforcement agency, police departments regularly provide copies of their ten-print cards to a central clearing and storage house. Among the leading fingerprint clearinghouses, as one might expect, is the Federal Bureau of Investigation. The FBI has served as a fingerprint clearinghouse since 1930 (Adams 1973). Typically,

when an agency submits a ten-print card to the FBI, it will receive in return a cumulative listing of all of the times that the clearinghouse indicates the individual has been arrested and fingerprinted.

In essence, fingerprints are used in law enforcement in two ways. First, they are used for general identification and identification confirmation, by comparing a known suspect's prints against existing records. Second, fingerprints can be used specifically to identify an unknown suspect's latent prints, those obtained at a crime scene or on some incriminating piece of evidence, by comparing these prints against those held by various fingerprint clearinghouses.

Occasionally, forensic technicians will come across an **impression** of a finger or palm print left in moist paint on a window sill or door. Or impressions may be found in other soft, pliable materials, such as window putty, butter, soap, and so forth. Another kind of fingerprint that crime scene investigators sometimes discover is an **imprint,** or viable fingerprint of a finger, palm, and occasionally, a foot. These prints are sometimes found on surfaces left in such media as dust, blood, dirt, grease, or any other substance that might serve as a kind of ink. Parents of small children are fairly familiar with these sorts of dirt imprints. They can be seen on the wooden jamb of the bathroom door or as track marks on the kitchen linoleum, moments after the children have been hurried in to wash their soiled hands after a hard day's play.

Shoe and Tire Impressions

In the same manner that a finger or a hand may leave an impression in dust, mud, or other pliable material, so too may a shoe or automobile tire. Usually, one thinks of these impressions as occurring in the outdoors. Often, these shoe and tire tread impressions are

Box 15.2

Ten Print Card

LEAVE BLANK

TYPE OR PRINT ALL INFORMATION IN BLACK
LAST NAME <u>NAM</u>   FIRST NAME   MIDDLE NAME

FBI   LEAVE BLANK

STATE USAGE	ALIASES	CONTRIBUTOR O R I	FL0120000 SO LAKE CITY FLA	DATE OF BIRTH <u>DOB</u> Month Day Year

SIGNATURE OF PERSON FINGERPRINTED

THIS DATA MAY BE COMPUTERIZED IN LOCAL, STATE AND NATIONAL FILES	DATE ARRESTED OR RECEIVED <u>DOA</u>	SEX	RACE	HGT.	WGT.	EYES	HAIR	PLACE OF BIRTH <u>POB</u>

DATE   SIGNATURE OF OFFICIAL TAKING FINGERPRINTS

YOUR NO. <u>OCA</u>

LEAVE BLANK

CHARGE

FBI NO. <u>FBI</u>

SID NO. <u>SID</u>   CLASS.

FINAL DISPOSITION   SOCIAL SECURITY NO. <u>SOC</u>   REF

NCIC CLASS - FPC

CAUTION

1. R. THUMB	2. R. INDEX	3. R. MIDDLE	4. R. RING	5. R. LITTLE

6. L. THUMB	7. L. INDEX	8. L. MIDDLE	9. L. RING	10. L. LITTLE

LEFT FOUR FINGERS TAKEN SIMULTANEOUSLY   L. THUMB   R. THUMB   RIGHT FOUR FINGERS TAKEN SIMULTANEOUSLY

Reel	Check Name*		ANA* Yes ☐ No ☐	Add D.O.B.* Yes ☐ No ☐	1	2	3	4	5
	Aliases for Input *			CHQU	6	7	8	9	10

Old F/P Class

Blocking Out	Blocking Out Reference	Classed By:

Frame	Old Height	Old Weight	Old Hair		
	Mod. P.O.B.* Yes ☐ No ☐	Add SSN* Yes ☐ No ☐	In NCIC Yes ☐ No ☐		Idented By:
	FDLE No.	Reel and Frame	Blocked Out By:	Mod. Reel and Frame* Yes ☐ No ☐	Verified By:

as distinctive as fingerprints. Like tools, these items frequently have identifiable flaws or nicks that show up in the impressions left in the mud, dirt, and even in the snow (Ojena 1984). These types of impressions are usually first photographed and then are cast in plaster or latex, depending on the medium in which the impression has occurred.

Fingerprints, shoe, and tire impressions have their greatest value to law enforcement agencies when they are found in locations to which only limited or authorized persons have access (Adams 1985). In public places and places of business, for example, prints found on a counter top or vending machine or virtually any other accessible object in the premises are reduced in value in a criminal investigation. Certainly, a good defense attorney can allege that the defendant may have touched some object when in the premises for some lawful purpose during normal business hours. Conversely, fingerprints of an intruder found in someone's private dwelling, where the suspected intruder had no authorization or legitimate access, become very incriminating pieces of evidence.

The Origin of Fingerprints in Forensic Science

The use of fingerprints for identification has a longstanding history in the criminal justice system. The origins of this technique have been attributed to the work of Alphonse Bertillon in France during the late nineteenth century. Bertillon was a records clerk for the Paris Prefecture of Police when in 1878 he began to develop a uniform standard of record-keeping for describing and identifying criminals (Johnson 1985). In 1883, after extensive work on his system, Bertillon made his first positive identification of a criminal recidivist. Two years later, he published his methods and findings in a book entitled *Identification Anthropometique* (Anthropometric Identification).

The Bertillon System, although somewhat primitive by today's standards, was a landmark breakthrough for criminal investigations during the nineteenth and early twentieth centuries. The system included fingerprints, among other anthropomorphic elements. By 1900 the Bertillon System had become the standard method for classifying criminal records in Europe and the United States (Johnson 1985).

Bertillon further contributed to the forensic sciences by introducing the idea of photographing a crime scene to preserve it, a means for casting footprints, and innovations in using handwriting analysis as an investigative tool.

At around the time as Bertillon was developing his ideas and methods of criminal recognition in France, several other "amateur" forensic scientists were working with fingerprints in England. Dr. Henry Faulds, Sir William J. Herschel, and Sir Francis Galton were working in this area.

Faulds, a Presbyterian missionary, was asked by the Japanese police in 1879 to assist in identifying a burglar from fingerprints left at the scene of the crime. Faulds did manage to do so and, in fact, developed a means for lifting the prints that resulted in identifying yet another thief (Johnson 1985).

While Faulds was working on his fingerprint methods in Japan, his countryman, Sir William J. Herschel, was developing his techniques in England. Herschel, a British magistrate, learned that there was an Asian superstition about manual contact with a business contract and a serious taboo against then violating the contract. The manual contact typically involved inking the fingers of involved parties and affixing prints of these fingers to the contract. In 1877, Herschel proposed that Indian prisoners held in British custody be made to place their fingerprints on their official records in order to discourage their *recidivism*. The proposal was rejected.

In 1888, Sir Francis Galton, a noted English scientist, was asked to discuss the Bertillon

System at a professional meeting he was to attend. During his preparation for this talk, Galton learned that Herschel had developed an extensive collection of fingerprints. Galton saw these fingerprints as a viable means of identifying people. Borrowing Herschel's fingerprint collection, Galton developed several critically important theories on fingerprints. First, Galton established that an individual's fingerprints remain the same throughout life. Second, Galton empirically established that no two individuals possess the same fingerprints. In short, no two fingerprints are identical (Johnson 1985). In 1892, Galton published his theories about classifying fingerprints in a book entitled simply, *Fingerprints.*

Lifting and Preserving Fingerprints

Because fingerprints have a longstanding and established tradition as a reliable means of identification, they are eagerly sought at major crime scenes. To preserve prints for later identification, several techniques are available. Certainly, a photograph provides one viable strategy. But, the ability of any law enforcement agency to identify a suspect from a latent print is only as good as the quality of this print. This is true whether the forensic technician is planning to photograph the print or lift it.

Lifting a print literally means carefully placing cellophane adhesive tape over the dusted print and then removing the tape from the surface. The dust particles adhere to the mastic on the tape in the outline of the print. This tape is then carefully readhered to a card, which is annotated with information indicating where it was taken.

Lifting copies of impressions is a slightly more complex activity. In this instance, a latex compound is gently brushed over the impression, which serves as a kind of mold. When the latex solidifies, it is peeled off. What results is a reverse image of the impression. By inking the latex copy and pressing it

against a print-card, a copy of the impression can be made for print comparison.

When photographing faint prints there is a possibility that normal room light may be inadequate. Forensic scientists, therefore, have sought ways to enhance the quality of a photographed print. Among the several current techniques of enhancement are various laser lights and combined laser and enzyme treatments (Menzel et al. 1984). At one point, the use of laser print enhancement was impractical since the device used was large and cumbersome. Machines often weighed as much as 400 pounds and were extremely costly to purchase. Today, however, portable laser print kits are both relatively inexpensive and lightweight, averaging only about thirty pounds.

DNA Fingerprinting: New Waves in Personal Identification

Although its use by law enforcement agencies and in courtroom proceedings remains controversial, the use of genetic fingerprinting is rapidly growing in acceptance (See Thompson 1989). The technique called **DNA fingerprinting** allows investigators to make positive identification of suspects based on DNA analysis of hair, blood, semen, or other body fluids or tissues.

Theoretically, genetic fingerprinting is an infallible matching of genetic material, or DNA, in a blood sample drawn from a crime suspect to the genetic print taken from some body fluid stain or strand of hair left at the crime scene. Although still not widely accepted in criminal courts across the country, the use of DNA identification was recently upheld in a Florida appeals court (*Andrews* v. *Florida*, 1988).

In this case, defendant Tommy Lee Andrews had been convicted of sexual battery and related offenses, partially on the basis of DNA analysis of his blood and of semen taken from the rape victim. During Andrews' trial, Dr. Michael Baird, an expert on DNA analysis, testified that there was a clear match. Dr. Baird also indicated that the chances that the matching DNA bands would be duplicated in some other person's cells was less than 1 in 839 million ("Criminal Justice Newsletter" 1988).

Andrews appealed on the grounds that the DNA tests were unreliable and that there were insufficient checks on the quality of the laboratory work. The Florida court of appeals, however, disagreed. The court noted that DNA testing has been successfully used in non-judicial settings for almost ten years and that extensive scientific literature on the subject already existed. Also, the laboratory had used control tests, using known DNA samples, to guard against possible faulty laboratory work in the Andrews case. As a final argument, the court stated that experts in the field of DNA analysis had testified that in the event of faulty testing, no results rather than erroneous results would be likely.

Several months after the October 1988 ruling of the Florida appeals court, California's attorney general, John Van de Kamp, announced that genetic fingerprinting would be used by his office when trying cases in California's criminal courts. In spite of the cautious approach most states have taken regarding DNA identification, the introduction of this technique into more criminal courts is likely to occur.

In March 1989 the FBI laboratory announced to the law enforcement community that it was prepared to accept physical evidence for DNA testing. Recognizing that such an announcement would result in an enormous increase in case submissions, the FBI laboratory established a guides for submission. Basically, the policy states that evidence for DNA testing must derive from a current, violent personal crime where appropriate standards are available for comparison ("FBI Bulletin" 1989). Essentially, this guideline represents cases of homicide, sexual assault, and violent aggravated assault in which suspects

have already been identified. Known blood samples from both the victim and the suspect usually are required for comparisons.

OTHER KINDS OF PHYSICAL EVIDENCE

Almost anything found at a crime scene may be used as evidence, provided that it is germane to the investigation. Even something as innocent as glass particles may offer an important clue in a criminal investigation and later become useful as evidence. For example, glass particles outside an automobile or on the rug of some premises below a window indicate the direction of the projectile that broke the glass. Later, glass particles may be found in the pants cuff of a suspect. Upon microscopic examination, these glass particles might be used to place the suspect at the scene of the crime (by matching them with particles at the scene).

The identification and comparison of various particles, fibers, and traces of substances as potential evidence fall under **forensic microscopy.** It was previously suggested that during the initial coarse examination of the scene, large items, relatively speaking, are located without the aid of magnification. During the microscopic examination, on the other hand, magnification, chemical treatment, enhanced illumination, and specialized technologies are all critical. In some instances, the dirt in which the intruder left a hand print may be as important a clue to his identity as the hand impression itself. Although the meaning or relevance to the crime may not be immediately knowable, once the nature of these dirt particles, or **microtraces,** are identified, they may be found to be very informative.

Collecting and Examining Microtraces

Skip Palenik (1988) suggests that there are five basic techniques typically used by forensic technicians when collecting microtraces:

1. Handpicking;
2. Adhesive tape;
3. Vacuuming;
4. Washing; and
5. Scraping. [Palenik 1988, 164]

Each of these techniques is discussed in Box 15.3.

Odontology as a Forensic Investigative Technique

Related to the more microscopic examination of physical evidence is an increasingly useful technique known as **odontology** or **bite-mark identification.** For example, cavalier burglars sometimes make themselves sandwiches and leave half-eaten remains on kitchen tables. Also, teeth are commonly used as weapons (both offensively and defensively) during assaults and sexual attacks.

Among the incriminating evidence used against Ted Bundy in his trial for killing two Florida State University students were comparison bite marks left in the breasts of the women by their killer and a casting made from a bite Bundy had taken from an apple while incarcerated.

By examining the impression of the bite mark in some object or the flesh of a victim and comparing it to a suspect's bite structure, an identification may be possible. Unlike fingerprints, however, bite-mark identification is not viewed as exacting. Even in the case of Ted Bundy, experts called in to identify the comparison bite marks could only claim that the markings could have been made by the same person.

Guns and Bullets

Among the more accurate television images of forensic science promulgated in the United States is that the most common type of physical evidence concerns guns and bullets. Perhaps because of the enormous number of

crimes each year involving shootings, the United States is teeming with firearms experts. Of course, as suggested in the beginning of this chapter, there is also the possibility of charlatans.

Less accurately portrayed in the media is the ease with which one can make a convincing identification of a bullet or cartridge fired from a particular gun. Although this is typically an important question in a shooting, it is not always answered as simply in the real world as it is in some police dramas on television.

Frequently, the bullets recovered in a shooting have fragmented or become significantly misshapen from their impact against bone, a wall, trees, or other solid objects. Also, the weapon that fired the bullet may have become damaged by rust, clogged with mud, worn, or intentionally damaged after use, making identification of a **signature** on either the discharged bullet or cartridge impossible.

In spite of the difficulties associated with it, the examination and identification of fired bullets, or what is more properly called **ballistics,** is an important area in forensic science. First, bullets and cartridge cases are typically the material left behind at a crime scene. Second, in many cases markings on bullets and/or cartridge cases created by a particular weapon are sufficiently unique that they are like fingerprints, hence the concept of the weapon's signature.

Typically, the essential question in a shooting is whether a particular weapon fired the bullet found. In order to answer this question, once a suspect and weapon are located, test firings are undertaken. Typically, this will involve firing the suspected weapon into a special tank filled with water. The water creates resistance to slow and eventually stop the bullet, but without causing serious damage to it. Also, water will not impart extraneous striations and markings on the soft lead of unshielded bullets. Jacketed ammunition (typically copper shielding) requires fewer

Box 15.3 _____

Microtrace Collection Techniques

Handpicking. Handpicking literally means the removal of particles from some medium by means of a gloved hand or some inorganic implement (tweezers, forceps, probes, magnets, and so forth). Handpicking is usually the first technique employed to locate and collect microtraces. It is useful for collecting particles that are numerous, large enough, or sufficiently color distinctive to contrast with their background. The shattered glass particles are an example of particles suitable for handpicking.

The major advantages to handpicking are its ability systematically to detect, recover, and isolate particles from contaminants in a single step. Identification of the location where the handpicked particles were found is relatively easy.

Adhesive Tape. Similar to the use of cellophane tape to lift fingerprints, cellophane adhesive tape is used to collect traces of minute particles from areas where handpicking may be ineffective. Once the particles adhere to the tape's mastic, they may be protected by folding a clean piece of tape over the particles. Another protective technique, originally advocated by Max Frei-Sulzer during the 1940s, places the strip of tape with the collected particles sticky side down on a microscope slide or plastic sheet (Frei-Sulzer 1951, Palenik 1988).

During examination of these particles, the slide can be placed directly under a microscope, or particular samples of the microtraces may be carefully removed. In removing samples, sections of the tape can be cut out, lifted, and used without damaging or contaminating the remaining particulates.

Adhesive tape is particularly useful for removing fiber fragments that might otherwise go unnoticed or undetected were simple handpicking used alone. Unfortunately, because adhesive tape depends upon its mastic to lift various minute particles, this technique is ineffective on wet, oily, or excessively dusty surfaces.

Vacuuming. The vacuuming technique of microtrace collection is regarded as a highly efficient, although non-discriminating strategy. Vacuuming can remove microscopic fragments of fiber or other substances from carpeting, fabric, and other woven materials. However, vacuuming collects *all* particulates in the area being covered and makes it necessary later to distinguish potentially useful microtraces from run-of-the-mill lint and dirt traces.

Forensic vacuums use very tiny filter cassettes to improve the technician's ability to identify specific locations where particles were found. Unlike the family Hoover, which may take weeks of household vacuuming before its filter bag is filled, these tiny filter cassettes take only a few seconds. Once they have been used, they are removed, bagged, and labeled to identify the location from which the dust has been obtained, just as with any larger pieces of evidence.

Washing. Washing, as a technique for collection of microtraces, is typically used to dislodge or loosen particles adhering to some medium. Some stains or deposits of mud or other soil harden significantly when dry. In order to remove pieces for examination and analysis, one might need to pick strenuously, potentially damaging materials that may be trapped below the surface of the stain. In such an instance, washing the stain to loosen and remove particles can be most useful.

Some stains, such as those caused by blood or seminal fluid, can be classified by Rhesus (Rh) factors and protein type, as well as being subjected to various other laboratory analysis tests. These traces can therefore be extremely useful in identifying suspects. These substances, however, tend to dry rapidly and create stains. Although moist stains, such as damp stains of blood or semen, may be collected on a blotter and allowing this to dry, dry stains on floors, fabric, and garments present slightly different problems. Frequently, one can successfully scrape some of the dry blood from a hard, smooth surface, such as a floor. Alternatively, however, a mild saline and water solution can be used to moisten the stain sufficient to blot it.

As Chapter Thirteen mentions, more and more forensic teams and investigative officers have grown concerned about the potential spread of AIDS from blood spatters—wet or dry—at crime scenes. Extreme caution is recommended, therefore, to both assure the sample is preserved and the safety of officers is maintained.

Scraping. Scraping can be a useful strategy in loosening stains, such as blood or semen, where little danger of damaging participates is apparent. Also, scraping can be a useful technique to dislodge microtraces from clothing. The usual procedure is to scrape the garment gently with a metal spatula. The garment should be held over some large, clean material (plastic garbage bags, or large sheets of paper, for example) to capture particles that fall.

Among the five microtrace collection techniques discussed, scraping is the least efficient. There are several reasons for this. First, running the spatula down the garment in an attempt to knock particles off the fabric is not efficient and many particles will remain lodged in the garment's fibers. Second,

and more serious, is the potential for nearly uncontrollable contamination from minute airborne particles. Traces of pollen, lint, dust, ash, and the like spin about us all the time. Anyone who wears eyeglasses can attest to that.

The damage these incredibly small particles can do is well understood by clean-room facilities workers where microchips and printed circuit boards are produced. Even a single particulate can destroy or irreversibly damage a microchip.

The scraping of a garment, then, not only loosens potential pieces of evidence, but large amounts of fibers and particles that are simply present in the air. Additionally, contaminants are likely to fall onto the capture sheet from the air itself.

precautions against potential damage when test-firing.

After test-firing and collecting the spent bullet, a comparison can be made of markings on the test slug and the one(s) obtained at the crime scene. Under magnification, both intentional tooling and rifling grooves left from the weapon's barrel and idiosyncratic irregularities in a barrel should become apparent.

Barrels of Weapons

As suggested above, a critical element in the identification of a bullet and the assertion that it came from a particular weapon is the markings left on a bullet by the weapon's barrel. Gun barrels typically leave significant markings on bullets that pass through them. Virtually all modern guns and rifles, with the exception of shotguns, possess internal barrel grooves known generally as **riflings.** A barrel's rifling results from one or another of several manufacturing methods, which leave grooves cut into the inner lining of the barrel. These grooves offer the bullet stability of flight by causing it to move with a rotary motion as it is propelled through the barrel. This activ-

ity, however, creates striations and markings on the bullet.

Variations consistently occur in the process of rifling a gun's barrel. These irregularities may be affected by flaws in the tools used to cut the rifling, different depths of cut, and even different methods of creating the riflings.

Computers and Forensic Investigations

The use of computers to automate fingerprint searching systems is becoming increasingly popular around the United States. Although the potential usefulness of comparison of latent fingerprints as a positive identifier has been known and accepted for a long time, its use on a practical level has been fairly limited. The obvious reason, of course, is that without a specific suspect in mind, it has been virtually impossible until recently to do a manual search of even all locally held tenprint cards.

Computers, however, manage very well with *image processing*, that is, using a mathematically created model image of the print, including the identification of up to 250 characteristics on each print (Buracker and Stover 1984). In addition to storing, searching, and retrieving these models, computer systems can reproduce them on a plotter or terminal screen.

The Automated Fingerprint Identification System (AFIS) rose to national recognition in 1985, when the Los Angeles police department identified and arrested Richard Ramirez as the notorious "Night Stalker." The Los Angeles police were assisted in their investigation by a computer built by the Nippon Electric Co. of Japan. AFIS sorted through 380,000 electronically stored ten-print cards and hit on a best fit with Richard Ramirez. Ramirez was arrested two days after his card was identified and charged with killing fifteen people. Experts have estimated that it would have taken a single fingerprint technician 67 years to make the same ten-print identification from manual files (Elmer-De Witt 1985).

In 1986, the Massachusetts State Police purchased a slightly more advanced version of AFIS than the one used in the Los Angeles investigation. The Massachusetts AFIS has the capacity to sort through 250,000 ten-print cards in just under three minutes and will report up to ten best hits.

Between November 1986 and August 1987, a total of 3,013 latent prints were entered and stored in the AFIS as a data base. Even with this preliminary data base, suspects in 215 cases, as well as 22 bodies, were identified.

An unanticipated benefit of this system has been the elimination of multiple jackets. In other words, the same individual arrested in different local jurisdictions may have used different names. By running the ten-print card through the system, aliases are identified and collapsed into a single file. As of August 1987, the Massachusetts AFIS had positively identified 737 criminal suspects who were using aliases (Governor's Conference, 1987).

In addition to increasing the statewide data base of the Massachusetts AFIS, the Massachusetts State Police are anxious to increase participation among neighboring states in a regional AFIS project. Such a multi-state venture would not only be the first of its kind in the nation, but might spur the development of various ancillary technology useful for criminal investigations.

Live Digital Fingerprinting

A related innovation in fingerprinting is the live digital fingerprint-scanning process. This scanning process permits one to scan a suspect's finger with an electro-optical system and to convert the resulting fingerprint image to a digital form. This digital information is displayed on a computer terminal and can be printed out on a ten-print card, transmitted from its originating site to some other site, or stored for later use (See Bennett 1987).

One digital scanning company, Fingermatrix Inc., of North White Plains, New York claims that fingerprint images produced from this process are far more detailed than the traditional ink-rolled process for ten-print card production. Also, Fingermatrix offers a complete support system for the AFIS, including the ability to scan existing, conventional ten-print cards.

The AFIS computers are being used in at least fifteen states and thirty cities and counties (Bennett 1987, Hall 1987). These systems have made an extraordinary impact on the ability of their agencies to identify suspects from latent prints. Unfortunately, in the absence of an inexpensive way for small law enforcement agencies to access these AFIS data bases, much of their potential utility is wasted. The sharing of fingerprint data among law enforcement agencies must certainly be the next step. The development of these fingerprint data base networks may be assisted by the advances being made in digital scanning and transmission of fingerprints.

Several law enforcement agencies in California have already begun using this live and latent fingerprint processing system in conjunction with their AFIS computers. AFIS computers already dramatically accelerate identification of suspects using less detailed rolled-ink prints. The potential for increased accuracy, and the ability of even small agencies to access fingerprint information through network sharing, is indeed amazing.

Expert Systems for Law Enforcement

"Expert System" computer bases are beginning to make their way into law enforcement investigations. Expert systems are part of a domain referred to as "artificial intelligence" (Hayes-Roth, Waterman, and Lenat 1983). These computer programs make various decisions and solve problems in ways that simulate human intelligence.

At the National Center for the Analysis of Violent Crime (NCAVC), there is considerable interest in harnessing the power of artificial intelligence systems for the investigation of crimes, especially in the analysis of psychological and criminal personality profiles (Reboussin and Cameron 1989). NCAVC is developing an expert system to perform exactly this analytic process. The NCAVC system, called PROFILER, has the ability to analyze faster and more efficiently than any single human investigator can.

The PROFILER system will never completely replace skilled human investigators and analysts. It will, however, significantly enhance the ability of human investigators and analysts to identify violent criminals.

SUMMARY

This chapter has examined generally the role of forensic science in criminal investigations. Following a brief description of how Col. Calvin Goddard came to establish the first American forensic crime laboratory, the chapter considered the nature of evidence. In this regard, evidence was divided into two major categories, direct and indirect evidence. Direct evidence was described as proof in itself of the guilt or innocence of a suspect. Con-

trasting this, indirect evidence was depicted as circumstantial or fragmented pieces of information that cumulatively suggested the possible guilt or innocence of an individual.

The chapter also detailed some of the problems with expert witnesses in forensic science. Attention was drawn to the delicate nature of truth and confidence in expert witnesses in criminal trials and investigations. Two categories of charlatans were identified: academites and careerists. Academites were sketched as persons purporting various scholarly academic credentials that do not exist. Careerists, in a similar vein, were described as fabricating various experiences and training qualifications.

The chapter briefly considered the admissibility of various sorts of evidence, differentiating between admissible and hearsay evidence. Admissible evidence was characterized as first-hand knowledge of a crime or suspect, or relevant physical evidence that met certain standards for admission. Inadmissible evidence was described as third-party information, or physical evidence that did not meet standards of admissibility.

A large portion of the chapter examined various strategies and technologies used to collect and preserve physical evidence during crime scene investigations. This section of the chapter began with a description of the coarse identification of potential pieces of evidence. This included consideration of large objects (weapons, furnishings, etc.) as well as latent fingerprints and similar imprints. Later, the chapter shifted focus to consider microtraces of evidence that may be located at crime scenes, on suspects, or on incriminating objects.

Finally, the chapter concluded with an examination of the usefulness of computers in criminal investigations. In particular, the Automated Fingerprint Identification System (AFIS) was detailed and considered.

REVIEW QUESTIONS _____

1. What is the central purpose of forensic science in criminal investigations?

2. Differentiate between "academites" and "careerists" as examples of charlatans in forensic science.

3. Under what circumstances would physical evidence found at the scene of a crime not be admissible in a court of law?

4. Why might a latent fingerprint lifted at the scene of the crime be unconvincing as a piece of evidence against a suspect in that crime?

5. How do "coarse" and "microtrace" examinations of physical evidence differ? How are they similar?

REFERENCES

Adams, Thomas F. *Law Enforcement*, 2d ed. Englewood Cliffs, N.J.: Prentice Hall, 1973.

Adams, Thomas F. *Police Field Operations*. Englewood Cliffs, N.J.: Prentice Hall, 1985.

Bennett, Robert A. "Refining the Art of Fingerprinting." *New York Times* (November 11, 1987): D10.

Buracker, Carroll, and William Stover. "Automated Fingerprint Identification—Regional Application of Technology." *FBI. Law Enforcement Bulletin* 53 (1984): 1–5.

"DNA Fingerprinting Upheld in First Appellate-Level Challenge" *Criminal Justice Newsletter*. 19 (December 1, 1988): 3–4.

Dunning, Wayne W. "Criminal Investigation and Criminalistics." In Dae H. Chang and James A. Fagin, eds. *Introduction to Criminal Justice: Theory and Application*, 2d ed. Geneva, Ill.: Paladin, 1985.

Elmer–De Witt, Phillip. "Taking a Byte Out of Crime. *Time*, (October 14, 1985: 96).

Frei–Sulzer, Max. "Die Sicherung von Mikrospuren mit Klebband." *Kriminalistik* 5 (1951):190–94.

"FBI Announces New DNA Policy." *FBI Bulletin.* Washington, D.C.: U.S. Department of Justice, Federal Bureau of Investigations (March 1989): 23.

Goddard, Calvin. "The Valentine Day Massacre: A Study in Ammunition–Tracing." *American Journal of Police Science* 1 (1930): 60–78.

Governor's Conference on Local Law Enforcement. Sponsored by the Massachusetts Committee on Criminal Justice, and the Massachusetts Criminal Justice Training Council, Needham, Mass. (September 16, 1987).

Hall, David G. "New Remote, Interactive Technology Enables Linkage of AFIS Systems." *The Police Chief* (October 1987): 61–63.

Hayes–Roth, F., D.A. Waterman, and D.B. Lenat, eds. *Building Expert Systems.* Reading Massachusetts: Addison-Wesley, 1983.

Johnson, David R. "The Triumph of Reform." In W. Clinton Terry III, ed. *Policing Society.* New York: Wiley, 1985.

Kirk, Paul. *Crime Investigation*, 2d ed. New York: Wiley, 1974.

Menzel, E.R., J. Everse, K.E. Everse, T.W. Sinor, and J.A. Burt. "Room Light and Laser Development of Latent Fingerprints with Enzymes," *Journal of Forensic Sciences* 29 (1984): 99–109.

Ojena, S.M. "A New Improved Technique for Casting Impressions in Snow." *Journal of Forensic Sciences* 29 (1984): 322–25.

Palenik, Skip. "Microscopy and Microchemistry of Physical Evidence." In Richard Saferstein, ed. *Forensic Science Handbook Volume 2.* Englewood Cliffs, N.J.: Prentice Hall, 1988.

Reboussin, Roland, and Jerry Cameron. "Expert Systems for Law Enforcement." *FBI Law Enforcement Bulletin.* (August 1989): 12–16.

Saferstein, Richard, ed. *Forensic Science Handbook Volume 2.* Englewood Cliffs, N.J.: Prentice Hall, 1988.

Thompson, Mark. "California Attorney General Endorses DNA Fingerprinting." *Criminal Justice Newsletter* 20 (March 1 1989): 1–2.

Waltz, Jon R. *Introduction to Criminal Evidence.* Chicago: Nelson–Hall, 1983.

Wilson, Charles. "Crime Detection Laboratories in the United States." In Joseph L. Peterson, ed. *Forensic Science: Scientific Investigation in Criminal Justice.* New York: AMS Press, 1975.

CASES CITED

Andrews v. Florida, No.87–2166 (1988).

Mapp v. Ohio, 395 U.S. 643, 644 (1961).

CHAPTER 16

THE FUTURE: EDUCATION, TRAINING, AND PRIVATIZATION IN POLICING

During recent years the number of pre-service and in-service police officers attaining baccalaureate-level educations has increased dramatically. This development is not entirely surprising, considering that education for police has been urged by police administrators since August Vollmer and Albert Schneider in 1917 and nationally since 1931 (National Commission on Law Observance and Enforcement, also called the Wickersham Commission). Although most American police departments do not require college educations of their entry-level recruits, the trend for police officers obtaining post-high school educations has been encouraged by the development of law enforcement and criminal justice academic programs. Additionally, financial support has been made available intermittently by federal and state scholarships. More recently, in May 1989, President George Bush announced to the nation a law enforcement plan that called for financial support of college students in exchange for two eight-week police training programs and a minimum of four years of police service following graduation from college. The national plan is reminiscent of an earlier plan by the New York City police department in 1984 to develop a "police corps." To date, the plan continues to be discussed but has not yet been successfully passed on the Senate floor.

Whether or not Bush's plan is successful, it is clear that the police are moving in the direction of increased numbers of college-educated line officers. Chapter Sixteen explores the merits and drawbacks to having police officers possess high levels of education. This chapter also will consider the debate over education versus field experience. In this regard, Chapter Sixteen considers the distinction between education and training in law enforcement. Finally, the chapter will explore the growing tendency in policing to obtain various police services from private vendors.

INTRODUCTION: POLICING AS A CAREER

Policing, as this book has tried to demonstrate, is not a static phenomenon. Instead, policing is a rather fluid and flexible activity that reflects both the needs and desires of the community and social structures of society. As each new layer is added to policing's social history, efforts to protect liberty increase.

In many ways, policing is likely to continue this pattern of bending and experimenting in its effort to accommodate community demands for safety and freedom while attempting to avoid infringement of citizens' rights. Because of this desire to accommodate the people they protect, the roles and functions of police officers are deeply influenced by the community they serve. During the recent past, members of communities have begun to work with police officials to identify serious crime and crime-related problems and to consider various alternative resolutions (See Skolnick and Bayley 1986; Smith 1986; Sherman 1986).

The purpose of this chapter is to review the way education and training in policing have been evolving, as well as their impact on the future of American law enforcement.

Throughout this book numerous issues relating to policing have been identified and discussed. For the most part these have all related to a general mandate in policing to protect and serve the community. In addition, issues corresponding to crime investigation, stress, and risk have also been considered. The comprehensive nature of these items and the complexity of law enforcement in general have required this book to offer only a scant look at each facet of policing. Nonetheless, this book has touched upon many of the major and timely aspects and elements commonly associated with policing.

It has also been the intention of this author to offer information about policing that was as realistic as possible. Often, students of policing foster highly idealistic, but equally unrealistic images of what and who the police are. As Chapter Ten expressed, this has created much consternation among new recruits and rookies as they begin their law enforcement careers.

In a study by M. Steven Meagher and Nancy Yentes (1986), police officers from two midwestern states were asked their reasons for becoming law enforcement officers. Meagher and Yentes (1986, 320) found, as many previous researchers have, that the principal explanations centered upon a "desire to help people and the [financial and occupational] security associated with the job of policing" (See also Milton 1978, Ermer 1978, Charles 1982).

Interestingly, the findings reported by Meagher and Yentes (1986) reflect nearly identical motivations from both male and female officers. In other words, both men and women indicate they have selected a career devoted to service, while neither expresses a desire to join the military or an authoritarian profession as a personal reason for joining the police force. The inference one can draw from the work of Meagher and Yentes, as well as from many previous investigators, is that the old notion that certain personality types enter policing in disproportionate numbers should be put to rest. As with any occupation, prospective members are concerned with financial considerations, job security, and advancement. During the recent past, many police officers have looked at higher education as a potential short cut to rapid advancement. Historically, however, the education movement in policing is a critical aspect in the modernization of the police as a social institution. It is important, therefore, to consider the role of higher education in law enforcement.

Higher Education and Police Officers

Among the more controversial elements associated with modern policing is the question of a need for college-prepared police officers. August Vollmer was among the earliest proponents of higher education for police officers. Vollmer urged adoption of a college education as a basic employment requirement as early as 1920. Yet little progress was made in this regard until the 1960s.

To a large measure, American law enforcement does not view higher education for police officers as valuable. It is only after modern police reform models and attempts to achieve the status of professionals (see Chapter Fourteen) emerged that education began to be seen as a positive item. In the 1960s, with the influx of federal money through such programs as the Law Enforcement Education Program (LEEP), police departments and American colleges and universities began to direct their attention to higher education for police officers. Money was made available both for officers who desired to pursue college educations and for colleges and universities desiring to develop police-oriented courses and programs. According to Richard A. Staufenberger (1980), only 184 institutions of higher education had established police-oriented programs

prior to 1967. But, by 1974, over 1,030 institutions had developed law enforcement courses and programs.

Staufenberger (1977; 1980) also reports, as examples of the increase in college-educated police officers, that in 1968 only 11 officers in the Dallas Police Department and 6% of the officers in Florida had college degrees. But, by 1975 the Dallas Police Department included 625 officers with completed bachelor's degrees, 21 officers with completed master's degrees, and over 450 officers actively pursuing college degrees. In Florida, by 1975, 23% of the state's officers had attended college, including 44 officers who had secured doctorates.

Several studies in the 1970s sang the praise of higher education for law enforcement officers. Bernard Locke and Alexander Smith (1976), for example, claimed that higher education reduced the tendency toward authoritarianism—a commonly employed personality description used of law enforcement officers during the late 1960s and early 1970s (See Chapters Nine and Fourteen). In 1967, the President's Commission on Law Enforcement and Administration of Justice concluded that "the complexity of the police task is as great as that of any other profession" (President's Commission 1967, 124). The Commission recommended that police departments begin to require a baccalaureate degree as an entry-level requirement. Few departments heeded the call in 1967.

In 1973, The National Advisory Commission on Criminal Justice Standards and Goals urged that police agencies begin gradually to require some college education among new recruits. They recommended beginning with a requirement of one year of college during 1973, an increase to two years of college by 1975, three years in 1978, and a four-year college degree in 1982 (National Advisory Commission 1973, 369). Again, few departments responded to these suggestions.

There were many involved in policing, however, who suggested that college educations could offer little for the average police officer (See Erickson and Neary 1975). The relatively boring and mundane activities usually associated with line-level policing were suggested as prime reasons why higher education for police officers might be a waste of time (Sherman and Bennis 1977).

In 1983, James Fyfe reported on a study he conducted for the International City Management Association. Fyfe's survey asked educational questions of police department administrators. Fyfe (1983) reports that among the 1,087 responding agencies, only four indicated that they required a four-year college degree as a condition of employment. Nearly eighty percent indicated they required a high school diploma or equivalency. It seemed increasingly clear that the various recommendations for college education as an employment requirement had not been meaningfully incorporated into policing ideology or police administration.

Several possible explanations have been offered for why police agencies failed to follow the various research and commission recommendations. Geoffrey Alpert and Roger Dunham (1988, 186) suggest that at least one reason for not following the recommendations may have to do with concern over the potential effect such restrictions might have for minority applicants. For example, the Urban League has argued that any educational requirements for entry-level positions should be relevant to that job. In the case of law enforcement, the Urban League maintains that a high school diploma or its equivalent should be the maximum requirement for entry-level positions (Reynolds 1980).

As a consequence, the maintenance of the lowest common denominator, minimal educational requirements, may be a detriment rather than a benefit. Although a wider range of minorities may be eligible for admission to the ranks of policing, the manifest appearance is a kind of lazy-racism, that is, the manifest appearance that there are no qualified minorities at higher educational levels—a subtle but racist attitude that is untrue.

Certainly, other service-oriented occupations such as nursing have not lowered their educational standards in order to accommodate much larger personnel needs than those occurring in policing. In fact, the trend in nursing is just the opposite. More and more, one finds hospitals eliminating diploma nurses (nurses who possess the status of a registered nurse, but who do not possess a baccalaureate degree). These diploma nurses are being replaced by college-prepared nurses—even to the extent of importing them from foreign countries. Also, one can find an increasing number of bed-side staff nurses who have masters degrees.

Minimal educational requirements create a misconception about the complexity and sophistication of modern policing. If it were the intention of police agencies to acquire additional warm bodies, then fixing the maximum requirement at a high school diploma or equivalent might be adequate. Police work, however, simply cannot be equated with dock work, automobile repairing, operating computer terminals, laboratory technical work, or any other semi-skilled occupation for which a high school education might suffice at entry level. Although this educational attitude may become an unpopular position, it is not unique to policing. Among the most strenuously fought battles in the profession of nursing today is the educational upgrading of bed-side (staff) nurses.

As in nursing, many people may question the need for police officers to possess more than very minimal educations. However, police work today requires rational and logical thinking, knowledge of other cultures, communication skills, writing and language skills, and a variety of other social and technical skills that come from a college-level experience, and not a weekend of cramming for the General Educational Diploma test (GED). High school and college experiences are vastly different. In most situations, one attends a high school located in the general vicinity of where one grew up. One attends along with many of the same peers one has grown up with in the community or with whom one attended middle and elementary schools. This homogenous experience is quite stilted when compared with the kinds of broader cultural and geographical experiences one typically can expect college to provide.

In truth, the requisite of a four-year college degree may be slightly more than an entry-level police officer needs immediately upon joining a department, and this may well be debated. However, it would seem reasonable to expect future officers to be involved with college programs or possess an associate's degree as a minimal educational level. As mentioned in Chapter Thirteen, a study by the Police Executive Research Forum recommends that colleges and universities direct their criminal justice programs toward liberal arts curriculum (Sapp et al. 1989). The study's implications are that academic college programs for police officers are indeed necessary, but not college programs that attempt to teach police skills.

Additional evidence of an increasingly college-educated police entry level is the recent congressional effort to pass the Police Corps Act of 1989. The bill was to create a new incentive for attracting college-educated, entry-level police officers. The bill provided for participating college students to secure federally guaranteed loans for their education. After graduating, up to $40,000 can be repaid by serving in either the state police or a local police department in the sponsoring state (American Press 1989). In 1990, a modified version of this bill was again brought to the Senate floor. In this version, officers already working also could qualify for financial incentives for college educations. Again the bill was not successful. However, lobbyists with the Police Executive Research Forum continue to support and promote this kind of educational bill.

The Police Corps was the idea of Adam Walinsky, a former aide to Robert Kennedy. The Police Corps promises three major benefits. Many urban police departments have difficulty attracting qualified minority re-

cruits. A Justice department survey has concluded that many inner-city minority youths would find the corps's "service-for-college" trade attractive. Second, the increase in college-educated, entry-level officers would improve the overall educational level of local police forces nationally. Finally, in time, a sizable number of civilians will gain a new appreciation for police officers and police work, since they would have served as police officers—even if for only four years (Kramer 1990).

Although compelling for academics and some police executives, the argument for increased levels of education for police officers is not overwhelmingly accepted by many police officials. As these police officials are quick to point out, a college education does not necessarily translate into better police work. Often, improvements in training and enforcement of training standards can provide as effective (or more effective) paths to increased quality policing. As Elizabeth Burbeck and Adrian Furnham (1985, 62) recently wrote:

Intelligence and education do not guarantee success in the police force, although they are of predictive use at the training school. Higher levels of education may paradoxically give rise to more dissatisfaction and higher wastage.

The question of police training requisites is itself problematic. For example, how many hours are necessary or sufficient during the academy to place officers safely in the field? What areas should be emphasized in the training program, and what proportion of hours should each area be given? At what levels should passing and failing be established? Should physical training be given equal, greater, or less time than more academic areas of study? Should rookie officers be permitted simply to begin police work after completing a classroom training program, or should they be required to have a structured field training experience first? And, finally, exactly what is the purpose or goal of police training to begin with? Unfortunately, a long and complicated debate is likely to arise, regardless of how one attempts to answer any of these questions. At least partially as a result of this circumstance, training is typically given a fairly low priority in nearly every police department across the country (Samaha 1988, 275).

Many police chiefs would prefer to do **on-the-job-training** rather than send their recruits to an academy. One reason for this is financial. While the recruit is attending the academy, the chief must pay an officer's salary without receiving the benefit of the officer's services.

Similarly, when it comes to in-service programs, police administrators are sometimes hesitant to pull officers from their usual duties in order to place them back in a classroom. Robert Meadows (1987) compared the perceptions of law enforcement training requirements as ranked by criminal justice educators (college and university professors) and police administrators. Meadows (1987, 8) reported that both groups similarly ranked the value of several training areas:

> Both groups ranked patrol and investigation, force and weaponry, and communications as being the most important. The respondents also ranked human relations training last.

It is interesting to note that both educators and administrators have ranked human relations training as least important for recruits to learn. However, and as Meadows (1987) explains, this may reflect uncertainty about how human relations training should be taught. This notion is not dissimilar to police educational questions raised by Lawrence Sherman's 1978 report, *The Quality of Police Education.* Sherman's report delved into the disagreement over what kind of educational model is most effective for police officers. For example, a liberal arts background may be too general, a criminal justice one too focused, and law enforcement training too technical. The Sherman report made a number of recommendations intended to improve the field of police education. For example, it was criti-

cal of the criminal justice programs that required instructors to possess police field experience as a requisite for hiring. It was clear that this requirement limited the number of more academically trained instructors from securing positions in these programs. Too, the report recommended that criminal justice course material begin to emphasize theoretical and ethical considerations relevant to law enforcement, rather than merely the mechanical procedures of policing. Nonetheless, the debate and controversy over police educational needs persists, and various interest groups perceive the training requirements and functions of police officers differently.

Experience as the Officer's Best Teacher

Another view of policing suggests that there is no substitute for street experience. Following this argument to its logical conclusion, neither material presented at the academy nor in the college classroom is as beneficial in dealing with confrontations in the real world. If this view of police learning is correct, then it follows that the best police officers should be the oldest, most seasoned field veterans. Also, the only persons who could adequately make comments and judgments in a supervisory capacity are those still actively working the streets. In effect, the argument is analogous to the absurd claim that in order to study drug addicts, one must first be a drug addict. Few police officers would, therefore, argue as stated here, that only actively working police officers are competent to assess, supervise, or educate recruits.

David Bayley and Egon Bittner (1984) indicate that, "what police say about how policing is learned [experientially] is not incompatible with attempts to make instruction in the skills of policing more self-critical and systematic." Bayley and Bittner even recommend a kind of blending of theoretically based material with more practical experiential learning strategies. In this regard, frank discussion of actual case studies and the kinds of decisions that went into each would be instructive. Bayley and Bittner warn, however, that there is an important distinction to be made between having instructors excite recruits with war stories and offering authentic case examples for illustrative purposes. Related to this, then, it seems necessary that instructors themselves be well educated both in law enforcement issues and material and in educational procedures and techniques.

The Value of College-Educated Police

The value of a police officer with a college education remains somewhat controversial. There is some research that suggests that college-prepared officers tend to perform their functions as police officers better than their non-college-prepared counterparts (See Sanderson 1977, Trojanowicz and Nicholson 1976).

For instance, Robert Trojanowicz and Thomas Nicholson (1976, 58) write that the college-prepared officer is:

Willing to experiment and try new things as opposed to preferring the established and conventional way of doing things; assumes a leadership role and likes to direct and supervise the work of others; uses a step-by-step method for processing information and reaching decisions; likes to engage in work providing a lot of excitement and a great deal of variety as opposed to work providing a stable and secure future; and he values himself by his achievement of status symbols established by his culture.

But, other research indicates that there is little difference in performance between college- and high school-prepared officers (See Weirman 1978, Miller and Fry 1978). For example, R.P. Witte (1969) compared two groups of police officers in the field. One group contained officers with college degrees, while the other was composed of high school graduates. Witte found that after six months, the crime rates in each group's area had remained relatively constant. Witte did report, however, that citizen complaints were fewer among the college-educated officers and that their response time in answering calls was faster than that of the high school-prepared officers.

Wayne Cascio (1977) and B.E. Sanderson (1977) found similar indirect evidence of a benefit from college-prepared officers. In Cascio's case, the higher levels of education among Dade County, Florida officers was associated with increased communication abilities, resulting in fewer on-the-job injuries during officer–resident interactions, fewer sick days taken each year, and fewer allegations of unnecessary use of force. Sanderson found that educational levels among officers on the Los Angeles Police Department could be positively correlated with performance during an officer's academy training period and later with the likelihood of promotions.

More recently, Lee Bowker (1980) concluded in his review of the extant literature on higher education and policing that college educations had a number of benefits for police officers. These benefits included higher morale, a decreased amount of dogmatism and authoritarianism, more liberal social attitudes, and fewer disciplinary problems and resident complaints (See Finckenauer 1975; Parker et al. 1976; Roberg 1978).

Regardless of the debate and controversy about college-educated police officers, there is a fairly strong tendency for officers interested in rapid advancement to secure college degrees. It is perhaps ironic that because so many officers have sought college and graduate school educations, the mere possession of a college or graduate school credential no longer assures rapid advancement.

For example, one study by Robert Fischer and his associates (1985) found that promotional chances are not enhanced by officers' possessing college degrees. Although most officers in the study who did obtain promotions possessed college degrees, it was not the degree that made, "a unique or essential contribution to the chances for promotion" (Fischer et al. 1985, 335). Stated slightly differently, so many officers have now begun to accumulate college degrees that such credentials no longer set them apart from other applicants for promotion. Fischer's and his associates' finding about the plenitude of college-prepared officers may provide at least a partial explanation for the dissatisfaction to which Burbeck and Furnham (1985) refer. Since college-educated police officers are becoming more prevalent, their job dissatisfaction may be attributed to the effects of the mundane and routine patrol work typical in policing. In other words, college-prepared officers may have gained social tolerance and a greater depth of knowledge in college, but they have also likely accepted the idea that college preparation is the ticket to advancement. Yet, in policing, experience continues to be a necessary requisite for command positions—regardless of one's educational achievements.

What is particularly interesting about the Fischer et al. finding is that it suggests that there are substantial numbers of college-prepared officers at all levels and ranks of law enforcement. In other words, policing is not administered disproportionately by overeducated ranking officers, nor is it commanded by undereducated, street-wise officials. Instead, there is apparently a far more heterogeneous mix of educational backgrounds.

From Man-at-arms to Police Scholar

It is necessary to emphasize that the historical transition from early watchmen to modern police officers has been slow. Egon Bittner (1980) accurately points out that the early men-at-arms could not be modernized simply by the infusion of scientific courses of study or the acquisition of academic degrees. The kinds of scholarly, scientific bodies of knowledge existing during the early days of law enforcement were inappropriate for creating police-scholars.

Also, many of the academics who instructed the scholarly courses in colleges and universities viewed police officers as unworthy of and not very interested in college educations (Bittner 1980). These assumptions, if true, in combination with officers' perceptions that college educations would not significantly improve their positions in the police department, further slowed the educating of police officers.

It should be stressed that regardless of on which side of the argument about degree requirements one stands, higher education in police work is certainly desirable. This is not to suggest that any course major in college is applicable to policing, although one might be tempted to make such a case, given the other life experiences and maturations college provides in general. This statement is intended to underscore the necessity in policing for officers to be educated in problem-solving and decision-making skills, along with knowledge of culture, psychology, technical writing, and computers. None of these areas can be adequately presented or mastered by students when presented in a programmed two- or four-hour module during the course of a fourteen- or fifteen-week academy class. As Bittner (1980, 79) expresses it:

> The transformation of the conception of policing from the model of man of arms to the model of the trained professional whose training stands in some relationship to scientific scholarship, naturally involves the mobilization of specifically delineated programs of study and instruction.

Naturally, the development of such programs and courses of study are not being advocated to foster an image of policing as more scholastic. Rather, the suggestion is to provide police officers with direction and scholarly course work in areas that will enhance their knowledge and abilities as police officers. In turn, police-officer recipients of graduate credentials who have been correctly schooled in scholarly methods and appropriate theories can eventually contribute to the scientific community in important and insightful ways.

A word of caution is also necessary concerning the potential in policing for officers to become *credentialists*. Credentialism typically involves one or the other of two types. First, it may involve an agency arbitrarily establishing a high educational requirement for a position or rank, but one that may bear little or no relationship to the job, for example, the requirement of a masters degree in any academic discipline as a requisite for becoming a police captain. The argument might be made that graduate school preparation, in general, provides a potential administrative supervisor with various necessary pieces of knowledge. However, it would seem reasonable to expect that a masters in a police-related or social-science field would offer greater benefit than, perhaps, a degree in zoology, mathematics, or geography. The second and closely related type of credentialism arises when an officer is in possession of a graduate degree—even one in a related field—and as a consequence believes he or she should be exempt from various service-time requirements.

Clearly, the American college and university system today has emerged as a means for manufacturing and distributing credentials much more than to providing edification and knowledge. As Christopher Hurn (1978, 39–40) states this position:

> Instead of saying that educational institutions teach skills that are necessary for the performance of complex occupations, it can be argued that educational credentials are used to ration access to high status occupations. . . . Those who have high levels of education do, of course, generally obtain higher status jobs than those with less education. But this does not seem to be because of the cognitive skills that educated people learn in school. It is the possession of the educational credentials, rather than the acquisition of the cognitive skills that those credentials denote, that seem to predict future status.

In the face of what may be termed an American fascination with credentialism, police officers must conscientiously avoid the temptation to secure the fastest, rather than the best, educational credentials. Some thought must be given to how useful a narrowly focused police technical degree might be after retirement. Similarly, police officers should consider whether diploma-mill degrees will be viewed as viable credentials by hiring agencies after retirement.

Police agencies also must be mindful to monitor the kinds of requirements they set for their administrative and supervisory personnel. If a masters degree—in anything—is a requisite for promotion, one might question whether it is necessary at all.

Is High School Preparation Enough?

The standard of a high school diploma as a basic requirement for entry-level police positions and other occupations has prevailed for many years. It can easily be argued that at one time this standard served a functional purpose, the identification of people possessing superior levels of formal education. But, today, where academic credential inflation has evolved enormously, the high school diploma no longer signifies—as it may have prior to World War II—above-average mental ability or a significant level of educational accomplishment.

Harry More Jr. (1985, 306) reports that in 1946, the U.S. Department of Health, Education, and Welfare claimed that less than one-half of the 17-year-old population had completed high school. By 1969, this figure had risen to over 78 percent. By 1985, just over 93 percent of American youths between the ages of 14 and 17 years old were enrolled in high school programs and the majority of them were expected to obtain their diplomas (Molotsky 1984, Bogue 1985). Certainly, the criterion of a high school diploma has become a minimum expectation, rather than an important factor in hiring personnel.

Many in our society, however, claim that while the general population has attained high levels of academic credentials and education, these laurels are unnecessary for basic police functions. In fact, writing during the early twentieth century, what some might consider the infancy of law enforcement, A.L. Cornelius (1929) wrote:

> *Policemen as a class are usually not well educated, skilled mechanically or industrially. They are men above average in physical strength and appearance who have lacked sufficient persistence to acquire an education or learn a trade.*

As More (1985) indicates, this attitude persists among many critics of police officers even today. The assumption is that issuing tickets, directing snarled traffic, and conducting permit inspections simply does not require high levels of education. But, these are not the sole responsibilities of most contemporary police officers. In fact, in many modern police agencies, these more mundane tasks have been delegated to civilian employees or private subcontractors (See Chapter Fourteen). Thus, contemporary police officers are charged with more essential and pressing tasks, such as reducing fear and anxiety about crime among community members, resolving major crimes, preserving constitutional rights, and assuring public safety in general. The necessity for police officers who are educated, articulate, tolerant of others, politically aware, and knowledgeable of the various social and cultural influences operating in the community they serve should be obvious.

Educational Directions for the Future

The argument about the value of college educations for police officers continues today, but with somewhat less intensity than it has previously had. Some of the previous problems involved confusion among both academics and police officials concerning whether college educations for police officers should be vocational training programs. Indeed, many of the early junior college programs, as well as a good many baccalaureate programs that arose during the LEEP years (the late 1960s and early 1970s), may have been more vocational than academic. Today, although some vocational programs persist, many of the early vocational programs have evolved into scholarly, academically oriented programs. Many of these programs are no longer designed exclusively for police officers. Rather, serious students of all aspects of criminal justice have begun to fill the seats in many criminal justice programs.

The debate over where training ends and education begins, and whether more than merely high school preparation should be a national standard for entry-level police officers, may not be settled soon. Yet there is growing appreciation among ranking police officials for the value of a wide-range and indepth knowledge in police and academic subjects. During the recent past, police researchers and police officials have begun to agree on many of their understandings of contemporary police issues. In keeping with this, one can expect a greater acknowledgment in all quarters of requirements in performance of police functions and their role in society.

Police work can no longer be viewed as an occupation of brawny but brainless people. It must begin to be seen as a skilled occupation of competitively educated, technically sophisticated, empathic and humane people. Too, reform and progress in policing must not be limited to the law enforcement community. Rather, as education and practice evolve in police circles, changes must consider the social contours, needs, and expectations of the community (Goldstein 1977, Radelet 1986, Berg 1990).

Until recently, law enforcement reform in America was guilty of "improving the police establishment without having given adequate attention to some serious underlying problems that grow out of the basic arrangements for policing in our society" (Goldstein 1977, 8). More recently, however, the gap between police and scholars has grown smaller and consideration of decision-making processes among police, accountability, ethics, broad educational bases, and control have become more than merely strategies for improved police administration. These areas have incorporated substantive social scientific theories, public opinions, and police needs. But, perhaps more important, recent police reforms have addressed both police and societal problems as related to one another.

THE PRIVATIZATION OF POLICING

As discussed in Chapter Two, the history of policing has been traditionally intertwined with privately and publicly supported efforts. Many businesses employ security guards garbed in uniforms that resemble those of the local police, including, in many cases, weaponry. The purpose of these private police officers, of course, is to secure their business employers against shoplifting and vandalism and to provide personal safety for patrons and employees. Private security officers have become common sights in the private sectors of society, such as shopping malls, department stores, on many college campuses, in the lobbies of fancy businesses, and in a growing number of apartment complexes and residential neighborhoods. However, they have also grown in their appearance in such public sector locations as official security for federal court buildings and courtrooms, as additional security in county sheriffs' jails, and in city run hospitals, parks, and recreational facilities.

In 1976, the report of the President's Task Force on Private Security stated that over one million people were employed in an estimated six-billion-dollar security industry in 1975. Although many of these individuals did have some form of security-related or law enforcement education, the vast majority did not. Unlike public police officers who must attend an academy and qualify through various examinations, most private police do not. Yet, as James K. Stewart, the former director of the National Institute of Justice, states in a recent report, "Nearly as much money is spent by governments to private security companies as is spent for public law enforcement by the federal and state governments combined" (Chaiken and Chaiken 1987, iii).

Many public officials and certainly police executives view the increasing use of untrained or semi-trained private security officers in public policing capacities as problematic. Other officials see the use of private police in the public sector as cost effective and necessary in order to operate efficiently. The privatizing of law enforcement functions, then, may have some serious implications in the face of efforts to professionalize policing.

Several attempts have been made to examine the relationship between public and private policing. In one study sponsored by the National Institute of Justice and undertaken by William C. Cunningham and Todd H. Taylor (1983), several problems of both public and private police are considered. Among other things, Cunningham and Taylor note that both systems do share many similar goals. Both, for example, seek to secure persons and property from harm, identify and prevent criminal activity, and recover stolen property.

The study also indicates that most law enforcement officers continue to hold a low opinion of the quality of contract security personnel, resulting in strain and discord when interacting with each other. Interestingly, 35 states require guards and patrol firms to be licensed, and over 80 percent of all private firms are regulated by state or local agencies (Chaiken and Chaiken 1987). Unfortunately, licensing typically represents filling out certain forms and registering with a local or state agency and not necessarily meeting any requirements or standards.

Although some efforts have been made to increase cooperation and collaboration between public and private police, strain, suspicion, and resentment of one another persist (Reiss 1985). For example, in Boston, Massachusetts, many colleges and universities employ campus police officers. Additionally, most campuses employ traditional contract security guards for fixed patrols in locations such as the bookstore, library, and administrations building or for late-night patrols of the buildings.

In some cases, such as Boston University, Boston College, and the University of Massachusetts at Boston, the campus police represent a full-fledged police department. Officers working in these departments must successfully complete the same fourteen- week academy training program required of all municipal police officers in Massachusetts and sponsored by the Massachusetts Criminal Justice Training Counsel. With the partial exception of certain traffic laws (Chapter 90 of the Massachusetts Motor Vehicle Law), these officers possess all the usual powers of arrest extended to municipal officers. These powers, however, are restricted for the most part to campus property and during their working shift. Even the larger proportion of regular campus police officers have been required since 1983 to attend a six-week police academy training course sponsored by the Massachusetts Criminal Justice Training Counsel.

Similarly, in Pennsylvania, many campus police departments require their officers to serve as "guards," until they have attended a regional police training academy and become fully sworn police officers. In other states, campus officers are partially warranted by the state and, while limited in their police powers, are actually state police officers.

Yet, because campus police officers are regarded by students and the public in general as glorified security guards, enforcing laws is sometimes difficult for these officers. Sarcastic jokes are sometimes uttered by full department campus police about their not being "real cops," as they arrest law-violating students. It would appear that public and private sectors, in the case of college communities, have become very closely related.

Privatization and the Provision of Adequate Police Services

Today, it would be almost impossible for communities to provide all necessary governmental services directly through public service employees. A mix of technical and specialized service needs have required the implementation of consultants, voucher systems, franchises, volunteers, inter-agency loans of personnel, and formal contractual agreements with vendors for an assortment of services.

Law enforcement organizations, as have other governmental agencies, increasingly find themselves faced with the task of considering the feasibility of alternatives to using exclusively police personnel to provide police services. Although not all alternatives may be feasible for every police agency, many agencies have innovated an assortment of cost-effective strategies for acquiring necessary services. These strategies include the use of civilian personnel—frequently as volunteers—sharing or mutually beneficial contractual agreements with agencies in other jurisdictions, and pay-for-service contracts with private vendors to allow police departments to offer a number of services they could not afford otherwise. In addition to these service acquisitions, many police organizations have services augmented by various public or governmental organizations. As Jan and Marcia Chaiken (1987) suggest, for example, neighborhood watch groups provide surveillance of local streets. Often, the only investment on the part of the local police is an officer's time during the initial organization of a watch group and periodically when an officer or officers provide technical assistance to the group.

In many jurisdictions, county agencies supplement various non-law enforcement functions that might otherwise be delegated to a police agency. For instance, county social services or community control counselors may conduct initial juvenile intakes when youths are arrested. Similarly, the county may offer services such as pretrial supervision of offenders or support services for victims.

Frequently, contracts for law enforcement support services are shared by county and municipal agencies or among several municipal departments in close physical proximity to one another. For example, throughout much of North Florida, the municipal police departments and county sheriffs offices all use the Florida Department of Law Enforcement's (F.D.L.E.) crime lab services in investigations of major robberies and homicides.

Even in larger cities, agencies frequently share certain support services that might otherwise be too expensive to be individually purchased and maintained. In Massachusetts, for example, the state police recently acquired an Automated Finger Print Identification System (AFIS). This computerized system enables the police to identify likely suspects from latent fingerprints. As of April 1987, 144 local police departments had submitted ten-print cards (fingerprint card records created during a booking) to the AFIS data bank. The submission of these cards entitles each agency to make requests for a search of the full data set when they identify latent prints during criminal investigations.

Even in this case, because of the sophistication of the AFIS system, the state police at least initially needed to contract with civilian computer experts to provide specialized training for the computer operators. Also, it was necessary to contract with private computer technicians to provide periodic service and maintenance of the system.

Contracts with private vendors in order for law enforcement agencies to obtain various technical support services are not as controversial as contracting for more direct policing services. But, as Cunningham and Todd (1983) report, in 1980, $3.3 billion was paid by government agencies to private security companies. This figure represents over four-fifths as much money as the federal and state governments spent jointly on public sector law enforcement ($4.1 billion).

For many police officials, the question is not whether to use private vendors, but which police functions can be carried out by persons other than sworn officers. For instance, a number of large cities have created job positions that lie somewhere between private citizen

and law enforcement personnel. It is fairly common to find civilian dispatchers who have little or no formal law enforcement training. A more recent innovation is civilian traffic officers (police cadets), who both direct traffic during peak hours at busy and congested intersections and issue parking citations. Yet, these traffic officers typically receive only very limited training, are unarmed, and not permitted full statutory arrest powers.

Even more controversial are the contracts with private vendors for security guards who operate essentially as de facto sworn officers—but who do not receive all the necessary training and who are not officially sworn. Among the leading governmental contractors in this regard is the United States Marshals Service. In March 1982 Chief Justice Warren Burger and Attorney General William French Smith agreed to have the U.S. Marshals Service provide security to the federal judiciary in an effort to both simplify and localize within judicial districts judicial security responsibilities.

The U.S. Marshals Service initially planned to employ 500 contracted security officers to provide courtroom security. This figure soon rose to well over 1,000 contract police to be employed annually by the Marshals Service (*The Third Branch* 1984). In addition to these courthouse and courtroom security officers, each of the 94 U.S. Marshals is empowered to spend up to $10,000 each year to secure private police for various local security needs. These local security needs include transportation and protection of federal witnesses and prisoners (Berg 1984).

Shifting Functions Among Private and Public Police Services

Ironically, the same service demands that led to the divergence from private to public policing over a hundred years ago have now surfaced to call for a resurgence of private police support. Police agencies in the United States, as described in Chapters Two and

Three of this book, sprang from the traditional English watch-and-ward systems. This style of policing mainly involved watching and symbolically serving as a deterrent to crime. Under traditional watch-and-ward systems, constables did not offer any proactive policing strategies—and few reactive ones. Their central purpose was to present a showing of police presence. Similarly, in today's society, there are public outcries for increased police visibility. A much louder shout can certainly be heard from the public for more uniformed officers on the street than for tax dollars to pay for expensive sophisticated investigative equipment (Stewart 1985).

Although basic demands for police protection have remained fairly stable during the past several decades, public sector police agencies have been unable consistently to provide for these demands. In part, this has been an unavoidable circumstance where a particular activity might offer unfair access to certain police functions for some and not for others. Neighborhood patrols by private services are illustrative of this point. By contracting directly with a private police firm, the neighborhood certainly obtains a greater degree of street surveillance than might be offered by the local public police agency. The local police benefit from this arrangement as well, since they are augmented by the private firm's personnel and presence on the neighborhood streets.

Another problem faced by the public police is their need to prioritize their activities and investigations. When an individual resident suffers a property loss from a burglary or robbery, the resident doesn't want to hear that the crime has low priority. In some agencies, calls to the station have begun to be screened and prioritized as they come in or referred immediately to other agencies, such as when a call comes in for emergency utility repairs.

Even where police agencies allocate sufficient funds to increase their numbers, a need for prioritizing calls and cases persists. As suggested above, some communities have realized that they have specialized needs that can only be addressed by a private police patrol.

SUMMARY

This chapter began with a brief consideration of policing as a career as well as the relationship between policing and higher education. The focus in these examinations and throughout this chapter was on the various attitudes and arguments related to the issue of how much education should be required of entry-level police officers. The question of differences between "training" and "education" were additionally considered.

As outlined in this chapter, training was described as involving various skill acquisitions, whereas education was depicted as a broader, more scientifically based accumulation of information and knowledge. As the chapter points out, the specific content of training, in itself, is somewhat problematic. In general terms, training was described as the material and information offered in the police academy, in vocational college programs, and in the field. In contrast to this, educations were described as more closely connected to scholarly college and university programs. The section concluded with the optimistic hope that current and future police reform will continue to move law enforcement in the direction of scholarly police advancements.

Finally, this chapter briefly reviewed another item of concern to law enforcement organizations, the privatization of policing and its potential impact. The chapter points out that private police and contracted law enforcement services in the public sector are not new. Yet, recent demands for various law enforcement services have required many police agencies to seek out greater amounts of private vendor service to augment their public law enforcement personnel. For some law enforcement officials, this has been viewed as a paradoxical and unsettling situation.

REVIEW QUESTIONS

1. What are several reasons police officers frequently state as influencing their decision to enter careers in law enforcement?

2. What are the basic arguments associated with the attitude that entry-level police officers do not require more than a high school diploma or equivalent?

3. In 1973 the National Advisory Commission on Criminal Justice Standards and Goals recommended that police agencies nationally begin to move gradually toward an eventual minimal requirement of a four-year college degree. How is it that over fifteen years have passed, yet few police agencies require a baccalaureate as a minimum educational requirement for employment?

4. How might one defend arguments that "experience is the police officer's best teacher"?

5. Why should future police educational reform efforts incorporate community concerns?

REFERENCES

Alpert, Geoffrey, and Roger Dunham. *Policing Urban America.* Prospect Heights, Ill.: Waveland, 1988.

American Press. "Plan Would Boost Nation's Police Force by 100,000." *Indiana Gazette* (July 12, 1989):1, 6.

Bayley David H., and Egon Bittner. "Learning the Skills of Policing." *Law and Contemporary Problems* 47(1984):35–59.

Berg, Bruce L. "Private Security in the Public Sector: The U.S. Marshal Service as a Case Example." Presented at the annual meeting of the American Society of Public Administrators' Conference on Privatization and Alternative Service Delivery. Cincinnati, Ohio (November 1984).

Berg, Bruce L. "Who Should Teach Police: A Typology and Assessment of Police Academy Instructors." *American Journal of Police* 9(1990):79–100.

Bittner, Egon. *The Function of Police in Modern Society.* Cambridge, Mass.: Oelegeschlager, Gunn and Haine, 1980.

Bogue, Donald J. *The Population of the United States: Historical Trends and Future Predictions.* New York: Free Press, 1985.

Bowker, Lee H. "A Theory of Educational Needs of Law Enforcement Officers." *Journal of Contemporary Criminal Justice* 1(1980):17–24.

Burbeck, Elizabeth, and Adrian Furnham. "Police Officer Selection: A Critical Review of the Literature," *Journal of Police Science and Administration* 13(1985):58–69.

Cascio, Wayne. "Formal Education and Police Officer Performance." *Journal of Police Science and Administration* 5(1977):89.

Chaiken, Marcia, and Jan Chaiken. *Public Policing—Privately Provided.* U.S. Department of Justice, National Institute of Justice. Washington, D.C.: U.S. Government Printing Office, 1987.

Charles, Michael T. "Women in Policing: The Physical Aspect." *Journal of Police Science and Administration* 10(1982):194–205.

Cunningham, William C., and Todd H. Taylor. "Ten Years of Growth in Law Enforcement and Private Security Relationships." *The Police Chief* 50(June 1983):30–31.

Erickson, James, and Matthew Neary. "Criminal Justice Education: Is It Criminal?" *Police Chief* 42(1975):38.

Ermer, V.B. "Recruitment of Female Police Officers in New York." *Journal of Criminal Justice* 6(1978):233–245.

Finckenauer, James O. "Higher Education And Police Discretion." *Journal of Police Science and Administration* 3(1975):450–57.

Fischer, Robert J., Kathryn M. Golden, and Bruce L. Heininger. "Issues in Higher Education for Law Enforcement Officers: An Illinois Study." *Journal of Criminal Justice* 13(1985):329–38.

Fyfe, James F. *Police Personnel Practices, Baseline Data Reports* 15 Washington, D.C.: International City Management Association, 1983.

Goldstein, Herman. *Policing a Free Society.* Cambridge, Mass.: Ballinger, 1977.

Hurn, Christopher. *The Limits and Possibilities of Schooling: An Introduction to the Sociology of Education.* Boston, Mass.: Allyn & Bacon, 1978.

Kramer, Michael. "From College to Cops." *Time* (March 15, 1990):19.

Locke, Bernard, and Alexander B. Smith. "Police Who Go to College." In Arthur Niederhoffer and Abraham S. Blumberg, eds. *The Ambivalent Force,* 2d ed. New York: Holt, Rinehart and Winston, 1976.

Meadows, Robert J. "Beliefs of Law Enforcement Administrators and Criminal Justice Educators Toward the Needed Skill Competencies in Entry-Level Police Training Curriculum." *Journal of Police Science and Administration* 15(1987):1–9.

Meagher, M. Steven, and Nancy A. Yentes. "Choosing a Career in Policing: A Comparison of Male and Female Perceptions." *Journal of Police Science and Administration* 14(1986):320–27.

Miller, J., and L. Fry. "Some Evidence on the Impact of Higher Education for Law Enforcement Personnel." *Police Chief* (August 1978):30–33.

Milton, Catherine H. "The Future of Women in Policing." In Alvin W. Cohn, ed. *The Future of Policing.* Beverly Hills, Calif.: Sage, 1978.

Molotsky, Irving. "31 States Gain in College Test Scores." *The New York Times* (December 19, 1984):B6.

More, Harry W. Jr., ed. *Critical Issues in Law Enforcement.* Cincinnati, Ohio: Anderson, 1985.

National Advisory Commission on Criminal Justice Standards and Goals. *Police.* Washington, D.C.: United States Government Printing Office, 1973.

National Commission on Law Observance and Enforcement (Wickersham Commission). *Report on Police.* Washington, D.C.: Government Printing Office, 1931.

Parker, L.C., M. Donnelly, D. Gerwitz, J. Marcus, and V. Kowalewski. "Higher Education: Its Impact on Police Attitudes." *Police Chief* (July, 1976):33–35.

President's Commission on Law Enforcement and Administration of Justice. *Task Force Report: The Police.* Washington, D.C.: Government Printing Office, 1967.

Radelet, Louis A. *The Police and the Community* 4th ed. New York: Macmillan, 1986.

Reiss, Albert J. Jr. *Policing a City's Central District—The Oakland Story.* U.S. Department of Justice, National Institute of Justice. Washington, D.C.: Government Printing Office, 1985.

Reynolds, Lee H. *Eliminators of Obstacle: Irrelevant Selection Criteria.* New York: Urban League, 1980.

Roberg, R. "An Analysis of the Relationship Among Higher Education Belief Systems and Job Performance of Patrol Officers." *Journal of Police Science and Administration* 6(1978):344–66.

Samaha, Joel. *Criminal Justice.* St. Paul, Minn.: West, 1988.

Sanderson, B.E. "Police Officers: The Relationship of a College Education to Job Performance," *Police Chief* 44(1977):62.

Sapp, Allen, David Carter, and Darrel Stephens. "Police Chiefs: CJ Curricula Inconsistent with Contemporary Police Needs." *ACJS Today* 17(1989):1, 5.

Sherman, Lawrence. "Policing Communities: What Works?" In Albert Reiss and Michael Tonry, eds. *Communities and Crime.* Chicago, Ill.: University of Chicago Press, 1986:343–86.

Sherman, Lawrence. *The Quality of Police Education.* San Francisco, Calif.: Jossey–Bass, 1978.

Sherman, Lawrence, and Warren Bennis. "Higher Education for Police Officers: The Central Issues," *Police Chief* 44(1977):32.

Skolnick, Jerome H., and David H. Bayley. *The New Blue Line: Police Innovation in Six American Communities.* New York: Free Press, 1986.

Smith, Douglas. "The Neighborhood Content of Police Behavior." In Albert Reiss and Michael Tonry, eds. *Communities and Crime.* Chicago, Ill.: University of Chicago Press, 1986.

Smith, Robert. "Accreditation: Impact on Police Departments," *The Police Chief* 54(1987):37–38.

Staufenberger, Richard A. "The Professionalization of Police: Efforts and Obstacles." *Public Administration Review* (November/December 1977):678–85.

Staufenberger, Richard A. *Progress in Policing: Essays on Change.* Cambridge, Mass.: Ballinger, 1980.

Stewart, James K. "Public Safety and Private Police," *Police Administration Review* (November 1985):22–26.

The Third Branch. "Federal Court Security Detailed by U.S. Marshals Service Director Morris." *Bul-*

letin of the Federal Courts 16(1984):1–3, 5–6, 8.

Trojanowicz, Robert, and Thomas Nicholson. "A Comparison of Behavioral Styles of College Graduate Police Officers vs. Non–College Going Police Officers." *Police Chief* 43(1976):57.

Vollmer, August, and Albert Schneider. "The School for Police as Planned at Berkeley." *Jour-*

nal of the American Institute of Criminal Law in Criminology (March 1917):875–80.

Weirman, C.L. "The Educated Policeman." *Journal of Police Science and Administration* 4(1978):450–57.

Witte, R.P. "The Dumb Cop." *Police Chief* 36(1969):38.

GLOSSARY

Academites. Individuals who purport to be experts, having or claiming to have certain academic credentials.

Accreditation. Formal recognition that an agency or institution conforms to some specific body of regulations or standards.

Active criminality. Active participation in any illegal behavior.

Acquittal. Legal confirmation that a defendant is innocent of the charges, following a criminal trial.

Addicts. Persons who habitually use and have an uncontrollable desire for various illegal and narcotic substances (heroine, cocaine, amphetamines, etc.).

Adjudication. The legal decision–making process through which guilt or innocence of criminal charges is determined.

Admissible evidence. Information and objects germane to a criminal trial case that meet certain rules of evidence, including safe transportation and a clearly recorded chain of custody.

Agrarian. A person or area organized around a farming life–style.

AIDS. See Human Immuno-deficiency Virus.

AIDS–Related complex. Prior to AIDS becoming active, persons testing positive and experiencing various illness complications, generally are referred to as ARC or AIDS–related complex.

Argot. A specialized language or jargon used by some group or occupation.

Androgynous. Possessing characteristics of both males and females; being at home with both masculine and feminine role characteristics.

Anomie. An inability to act appropriately because one does not understand the rules of the game; social normlessness or normative confusion.

Antiquity. Referring to ancient times, typically periods prior to the Middle Ages.

Arraignment. A formal hearing before a judge or magistrate, in which the accused is read the charges, informed of legal rights, and is asked to enter either a guilty or not guilty response to the charges.

Arrest. The action of stopping and detaining an individual for the lawful purpose of restraining this individual until formally charged with some law violation.

Arrest warrant. A formal court order issued by a judge or magistrate directing that a specified individual be brought in and detained in order to respond to criminal charges.

Assault. Placing an individual in fear or apprehension of being harmed; reasonable apprehension of immediate or offensive contact by another; often connected with the concept of battery (see *Battery*).

Assize of arms. An ancient statute in England that decreed that all able–bodied men respond to an alarm cry, and chase after a law violator.

Authoritarianism. A rigid, hierarchical view of social relations, usually accompanied by intolerance of other view points, and the belief that rules should be strictly followed. In policing, often associated with a personality and behavioral style which involves blind obedience to rules and authority.

Automated Fingerprint Identification System (AFIS). A computerized system that stores fingerprint record cards in its a data base and can rapidly match latent prints found at crime scenes or identify suspects who have been arrested.

Bail. Money or property posted by a defendant (or someone in the name of the defendant) to secure a pretrial release from jail and ensure that the defendant will return to court for trial. If defendant fails to appear for trial, money or property are forfeited.

Bail bondsman. An individual who contracts to pay another person's bail in exchange for a fee, usually about ten per cent of the total bail amount.

Ballistics. The scientific study of bullets and their tell–tale markings. By making comparisons of marks left on bullets, they can be matched to the weapon that fired them.

Baton. A club used by police officers as a tactical weapon.

Battery. The unlawful touching of another person without consent, usually rough or potentially injurious. In connection with assault ("assault and battery"), the literal touching or placing of an individual in fear or apprehension of being touched.

Beat. The basic geographic unit of patrol; the area a patrol officer is assigned during a tour of duty.

Bill of indictment. A written document used in grand jury systems by the state's prosecutor asking grand jury members to charge a suspect with a crime.

Block watches. An organized neighborhood group that serves as the eyes and ears of the police, contacting the local authorities when suspicious people are noted.

Blue Devils. Derogatory slang for Sir Robert Peel's Metropolitan Police Force; refers to the blue coats worn by the Day Police, who preceded the Metropolitan Police.

Bobbies. Affectionate nickname for British constables, derived from the name of Sir Robert Peel.

Booking. Formal record of arrest, involving identification of the suspect (name, address, photograph, and fingerprinting); listing of offenses with which the suspect is charged; name of the arresting officer, and the name and address of the complainant (if other than the officer).

Boom towns. During the gold rush of 1849, towns that sprang-up or burst open across California almost over night.

Bribery. The illegal offering of money, property, or favor, in exchange for access to some desired goal or exchange of favors.

Bureaucracy. An administrative system used by formal organizations to improve uniform effectiveness and efficiency, including a hierarchical ranking of organizational members, rules, communication linkages, and records.

Burglary. Unlawful, forced entry to a building in order to commit a felony (usually a theft).

Buttering. Intentionally issuing bad or worthless checks.

Byzantine. Used as an adjective, it refers to characteristics associated with the ancient Byzantine Empire.

Call–for–Service. Police calls for any activity other than to enforce law or restore civil order to a situation.

Careerists. Alleged forensic experts who augment their experiential training and qualifications by fiction or fraud.

Case law. Legally binding interpretations of written laws; previous interpretations of past court cases that have established precedence or custom in the legal system.

Castrum. Latin term for castle, market, and city.

Cavalry. Soldiers who traditionally fought while mounted on horseback.

Chain–of–Custody. Accurate records indicating who has received and who has returned the evidence, including times, dates, and signatures of all parties handling evidence.

Charge. The formal description of a law violation of which a suspect stands accused.

Cigarette boat. Speed boats frequently the vessel of choice of drug smugglers.

Circumstantial evidence. Evidence offered in court, although indirect, that is germane to the case being heard (See also Ad*missible evidence*).

Citizen's arrest. The constitutional right of every person to take a suspect into custody (place them under arrest). Rules of citizen's arrest vary in different jurisdictions.

Civil law. Body of laws and torts, distinguished from criminal laws as those pertaining to private and civil matters.

Civil rights. Refers to those civil liberties guaranteed by the Bill of Rights of the U.S. Constitution, including various limitations on the authority and privilege granted police officers in the United States.

Clearing cases. Taking police cases off the open records either because a suspect has been arrested (cleared by arrest), been adjudicated (cleared by conviction), or to allow other cases to be investigated (cleared to a pending file).

Common law. Early English law built upon the tribal customs of Anglo–Saxons, feudal rules and procedures, and traditional ways of life among village peasantry; became the standardized law of England and later the basis for much of U.S. criminal law.

Community policing. A police strategy that strives to reduce fear, increase community awareness about safety and crime, and maintain order, rather than direct crime interdiction.

Complaint. A sworn written statement asserting that a specific individual has committed a law violation.

Conflict perspective. The view of the American justice system as a collection of diverse groups, each vying for dominance and self–interest in society. Criminal laws, then, are seen as attempts by the dominant group to maintain its position by suppressing other groups.

Consensus perspective. The view that most people in society agree upon certain common goals, values, and social standards for behavior. Crimes, then, are seen as violations of these shared standards for behavior.

Consent. The voluntary participation of an individual, such as granting permission for police to conduct a search.

Constable. Originally seen as the peacekeeper in early English and colonial American towns; today, a municipal official similar to a sheriff, responsible for preserving public peace, as well as serving various civil processes.

Contraband. Any item for which possession is formally a violation of law or institutional rule (such as in hospitals or prisons); including firearms, and drugs.

Conviction. The judgment of guilty in a criminal court case.

Cop–speak. A jargonized version of police language.

Corruption. The tainting of integrity and moral principle through acceptance of bribes, graft, or favors.

Court of the star chamber. An early English court whose members were appointed by the King; court met in a star–shaped chamber, where "enemies of the Crown" were tried. If defendants failed to provide the court with a confession, they would be tortured until they did. The defendants were later executed on the weight of their confessions.

Covert. Activity performed surreptitiously.

Credentialist. Someone who acquires many training certificates and/or academic credentials in order to suggest having greater expertise in an area than they actually possess.

Crime. Violation either of social norms and rules (societal definition) or of codified bodies of law (legal definition).

Criminal justice. The institutional system devoted to preventing, detecting, apprehending, adjudicating, punishing, correcting, and reintegrating individuals who commit criminal behavior.

Criminal law. Codified body of laws that define lawful and unlawful behavior, establish punishments for violation, and whose enforcement is backed by the political force of the society.

Criminologists. Persons involved in the study of crime, criminals, social responses to criminal behavior, and the evolution of laws and legal systems.

Criminology. The systematic study of crime, criminals, and social responses to criminal behavior.

Crushers. Derogatory slang used to describe Sir Robert Peel's Metropolitan Police Force.

Culpability. The quality or state of being blameworthy; the amount of responsibility one deserves for a particular offense.

Culture. The social inheritance of a group or people, including ways of life and behavior.

Curtilage. The area of property commonly in use by the residents of a dwelling; typically, the land and buildings near the main residential dwelling, but may extended into fields and acreage which is used routinely by the owner.

Custody. Placing an individual or property under lawful control or maintaining protective responsibility for an individual or item of property (as in evidence).

Cynicism. The attitude or belief that people are self-interested and motivated singularly toward personal gain.

Deadly force. The amount of force likely to cause serious bodily injury or death.

Deep cover. Undercover police operations that exceed the daily shift of an officer and may require the officer to alter appearance, residence, and identity for the duration of the investigation.

Defeminization. Casting off traditionally associated feminine role characteristics by women and imitating masculine attributes.

Defendant. The individual who stands accused in a criminal or civil court case.

Delinquency. Refers to youthful misconduct and law violations.

Desocialization. The striping away of one's self within an institution in order to later replace this with the institution's desired orientations, goals, and values.

Detective. A category of police officer responsible for the investigative end of a police case (gathering evidence, interviewing witnesses and suspects, etc.).

Detention. Restraining a suspect prior to court appearance.

Determinate sentencing. Refers to fixed (flat) terms of incarceration; the attaching of a specified number of years of incarceration to each element of a crime.

Deterrence. An attempt to prevent criminal activity before it occurs; philosophically is linked to punishment theory in which the expectation of a severe punitive response is intended to discourage criminal behavior.

Deviance. Non-conformity to social norms; exceeding the social tolerance of a group, community, or society.

Direct evidence. Evidence offered by an eyewitness to a crime and germane to the case.

Discretion. The ability of an individual to use personal decision making abilities to determine actions. In the case of police, includes whether to ticket or arrest, what crimes to charge an individual with.

Domicile. A place of residence.

Double-marginality. A feeling among some black officers that they are seen by their white colleagues as likely to be lenient with blacks in the field, at the same time as they are subjected to overt racism and discrimination.

Due process. The essential element in constitutional law that assures a person rights to privacy, limits the intrusions government can lawfully make into the affairs of an individual, and safeguards the individual from arbitrary or unfair state procedures in judicial and administrative actions.

Election riot. A major civil riot in New York City in 1934, so extensive that police alone could not restore order, and the National Guard was called in to assist.

Empathy. The ability of one person to place oneself in the role of another to better understand how the other person feels or thinks.

Enclosure system. The conversion of farm land to sheep pastures in England during the early parts of the

Industrial Revolution.

Enforcement priorities. When a police agency establishes a particular or set of particular law violations to concentrate on, sometimes referred to as *selective enforcement*.

Entrapment. The initiating of a crime by a law enforcement agent to induce someone to take part in the crime's commission. Because it is illegal, the claim of entrapment is used by felony suspects as a defense plea.

Evidence. Sworn statements, material, or microtraces that offer information (directly or indirectly) about the guilt or innocence of a defendant in a court trial.

Exclusionary rule. Restricts admissible evidence only to that which has been lawfully obtained (See *Admissible evidence*).

Excused for cause. During *Voir Dire,* an attorney's challenge of a potential juror to eliminate the person from the jury panel when answers to questions demonstrate the potential juror's unsuitability to serve. Most jurisdictions have some limit on how many challenges with cause an attorney may use.

Fair access to law enforcement. Refers to a doctrine that all persons are entitled to equal police protection and services.

Felony. A serious law violation that carries a penalty of a prison sentence (either at state or federal level) or execution. Typically, prison sentences are for durations of greater than one year (two years in some jurisdictions).

Feud. A prolonged mutual antagonism between two or more parties.

Feudalism. The social and political system that flourished throughout much of Western Europe during the nineteenth to fifteenth centuries. The system revolved around a landed lord, or *Thane,* who had the services of tenants (serfs) to work and protect the land.

Fine. A monetary remedy that a convicted person may be required to pay, either in addition to or instead of other punishments.

Fingerprint. The imprint or impression left by the raised ridges (friction lines) of an individual's fingertips.

Fleeing felon rule. A common law rule, that prior to 1985 (*Tennessee* v. *Garner,* 105 S.Ct. 1694, 1985) permitted police officers to shoot any fleeing felon. After the Supreme Court ruling in *Tennessee* v. *Garner,* state laws significantly modified their specifications and the circumstances under which an officer can lawfully fire at fleeing felony suspects. Speaking generally, these modifications require that the escaping suspect possess an imminent threat to other people or society.

Fluid patrol. A style of police deployment that provides for shifting patrol personnel hour by hour into sections of the community where and when crime data indicate the greatest need.

Foot patrol. Style of police patrol in which officers walk an assigned area.

Forensics. Using various aspects of the natural and medical sciences to solve a crime.

Forgery. The falsification or altering of a public record, financial instrument, or other written instrument in order to defraud or deceive another person.

Forty–niners. Nickname given to pioneers who traveled to the West Coast to prospect gold in 1849.

Frankepledge. A mutual responsibility system established by the French; served as basis for the English tithing system; imposed on Englishmen by the Normans as a kind of compulsory collective bail fixed for individuals.

Fresh pursuit doctrine. The ability of police officers to cross jurisdictional limits to continue the uninterrupted pursuit of a fleeing felony suspect.

Friction ridges. Ridges on the surfaces of fingers, palms of hands, toes, and soles of feet. These ridges tend to be parallel to each other and are unique in pattern to each individual.

Frisks. Also called "Terry

Stops," provide police officers with the legitimate right to pat down the outer garments of a suspect or suspicious person stopped for questioning, provided the officer has reason to believe the stopped person may be carrying a weapon.

Functionalism. A sociological approach that emphasizes the idea that society is composed of many interdependent parts. A functionalist approach stresses the need for social cooperation and a consensus on social values and norms among societal members.

Gold coast. Nickname for the coast of California; originated during gold rush of 1849.

Good faith exception. Legal provision that permits the introduction of evidence even when the warrant executed to obtain it is faulty. The good faith exception is permitted provided the police demonstrate they acted with good faith and to the best of their knowledge and ability when obtaining the warrant.

Grand jury. A group of citizens impaneled to evaluate information and evidence used to determine whether a crime has been committed and whether sufficient grounds exist to justify charging an individual.

Grass eaters. Term used in the Knapp Commission report to describe police officers who routinely received small payoffs for ignoring certain activities such as gambling and prostitution.

Headborough. An elected head man of the hundred; presided over monthly meetings to discuss various problems or needs of the hundred. Also called a *Reeve*.

Hearsay evidence. Second or third party information (as compared with direct evidence) for which the individual does not have personal knowledge.

Hellenistic. Refers to ideas and customs associated with a period of time in Greece after the conquest by Alexander the Great, characterized by a blend of Greek and Roman styles of culture; around the second century.

High-risk for AIDS. Categories of persons who are more likely than some other categories to contract AIDS.

Home security survey. A common activity undertaken by neighborhood watch groups; involves an inventory of safety and security items which watch group members use to assess how secure their own homes are.

Homicide. The killing of one person by another.

Hue and cry. An alarm used in medieval England when the villagers needed to raise a group to pursue an offender.

Human Immunodeficiency Virus. Commonly called HIV. Infects and destroys white blood cells, which are used by the body to fend off infections and illness.

Hundred. During medieval England, a population and geographic arrangement containing ten tithings, which equaled 100 families (See *Tithing*).

Hundred court. Designed to ensure that all eligible men were enrolled in a tithing and thus pledged for their good behavior and that of one another; also known as the *Sheriff's Tourn*.

Image processing. Use of computers to plot, draw, store, and transmit images.

Immunity from prosecution. An exemption from legal responsibility; certain categories of people who cannot be prosecuted even if they intentionally break the law (certain diplomats).

Incapacitation. A theory of punishment that removes the offender from society so he or she cannot commit additional crimes; placing an individual out of commission.

Incident report. A basic record–keeping device used by most police agencies to note police officers' responses to service and law enforcement calls.

Incommunicado. The detaining of an individual while depriving the person of any ability to communicate with others.

Incriminate. The appearance of guilt as the result of some evidence.

Indeterminate sentencing. A duration of incarceration with both a stated minimum and maximum amount of time to serve. After serving the minimum time, the prisoner becomes eligible for parole.

Indictment. The written accusation by a grand jury charging an individual with a felony.

Indigent. A person who lacks sufficient financial resources to obtain basic necessities such as food and shelter.

Informal social control. All of the informal ways in which people are discouraged from deviant or illegal behavior; mechanisms designed to increase conformity to norms and laws.

Informant (tipster). An individual who provides information to law enforcement officers.

Information. Similar to an indictment; formal written document used to demonstrate probable cause exists to charge an individual with a crime; used in jurisdictions where a grand jury system does not exist.

Initial appearance. A suspect's appearance before a magistrate to be charged and to enter a plea. In some cases bail will be set during the initial appearance.

Institutional discrimination. The denial of opportunities and equal rights as the result of the normal operation of an organization or agency.

Intent. Intentional action.

Interactionism. A sociological approach that views reality as influenced by how people define their situations; their reactions to the behavior of others.

Internal corruption. A category of police corruption that occurs among officers involved in bending or breaking agency rules, regulations of the criminal law.

Investigation. The inquiry undertaken by law enforcement officers to solve a crime and to identify and apprehend the offender(s) responsible.

Jail. A holding facility often located in a local police station or sheriff's office; used temporarily to detain suspects prior to their trials. Jails may additionally contain persons who have been tried and given short sentences.

Joust. A combat between two knights on horseback on an enclosed field in medieval England.

Judge. A individual empowered to offer an authoritative opinion about conflicting issues offered by two parties with decisions to be based upon the merits of each side's argument.

Judicial. Relating to the judgment or decision-making process of judges.

Judiciary. A term that refers to judges as career members of the system of courts in a given area.

Jurisdiction. As regards police, the geographic area to which their law enforcement authority is restricted. Similarly, for courts, the geographic area from which court cases can be heard.

Jury. A group of people impaneled and sworn to determine fairly the guilt or innocence of a defendant in a court case.

Justice. The equitable disposition of disputes established in the writings of Plato around 400 B.C.

Juvenile. A youth under legal age for certain privileges, and who because of youthful age is tried in juvenile or family court rather than criminal court. Under some circumstances, such as excessive brutality, a juvenile may be petitioned to criminal court, where the juvenile will be tried as an adult.

Kin police. A system of policing associated with primitive cultures. This system involves the family members of an injured or offended party to locate and punish the individual responsible. This style of policing easily disintegrated into bloody feuds.

Kiting. Knowingly writing a check for an amount of money that exceeds the balance, with the intention of adding sufficient funds to the account prior to the check's negotiation.

Knapp Commission Report.

The report resulting from a lengthy investigation of police corruption in New York state in 1972. The report described massive graft and corruption at all levels of the New York City Police Department.

Larceny. The taking and carrying away of personal property of another with the intention of depriving the owner permanently of its use.

Latent. Consequences that are not obvious or recognized by participant in a system; unintended outcomes.

Latent print. The finger, palm or foot print left on objects at scene of a crime (See *Fingerprint*).

Law Enforcement Assistance Administration (LEAA). A federal agency established in 1965 to administer aid to local justice systems. The intention was to encourage improvements in police departments, particularly in the areas of police officer education and training strategies. Money for educational programs was provided through the Law Enforcement Education Program (LEEP). Many of the criminology and criminal justice programs at colleges and universities today were started by funds from LEAA.

Law enforcement calls. Police response to calls that result in the enforcement of law rather than the provision of some (social) service.

Law enforcement officer. One sworn to preserve the peace and maintain social order.

Lex talionis. Retaliatory principle attributed to the Code of Hammurabi; the punishment for an equivalent offense; often described as "an eye for an eye."

Light cover. Undercover police operations that last only the duration of the officer's duty shift (about eight hours).

Line officer. The uniformed patrol level of police organizations.

Line-up. A procedure in which a witness views a group of individuals, including a suspect in the crime. The witness is asked to identify the suspect. If an identification is made, and the witness points-out the suspect, this identification may be used in court.

Magna Carta. A document issued by King John of England on June 15, 1215; provided Englishmen with rights to due process, trial, and other legal protections and rights.

Mala in se. Behavior innately evil and immoral, including murder, rape, and aggravated assault.

Mala prohibita. Behavior that is illegal because a statute or ordinance prohibits it; crimes that reflect the breaking of social norms of particular times or community needs. Parking laws are an example of mala prohibitum crimes, as are

drinking–age restrictions.

Malice. Intentional harm.

Mandate. A formal order or responsibility; an obligatory duty.

Manifest. Consequences and outcomes obvious to, and intended by participants.

Masculine. Stereotypic characteristics associated with being male.

Meat eaters. Term used in the Knapp Commission Report to describe corrupt police officers who actively used their position to secure bribes.

Microtraces. Minute particles used as evidence in forensic investigations of crimes.

Miranda warning. The requirement that police officers advise suspects of their constitutional rights about self–incrimination prior to asking them any questions. The warning also informs the suspect that he or she is entitled to counsel by an attorney before making any statement that can be used against the suspect in court, and that counsel will be provided, even if the suspect cannot afford it.

Misdemeanor. A crime less serious than a felony; behavior punishable by a short jail sentence and/or a fine.

Mitigating circumstances. Information about a criminal's state of mind prior to or during the commission of an illegal act, which may reduce criminal responsibility; information a judge or jury may consider in determining the extent of blameworthiness of a defendant.

Mobile patrol. Patrolling some area by means of a conveyance other than walking.

Modus operandi. A distinct style or pattern characteristic of a criminal's behavior.

Molly Maguires. An alleged terrorist group during the 1870s that sought to secure safety codes and rights for coal miners in Pennsylvania.

Morals. Pertaining to internalized values about social behavior and conformity to norms, rules, and law.

Mounted Officers Patrol. Established in 1748 by Henry Fielding. This policing group rode horses along the crime–infested roads leading to London in order to maintain safe passage for travelers.

Mules. A term to describe people smuggling drugs into the country.

Myth of full enforcement. The idea that all laws are enforced with equal intensity all of the time.

Narc. Slang for undercover narcotics investigators or undercover police officers in general.

New professionals. Contemporary label used for certain categories of workers, such as architects, social workers, teachers, bankers, and accountants. While these work categories do

not conform to most definitions of traditional professions, they have nonetheless been awarded the nominal status of professions.

Nolo contendere. Literally means "I will not contest it." This plea is entered in criminal cases implying but not actually admitting guilt. Since no admission of guilt is actually offered, a plea of nolo contendere cannot be used against the defendant in any later civil proceeding that might arise.

Norms. Guidelines for behavior; social standards of conduct and deportment in various places and times.

Offender. A person who has violated the law.

On call. When an officer is prepared to go on duty upon receipt of a telephone call.

Ondontology. The use of bite marks as a means of identifying criminals.

On–the–job–training. Learning basic skills for a given job while actually working in the field.

Open field doctrine. Refers to the ability of police lawfully to enter private property in order to seize contraband clearly in view, even in the absence of a search warrant (See *Search warrants* and *Plain sight doctrine*).

Operation I.D. A segment of community policing sometimes associated with neighborhood watch operations. Involves initiating or

in other ways marking personal property such as stereo equipment, televisions, and appliances and registering these items with local police. In the event of a theft, the "IDs" (identification marks) can be used to ensure proper return of the item.

Order maintenance. A primary mandate for police officers to maintain control and peace in the community.

Ordinance. A publicly enacted law prohibiting certain actions and enforced by governmental sanctions (fines and/or jail).

Outsider. Someone outside of or not a member of a group and therefore not fully accepted or able to fully understand the language, values, or behavior of group members (insiders).

Paramilitary. Patterned after or associated with military organizations; the use of military ranking and organizational system.

Pariah. A person or group rejected and cast out from society; nomadic guests in various host cultures.

Parliament. A formal council used to discuss public concerns; a political governing body in England.

Parochial. Of or related to the control or influence of a church parish.

Parole. The release of a prisoner prior to serving a full sentence. Parole is a privilege that must be earned and then maintained through a contractual agreement. Violation of this agreement can result in the parolee's immediate return to prison.

Peacekeeping. A principle function of the police (See *Order maintenance*).

Peelian reform. Standards for law enforcement hiring and operations established by Sir Robert Peel in 1829. Peel's twelve recommendations are still the cornerstone of modern police hiring standards in the United States.

Perjury. Lying while under oath; willfully making a false statement while asserting its truthfulness.

Plain sight doctrine. Refers to the ability of police officers to establish probable cause for a warrantless arrest if they see contraband in plain sight.

Police agency accreditation. Standardized rules and procedures set forth by Commission on Accreditation to upgrade and maintain a high level of performance among accredited police agencies.

Police discretion. The range of choices police officers have at their disposal; including whether to ticket, counsel, refer, arrest, detain, talk with, or even shoot a suspect.

Police professionalism. The attempt to convey the idea that modern police officers

are qualified for and skilled at their jobs. The push for police professionalism has led to increased educational requirements for entry-level officers, better equipped departments, and more clearly articulated department policies and procedures.

Police state. Governmental rule by force that uses networks of secret police to maintain social and civil order.

Police subculture. A social network providing officers with emotional support, empathic understanding, like values, beliefs, and shared ways of seeing and doing things.

Police work. The activities undertaken by police officers. Often refers to law enforcement tasks associated with patrol work.

Practical norms. The everyday rules that guide our behavior regardless of whether these behaviors stretch social tolerance.

Precinct. A geographic area including several sectors; used administratively to coordinate the activities of patrol officers.

Pre-emptory challenge. During *voir dire*, a prospective juror may be eliminated by either state's counsel or defense counsel without specific reason. The number of pre-emptory challenges depends upon both a given jurisdiction and the kind of case.

Presumption of innocence. The maxim in American justice that a "person is innocent until proven guilty." This maxim provides the justification for bail prior to trial.

Presumptive sentencing guidelines. Policy established by a state's legislature conveying the specific sentences for various crimes. Sentences vary according to jurisdictions, but all carry the full weight of the law.

Proactive policing. A strategy in policing in which the police organization takes the initiative in seeking out and apprehending criminals and preventing crimes.

Probable cause. Facts and information that would lead the average person to believe that a crime has been or is about to be committed.

Profession. In the traditional sense, certain careers characterized by established standards for behavior, entrance restrictions, educational and performance requirements, a code of ethics, self-regulation and sanctioning abilities.

Professional. In contrast to an amateur, one who possesses certain specialized knowledge and skills and who is paid for this knowledge or skill.

Prosecutor. Official representative of the state in criminal court proceedings.

Protect and serve. A widely used motto for police officers. This motto is given to loosely outline the breadth of services police officers provide to their communities.

Public defender. Employed by the state, attorneys who defend persons accused by the state of criminal offenses; public defenders counsel accused persons who cannot afford to retain private counsel.

Queue. A line of persons or objects.

Railway Police Acts. State statutes during the nineteenth century that empowered proprietary guard forces employed by the railroads with full police powers.

Rattle watch. A night watch group in New Amsterdam circa 1664; members carried wooden rattles to announce their presence and allow would–be law breakers to flee before confrontation with the watchman.

Reactive policing. A policing strategy in which police officers respond to the complaints of residents, or investigate criminal activity only after it has occurred.

Recidivism. The repetition of criminal behavior; usually associated with a released prisoner being apprehended for committing another crime.

Reeve. An elected head man of a hundred (See *Headborough*).

Reference group. The peo-

ple in one's friendship group or primary group one looks up to and desires to emulate. May also include celebrities or fictitious characters one admires.

Release on recognizance (ROR). Releasing a person accused of a crime with no monetary bail required; ROR occurs when the defense has demonstrated the accused is a stable member of the community not likely to flee or fail to return for trial.

Resocialization. The replacement of one set of values, orientations, beliefs, and attitudes with another.

Rifling. The internal grooves in the barrels of most modern rifles (except shot guns).

Ritual. Routine procedures that take on great meaning for their performer.

Robbery. The use or threat of force in order to steal money or property from another person.

Role. Expectations (patterns) of behavior associated with a given category or position.

Rotten pockets. Several corrupt police officers who band together within a single precinct.

Sanctions. Penalties or punishment invoked when a person violates norms or laws.

Search and seizure. Inspection of a person, property, vehicle, or premise by police and confiscation of con-

traband or evidence. With the exception of certain circumstances, the search must be accompanied by a search warrant for the confiscation of evidence to be lawful (See *Search warrant*).

Search warrant. A formal writ issued by a judge or magistrate permitting police officers to search specified areas and seize certain items of evidence. Warrants can only be obtained after the police demonstrate a reasonable cause to search.

Secret police. Police or a security organization designed to provide a political leader with special services and protection.

Sector. A geographic unit containing several beats and used administratively to supervise and coordinate the activities of patrol officers (See *Beat*).

Selective enforcement. The prioritizing of laws to enforce, usually to temporarily focus police actions in a given area for a brief period of time.

Self–incrimination. Causing oneself to appear guilty of a crime through word or action.

Semi–profession. A way of describing certain new professional groups.

Sentence. The sanction imposed upon a defendant by a court after conviction of a crime.

Shadow-box professionalism. Refers to the idea that

some occupations attempt to professionalize by imitating attributes of more traditional professions. However, rather than successfully replicating various necessary characteristics, shadows or near–replications occur.

Sheriff. The chief law enforcement official in a county.

Shire. A geographic area in medieval England about the size of a county.

Shire–reeve. The head law enforcement official of a shire in medieval England (See *Shire*). *Shire reeve* was the forerunner of the title and role of sheriff.

Sociological. Referring to the systematic study of social behavior.

Social control. All of the social efforts used to discourage people from rule or law violating behavior.

Social response. All of the social sanctions imposed by society to punish and discourage rule, norm, and law violating behavior.

Socialization. Learning one's cultural way of life; in policing, learning about police values, norms, and social roles (See *Subculture*).

Statute. A law passed by the legislature of a state.

Statute of Winchester. King Edward the first's attempt to reaffirm the old tradition of mutual responsibility in 1285. Reestablished a version of the Saxon hue and cry system, and made it a crime to conceal or protect felons.

Stings. Undercover police operations that lull criminals into a false sense of security as these criminals attempt to fence stolen goods to officers. Some stings involve misleading suspects who have eluded authorities into believing they have won some contest in order to ensure their presence somewhere and their willingness to identify themselves. Once they have positively identified themselves, they are taken into custody.

Street experience. The experiential knowledge gained from years of working as a police officer, regardless of one's level of formal education.

Stress–reaction training. An attempt to draw out character flaws among new police recruits during the first day of police training. Involves the use of anxiety to elevate stress.

Subculture. A group that in addition to participating in mainstream social life shares certain values, norms, goals, and lifestyles distinguishable from the mainstream.

Subpoena. An order to appear issued by a court. The subpoena indicates the date, time, and location at which the person must appear.

Summons. A document issued by a court notifying a person that he or she has been charged with an offense. A summons tells the person to appear in court to respond to the charges.

Symbolic. Anything identified by humans as standing for something else; an arbitrary affixing of meaning to an object, as in the American flag representing liberty and democracy.

Team policing. A policing strategy that involves the use of several officers, often with diverse but complimentary special skills, working as a group.

Ten–print card. Used to record the fingerprints of suspects during the normal booking procedure.

Thief–takers. Another name for the Bow Street Runners.

Thin Blue Line. Expression referring to traditional municipal police officers' blue uniforms. The expression conveys the idea that police officers represent society's line of demarcation between conformity and chaos.

Tithings. In medieval England, a group of ten families who joined together for mutual protection and who were responsible for one another's behavior.

Tort. Derived from the concept of torturous harms; the body of law pertaining to non–criminal wrongs and damages to property, persons, and reputations.

True Bill. The official statement issued by a grand jury charging an individual with a criminal of offense.

Truncheon. A short club carried by early constables and a forerunner of modern police batons.

Tun. A village containing a tithing (See *Tithing*).

Underclass. Lower–level social strata.

Uniform Crime Reports. Statistical rates of crime and other related data collected and issued annually by the Federal Bureau of Investigation (FBI). The data contained in these reports is limited to reported or known crimes and is therefore only a partial reflection of the total number of crimes committed each year.

Unreasonable force. The use of more force than is required to bring a situation under control.

Verdict. The findings of a jury or judge after hearing all of the evidence in a trial.

Vice crimes. Crimes associated with moral depravity or corruption.

Victimless crimes. Crimes debatably associated with having no victims; includes gambling, substance abuse, prostitution, and other vice crimes.

Vigilante. An individual who side–steps legal channels and takes retaliatory action against an offender.

Voir Dire. Literally, "to speak the truth;" the process of questioning potential jurors to determine their appropriateness for impaneling. The prosecutor and defense attorney each may challenge potential jurors. Those that either finds unacceptable are eliminated from the panel, which becomes the jury.

Voluntary consent. In effect, when one consents to allow police to search one's person or premises.

Watchman–style policing. A style of policing that stresses reactive rather than proactive policing strategies (See *Reactive* and *Proactive policing*).

Watch system. An early system of policing in which watchmen walked the streets to guard against fires, breaches of peace, and to sound an alarm if they observed a crime.

Weltanschauung. A world view, or mind set; a particular ideology.

Women's bureaus. Used during the early twentieth century to house women police officers.

Subject index

Name Index